Bridging Design and Fandom: Fan Studies and Design Research in Conversation

EDITED BY

NAOMI JACOBS

Lancaster University, UK

emerald PUBLISHING

United Kingdom – North America – Japan – India – Malaysia – China

Emerald Publishing Limited
Emerald Publishing, Floor 5, Northspring, 21–23 Wellington Street, Leeds LS1 4DL

First edition 2026

British Library Cataloguing in Publication Data
A catalogue record for this book is available from the British Library

ISBN: 978-1-80592-662-7 (Print)
ISBN: 978-1-80592-659-7 (Online)
ISBN: 978-1-80592-661-0 (Epub)

INVESTOR IN PEOPLE

Bridging Design and Fandom

For Rachel

Contents

Part 5: Sustainability

About the Editor

Dr Naomi Jacobs is a Lecturer in Design Policy and Futures Thinking at Lancaster University, and Co-Director of Imagination Lancaster, the Design-led research centre based in the School of Arts. Her interdisciplinary research spans Design Research and Fan Studies and focuses on interactions; between individuals, communities, disciplines or sectors and between people and technology and the media they consume. Her work often uses speculative methods to consider ethical implications of new and emerging technologies in contexts such as food, fashion, public space and fandom.

About the Contributors

Atanur Andıç is an Assistant Professor of Communication Design at Özyeğin University, Faculty of Architecture and Design. He completed his PhD in Arts, Technology and Emerging Communication from the University of Texas at Dallas and his M.A. in Communication Sciences from Kadir Has University. His dissertation examined the politics of 3D model making and the publics it constructs. His research explores new media, fan studies and digital humanities, focusing on how emerging technologies shape cultural production, platforms and everyday practices of participation and authorship.

Sejal Changede is a Lecturer in Design at the Open University. Her work focuses on how design can contribute to developing more sustainable ways of living, particularly through exploring traditional knowledge systems. Her work is interdisciplinary, crossing design, sustainability, material cultures, fan studies and emerging technologies, exploring connections between traditional craft knowledge and contemporary making. Recent projects include developing frameworks for regenerative heritage greenspaces and creating curriculum for Design for Transformation.

Paul Coulton is the Chair of Speculative and Game Design at Imagination Lancaster, the Design-led research centre based in the School of Arts at Lancaster University. His practice uses research through design to create experiential futures which deliberately mix a present experience with a speculative future that are concretised by combining immersive scenarios with artefacts produced as design fictions or speculative designs.

Sabina Fazli is a researcher in the Collaborative Research Centre Human Differentiation (SFB 1482) at Johannes Gutenberg University Mainz, Germany. Based at the Obama Institute for Transnational American Studies, she works on a subproject examining contemporary periodical cultures. Her research focuses on the British style press of the 1980s, independent magazines and zine media. She holds a PhD in English Literature from Georg August University Göttingen, Germany. She is a co-editor of the *German-language handbook Handbuch Zeitschriftenforschung* (2022) and a forthcoming special issue of *DIY, Alternative Cultures & Society* on zines (2026).

Hamed Goharipour is an Assistant Professor of Urban Studies at The College of Wooster. His research examines the urban legacy of sporting mega-events and how host cities function before, during and after the Olympic Games and FIFA World Cup. He studies the use and control of public space, city securitisation and social and environmental impacts, with close attention to each host city's context. Recent projects include Tehran 1974, Rio 2016, Qatar 2022, Paris 2024. His work appears in Cities, Qualitative Research, Soccer and Society and Frontiers of Architectural Research, with books and chapters published in English and Persian.

Roberto Huertas Gutiérrez is a Lecturer and a researcher at Universidad Carlos III de Madrid, where he is completing his doctoral dissertation within the research group "Television–Cinema: Memory, Representation and Industry (TECMERIN)" under a predoctoral training contract. His work explores the relationship between television and society, with a particular focus on contemporary television comedy.

Matt Hills is an Honorary Professor at the University Bristol, having formerly been a Professor of Fan Studies at the University of Huddersfield. Hills is the author/editor of multiple books on fandom and *Doctor Who*, including *Fan Cultures* (Routledge, 2002), *Triumph of a Time Lord* (I.B. Tauris, 2010), *Doctor Who - The Unfolding Event* (Palgrave-Macmillan, 2015) and *Adventures Across Space and Time: A Doctor Who Reader* (co-editor; Bloomsbury Academic, 2023). Hills has also published related work in journals such as *Journal of Fandom Studies, Transformative Works and Cultures, Science Fiction Film and Television, Celebrity Studies* and many others.

Christopher Housseaux is a doctoral student, a research assistant and a Lecturer at the University of Montreal. He is interested in the uses of digital platforms for sociopolitical mobilisation and the forms of inclusion and exclusion that occur in online communities. His thesis focuses on the mechanisms of inclusion and exclusion experienced by neurodivergent fans in fandoms.

Bethan Jones is a Research Associate in the School of Journalism, Media and Culture at Cardiff University, where she is undertaking research into the way the past is remediated/animated through algorithmic systems, and with what consequences. She has written extensively about fandom, true crime, media tourism and participatory cultures, and her work has been published in *Television and New Media*, *Convergence* and *Transformative Works and Cultures*, among others. Bethan is also a co-editor of *Crowdfunding the Future: Media Industries, Ethics, and Digital Society* (Peter Lang, 2015) and *Participatory Culture Wars: Controversy, Conflict, and Complicity in Fandom* (University of Iowa Press, 2025)

René H. Kerschbaumer, PhD, is a Research Associate and a Lecturer at the Department Marketing & Sales at CAMPUS 02 University of Applied Sciences in Graz, Austria. He further serves as the head of the Josef Ressel Centre for Platforms and Digital Ecosystems at CAMPUS 02. René is best known for his work on subscription and platform commerce and researches in the fields of consumer behaviour and e-commerce. His work has been published in the

Journal of Business Strategy, the *International Review of Retail, Distribution, and Consumer Research* and the *Journal of Consumer Behaviour*.

Nicolle Lamerichs is a Senior Lecturer and the team lead at Creative Business, HU University of Applied Sciences, Utrecht. She is the programme coordinator of the MSc Sustainable Business Transition. Lamerichs holds a PhD in media studies from Maastricht University (2014). She has published and edited several books on fandom, such as *Productive Fandom* (2018), *Affect in Fandom* (2025) and the Dutch monograph *Leven als Fan* (2024). Through peer-reviewed articles and chapters, she has contributed to the study of media culture, cosplay and game practices. Her current research focuses on participatory culture on digital platforms, specifically in relation to identity, sustainability and play.

Lies Lanckman is a Senior Lecturer in Film at UWE Bristol. She is the co-founder of NoRMMA, the Network of Research: Movies, Magazines, Audiences, and the editor of Star Attractions: Twentieth-Century Movie Magazines and Global Fandom (2019) and Stars, Fan Magazines and Audiences: Desire by Design (2022). The main focus of her research is Hollywood history of the 1920s–1940s; particular research interests include stardom and fandom, fan magazines, issues of censorship, and the career of Norma Shearer.

Violet Owen undertakes research situated at the intersection of technology, design and society. Her work investigates how emerging technologies can be designed to support learning, creativity and long-term sustainability, spanning generative artificial intelligence (AI) education for primary schools, immersive interactive experiences and Research through Design methods that foreground play, experimentation and engagement with complex sociotechnical issues. Drawing on fan studies and gaming communities, she examines how emotional attachment and collective practices influence repair, maintenance and technological lifespans, offering insights for future technology design practice. She further conducts research in Creative Evaluation, developing participatory, design-led approaches that offer organisations alternatives to traditional impact measurement.

Sofie Stobberup Rasmussen is an art historian and former PhD researcher at the University of Southern Denmark with experience from the National Museum of Denmark. Following the COVID-19 pandemic, she paused her doctoral studies to focus on her museum career. With tourism now revitalised, she incorporates post-pandemic perspectives into her research on media tourism and cultural heritage, publishing findings from her broader field study on Harry Potter tourism (2016–2024), which examines how iconic literary culture and popular media shape tourism practices in Denmark and the United Kingdom.

D. Rodriguez is the Music Cataloguer at the Marta and Austin Weeks Music Library at the University of Miami. They research recorded music cultures, with particular attention to contemporary pop genres, practices of listening and fandom.

Hong Shen is an Assistant Professor in the Human-Computer Interaction Institute at Carnegie Mellon University's School of Computer Science, where she directs the Collective AI Research and Evaluation (CARE) Lab. Her research focuses on human–AI interaction and the development of safe, responsible and aligned AI systems. Her work has been published in and received awards from leading venues such as ACM CHI, CSCW and EMNLP and has been featured in *Forbes*, *Wired*, BBC and *The Guardian*. She is a recipient of the Google Research Scholar Award, the Microsoft AI and Society Fellowship and the Google Policy Fellowship.

Michael Stead is a Lecturer in Sustainable Design Futures at Imagination Lancaster, the Design-led research centre based in the School of Arts at Lancaster University. His practice-led research explores the environmental, social and economic opportunities and challenges emerging technologies including Internet of Things, AI and Digital Fabrication pose for redressing climate change and engendering climate justice. Advancing approaches including Speculative Design, Regenerative Design and Participatory Design, he is developing innovative regenerative tools and strategies with local community partners, policymakers and wider industry that support adoption of sustainable and equitable technologies, practices and infrastructures across future society.

Asier Gil Vázquez is a Lecturer and a researcher in the Department of Communication at Universidad Carlos III de Madrid, where he obtained his PhD in 2020. He is also a member of the TECMERIN research group and of the UC3M University Institute of Spanish Cinema. His research focuses mainly on the history of film and television in Spain, with particular attention to the work of actors and actresses.

Zilu Wang is a researcher at King's College London whose work examines the cultural dynamics of contemporary internet platforms. Her research focuses on short-video ecosystems such as Douyin/TikTok, where she studies how recommendation algorithms, creator cultures and emerging platform norms shape everyday expression and digital labour. More broadly, she is interested in the governance of algorithmic media, platform power in China and beyond and the ways users negotiate identity and agency within highly datafied environments.

Wolfgang J. Weitzl, PhD, is a Full Professor of Digital Marketing at the Institute of Digital Business, University of Applied Sciences Upper Austria, and Senior Research Fellow at the University of Vienna, Austria. His research focuses on digital consumer experiences created by various marketing instruments (e.g., human/virtual influencers, online reviews) and mediated via diverse online channels as well as various technologies (e.g., augmented reality, virtual reality). He has published, among others, in the *Journal of Business Research*, *European Journal of Marketing*, *Computers in Human Behavior*, *Internet Research*, *Journal of Research in Interactive Marketing*, *Electronic Commerce Research* and *Journal of Product & Brand Management*.

Qing Xiao is a PhD student in the Human–Computer Interaction Institute at Carnegie Mellon University. His recent research investigates AI companions and the forms of intimacy, dependency and vulnerability that arise in these emerging human–AI relationships. In this line of work, he investigates how affective design choices in AI companions, and even in general-purpose Large Language Models, may offer comfort to users but also carry the risk of manipulative influence and the development of emotional attachment. His very recent research agenda advances a framework termed user-driven alignment, which develops design and governance strategies to mitigate manipulative dynamics in AI companion systems.

Acknowledgements

This book is dedicated to Professor Rachel Cooper, OBE, who passed away in 2025. Rachel employed me on an interdisciplinary project at Imagination Lancaster despite my lack of any knowledge of design, and through her steadfast support and mentorship I learned what design research was – thus without her, this book would not exist. She is a great loss to the entire design community and will be much missed.

The work of this book was also supported through the Beyond Imagination project, funded by Research England, through which I was employed as a Lecturer in Design Policy and Futures Thinking. Beyond Imagination also provided funding for the 2023 symposium on Fan Studies and Design Research from which some of the work in this book emerged. I am very grateful for this support.

I would also like to thank the fan studies community, particularly the Fan Studies Network and Fan Studies Network North America, for providing a welcoming and supportive space in which to foster exciting, interdisciplinary research. In particular, I need to thank JSA Lowe for introducing me to the idea that it was even possible to do academic research about fandom. In addition, the support of the many and various fan communities I have been part of over the years is indispensable – you know who you are.

Finally, I would like to offer thanks to everyone who has helped make this book a reality, including peer reviewers, Emerald, colleagues, family and friends.

Chapter 1

Introduction: Bridging Design and Fandom

Naomi Jacobs

Lancaster University, UK

Abstract

In this introduction, the author introduces the fields of design research and fan studies and discusses how they have prior under-explored synergies. The introduction provides a background to this book, introduces design and fandom as fields of study and surfaces their commonalities. The author provides a new framework for thinking about design *for*, *into* and *through* fan studies research and uses it to locate the wide-ranging research that will be presented in the following chapters. The introduction concludes by introducing each section of the book and the work which it contains.

Keywords: Fan studies; design research; research through design; methodologies; interdisciplinarity

Why This Book?

There may not initially seem to be an obvious connection between design research and fan studies. Why are they being brought together here for the first time? My belief, which I will explain below, is that these academic fields should be working together more closely; that together they create fertile ground for new and exciting research areas. The goal of this collection is to bring those opportunities to the surface and to showcase existing links. In doing so, we can uncover new productive ways of exploring what it means to be a fan and research fans, what design and design researchers bring to the world and what happens when these two practices and research fields come together.

Bridging Design and Fandom, 1–13

doi:10.1108/978-1-80592-659-720261001

Some of my belief in the importance of this coming together I attribute to my own somewhat idiosyncratic interdisciplinary career, which has opened my eyes to the ways that these two seemingly unrelated areas of research have much in common. I have not had a traditional entry point to either of these fields. I do not have a degree in any of the areas most common as grounding for fan studies such as media and cultural studies or literature. Nor do I have any formal training in design. However, I have been working as a design researcher for over a decade at Imagination Lancaster, the renowned, interdisciplinary, design-led research centre at Lancaster University. I have also been a fan, involved in fan communities both on and offline, for over 30 years – since I was a teenager. Coincidentally, it was not until I was learning about design research for the first time (while working on a project at Lancaster about interdisciplinary collaboration and 'digital public space') that I discovered that not only could fans be a topic of academic research but that fan studies was a well-established field. Since then, I have carried out research in both these areas and seen how they can draw together. At the 2016 Fan Studies Network Conference, I attended a roundtable session discussing methodologies in fan studies and was intrigued by the fact that many methods associated with design research (such as participatory action research) seemed like they might be useful in a fan studies context despite little awareness of these at the event.[1]

In March 2024, I organised a Symposium on Design and Fan Studies held in Lancaster, which was intended to bring these two research areas into conversation. I was surprised and gratified to see how much interest there was from both design and fan studies researchers. Several of the contributions to this edited collection have their origins in work which was initially presented at that event.

The work presented here will have relevance to those familiar with fan studies research or design research. However, because there is so little existing work or training which considers these together, there is no expectation that readers will be equally comfortable with both. In this introduction, I will therefore first provide readers an initial grounding in what is meant by design research and fan studies research.

Design and Design Research

To talk about design research, we should first talk about design. But what is design? Ranulph Glanville noted that 'Designers do not describe the world as it is, but rather they change the world (no matter how tiny the change) by making new objects, services, processes, etc.' (Glanville, 2023, p. 45). Bruce Archer, much earlier, suggested design research relates to knowledge of 'embodiment of configuration, composition, structure, purpose, value and meaning in man-made

[1]These reflections resulted in an article in a special issue of Transformative Works and Cultures on Methodologies encouraging fan studies to borrow methods from other disciplines including design research (Jacobs, 2020).

things and systems' (Archer, 1981, p. 31). Design could therefore be summarised as the process of intentional creation by humans for a purpose. As Herbert Simon puts it, 'devising of courses of action aimed at changing existing situations into preferred ones' (Simon, 1996). This often results in designed artefacts, the 'human-made world' (Cross, 2001). However, other more intangible things are also constructed by humans and hence designed, such as cities, services, policies or futures. The problem-solving aspect of design is also important, particularly when distinguishing design from art. Design is particularly good at addressing so-called 'wicked problems' (Rittel & Webber, 1973) arising out of social systems. These are complex and ill-defined, each one being unique, and do not have a single 'true or false' solution but must be incrementally addressed with 'good or bad' solutions.

Modern design education has developed various ways to teach how designers create 'things' to solve problems, with different codified processes which identify, as Nigel Cross famously calls them, 'Designerly ways of knowing and thinking' (Cross, 2024). In 2005, the British Design Council popularised the 'double diamond' (Fig. 1.1) as a model for describing the process of design. It was based on earlier work by Bela Bathany who proposed a 'divergence-convergence' model (Banathy, 1996).

The double diamond describes how designers should take a wide, open-minded approach to seeking new potential solutions, before focusing down on one possibility, followed by considering many options of how this might be achieved and then becoming focused again to deliver potential outcomes. It demonstrates how design involves iterative practice, which may in fact go through multiple cycles of exploring, prototyping, testing and refining. There are also specific approaches that can be taken while undertaking such a process: for example, user-centred design involves at each stage consideration and centring of users and their needs. Inclusive design takes the starting point that considering diversity and creating designs that enable use by people with a range of abilities and backgrounds makes better designs for everyone. More-than-human design

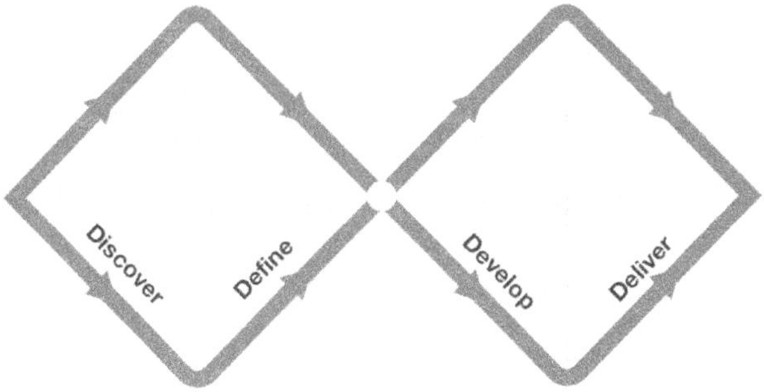

Fig. 1.1. The Double Diamond by the Design Council.
Source: Licensed under a CC BY 4.0 license.

considers not just people in the design process but looks wider to include, for example, animals and the broader ecosystem. Developing and examining the theory behind these kinds of approaches is one aspect of the field that is called design research.

When Bruce Archer was defining design, he was doing so in an attempt to also define design research, which at that time (in the 1980s) was a new and emerging field of academic study, still trying to find its place. The origins of this field can be found in the 1960s, with Herbert Simon being one of the first to separate out design as its own academic subject and form of research as distinct from the sciences and the humanities (Simon, 1996).

If, as we have discussed, design is the process of intentional creation by humans for a purpose, then design research is the study of that purposeful creation, its methods, practices and outputs. But Design Research as a field of academic study is a multi-faceted thing. Christopher Frayling (1994) famously distinguished between different ways that design (and art) could intersect with research. Research *for* design, he proposed, is the process of discovery that is undertaken as preparation for creating a designed object. Research *into* design is instead an examination of design and designers; research that creates knowledge about design. The third type is research *through* design, which is becoming the focus of much modern design research.

Research through design is a research method and practice through which the act of creation itself is a means of developing new knowledge: 'learning through doing' (Green & Lindley, 2024). Archer (1995) relates this to action research, a method whereby the researcher works with communities or other real-world contexts to make change and through this process understand the outcomes. Archer suggests that 'It is when research activity is carried out through the medium of practitioner activity that the case becomes interesting'.

Fans and Fan Studies

Fan studies is also often concerned with practitioner activity. It the study of people who are fans, the cultures of fan communities (often called 'fandom'), the practices carried out in association with these and their implications for society. As an interdisciplinary academic field, it is generally agreed to have begun in the 1990s and can be considered in the process of emerging as its own discipline (Jacobs, 2020).

Such fan practices are not at all new. Henry Jenkins, in his 1992 book 'Textual Poachers' (considered to be one of the key founding works of the field) talks about the origins of the word fan as a shortening of 'fanatic' in the late 19th century. It was applied initially to those following professional sports teams, before its expansion to encompass a wider range of 'devotees'. However, it is possible to identify many examples throughout history of people who felt heightened affective responses to a celebrity, creative work, musical act or sports team, who sought community with others who felt similarly and found ways to express their response creatively (for some examples see Fuller-Seeley, 2017).

Before the 1990s, research into fans tended to be disparate, and often pathologizing or dismissive – reducing fans to the 'obsessed individual and the hysterical crowd' (Jensen, 1992, p. 9). There are gendered associations to these categories. Indeed, much of the scorn given to major cultural fan movements such as Beatlemania, despite their significance as economic drivers, is likely because those taking part were primarily young women – historically, routinely dismissed in conceptions of acceptable fan practice (Scott, 2019). However, Jensen, Jenkins and a number of others writing in the early 1990s sought to reclaim fan practice as both a potentially positive force and worthy of academic study.

Production is a key element of fan behaviour. Fiske (1992) identified three types of fan productivity; semiotic production (creating meanings for oneself through interaction with a source text) enunciative productive (creating public, shared meaning making through speech or social expression such as clothing) and textual production (creating new texts outside of traditional commercial modes that are in conversation with both the source material and the semiotic, enunciative fan ecosystem surrounding it). Much early fan studies scholarship originated in media and cultural studies and related disciplines; thus, scholars were particularly interested in this textual production which often challenged or subverted the beloved source material: the 'poaching' of Jenkins' title.

Fan studies research has thus often focused on fans of media properties such as books, films and TV shows who follow modes of gift-economy based productive practice. These were pioneered by (primarily female) Star Trek fans in the 1960s and 1970s, who for example shared creative transformative content in fanzines and at conventions, produced video edits that reconfigured the beloved show into new paradigms and wrote fanfiction that told new stories about worlds and characters – often incorporating new readings of the text such as female-centric or queer perspectives. This is an extension of historical precedents such as Sherlock Holmes fans who have for over a century written their own versions of the stories and characters, performed immersive pretence that the text was 'real' (Rosales, 2022) and even organised mass campaigns appealing to the author to move the story in ways that they preferred or continue it after it was considered complete.

Analysis of such textual production takes various forms, for example doing deep textual analysis on fanfiction, using modern techniques from the digital humanities to uncover broader trends in this literature and its associated metadata (Black, 2020) or analysing fan art from a perspective of iconography (Nielsen, 2021). However, fan studies also encompasses topics that go beyond the texts themselves. Since the 1990s, digital technologies have significantly altered the speed and breadth of fan practice, if not necessarily its nature. Fans have always been early adopters of new technology (see Booth, 2017), and social media and digital spaces have become key venues for fandom activity. Gray et al. (2007) highlight the importance of fan studies to help understand such technologies of mediation on a wider scale because 'studying fan audiences allows us to explore some of the key mechanisms through which we interact with the mediated world at the heart of our social, political, and cultural realities and identities' (p. 10).

Recently, fan studies has been moving towards a more inclusive and critical approach, for example considering the impacts of systemic racism on who has traditionally been made welcome or unwelcome in fan spaces and fan studies (Martin & Griffin, 2024). There is also research on the actions that fans take in the world as individuals or collectives, for example fan activism where fandoms can prompt social movements to take charitable, political or other action (Scott, 2019). Fan activity is now examined which goes beyond fans of media texts; research on sports fans for example, which has often taken place outside the field, is being increasingly welcomed into it (Ford, 2014). Modern critical fan studies considers the practices of fandom that have more negative impacts, sometimes called toxic fandom or antifandom, but which Stanfill (2024) categorises in the title of their book as 'Fandom is Ugly'. Many such ugly impacts can be seen to spread outside of what are traditionally considered fan spaces, for example increasing interactions between fan behaviours and spheres such as politics, disinformation and conspiracy theories (Petersen, 2022).

It is therefore important when thinking about the breadth of fan studies to consider the difference between 'being a fan' and 'being in a fandom' as these can be very distinct and in fact each cover a myriad of practices. It is indeed also important to not generalise 'what fans do' and to speak about fandoms (plural) or a fandom rather than fandom in general, as we consider multiple overlapping and intersecting communities (Garrison & Jacobs, 2020) that may have large differences in behaviour and practice even if they share a focus (such as a film, celebrity, sport or political affiliation).

Design and Fandom in Conversation

Intrinsic to design, and by extension design research, is the ability to look at what exists and consider alternatives. And this urge should be familiar to many people who have engaged with fans and fandom. A well-established notion in fan studies scholarship, originating in a post on the Dreamwidth platform by Obsession_inc (2009), is the idea that fan activity can be broadly categorised into two types: affirmational fandom and transformational fandom. Affirmational fandom describes activities which celebrate and allow one to re-experience the beloved text. This includes for example collecting merchandise, analysing and categorising content (such as solving 'mysteries' in the text, or making ranked lists of which are the 'best' films or episodes in a particular show) and meeting celebrity idols. Transformational fandom by contrast is described as 'laying hands upon the source and twisting it to the fans' own purposes' (obsession_inc, 2009). This includes reinterpretation and reinvention of source material, creating new content such as fanfiction, art or remix videos or analyses that present new radical interpretations of the text.

Returning to Glanville's assertion that designers change the world by making new objects, services or processes, I would argue that this process of change through creation also describes many of the activities that fans carry out. In particular, transformational fandom is all about changes. Such change may be in obvious ways, for example writing new versions of stories that surface hidden or missing features of the original text, such as queer representation. However, even something as affirmational as making a list of favourite episodes of a television series is making a change, by identifying and prioritising a knowledge base of what defines a 'good' episode. And the actions of fan communities can create wider change in the world, such as activism, or designing new structures and platforms for digital archiving (Fiesler et al., 2016).

As discussed above, fans have a strong affective response to the objects of their fandom. But emotional and affective responses are also important in design. Glanville (2023) noted that '[o]ne element in the designerly is delight' (p. 20). Delight is a key driver for fans, who create for their own delight, as Glanville goes on to suggest should apply to design as well: 'to whom should we aim to bring delight? To the world at large, to the immediate users and also to those who make it, the designers' (p. 21). Fans are often first movers, those with the strongest feelings and motivation to be involved. They are the 'extreme users' that designers may particularly consider when using an inclusive design approach. Fans also are often undertaking design processes themselves, eager to solve problems and overcome challenges that interfere with the 'ideal' fan experience. For an example of this we can look to the way digital tagging conventions and metadata have been developed by fans, appropriating features of platforms such as Tumblr or Delicious that were never designed for a fan audience and creating complex and innovative design solutions that allowed detailed customisation of the site.[2]

Design follows divergent and convergent iterative processes, considering many different possibilities and futures before choosing where to focus to make a desired change. Similarly, fan creativity is often divergent and transformative, imagining multiple and often contradictory stories and meanings; often held simultaneously by a single individual. Fans love to imagine what-if options, multiple 'alternate universes' and playful explorations before converging on a new path to create something that expresses that possibility, either individually or as a collective shared imaginary. This can even be used to playfully extrapolate and iterate on beloved fan objects that do not exist at all, such as the Tumblr phenomenon 'Goncharov' (Ward & Price, 2025).

Bridging Design Research and Fan Studies

There are, as outlined above, interconnected relationships between design and fan practice, which are both playful, explorative and use fiction as a key tool to consider possibilities and create new knowledge. We should therefore not be surprised to find commonalities between design research and fan studies, which

[2]For a discussion of the history of fans appropriating the tagging systems on Delicious and interacting with its designers, see Cegłowski, 2013.

are both interdisciplinary disciplines that take a bricolage approach to theory and methods to explore complex societal challenges (Jacobs, 2020).

Interactions between design research and fan studies may take multiple forms, as will be demonstrated by the chapters in this collection. Fan contexts open exciting areas in which to explore design practice or design impacts. Foregrounding the design practices of fans brings new insights for fan studies researchers. Fan audiences may be a cohort that are underexamined by design researchers when examining theories of design. And looking at how fans and designers each approach and engage with wicked problems such as sustainability can give deeper insight into these challenges.

As David Philip Green and Joseph Lindley put it in their film of the same name, design research gives 'permission to muck about' (Green & Lindley, 2024). One could suggest that fans and hence fan studies scholars (many of whom are themselves 'aca-fans', straddling research and fandom) have been 'mucking about' for a long time.

This book is divided into five sections, each of which contains work addressing a current topic of focus or grand challenge which speaks across both design research and fan studies. When reflecting on the contributions to this collection, you are invited to consider how they might fit within a research framework of *design in fandom* based on Frayling's (1994) categorisations of research *into*, *for* and *through*.[3]

Research for design in fandom – Undertaking research that allows us to design solutions to improve things for fans or respond to the impact of fan behaviour. This might include design that helps address fan-specific needs or problems or addresses larger 'wicked problems' represented in fan spaces and activities relating to, for example, sustainability, decolonisation, inclusion and equity, or the societal impacts of new technologies.

Research into (about) design in fandom – Studying, for example, the ways that fans use design in their fan practice, the way that design is used to engage with fans (for example by commercial organisations developing products or experiences, or between-fan engagement) and the way that designed artefacts and their affordances are designed by fans or impact on fan practices.

Research through design in fandom – Using design practice to create things and through this process develop new knowledge about fans and design; this practice may be done by or in collaboration with fans as well as researchers, through participatory work, action research and as so-called 'aca-fans' who are within both fandom and the academy.

The first section of this book deals with *platforms and affordances*, broadly conceived. Platformisation is an area of increasing interest for fan studies scholars and for design. Platforms of mediation, that enable and facilitate communication between users, form the basis of much of our modern digital society, especially for fans for whom sharing and communicating is a key facet of

---

[3]It is important to note that these are not mutually exclusive categories, and an individual piece of scholarship may straddle multiple approaches.

fan practice. While digital platforms have an undeniably powerful role in today's culture, media platforms are not just digital, as demonstrated by the first chapter in this section. Here, Lies Lanckman takes a historical perspective to examine film magazines from the early 20th century. The mediation performed by these as a platform and the design of the affordances that construct their uses and are developed for, with and by their users, provide an example of research into design in fandom and preface some of the power of platform affordances that shape modern digital spaces. D. Rodriguez also uses a historical, though more recent, case study. They examine the now-closed digital livestreaming platform VLIVE and how its affordances were designed for and shaped by its community of K-pop fans. Combining this focus on affordances with Actor Network Theory, the chapter demonstrates how VLIVE encouraged and enabled specific fan behaviours through its design, influencing wider K-pop fandom. The final chapter in this section by Christopher Housseaux describes how fans can appropriate and manipulate platforms for their specific needs, undertaking what Adrienne Shaw (2017) describes as negotiated or oppositional responses to affordances. Using the concept of 'creative digital practices' and relating it to hierarchies of digital activism, Housseaux describes how BTS ARMY fans creatively adapt platforms (including Twitter, now known as X, and YouTube), leveraging and reinventing affordances, thus enabling uses that may have been unintended by their designers.

Section 2 focuses on *digital fan design*, dealing specifically with how fans use digital technology in the process of design and how design approaches might improve digital technologies intended for use by fans. Considering the interaction between fandom and digital technology is crucial since fans are often early adopters of such technology (Booth, 2017). Continuing the theme of platforms, Atanur Andıç discusses Sketchfab, a platform which is used to view, store and share digital 3D models. These models, which are designed using a range of specialist software, sit within an infrastructure of professionalised design practice but are also produced by fans. Working within this environment, professional artists and designers but also cultural institutions and fans share content. Fan artists creatively use the tagging and metadata systems of the platform to make fanart and fan designs visible and findable for members of their community. Andıç considers not only how fan designs are shared on the platform but also how the fan gift economy interacts with other systems of monetisation and credit for creative labour through the use of, for example, Creative Commons licences. In the next chapter, Wolfgang J. Weitzl and René H. Kerschbaumer take a different approach, looking not at design by fans, but at the design of technology that is specifically intended to cater to fans. In their chapter, which might be categorised as research for design in fandom, they examine the design of virtual influencers: computer generated social media avatars that, in order to be effective as a marketing mechanism, must cultivate their own fandom. By examining the complex relationships that form between these virtual influencers and people who engage with them, Weitzl and Kerschbaumer engage with notions of trust, authenticity, identification and anthropomorphism. They also discuss parasocial relationships that form between influencers and fans, noting that in the case of virtual influencers, these relationships may resemble those that form with fictional characters within narratives. This allows them to present a roadmap of recommendations for designing more effective virtual influencer campaigns. Finally in this section, Qing Xiao, Zilu Wang and Hong Shen also discuss parasocial relationships but return to the digital design practice of fans. They focus on those who use AI technology to design interactive chatbots based on favourite characters – comparing this to the creative work that goes into other transformative works such as fanfiction. They note that these chatbots are often created through bottom-up fan community design practices, where affective and emotional connection to the characters informs creative labour yet may come into conflict with underlying biases and norms in the AI models. As in Andıç's chapter, questions emerge relating to monetisation and tensions between gift-based community norms and commercialisation.

This theme is picked up further in Section 3, which considers *making, sharing and selling*; the complex systems of fan design labour and affective production which intersect with both the gift economy and more commercial economic models. This includes considering the design of products and services by or for fans and how monetisation can intersect and be overlaid upon fan practices that may be commonly thought of as purely non-profit, forming hybrid economies. In the first chapter of this section, Sabina Fazli analyses independent ('indie') magazines as a site of implicit fandom, led by affective labour and implemented through design expertise. These magazines are not only produced by highly skilled designers but aimed at a design-literate audience who can appreciate these skills. While not necessarily self-identifying as fans, Fazli argues that fan affect – specifically an interest in the design of the print magazine as a medium – is a key driver of their production and circulation, and combined with the postdigital material turn, encourages participatory making. While these magazines are not highly profitable, they are commercially sold. Sale of fan work is also discussed by Roberto Huertas Gutiérrez and Asier Gil Vázquez. They focus on graphic designers who use fan art to reimagine and reinterpret their fandom focus – in this case the Spanish television comedy *Aquí no hay quien viva* – and subsequently monetise this production. Huertas and Gil Vázquez use iconicity as a frame for discussing how design choices can graphically or materially encode critical interpretation and shared affective responses to beloved media, and how this can be capitalised on by designers working in this space. The final chapter in this section, by Matt Hills, similarly examines fan-designers selling their work and explores multiple forms of cultural capital that come into play when fandom is professionalised through fan-created merchandise. Hills unpacks Bourdieusian theories as they apply to both design research and fan studies, noting the cultural capital that designers possess and reproduce, and the approach of second wave fan studies to the cultural capital accrued and deployed by fans and fantrepreneurs. He suggests that other types of cultural capital such as digital cultural capital, attention capital and corporate cultural capital have key roles in unlicenced merchandise such as that created by the two Doctor Who fans in his case studies.

In Section 4, we turn to *tourism and urban space* as place-based sites for fan design. Fan tourism is a burgeoning global industry, supporting local and national economies. There are many ways in which design can intersect with these located fan experiences, from spatial and service design, to memorabilia. The chapters in this section include a variety of different types of fan focus and fan practice. The section opens with work by Hamed Goharipour, bringing together two topics that are both under-explored in fan studies: sports fandom and urban design. In this case study of football fans attending the 2022 FIFA World Cup in Qatar, Goharipour examines how spatial design of the Souq Waqif marketplace enabled positive interactions between fans and locals. He surfaces the specific connections and interactions that uniquely emerge when fan groups are among the people engaging with and in a shared space, providing insights and recommendations into how design contributes to shaping these experiences and how fan affect and community can in turn shape spaces. Sofie Stobberup similarly explores the design of multiply layered experiences and meaning in urban and other spaces, in her chapter examining locations where Harry Potter related tourism takes place. She focuses on heritage, considering how placemaking is shaped by ground-up tourist practices as well as brand management by sites and practical design considerations. Many of these public spaces have multiple heritage functions which must be negotiated; shared by media fans, those interested in the historical significance of the locations, and (in urban spaces) functional use by local people. Finally in this section, Bethan Jones turns towards sustainability concerns when fan tourists make location visits that can result in ecological damage. She builds on the previous chapter by also discussing Harry Potter screen tourism, as well as exploring a site visited by Game of Thrones fans. Jones proposes that a participatory co-design approach to screen tourism, where collaboration with fans happens early in the production process, can help protect potentially vulnerable sites from negative environmental impacts. This chapter highlights that environmental sustainability is often aligned with the values of fandom, something that the next and final section explores in more detail.

The final section takes up a focus specifically on *sustainability*, considering ways in which more sustainable fan practices can be encouraged and designed for. This addresses one of the major topics of our time. Environmental impacts of fandom can be considerable, as Jones' chapter highlights, but considering these challenges from a design lens can provide new approaches to this so-called 'wicked problem'. We can also consider sustainability from a multi-pronged perspective, not only considering environmental sustainability but also economic and social sustainability as per the 'triple bottom line' (Elkington, 1997). In the first chapter in this section, Sejal Changede and Naomi Jacobs use the 'quadruple bottom line' to explore meaning as a key factor in sustainable fandom. They pick up some of the conversations around merchandise, labour and consumption from Section 3 but consider this specifically in terms of sustainability. This work considers the objects that fans create, share and buy, exploring ways that fan objects might be made more environmentally sustainable. They foreground personal history and meaning as a key factor in sustainable practice but also take sustainable design lessons from traditional knowledge. Violet Owen, Michael Stead and Paul Coulton take up further this focus on meaning-making as a key factor in sustainable practises, looking specifically at videogames, consoles and related objects. They explore how working with and learning from videogame fandoms might support more sustainable attitudes to technology design and challenge the 'throwaway culture' that can contribute to electronic waste. They suggest that video game fans have a 'culture of care' that can be understood as a form of fan activism and that the emotional meaning attached to gaming objects can lead fans to overcome planned obsolescence through activities such as modding, archiving and repair. In this way, they propose that gaming cultures can form a blueprint for sustainable design that resists invisibility and inconspicuousness of devices to foreground emotional connection. Finally, to close this section and the book, Nicolle Lamerichs takes a research through design in fandom approach, creating a Sustainable Fandom Canvas tool and exploring how it can be used to help develop 'sustainable fandom'. The Canvas is designed to be used by fans and organisations to consider social benefits, ecological benefits and innovation in fan culture, and ideate for ways to improve sustainability across multiple axes such as material culture, digital productivity, transport and the circular economy. Lamerichs outlines, through examples, how the tool can be used in practical settings and encourages a co-creation approach, where fans and other consumers play a key role in supporting sustainable design. The tool is offered for use in workshops and teaching contexts to support a reflective system-thinking approach.

Such design research outputs are not only a practical tool for supporting sustainability but a call for action in facilitating change for social good in fandom and elsewhere. As readers reflect on such tools for change, I hope that the contributions of the book as a whole and the intersections between design and fan studies become clear.

References

Archer, B. (1981). A view of the nature of design research. In R. Jacques & A. James Powell (Eds.), *Design, science, method.* Westbury House.

Banathy, B. H. (1996). *Designing social systems in a changing world.* Springer.

Black, S. R. (2020). Adding a digital dimension to fan studies methodologies. *Transformative Works and Cultures, 33.* https://doi.org/10.3983/twc.2020.1725

Booth, P. (2017). *Digital fandom 2.0: New media studies.* Peter Lang.

Cegłowski, M. (2013, September 6). *Fan is a tool-using animal.* https://idlewords.com/talks/fan_is_a_tool_using_animal.htm. Accessed on November 25, 2025.

Cross, N. (2001). Designerly ways of knowing. *Design Issues, 17*(3), 49–55.

Cross, N. (2024). *Designerly ways of knowing and thinking* (2nd ed.). Springer.

Elkington, J. (1997). *Cannibals with forks: The triple bottom line of 21st century business.* New Society Publishers.

Fiesler, C., Morrison, S., & Bruckman, A. S. (2016). An archive of their own: A case study of feminist HCI and values in design. In *Proceedings of the 2016 CHI conference on human factors in computing systems* (pp. 2574–2585).

Fiske, J. (1992). The cultural economy of fandom. In L. A. Lewis (Ed.), *The adoring audience: Fan culture and popular media* (pp. 30–49). Routledge.
Ford, S. (2014). Fan studies: Grappling with an 'Undisciplined' discipline. *Journal of Fandom Studies*, *2*(1), 53–71.
Frayling, C. (1994). Research in art and design. *Royal College of Art Research Papers*, *1*(1), 1–5.
Fuller-Seeley, K. (2017). Archaeologies of fandom: Using historical methods to explore fan cultures of the past. In *The Routledge companion to media fandom* (pp. 27–35). Routledge.
Garrison, S. T., & Jacobs, N. J. (2020). Life as a networked fan. *AoIR Selected Papers of Internet Research*. https://doi.org/10.5210/spir.v2020i0.11216
Glanville, R. (2023). The sometimes uncomfortable marriages of design and research. In P. A. Rodgers & J. Yee (Eds.), *The Routledge companion to design research*. Taylor & Francis Group.
Gray, J., Sandvoss, C., & Harrington, C. L. (2007). Introduction: Why study fans? In J. Gray, C. Sandvoss, & C. L. Harrington (Eds.), *Fandom: Identities and communities in a mediated world* (pp. 1–16). NYU Press.
Green, D. P., & Lindley, J. (2024). *Permission to muck about* [Film]. Design Research Works. https://designresearch.works/permission-to-muck-about/
Jacobs, N. (2020). Interdisciplinary methodologies for the fan studies Bricoleur. *Transformative Works and Cultures*, *33*. https://doi.org/10.3983/twc.2020.1665
Jenkins, H. (1992). *Textual poachers: Television fans and participatory culture*. Routledge.
Jensen, J. (1992). Fandom as pathology: The consequences of characterization. In *The adoring audience* (pp. 9–29). Routledge.
Martin Jr, A. L., & Griffin, M. (2024). Putting the 'Black' in fan studies. *Transformative Works and Cultures*, *44*. https://doi.org/10.3983/twc.2024.2815
Nielsen, E. J. (2021). The iconography of fanart. In P. Booth & R. Williams (Eds.), *A fan studies primer: Method, research, ethics*. University of Iowa Press.
Obsession_inc. (2009, June 1). *Affirmational fandom vs. transformative fandom*. https://obsession-inc.dreamwidth.org/82589.html. Accessed on November 25, 2025.
Petersen, L. N. (2022). *Mediatized fan play: Moods, modes and dark play in networked communities*. Routledge.
Rittel, H. W. J., & Webber, M. M. (1973). Dilemmas in a general theory of planning. *Policy Sciences*, *4*(2), 155–169.
Rosales, L. N. (2022). "Fannish sensibilities": Fissures in the Sherlock Holmes fandom. In B. Kies & M. Connor (Eds.), *Fandom, the next generation*. University of Iowa Press.
Scott, S. (2019). *Fake geek girls: Fandom, gender, and the convergence culture industry*. New York University Press.
Shaw, A. (2017). Encoding and decoding affordances: Stuart hall and interactive media technologies. *Media, Culture & Society*, *39*(4), 592–602.
Simon, H. A. (1996). *The sciences of the artificial* (3rd ed.). MIT Press.
Stanfill, M. (2024). *Fandom is ugly: Networked harassment in participatory culture*. New York University Press.
Ward, E., & Price, L. (2025). "The real Goncharov was the fandom we made along the way": Goncharov (1973) as information creation. *Journal of Documentation*, *81*(4), 870–889.

Part 1

Affordances and Platforms

Chapter 2

Defying Gravity: Solving the 'Wicked Problem' of Film Fandom in the Pre-Digital Age

Lies Lanckman

UWE Bristol, UK

Abstract

In this chapter, the author investigates the classic Hollywood fan magazine as a fan platform for the pre-digital age and highlights particularly the affordances it offered to its readers.

In doing so, the author firstly frames this magazine as an object designed in the early 1910s to resolve a 'wicked problem'; that of managing the parasocial relationships between a growing number of enthusiastic fans and their increasingly distant idols, the Hollywood stars. The author then looks at five issues of *Photoplay* magazine in detail and determines how the magazine developed from 1915 to the later 1930s in terms of fulfilling this purpose, focusing particularly on participatory sections such as fan letter departments, competitions and, importantly, the often-overlooked Questions and Answers section.

The author argues these sections not only created a space for fans to converse – with the magazine's editors and with each other – about the objects of their fandom but also helped shape the magazine itself, prompting a series of optimisations which improved the user-friendliness of the magazine's design. Over the course of the 1920s–1930s, a number of new departments, focused on star and studio addresses, as well as film reviews and casts, gradually helped facilitate the booming business of being a fan.

Bridging Design and Fandom, 17–32

doi:10.1108/978-1-80592-659-720261002

Keywords: Classic Hollywood; fan magazines; *Photoplay*; stardom; fan letters

Introduction

A staple of film fandom from the 1910s to the 1970s, the fan magazine has been succinctly described by Anthony Slide as 'fundamentally a film- and entertainment-related periodical aimed at a general fan, an average member of the moviegoing public who more often than not was female' (Slide, 2010, p. 12); it was, in short, a widely accessible movie magazine published for, not by, fans. Its long history started with the publication of the American title *Motion Picture Story Magazine* in February 1911 and during the following decades dozens of others followed, in the United States and throughout the world, with some other well-known American titles including *Photoplay* (from 1911), *Picture Play* (from 1915) and *The New Movie Magazine* (from 1929).

These magazines, both affordable and widely read, have in recent decades been used relatively widely by scholars, primarily to investigate the public personae of classic stars – as proposed by Richard Dyer in his seminal 1979 work *Stars* and demonstrated, for example, in Tamar Jeffers McDonald's work on Doris Day (2013) – as well as to examine how these magazines articulated and impacted certain cultural shifts more broadly, for example in Sumiko Higashi's work on *Photoplay* and 1950s consumer culture (2014). Until recently, however, they have been largely ignored as resources for the study of historical fans and audiences – of their actual, rather than hypothetical, readership. As Marsha Orgeron, who *has* done such work, described it, there has been a 'tendency to abandon fans' reactions at the theoretical level' (Orgeron, 2009, p. 3).

My own work on fan magazines has also attempted to remedy this; in this context, I have primarily focused on fan letter sections and assessed their reliability as sources (Lanckman, 2019), investigated 'recurring fans' in these sections (Lanckman, 2020) and focused on particular threads of conversation within these sections (Lanckman, 2021). This work has been useful in unearthing a great number of individual movie fans, but it has also tended to take a very zoomed-in approach, focusing on one single aspect of the fan magazine's structure and also usually on one particular moment in time. In this chapter, then, I want to look at the fan magazine more holistically, throughout its early history, both in terms of what it presented to fans and in terms of how they used the material provided to them – essentially, its affordances.

Fan Magazines and 'Wicked Problems'

In this context, I want to look at the fan magazine as a designed object – a periodical intentionally created, from 1911 onwards, to fulfil a specific purpose. In particular, I would argue the fan magazine was developed as a partial solution to a 'wicked problem' of early 20th century culture, i.e. an open-ended, socially complex problem with no clear true/false solution (Buchanan, 1992, p. 97). This is the problem, or challenge, of managing the parasocial relationships between the increasing number of movie fans and the objects of their fandom within the rapidly developing movie industry.

This problem emerged with particular urgency at this time because, as the movie industry consolidated into a fully-fledged business in the 1900s–1910s, the distance between filmmakers and their audiences increased. This happened in several ways, including the emotional, since the development of stardom as a promotional technique involved the essential 'elevation' of stars above the realm of ordinary humans, in its turn feeding into a broader distinction between people who were active inside and outside the industry. On a more practical level, the increased distance also translated into geography; between roughly 1910 and 1915, the American film industry moved from its birthplace on the more densely populated East Coast to its new home on the – for most of the US population, then as now – more distant West Coast, to Hollywood.

The fan magazine, then, stepped in to manage this developing relationship between film audiences and film professionals in different ways, aiming to encourage, but also to steer and control, particular modes of reception and fandom. In this way, I frame it here as a form of fannish conduct literature,[1] which attempted to imbue in its – mostly young and female – readers a particular way of approaching their fascination with Hollywood. In this chapter, I will therefore consider the ways it encouraged and discouraged particular fan interests and behaviours within its pages.

Secondly, though, I will also consider the fan magazine as a potential, pre-digital fan platform, investigating the specific affordances provided through its design and structure and considering how fans were constrained by but also used these affordances to engage in a level of interactivity and to develop a relationship with the world of Hollywood on their own terms. The fan magazine was obviously, by necessity, a heavily mediated platform in this regard – but nonetheless I wish to argue here that even if it was never quite a democracy, it was at least an instance of mildly enlightened despotism.

To investigate the above, I will consider five representative issues of *Photoplay* magazine, the second ever fan magazine to be published (shortly after *Motion Picture Story* Magazine) and probably the most consistently popular one from its first publication as a fan magazine in 1912 to its final closure in 1980. Specifically, I will look at the June issues of the years 1915, 1920, 1925, 1930 and 1935 and use this broad chronological sweep to understand how fan magazines and their perception of film fandom developed over the first few decades of their existence as well as the way this development might have been steered by the ways people engaged with their contents.

In each of these issues, I will think about the kinds of contents the magazine fed its fans and how these contents invited fans to think about, conceptualise and

---

[1]The term "conduct literature" describes a kind of didactic literature which prescribes 'proper' behaviour for its readers. It includes, for example, etiquette guides like Emily Post's *Blue Book of Social Usage*, which was very popular during the heyday of the fan magazine.

relate to the movie industry. At the same time, I will also consider the ways the fan magazine invited fans to be active participants in the culture it created and how fans engaged with these invitations.

June 1915: Shaping Early Film Fandom

The June 1915 issue is a good example of the way early fan magazines navigated these issues, demonstrating the aspects of film culture their readers were expected and encouraged to take an interest in.

This issue is particularly interesting in that it clearly established stardom as a primary, but relatively new, point of focus for film fandom, according it the importance it would retain throughout *Photoplay*'s long history and into the present day. In this regard, it illustrates the recently completed transition from 'picture personality' to 'star', as outlined by Richard deCordova. While in the earliest years of the film industry (until 1913–14), audiences were expected to restrict themselves to 'professional knowledge of the actor' (deCordova, 1990, p. 98) referred to as a 'picture personality', after this time, the 'private lives of the stars were [also] constituted as a site of knowledge and truth' (p. 98). As opposed, then, to the very earliest issues of fan magazines, which quite literally recapped 'motion picture stories' in a short story format, the content of this issue clearly shows this shift to a focus on the private lives of stars, with articles focusing on the homes of the stars, their baby pictures, and so on.

It also showed this encouragement of star adulation in more subtle ways, such as through the design of the magazine, which at this point started with a 'Popular Photoplayers' section; this section contained over a dozen full-page star portraits, complete with decorative borders and clearly printed for the purpose of cutting-out and display or preservation. A readers' letter printed in this same issue, exhorting the magazine to 'print as large a picture on every page as you can' (p. 152), appears to indicate that fans happily adopted this practice.

At the same time, the magazine also included, from its inception, a degree of fan participation, moving beyond the prescriptive and encouraging active reciprocity in a number of ways. Firstly, it did so by promoting contests and competitions – which were a key part of encouraging active fandom throughout its entire history – as I will outline throughout this chapter. Later on, such contests and competitions would be connected to the composition of the greatest fan letter or a crossword or visual puzzle – but at this early stage, they could also take a different format: that of a screenwriting competition.

This demonstrates again my point about the growing distance between filmgoers and filmmakers at this time. Throughout its history, the film industry used the lure of stardom, of direct participation in the glamorous movie world, as a way to keep fans captivated, and later fan magazines happily participated in this. This 1915 issue does a similar thing but with two major differences: firstly, it focused primarily on screenwriting, rather than acting, as a potential career, and secondly, it presented this as a realistic career path, rather than a distant dream.

At this early stage in the development of the Hollywood film industry, there was a clear sense that film fans could realistically find work in the industry.

The Diamond from the Sky competition advertised on the first page of this magazine issue illustrates this fact: this 1915 film was made as the result of a screenplay competition in the *Chicago Tribune*, and now the North American Film Corporation was offering $10,000 to the 'man, woman or child' who provided a suggestion for a potential sequel (p. 3). While the magazine acknowledges the screenwriting industry is a competitive one – for example in its regular 'Hints on Photoplay Writing feature' – it is nonetheless presented as one a *Photoplay* reader could realistically enter. This would change in years to come, as the distance between fan and industry increased further.

In terms of 'pure' fan participation – participation by fans as *fans*, rather than as aspiring screenwriters – readers were also encouraged to contribute to the magazine directly through fan letter sections, which the magazine would feature throughout the history covered here. At this stage, two fan letter sections existed: one, 'Seen and Heard at the Movies', published 100-word, humorous anecdotes about the moviegoing experience and offered a 5-dollar prize while the 'Rocks and Roses' section printed readers' letters on any film-related topics. The magazine published full names and locations for each letter – which, as my previous work has noted (Lanckman, 2020), enables us to locate particular letter writers in historical census records and therefore prove their existence – and covered, in this issue, such topics as praise of the magazine, the legitimacy of film as an art form and the aforementioned concern for the size of printed star images (p. 152).

In this chapter, though, I want to privilege another fan participation section, which the magazine ran for most of its early existence: this is the Questions and Answers section. This section has not received much scholarly attention, perhaps because – compared to readers' letters sections or glitzy competitions – it was an unassuming one, usually consisting of pages upon pages of small-print answers to readers' (unpublished) questions, provided by the magazine's editorial staff (see Fig. 2.1). Nonetheless, I want to argue that this section is extremely valuable for those interested in the magazine's priorities, its readers' interests and, crucially, the way the magazine design developed as a result of careful negotiation between these two factors. One important aspect of the section to bear in mind in this context is its sheer size; in this early issue, the 'Questions and Answers' section took up a staggering *13* (of 172) pages, marking itself out as a key feature.

This importance is apparent in a number of ways. This June 1915 iteration, for example, compared to earlier ones, demonstrates once again the evolution from 'picture personality' to 'star' and the fact that readers were no longer discouraged, at this stage, from taking an interest in the personal lives of their stars. While, for example, the header of the Q&A section – then called 'The Question Box' – in November 1912 instructed readers that 'Information as to matrimonial alliances and other purely personal matters will not be answered'. (p. 124), the June 1915 header, on the other hand, merely told readers not to ask questions 'about religion or photoplay writing' (p. 153).

Indeed, aside from frequent questions about the casts and plots of particular films, questions about stars' private lives and their 'matrimonial alliances' were

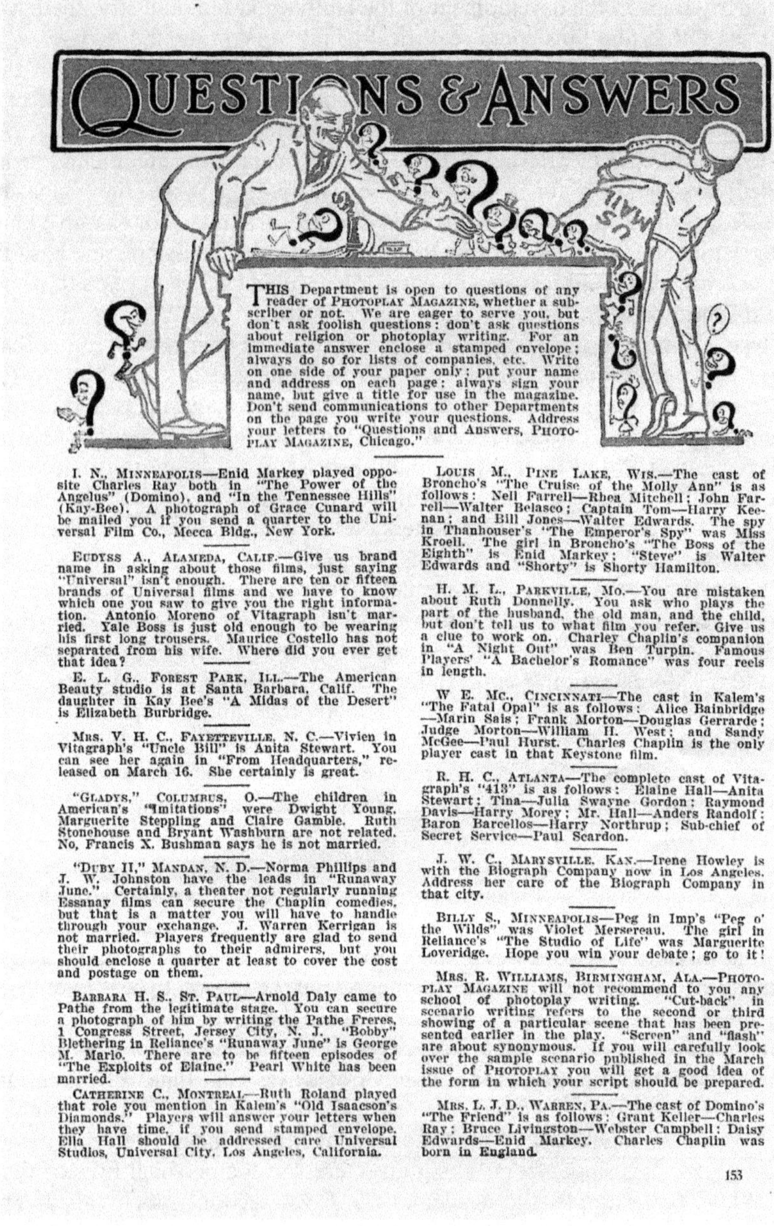

THIS Department is open to questions of any reader of PHOTOPLAY MAGAZINE, whether a subscriber or not. We are eager to serve you, but don't ask foolish questions; don't ask questions about religion or photoplay writing. For an immediate answer enclose a stamped envelope; always do so for lists of companies, etc. Write on one side of your paper only; put your name and address on each page; always sign your name, but give a title for use in the magazine. Don't send communications to other Departments on the page you write your questions. Address your letters to "Questions and Answers, PHOTOPLAY MAGAZINE, Chicago."

I. N., MINNEAPOLIS—Enid Markey played opposite Charles Ray both in "The Power of the Angelus" (Domino), and "In the Tennessee Hills" (Kay-Bee). A photograph of Grace Cunard will be mailed you if you send a quarter to the Universal Film Co., Mecca Bldg., New York.

EUDYSS A., ALAMEDA, CALIF.—Give us brand name in asking about those films, just saying "Universal" isn't enough. There are ten or fifteen brands of Universal films and we have to know which one you saw to give you the right information. Antonio Moreno of Vitagraph isn't married. Yale Boss is just old enough to be wearing his first long trousers. Maurice Costello has not separated from his wife. Where did you ever get that idea?

E. L. G., FOREST PARK, ILL.—The American Beauty studio is at Santa Barbara, Calif. The daughter in Kay Bee's "A Midas of the Desert" is Elizabeth Burbridge.

MRS. V. H. C., FAYETTEVILLE, N. C.—Vivien in Vitagraph's "Uncle Bill" is Anita Stewart. You can see her again in "From Headquarters," released on March 16. She certainly is great.

"GLADYS," COLUMBUS, O.—The children in American's "Imitations" were Dwight Young, Marguerite Steppling and Claire Gamble. Ruth Stonehouse and Bryant Washburn are not related. No, Francis X. Bushman says he is not married.

"DUBY II," MANDAN, N. D.—Norma Phillips and J. W. Johnston have the leads in "Runaway June." Certainly, a theater not regularly running Essanay films can secure the Chaplin comedies, but that is a matter you will have to handle through your exchange. J. Warren Kerrigan is not married. Players frequently are glad to send their photographs to their admirers, but you should enclose a quarter at least to cover the cost and postage on them.

BARBARA H. S., ST. PAUL—Arnold Daly came to Pathe from the legitimate stage. You can secure a photograph of him by writing the Pathe Freres, 1 Congress Street, Jersey City, N. J. "Bobby" Blethering in Reliance's "Runaway June" is George M. Mario. There are to be fifteen episodes of "The Exploits of Elaine." Pearl White has been married.

CATHERINE C., MONTREAL—Ruth Roland played that role you mention in Kalem's "Old Isaacson's Diamonds." Players will answer your letters when they have time, if you send stamped envelope. Ella Hall should be addressed care Universal Studios, Universal City, Los Angeles, California.

LOUIS M., PINE LAKE, WIS.—The cast of Broncho's "The Cruise of the Molly Ann" is as follows: Nell Farrell—Rhea Mitchell; John Farrell—Walter Belasco; Captain Tom—Harry Keenan; and Bill Jones—Walter Edwards. The spy in Thanhouser's "The Emperor's Spy" was Miss Kroell. The girl in Broncho's "The Boss of the Eighth" is Enid Markey; "Steve" is Walter Edwards and "Shorty" is Shorty Hamilton.

H. M. L., PARKVILLE, MO.—You are mistaken about Ruth Donnelly. You ask who plays the part of the husband, the old man, and the child, but don't tell us to what film you refer. Give us a clue to work on. Charley Chaplin's companion in "A Night Out" was Ben Turpin. Famous Players' "A Bachelor's Romance" was four reels in length.

W E. MC., CINCINNATI—The cast in Kalem's "The Fatal Opal" is as follows: Alice Bainbridge—Marin Sais; Frank Morton—Douglas Gerrarde; Judge Morton—William H. West; and Sandy McGee—Paul Hurst. Charles Chaplin is the only player cast in that Keystone film.

R. H. C., ATLANTA—The complete cast of Vitagraph's "413" is as follows: Elaine Hall—Anita Stewart; Tina—Julia Swayne Gordon; Raymond Davis—Harry Morey; Mr. Hall—Anders Randolf; Baron Barcellos—Harry Northrup; Sub-chief of Secret Service—Paul Scardon.

J. W. C., MARYSVILLE, KAN.—Irene Howley is with the Biograph Company now in Los Angeles. Address her care of the Biograph Company in that city.

BILLY S., MINNEAPOLIS—Peg in Imp's "Peg o' the Wilds" was Violet Mersereau. The girl in Reliance's "The Studio of Life" was Marguerite Loveridge. Hope you win your debate; go to it!

MRS. R. WILLIAMS, BIRMINGHAM, ALA.—PHOTOPLAY MAGAZINE will not recommend to you any school of photoplay writing. "Cut-back" in scenario writing refers to the second or third showing of a particular scene that has been presented earlier in the play. "Screen" and "flash" are about synonymous. If you will carefully look over the sample scenario published in the March issue of PHOTOPLAY you will get a good idea of the form in which your script should be prepared.

MRS. L. J. D., WARREN, PA.—The cast of Domino's "The Friend" is as follows: Grant Keller—Charles Ray; Bruce Livingston—Webster Campbell; Daisy Edwards—Enid Markey. Charles Chaplin was born in England.

153

Fig. 2.1. The First Page of the 'Questions and Answers' Page in *Photoplay*, June 1915.

the bread and butter of the section, with many readers clearly fascinated by the marital status – or marital happiness! – of various stars and the state of the Mary Pickford/Owen Moore marriage a particular topic of discussion. One additional specific avenue of inquiry was addressed through a particular note entitled 'No – They're Not Dead', inserted on the second page of this section and addressing the persistent death rumours surrounding particular stars, like Charlie Chaplin (p. 154). This insert allowed the magazine to frame itself as a reliable expert on the private lives – or deaths! – of the stars, noting it 'has staff correspondents at the front wherever photoplays are being produced and if there was any news, you shall have it as soon as the current magazine can be gotten off the press' (p. 154).

The 'Questions and Answers' section went beyond mere matters of life and death, however, and was also consulted about more practical concerns. This included once again the business of screenplay writing, despite its disclaimer that it would not answer such queries; several responses dealt with, for example, the business of negotiating a fair price with movie studios (p. 155). It also, crucially, included advice on the business of being a fan and gave useful advice, such as to include a stamped envelope if writing to a star and hoping for a response and to include 25 cents if writing to a studio for a star's photograph (p. 156). To facilitate this – and to pre-empt at least some of the queries the section frequently received – the magazine inserted a 'Studio Directory' directly into the Q&A section, where readers could locate the addresses to write to (p. 156).

Other questions were directed at the magazine itself, including a question about ordering back issues (p. 168) and one requesting an interview with a favourite (p. 156) – which the editor promised to grant. There is a real sense here that the magazine was happy to respond to people's demands – so long as these fit within the basic remit, and within the kind of fandom they wished to encourage – and this extended to the facilitation of fandom as a space for people to meet other, likeminded readers of *Photoplay*. One note in the Q&A section, for example, involved the forwarding of one writer's letter to another – since the magazine often held, though did not publish, the addresses of each writer – while elsewhere, the editor acknowledged this need for contact as something the magazine would consider addressing. In this context, he told a reader that:

> You'll have to wait a little on your wild desire to correspond with your friends. Half the people sign their names just as you do, and don't give any address, but we're going to try to work out a scheme so that you can get together. (p. 166)

Here, the magazine comes close, even at this early stage, to becoming something like a pre-digital fan platform where readers might meet fellow film enthusiasts and make new friends. This also highlights the 'Questions and Answers' section specifically as the site of real interactivity, even dialogue, between fans, between fans and the magazine, and between fans and the movie world.

At the same time, crucially, it also set up this section as one steering what the magazine would look like in the future, giving the editors a sense of what fans needed from their beloved *Photoplay*. The 'Studio Directory' section, for example, is the first instance of the magazine's format clearly reflecting the requests voiced by fans through the 'Questions and Answers' pages, and, as I will demonstrate over the course of this chapter, it would not be the last.

June 1920: A Fandom in Flux

The June 1920 issue gives us a sense of how this development progressed across the subsequent five years. This is apparent from the first pages of the magazine issue: the Table of Contents layout, which in the June 1915 issue was very straightforward and merely involved a list of features and page numbers, was now more complex and highlighted a handful of key magazine features in a series of text boxes on the right-hand side of the page. This allowed the editors to steer readers towards certain features, which, I argue, once again fulfilled the double role of, on the one hand, shaping the way fans took an interest in the film industry and, on the other hand, improving user friendliness by highlighting features fans might be particularly interested in.

This is especially true in case of the first text box, which runs all the way down the first of the two TOC pages and which provides a list – with page numbers – of all the films reviewed in the 'Shadow Stage' review section of the magazine (see Fig. 2.2). The text above the list of films advises 'Save this magazine – refer to the criticisms before you pick out your evening's entertainment. Make this your reference list' (p. 5), which itself underlines the user friendliness aspect: readers no longer had to leaf through the magazine to check if a particular film they were interested in was covered in this issue. In this sense, the detailed nature of the section makes it function in a similar way to a hyperlink.

It also demonstrates a further development in terms of the types of content the magazine sold and promoted to its readers; while the June 1915 issue still focused relatively heavily on publishing short stories – essentially recapping the plots of particular films – this 1920 issue had completely moved on from this and instead showed a focus on film criticism, on the one hand, for example through the aforementioned new 'Shadow Stage' section and on the lives of the stars on the other hand.

Even more so than in 1915, stars were now clearly at the heart of everything, with the idea of digging into the private lives of the stars a key attraction presented to readers. Articles focused on this topic included 'The Pickford-Fairbanks Wooing' – about the new marriage of Douglas Fairbanks and the recently-divorced Mary Pickford – and 'The Confessions of Theda Bara', which tapped into the idea of the fan magazine as the source of 'secret' information about beloved performers. Another section flagged up in a text box accompanying the Table of Contents also underlined this increased focus on stars and, indeed, the close relationship between the magazine, Hollywood, and the fans: this was a new fashion section purportedly written for the magazine by star

The World's Leading Motion Picture Publication

PHOTOPLAY MAGAZINE

JAMES R. QUIRK, EDITOR

VOL. XVIII No. 1

Contents

June, 1920

Cover Design, Katherine MacDonald
From a Pastel Portrait by Rolf Armstrong.

Rotogravure 19
Helene Chadwick, Peggy O'Dare, Bill Farnum, Helen Ferguson, Raymond Hatton, Marion Davies, Jane Novak and Dorothy Gish.

The Welcome Wolves Editorial 27

They Both Rebelled 28
Two Shooting Stars Swap Firmaments.

Broadway's Royal Family Ada Patterson 30
The Remarkable Story of the Barrymores.

Beauty Her Great Handicap Julia Regis 34
Katherine MacDonald's More-Than-Skin-Deep Troubles.

Dollars and the Woman Nanon Belois 36
A Splendid Lesson in a Beautiful Story.

The Family Circle Margaret E. Sangster 41
A Heart to Heart Talk.

Noncensorship Howard Dietz and Ralph Barton 42
From Soup to Nuts, a Merry Menu.

West Is East Delight Evans 44
A Few Impressions.

(Contents continued on next page)

Editorial Offices, 25 W. 45th St., New York City

Published monthly by the PHOTOPLAY PUBLISHING CO., 350 N. Clark St., Chicago, Ill.

EDWIN M. COLVIN, Pres. JAMES R. QUIRK, Vice Pres. R. M. EASTMAN, Sec.-Treas.
W. M. HART, Adv. Mgr.

YEARLY SUBSCRIPTION: $2.50 in the United States, its dependencies, Mexico and Cuba; $3.00 Canada; $3.50 to foreign countries. Remittances should be made by check, or postal or express money order. Caution—Do not subscribe through persons unknown to you.

Entered as second class matter Apr. 24, 1912, at the Postoffice at Chicago, Ill., under the Act of March 3, 1879.

Pictures Reviewed in the Shadow Stage This Issue

Save this magazine—refer to the criticisms before you pick out your evening's entertainment. Make this your reference list.

Page 66
Dr. Jeckyll and Mr. Hyde ...... Paramount-Artcraft
Page 67
In Search of a Sinner .. First National
The Idol Dancer .. Griffith-First Nationl
Page 68
Dangerous Days .... Goldwyn
A Child for Sale ..... Ivan Abramson
The Family Honor .... Vidor-First National
Excuse My Dust . Paramount-Artcraft
Mary Ellen Comes to Town ..... Paramount-Artcraft
Old Lady 31 .... Metro
Page 95
His House in Order .... Paramount-Artcraft
Duds .... Goldwyn
The Village Sleuth .... Paramount-Artcraft
Page 99
The Harvest Moon .... Gibralter-Hodkinson
Daredevil Jack .... Pathe
Locked Lips .... Universal
The Torchy Comedies ..... C. C. Burr
Haunted Spooks .... Rolin-Pathe
Alarm-Clock Andy .... Ince-Paramount-Artcraft
The Stolen Kiss .... Realart
The Lost City .. Warner Brothers Serial
Polly of the Storm Country ..... First National
Molly and I .... Fox
Love Without Question .... Jans
The Emotional Miss Vaughn ... Pathe
Simple Souls .... Pathe
Shore Acres .... Metro
The Woman Game .... Selznick
A Manhattan Knight .... Fox
Sooner or Later .... Selznick
Partners of the Night ...... Goldwyn
Page 116
The Sporting Duchess ..... Vitagraph
The Evil Eye .... Hallmark
The Daredevil .... Fox
The Beloved Cheater .. Robertson-Cole
The False Road . Paramount-Artcraft

Copyright, 1920, by the PHOTOPLAY PUBLISHING COMPANY, Chicago.

5

Fig. 2.2. The Table of Contents for *Photoplay*, June 1920.

Norma Talmadge. In this way, the magazine presented itself as not only providing private information about stars but also as a direct conduit *to* the stars – and their tastes – themselves, with a star here presented as sharing her fashion advice with readers, thus helping 'the extension of fan partialities into everyday living' (Staiger, 2005, p. 105).

In terms of active participation by fans, the magazine still contained some references to screenwriting as a career option – particularly through targeted advertisements – but had largely moved away from this; instead, the magazine told the story of Lois Lee, who won its 'first and last Beauty and Brains contest' four years ago and became a film star (p. 88). At this point, clearly the emphasis had moved away from realistic career advice, into the dream world of a sudden discovery and subsequent screen stardom – which, as the emphasis on 'first and last' indicates, was now, in 1920, largely out of reach. Indeed, the idea of practical participation was, in 1920, almost entirely focused on fandom: the distance between star and fan was now so great that fans were unlikely to break into the film industry but might nonetheless play a role of their own, either through winning competitions or communicating with the magazine in other ways.

Another text box positioned next to the Table of Contents emphasised both these aspects simultaneously, flagging up a multi-month letter competition the magazine was running. The June 1920 issue published the winners of the previous iteration, in which readers were asked to send in letters focused on 'What Motion Pictures Mean to Me', and invited responses to the next one, focused on 'How Would You Run a Motion Picture Theater?' (p. 6). The magazine paid $25 for the winning letter – like that published in this issue, from a self-styled 'old maid' who felt she could relive her youth through the movies – and $15 and $10 as runner-up prizes. This month's topic was particularly interesting from the point of view of fan participation in the movie industry, as it invited readers to reflect on how to target a theatre to a particular audience, how to successfully market it and so on – essentially performing some audience research of their own.

Published fan letters had clearly become a key cornerstone of the magazine's promotion of fan participation since 1915; aside from the above competitions, this issue also featured several standard letter sections which did not award prizes. This included 'Why-Do-They-Do-It', which called out 'absurdities in pictures' such as continuity errors – once again underlining the film-critical angle of the 1920 iteration of the magazine, inviting fans to work as film critics themselves. Another section, entitled 'What Do You Think?' simply presented readers' letters on any topic, with one letter directly addressing a previous letter writer on the topic of the price of clothing.

Finally, the 'Questions and Answers' section reappeared; it was still 13 pages long – taking up about 10% of the magazine! – and still contained a similar disclaimer at the top, asking fans not to ask about 'religion, screenplay writing, or studio employment' (p. 153). This time, however, the text also noted that 'Studio addresses will not be given in this Department, because a complete list of them is printed elsewhere in the magazine each month'. Such a list had already been included the 1915 issue of the magazine but had now been moved to a more prominent position near the front (p. 16) and was explicitly framed here as a response to previous reader queries, which tended to ask for these addresses to enable correspondence with stars.

The questions and answers included in the section itself were still wide-ranging, including the love lives of stars, the plots or casts of particular films, as well as how to acquire back issues of the magazine – but also continued the parasocial elements which had already been present previously, with one answer casually claiming 'I have handed your poems to the Gish girls – that is, to Lillian, who will see that Dorothy reads the verses you dedicated to her' (p. 96). This answer again emphasised the sense of direct contact through the magazine, establishing the anonymous editor as a Hollywood insider and giving fans a real sense of closeness to the stars.

Interestingly, the editor himself – because regardless of his/her real identity, he was depicted as a man in the header image – was also the subject of a great deal of parasocial exchange, calling fans his 'correspondents' (p. 113) and responding to speculation about his name and identity (p. 103). This section also gives a sense of ongoing conversation, in that some writers were clearly recurring fans (as I have previously discussed in terms of fan magazine letter sections (Lanckman, 2020); here, proto-Goth reader 'The Mystic Rose' is engaged with the editor in a debate about vampires on screen, who ends his response by saying 'Lift the old knocker again soon'. (p. 108) and inviting further discussion. Indeed, a further search for this reader finds several later mentions, including one in the *Photoplay*, August 1922 issue, where the editor calls her 'one of my favorite and favored correspondents' and compliments her ongoing 'good sense' and humour (p. 89). The humble 'Questions and Answers' section therefore aided the magazine in becoming an at least partially interactive fan platform.

June 1925: Facilitating Fandom Further

The June 1925 issue continued the 1920 pattern in terms of the layout of the table of contents, again including an extensive list of reviews, with page numbers, as well as encouragement to the reader to 'make this your reference list' (p. 5). Like in 1920, the magazine continued its overall focus on film criticism and stars, which were the key topics its contents encouraged readers to be interested in – but, in the intermediate five years, it had also again adjusted to the specific requirements readers might have in this context, as highlighted through the 'Questions and Answers' section.

This can be seen most clearly through the addition of two new departments. Firstly, the magazine now included a section entitled 'Brief Reviews of Current Pictures'. This section presented brief comments, usually in one sentence, of all films it had reviewed in the past six months – therefore pre-emptively answering a number of questions previously answered individually – while also indicating in which back issue – another frequent topic in the Q&A section – the full review could be found. It did so, the editor explained because 'most photoplays do not reach the great majority of the country's screen theaters until months later' (p. 10), and readers therefore needed to be able to read about films after they had first been released and reviewed. Another section added in direct response to Q&A queries was 'Casts of Current Photoplays', which included a full cast list of every movie reviewed in the issue; casts were another frequently requested piece of information, with the Q&A section encouraging people to include their address so a personalised answer could be sent to them, since printing such answers would take up a lot of space.

The magazine had also increased its interest in – mediated – interactivity further, firstly through the inclusion of a cut puzzle competition which, so the magazine promised in enormous letters next to the Table of Contents, offered $5000 in prize money with a staggering $1500 as its first prize – an impressive sum even today (p. 6). The contest, which spanned four months, invited readers to reassemble the cut-up faces of a number of stars, with an eight-line poem underneath each picture providing biographical detail (see Fig. 2.3). These lines – including things such as 'The eyes have found romance in France' (p. 60) and 'The hair is, at polo, a player of note' (p. 61) – required an impressive and broad-ranging knowledge of the details of stars' lives and emphasised the way the magazine had, for years now, framed this kind of knowledge as key to 'correct' movie fandom. Indeed, this competition – challenging even for the 21st century fan armed with an online search engine – required genuine fannish skill, built up over a long period of fan magazine readership, as opposed to, for example, the 1920 fan letter writing competition, which was much more straightforward.

Nonetheless, letter writing, too, still formed a major part of the way the fan magazine invited fan interactivity in 1925. Firstly, it moved the regular fan letter section – now named 'Brickbats and Bouquets', as it would remain for much of *Photoplay*'s history – to the front of the magazine, but it also contained some additional, special features which were also letter-based.

One example is a competition in which long-established star Mary Pickford purportedly asked the readers of *Photoplay* for ideas as to which kinds of pictures she should play in. The winning suggestion would receive $50, but the most remarkable thing about the competition was the fact that the letters should be sent, not to the magazine but directly to Pickford's Beverly Hills home, Pickfair. It is unclear how this unfolded in reality, but at the very least, this would give readers the sense of direct communication and interaction with the star because they would literally be addressing their suggestions to her private home. Another section of the magazine, not competitive but equally emphasising this sense of parasocial relationships with the stars, printed letters from fans to the widow of deceased actor Wallace Reid, who died two years previously. The phrasing of these letters demonstrates the extent to which people framed distant stars as, if not friends, then still close acquaintances; for the most part, the letters are formal expressions of condolence, assuring Mrs Reid 'of the continued sympathy of myself and my family for you' (p. 81).

At this stage, the magazine was clearly aware of the fact that it placed a lot of emphasis on both fan participation and interactivity through readers' letters and published a very self-aware, two-page humorous spread in which fans could send a 'coupon' to censor Will H. Hays because, after all, 'You too can write

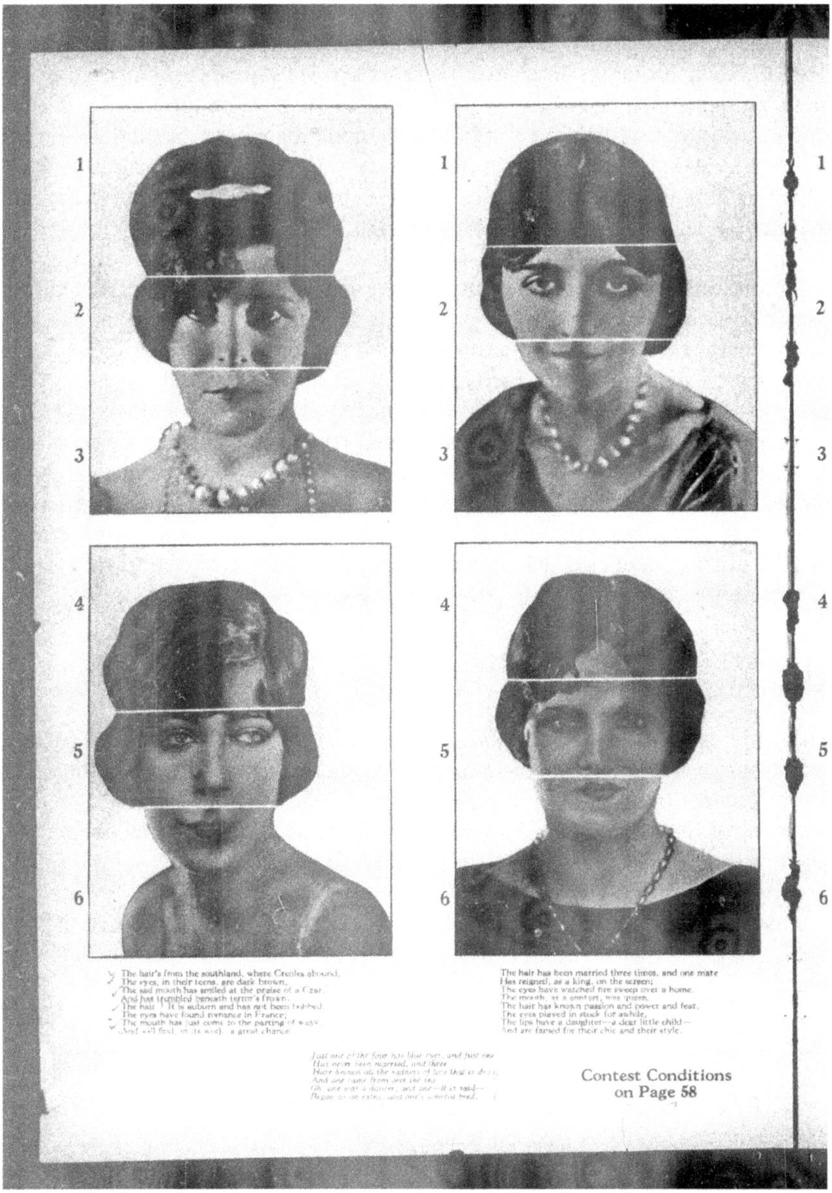

Fig. 2.3. The First Page of the 'Cut Puzzle Competition' in *Photoplay*, June 1925.

complaints! Uplift the movies in your spare time!' Potential features to be eliminated included such dangerous influences as 'knock-kneed bathing girls', 'Rod LaRocque's tailor' and indeed 'censors' (p. 41). A real coupon, on the other hand, was included elsewhere in the magazine, as it – for the fourth year in a row – sought votes for its 1924 'Photoplay Medal of Honor', a solid gold medal which it awarded to the best picture of every year (p. 52). The magazine would issue this film award, both significantly older and significantly more democratic than the Oscars, until it closed down in 1980.

The 'Questions and Answers' section had – finally – shrunk down by this point and was now a mere three pages long. In a sense, it had contributed to its own obsolescence, as the magazine increasingly introduced regular sections which answered the kinds of questions which had previously filled 13 full pages, and made space for interactivity – a frequent request in the Q&A section – through other aspects, such as the expanded readers' letters pages. At this stage, the questions and answers covered tended to be quite specific and not include full synopses or casts: instead, people asked about the marital status, height or hair colour of particular stars as they always had, about reviews of films from a few years ago (which were therefore not included anymore in the 'Brief Reviews' section, which only went back six months) or about which studio to write to in order to contact particular stars.

June 1930 and Beyond

The June 1930 issue of *Photoplay* continued, in many ways, the basic setup established by 1925, such as the *Photoplay* medal of honour, the inclusion of star puzzle competitions with large prizes, the privileging of fan letter sections near the front of the magazine and so on. Nonetheless, a few additional tweaks were made, and these continued the path of user optimisation already set out in 1920 and 1925.

One such tweak happened to the 'Studio Directory', which had been included since 1915, but which had always posed the problem that people might not necessarily know which studio 'their' star currently worked for. Historically, this had been a regular question in the Q&A section, but by 1930, the 'Studio Directory' section had become 'Addresses of the Stars', where each studio address became a heading above a list of stars currently working for that company. This demonstrated, firstly, another development in user friendliness as a direct consequence of a frequently asked question while also underlining again the transformation of the representation of Hollywood as a place one might one day work into a dream world inhabited by fabulous yet distant stars. After all, while studio addresses in 1915 were provided primarily, or at least partly, to benefit aspiring screenwriters, their inclusion by 1930 was entirely, and solely, framed as a way for fans to write to stars.

Another added feature was 'Ten Years Ago in *Photoplay*', which reflected on some of the materials published by the magazine 10 years earlier, in June 1920 – recapping, for the most part, the stories of the stars of that era but also reflecting briefly on the 'What Motion Pictures Mean to Me' competition run at this time. At this point, the fan magazine was clearly a periodical with a history, which assumed at least some of its readers had been reading and enjoying the magazine for years and had been trained in fannish practices through its coverage of Hollywood. By 1935, this section had expanded into 'Screen Memories from *Photoplay*' and covered material from 5, 10 and 15 years earlier, once more showing itself to be a periodical keenly aware of its history.

In addition to the above additions, the Table of Contents was restructured from 1930 onwards, in that the magazine's features were no longer simply listed in numerical order but were now categorised in ways that made the magazine easier to navigate for its readers – collecting articles about stars under the heading 'Personalities', for example, while another category called '*Photoplay*'s Famous Reviews' contained various film reviews. The most interesting category, however, singled out at the right-hand side of the page and therefore particularly prominent, was called 'Information and Service' and contained many of the magazine departments outlined here as improving the user friendliness of the periodical, including 'Casts of Current Photoplays', 'Brickbats and Bouquets', 'Addresses of the Stars' and indeed 'Questions and Answers' (p. 5).

Conclusion

It has been my contention in this chapter that the 'Questions and Answers' section, which has barely been investigated and has been continually overlooked in favour of more glamorous fan magazine features, has been the most instrumental in terms of both steering film fandom into acceptable channels but also responding to fannish needs and honing the magazine accordingly. In doing so, as might perhaps be expected, it made itself obsolete; while the 1930 section still featured three pages, it was reduced to a single page by 1935 and mainly concerned itself with providing full, paragraph-length biographies of particular stars. In the October issue of 1937, the section suddenly vanished, never to return – even as other interactive sections, such as the readers' letters pages I have discussed at some length, would proliferate for years to come.

Nonetheless, through its willingness to engage with and respond to a wide range of fannish queries over the 25 years of its existence, the section impacted the magazine in countless ways, doing more than any other section to resolve the 'wicked problem' of managing the early years of a burgeoning Hollywood fandom. It did this both through fostering and steering fans' interest in stars and stardom, and by prompting the magazine to invest more space in interactivity, through letter sections and through other additions, such as the 'Fan Club Corner' which had emerged by 1935.

Through an analysis of this section especially, and of *Photoplay* magazine more broadly, then, I have demonstrated in this chapter how the fan magazine developed as a platform through the first three decades of its existence. Across this time, it underwent an iterative design process steered in part by fan input and fine-tuned the affordances it offered to its readers – leaving behind a well-informed and well-trained fan base and shaping the parameters of Hollywood fandom for years and decades to come.

References

Buchanan, R. (1992). Wicked problems in design thinking. *Design Issues*, *8*(2), 5–21.

deCordova, R. (1990). *Picture personalities: The emergence of the star system in America*. University of Illinois Press.

Dyer, R. (1979). *Stars*. British Film Institute.

Higashi, S. (2014). *Stars, fans, and consumption in the 1950s: Reading Photoplay*. Palgrave Macmillan.

Jeffers McDonald, T. (2013). *Doris Day confidential: Hollywood, sex and stardom*. I.B. Tauris.

Lanckman, L. (2019). In search of lost fans: Recovering fan magazine readers, 1910-1950. In L. Lanckman & T. Jeffers McDonald (Eds.), *Star attractions: Twentieth-century movie magazines and global fandom*. University of Iowa Press.

Lanckman, L. (2020). Fans, community, and conflict in the pages of Picture Play, 1920–38. *Transformative Works and Cultures*, (33).

Lanckman, L. (2021). "They took our jobs!": Politics and xenophobia in the Golden Age fan magazine. In P. Booth & R. Williams (Eds.), *Fan studies primer: Method, research, ethics*. University of Iowa Press.

Orgeron, M. (2009). "You are invited to participate": Interactive fandom in the age of the movie magazine. *Journal of Film and Video*, *61*(3), 3–23.

Photoplay. (1912). *III*(4). Photoplay Publishing Co.

Photoplay. (1915). *VIII*(1). Photoplay Publishing Co.

Photoplay. (1920). *XVIII*(1). Photoplay Publishing Co.

Photoplay. (1922). *XXII*(3). Photoplay Publishing Co.

Photoplay. (1925). *XXVIII*(1). Photoplay Publishing Co.

Photoplay. (1930). *XXXVIII*(1). Photoplay Publishing Co.

Photoplay. (1935). *XLVIII*(1). Macfadden Publications, Inc.

Slide, A. (2010). *Inside the Hollywood fan magazine: A history of star makers, fabricators, and gossip mongers*. University Press of Mississippi.

Staiger, J. (2005). *Media reception studies*. New York University Press.

Chapter 3

We Remember K-pop: A Study on the Mutual Constitution of the VLIVE Livestreaming Platform

D. Rodriguez

University of Miami, USA

Abstract

Founded in 2015 by Naver, South Korea's largest internet corporation, VLIVE was designed to be the premier livestreaming portal for K-pop idols, matching the technological capabilities of its parent company with its business ties in the K-pop industry to create a multi-sided platform that housed on- and offline fandom practices. This chapter recounts the genre's move from traditional broadcast channels to online media to show how this informed VLIVE's goals and intended audience. Drawing from science and technology, platform and fandom studies, this chapter utilises actor-network theory to explore how VLIVE's multifaceted affordances were co-created within a complex web of objectives. The multi-layered quality of actors along with their inter-relationships ultimately afforded the platform a tightly-knit, born-of-the-culture authority that fostered a sense of community within fandoms and K-pop fandom as a whole. As VLIVE sustained a cultural shift in the modes of K-pop fandom in the late 2010s and early 2020s, it became a place where these actions were formalised as practice. Tracing these threads through VLIVE's closure in 2022, this chapter concludes by looking at the consequences of platformisation on community-making in K-pop, focusing on related technomusical ventures and the increasingly antagonistic positioning of fans within these platforms.

Bridging Design and Fandom, 33–48

doi:10.1108/978-1-80592-659-720261003

Keywords: VLIVE; K-pop; livestreaming; multi-sided platforms; fan labour; actor-network theory

Introduction

The increased consideration of the *platformisation* (Poell et al., 2022) of fandom spaces, together with case studies on particular platforms (Alberto et al., 2024), has answered the call towards platform studies by fan scholars. Whereas YouTube was once the touchstone for exploring the role of platforms in K-pop (Oh & Lee, 2013), this work has become more diverse through investigations of other platforms like Bubble (Lee & Prey, 2023), Weverse (Bollmer & Tillerson, 2025; Song, 2021) and VLIVE (Aisyah & Nam, 2017; Ham & Lee, 2020; King-O'Riain, 2021).

VLIVE, or V App, is a reminder that the specific contexts in which a platform arises, as well as the totality of the experience it affords both its users and its creators, should not be taken for granted. Following Bollmer and Tillerson's (2025) work on Weverse, this chapter aims to relate what VLIVE was as a fan platform designed by and for the K-pop community through a close reading of a selection of its affordances, the practices upon which they were built and how these practices reflexively developed through investment in and engagement with the platform. Unlike the authors above, a walkthrough approach from the homepage onward is not possible because VLIVE is no longer accessible in its original form nor are its pages publicly retrievable through sites like the Internet Archive's Wayback Machine. What is left of the platform are the 'residues of digital performance' (Lothian, 2013, p. 551) found in press clips, scholarship, fandom comments and discussions, and fandom archives, the latter in which I include my own memory, as well as the idiosyncratic selection of pages I archived before the platform's closure (https://conifer.rhizome.org/dxr960/vlive-archive). Building from and in service of this provenance, my analysis moves away from 'quantitative indicators of platform dominance' (Poell et al., 2022, p. 179) and instead turns towards actor-network theory (ANT) to examine the network inscribed within VLIVE's development as a locus of K-pop activity. This chapter begins with a historical overview of K-pop and the role that broadcast technologies and platforms have had in shaping its business and performance practices before turning to a selection of the more particular and salient elements of VLIVE.

K-pop's Broadcast History

K-pop does not refer to all Korean popular music; its formalisation as its own sub-genre is a phenomenon of the late 1980s and early 1990s, culminating in the debut of Seo Taiji and Boys in 1992. K-pop as we hear it today – its sounds, venues of communication and consumption, and methods of industrial organisation – find their core here and in the 1997 International Monetary Fund Crisis. Not only were the cultural industries to be part of the country's recovery via globalisation

(Kim, 2018, p. 28), this sector was pursued *because* of its potential to expand other industries, particularly information and communications technologies (ICT) (Kwon & Kim, 2014, p. 426). Thirty years on, much research has been done on K-pop's musical sensibilities and logic (Fuhr, 2016; Lee, 2004), as well as its business structure and community formation(s) (Jeon et al., 2023; Kim & Kwon, 2022).

The repeal of the Basic Press Act of 1980 had opened the broadcast market, allowing for cable and satellite television in the early 1990s. Despite strict censorship, the 'practice of popular music was settled around the power of television' (Lee, 2017, p. 40) to the point that televised live performance on talent- and weekly-style programming became 'the most important platform' for music promotion (Shin & Kim, 2013, p. 262). The performance practice of comebacks was formalised here, with idols promoting singles by performing on shows like SBS's *Inkigayo* (1991–) and KBS's *Gayo Top 10* (1981–1998). To be a K-pop idol necessarily meant to engage in these 'multimedia performance[s],' later expanding to include other formats such as talk, reality and variety programming (Kim, 2018, p. 2). Idol variety broadcasts see peak popularity in the early 2000s, followed by survival shows built on the weekly contest premise, now crucially featuring idol trainees up for debut. This programming expanded the venue of performance from the cordoned space-time of the stage to the once-private practice rooms and beyond, but did so through coordinated production between entertainment companies and broadcast producers.

The genre's third revolution came with the arrival of YouTube in December 2005, with Mnet – a music broadcast channel – and SM Entertainment creating YouTube channels in 2006 and the remainder of the 'Big Three' – JYP Entertainment and YG Entertainment – creating theirs in 2008. From here on, music videos became the 'central media of transmission' of K-pop's global presence (Fuhr, 2016, p. 108), with the touchstone being Psy's 'Gangnam Style' (2012), the first video to reach one billion views on YouTube. Despite this, K-pop's rising reputation as a primarily online phenomenon (Kim, 2018, p. 2) necessarily involved other video formats. Vlogs and documentary-style videos started granting audiences an insider's perspective on the construction of on-stage performance, leading to the greater incorporation of intimacy as a core value of the genre. Series like 2NE1's *2NE1 TV* – first broadcast on Mnet in 2009 with later seasons uploaded to YGE's YouTube channel – present this performance practice still in development. YGE's camera operators drift in and out while the producers and artists question their own unscripted reactions as they vacillate in acknowledging the operators' presence. Here, the physical and temporal black boxes of the studio, the time-spaces before and after songs are produced, recorded and reproduced, become another stage for performance.

This documentary-style practice evolves through the concurrent rise of livestreamed video. While livestreaming was used primarily for concerts, there was no formal industry-wide agreement on the companies with which to partner. Broadcast channels and networks like Mnet and MBC used YouTube Live (2011) to stream special events like the Mnet Asian Music Awards (MAMA), later expanding to livestreaming their regular broadcast programming (Jung, 2017). Ustream (2007) was used by entertainment companies to stream fanmeetings, with the CEO of Ustream Korea noting that it could become a 'more specialised' platform for global K-pop content distribution over its competitors (Lee, 2012). Suk-Young Kim justifiably expounds on Arirang TV's *After School Club* (ASC), streamed online through Google Hangouts (2013), because it '[brokered] the spread of technology itself' through its early adoption of the platform and because of its revolutionary interview format (Kim, 2018, p. 79). Hosts would interview idols in a mix of Korean and English (with English translations typed in real-time on-screen) while fans would be shown on a stage monitor asking scripted questions, presenting their fanart and performing covers all through their webcams. This active incorporation of fans constituted an 'unusual role reversal' that realised the show's ambition to reach dedicated international fans (Kim, 2018, p. 79). As more platforms launched – Twitter's Periscope, Facebook Live and Naver's VLIVE in 2015, Instagram Live in 2016 – livestreaming was further normalised as a way for entertainment and broadcast companies to connect with audiences and for fans to access 'contents' internationally.

K-pop's K-pop Platform

It is with(in) this history that Naver, South Korea's foremost online corporation, props up VLIVE as a site for K-pop in 2015. Following Naver's pursuit of services featuring user-generated content as a business diversification strategy (Oh, 2023), the goal of VLIVE was to act as a home-base for overseas fans of K-culture broadly – and K-pop specifically – by facilitating live interaction between artists and fans. Much like Ustream, VLIVE was designed to address the limited functionality of domestic channels for reaching an international audience; its default interface in English is one testament to this, as is its release on mobile devices first and desktop second (Park, 2015). VLIVE was designed as a livestreaming platform for idols, with each channel belonging to an entertainment company, idol or K-content creator. While the user interface changed over the years, a livestream on the app usually displayed (a) the name of the channel and video, (b) VLIVE and heart icons, (c) a view counter, counting *total* hits, (d) a heart counter and its paid counterpart, VLIGHTSTICK, (e) a live chat box and (f) a date for replays.

To make sense of how the platform's affordances spoke to the nature of the relationships between the actors inscribed within them, it is helpful to turn towards ANT and action nets. I do so, much in the same way Cavanagh (2015) does, keeping in mind that '[t]his framework is provisional... a provocation for future fieldwork, critique, and reflection' (2015, p. 410). This application of ANT is presented as a supplement to other conceptualisations of the K-pop industry, like systems in Jeon et al. (2023) or the ecology model in King-O'Riain (2021).

Lindberg and Czarniawska (2006) note that organisations begin as action nets, where roles are not firmly established and any singular action can be dispersed throughout the net (2006, pp. 293–294). Establishing venues of communicative actions is what later enables the formation of actors, and subsequently networks, with identity and authority precipitating from things like capital.

Naver's Google-like domestic monopoly and how it would be processed and translated through the K-pop community at the time of VLIVE's debut would be one example.

Unlike nets, networks are created when 'actors 'translate'… or 'inscribe' other actors into 'programs of action' and align these interrelations (Krieger & Belliger, 2014, p. 57). Actors are not exchangeable in a network. They are constructs of associations that are mutually, continually and reflexively translated and reprocessed (Lindberg & Czarniawska, 2006, p. 294). ANT is an amenable framework for fan studies, as it implicates the author-observer as an ontological actor, where 'describing an actor-network amounts to participating in the construction of an actor-network' (Krieger & Belliger, 2014, p. 90). This chapter is a self-conscious act of fanship, then, with my inscription in this K-pop network informing the following selection and translation of actions and actors.

Following Bruno Latour's work, particularly Latour (1994, 1996), this investigation reproduces ANT's theoretical pitfalls of ambiguity between the individual and the collective (King, 2024) though this is not overtly consequential as a top-level review of VLIVE and its participant network(s). What is particularly consequential is *first,* the heterogeneity of networks or how actors are not limited to the human (Latour, 1994, p. 35). ANT allows for a technological platform like VLIVE to be configured as an action and actor, meaning that a platform's affordance can also be configured as an action exchanged between actors. This is a process of translation that 'inscribes' a resultant reaction, or even practice, in and from others (Latour, 1994). An illustrative example here would be the heart icon superimposed on livestreams, which prompted a floating heart after being tapped. Idols on camera would mime the action of tapping where they knew the icon to be, making it seem as if they were causing the hearts to flutter while also prompting fans to act. This is a practice that arose from the user interface of the application and elicited continued engagement from all users. *Second*, the consideration of networks and actors without prejudice regarding scale (Cressman, 2009, p. 5) pushes for an examination not of distance but of how associations are strengthened and weakened (Latour, 1996, p. 371). ANT therefore bypasses the question of the *possibility* of agency of smaller actors – a topic well-traversed in fan studies vis-à-vis fans versus corporate institutions – instead focusing on the translative actions that constitute and determine the value of these associations. Examining how these connections are achieved and translated into *programmes of action* leads to a better understanding of how programs can be layered or how actors can be networks in and of themselves.

Exclusivity

From inception, VLIVE was figured explicitly as a collaboration where 'Naver [would] provide its expertise in platform operations and marketing, while talent agencies [would] provide the content' (Park, 2015). This meant that, unlike YouTube or Periscope, not everyone could broadcast on VLIVE – only idols and industry-aligned institutions could create channels and videos (Lim, 2015). Partnerships with JYPE, YGE and SME were first realised through 23 channels for artists including Twice, BIGBANG and BTS. With this practice, Naver functioned as an ontological gatekeeper of K-pop, much like the entertainment companies. Oh (2018) speaks to the use of K-pop by entertainment companies and the South Korean government to create and market an imagined K-pop-centric Seoul. As a localised alternative to outsiders like YouTube, VLIVE functioned as a sort of virtual counterpart to what Oh explores with the Gangnam district. Naver iteratively manufactured a sense of authority as a Korean company through the major platform affordance of its strong associations with domestic K-pop partners and the buy-in from their idols. Exclusivity differentiated VLIVE from its contemporaries (Seo, 2018), which translated into becoming the preferred livestreaming platform through sustained use over time.

VLIVE's exclusive access to idols was further manifested through the subsequent practice of livestreaming outside of traditional performance spaces, with the platform transforming the communicative boundaries (i.e., what is considered on- or off-stage) and actions between idols and audiences. VLIVEs could be filmed in a studio with a script, but they could also be filmed in a dorm room on a smartphone without extra production crew present. Streams like the latter, where an idol would answer chat questions, were the most common type on the site (Ham & Lee, 2020, p. 8), to the point idol livestreams came to be known by the term 'VLIVEs' themselves. VLIVE aesthetics were different, the physical requirements were lower and, whether perceived or real, VLIVE was regarded as the venue that allowed for more intimate and authentic performances (King-O'Riain, 2021); it was the actor that achieved aligning the inter-related actions of companies, idols and fans, thereby creating a standard of performance, or *programme of action(s)*, characterised by intimacy and proximity. The overwhelming adoption of the platform and the subsequent centralisation of communicative performance cannot be overstated: VLIVE reshaped when, how and how much communication could happen between idols and fans (_Tinky_Winkyy, 2021).

Time-Based Design

VLIVE further employed what Neeley and Mages (2025) term *time-based design* to bolster this intimacy between physically distant users (p. 16). Generally, livestreams afford users the experience of *kairotic time* or time that is 'not defined at an *instant* of arrival, but...understood in the *unfolding gestures* that bring one toward and away-from these touchpoints' (Neely & Mages, 2025, p. 17). Kairotic time is value-laden: the process of value creation is one that occurs within and without oneself, leading to a dynamic and interdependent reality that is meaningful because it is shared (Neely & Mages, 2025, p. 17). In the case of VLIVE, a livestream notification was the unfolding gesture that opened to a connected fandom experience. Community was not a product of liveness itself but of the collaborative production of kairotic time, which on VLIVE involved artists interacting with fans through the chat and fans interacting with fans through the artist. A regular afternoon could now be a shared meal with an idol on stream or the night before a concert a chance to mutually shake out the nerves before the big day. Time passes regardless, but a livestream effectuates meaningful time, the significance of which unfolds after a stream is over through the translation of fandom memories into narrative histories. Put another way, a fan watching an idol's debut VLIVE years later is still afforded community because the meaning of that moment is constructed through the actors within the stream, *as well as* those beyond it who continuously weave chronology into a common, shared history that acts as a foundation for that fandom's identity.

VLIVE's own chronological organisation foregrounded this kairotic potential, as chronological order is what provided the 'raw material for kairotically-organized narratives' (Czarniawska, 2004, p. 776). Livestreams were not ephemeral but were housed alongside music videos, tour diaries and other video content, creating channels that preserved comprehensive histories of artists. This was all the more notable as common practice still locates title track music videos on an entertainment company's YouTube channel, not on an artist's own channel. Unlike YouTube, the arrangement of newest to oldest extended through to the homepage and search function. Algorithmic recommendations were also present but the default structure being chronological resulted in a platform that was, in practice, an archive for individual idols *and* K-pop generally.

VFansubs

K-pop fans have long been translating and distributing material in blogs and forums. Entertainment companies also translate materials, usually limited to official or scripted contents like concerts and usually limited in languages. To address one of the biggest barriers to entry to Korean popular culture (World Association for Hallyu Studies, 2023, p. 17), Naver launched the VFansubs platform on VLIVE in 2016. VFansubs provided both a webpage application where fans could contribute translations in multiple languages and a team of professionals to control quality before publishing. Subtitling is normally technologically involved, including downloading and uploading files, translating, editing, timing and encoding, using various software throughout (Condry, 2013, p. 173). In contrast, VFansubs simplified fansubbing into a two-step process: a timer would break up a video into translatable chunks for a translator who could work from the original or other translation (Aisyah & Nam, 2017). As an integrated webpage, no down- or uploading was necessary, and no encoders were needed to unite files.

VFansubs contributed to fans' *social capital* (Hills, 2002) through the gamified aspects of the page, such as leaderboard rankings and the affordance of collaboration from the division of labour. In terms of *cultural capital* (Fiske, 1992), fansubbers became explicitly inscribed in Naver's twenty-step transmission process (Kim, 2019), sharing their cultural knowledge with and for other fans and sustaining this expertise through this practice. Copyright for translations were split between the Fansubs team and the translator (*Terms of Use*, 2022), and translations were cosigned through Naver's Korean–English dictionary, where links to timestamped translations would appear as usage examples. Through VLIVE, Naver turned a process that necessitated multiple instances of copyright infringement into a process sanctioned by the platform and entertainment companies, legitimising fansubbing practices; through the labour of fans and the Fansubs team, VLIVE became known by fans, idols *and* entertainment companies as the place to go for translated content over sites like YouTube (Aisyah & Nam, 2017). This is due in part to common translator interjections explaining specific cultural jokes or phrases and to the quick turnaround unmatched by entertainment companies' 'official' translations (Aisyah & Nam, 2017). On a surface level, this mirrors how translations in ANT have an active, creative dimension and are not merely a 'shift' in vocabulary (Latour, 1994, p. 32). On a deeper level, the legal and technological coordination of labour between actors here established lasting expectations of social and semiotic access to K-pop worldwide.

Copyrighted Music

The use of musical recordings is governed by copyright law. Music copyright in South Korea is split into the copyright afforded to the composition and the neighbouring rights afforded to the performers and owners of the recording. For platforms like VLIVE with a variety of video types, economic rights and royalty rates are dependent on the application of the appropriate legal definition of usage (Copyright Act, amended by Act No. 17592, 11 August 2020, 1957). Platforms negotiate licences for compositions with performance rights organisations (PROs) and negotiate licences for recordings through trade associations or agreements with distributors and labels (RIAA, n.d.). Users can then upload content with music attached without having to reach out to composers or labels themselves. For most K-pop artists, the Korean Music Copyright Association (KOMCA) is responsible for negotiating licences and determining royalty rates for compositions.

Licences almost never cover the use of music in livestreamed video, with any unlicensed usage subject to takedowns, fines and more. During one Instagram Live where Stray Kids's Felix played Florence + the Machine's 'Dog Days Are Over', Instagram automatically cut the stream not a minute after the song was finished. Felix's apparent confusion and chagrin at having to start another livestream is a consequence of VLIVE's dominant influence in K-pop.[1] Unlike its contemporaries, VLIVE licenced compositions and paid out royalties for all of its paid and free, video and audio, on-demand *and* streaming content. Though the Federation of Korean Music Performers (FKMP) and the Recording Industry Association of Korea (RIAK) did not respond to requests for

[1]This information is sourced from a fan-recorded (or, bootleg) version of this livestream. While available online, it is not cited directly for ethical reasons.

confirmation on the collections process, the widespread use of recordings on VLIVE, along with the strength of the relationships between Naver, entertainment companies and artists, makes clear that neighbouring rights were also paid out though rates for content like livestreamed concerts were still being negotiated as the technology was being launched (Kim, 2020).

In practice, licencing music use gave artists the platform to be artists. Examples on VLIVE included:

- *Cover & Freestyle*, featuring the members of NMIXX freestyling over songs like Taylor Swift's 'Shake It Off';
- *RetD*, a radio-style, usually audio-only, series led by Stray Kids's Hwang Hyunjin;
- *We Remember K-pop,* a series where Seventeen's Boo Seungkwan would provide historical reviews and commentary on K-pop hits of years past;
- *Chan's Room*, a weekly series hosted by Stray Kids's Bang Chan playing recent comebacks, music videos and even composing and recording on camera.

NMIXX being Swifties showcased how the use of music allowed idols and fans to listen together, thereby sharing the experience of being a fan *and* being in a fandom. Auslander (2023) stresses that performance is 'predicated on the distinction between performer and spectators' or that idols were still idols even in these shared moments (p. 26). There is no doubt idols were performing in their livestreams: singing covers, freestyling dances and laying down vocals. However, turning back to Latour's emphasis away from frameworks of distance (1996), one of the affordances of music here was the active inscription of idols into a fan *programme of action*, with this enacted fanship functioning not as a negation but as a layering of identity. The translative work of VLIVE in elucidating these layers reveals the fractal nature of the network (Krieger & Belliger, 2014, p. 57), wherein actors are actor-networks unto themselves, full of connections to and translations of other inspirations and artists. When listening to K-pop in particular, the presence of music provided an opportunity to contextualise idol performance and reinforce community between idols and hence between idols and their respective fandom(s). In other words, music acted as a 'corroboration' of the authenticity of idols as performers in the industry and as fans of the genre (King-O'Riain, 2021, p. 2823), adding yet another layer of proximity between idols and audiences. The exclusive collocation of K-pop artists' channels on VLIVE supported this affordance, further justifying VLIVE's 'home' reputation within the slate of other K-pop platforms.

Multi-Sided Platform (MSP)

An MSP affords a shared construction of value between various user bases, with the platform itself acting as a mediator that filters and guides these points of contact and transaction (Song, 2021, p. 174). To supplement its free video content and smaller paid features (e.g., VLIGHTSTICK), VLIVE opened venues of monetisation for entertainment companies, including VLIVE+ in 2016 and CH+ (Channel+) in 2017. The latter was a monthly subscription to individual channels and included exclusive posts and videos. The former included access to one-off content such as VLIVEs and livestreamed concerts. BTS's sold-out 2019 Wembley concert, for example, was offered through VLIVE+ as a livestream and video-on-demand. The revenue collected was shared between the platform and the entertainment company while the development of the infrastructure to support such high-volume traffic was primarily headed by Naver. Naver's IT competency and capital played a key role in handling payments, exploiting the company's existing cloud infrastructure in Europe, expanding servers and quickly employing submarine communication cable operators to connect to Wembley directly (Kim, 2019). As the alignment of inter-industrial actors, VLIVE+ positioned VLIVE as a 'hybrid composite' actor with 'distributed competencies' (Krieger & Belliger, 2014, p. 96) that had both capital and the know-how regarding when and where to deploy it.

Fanship

CH+ provided the foundations for an extended, paid service called Fanship that was launched in 2019 to provide a more fan club-like experience. Fanship was a yearly membership to a particular channel, giving access to exclusive posts, videos and chat rooms with artists. Unlike CH+, it also included physical goods like merchandise and access to concert presales. By rerouting and centralising these varied transactions between entertainment companies and audiences, fandom activities that might happen offline, like purchasing merchandise or using light sticks, were folded into the online platform experience. Fanship strengthened VLIVE's mediation of fan action by aligning on- and offline modes of K-pop fanship and funnelling this activity through one platform.

Beyond LIVE

The digital fanship and fandom practices afforded by VLIVE+, CH+ and Fanship fed into and were continued by Beyond LIVE. In 2020, Naver and SME partnered to address the impact of the COVID-19 pandemic on live music by creating Beyond LIVE to stream concerts exclusively for virtual audiences (Suh, 2020). This eventually led SME and JYPE to establish a production company by the same name (KoreaTech Today Editor, 2020). As the alignment of financial and technological capital, Beyond LIVE was leveraged to reconfigure the limitations of virtual space as possibilities (Hong, 2020). Notable stream stability, pre-recorded bits and non-diegetic transitions produced a smooth concert performance (Hong, 2020). High-definition video and a multi-cam view – a practice made popular as an extension of 'fancams', or fan-made videos of individual idols performing on broadcast shows – enabled fans to focus on their biases, or their favourite idols. Augmented reality, extensive graphics and the 'Cheering

Stick Sync Play Service' that could synch fans' physical light sticks to the concert produced a uniquely mediated and avant-garde experience of a concert's shared time-space (Kim, 2020). Through Beyond LIVE, VLIVE reacted to the live performance practices of idols and audiences and translated them into a tailor-made digital space. The combination of these elements created a consciously different mode of performance that helped propel K-pop's popularity worldwide despite the global stoppage on live gatherings. Furthermore, it exemplified the genre's elevation of technology as a core aspect of its form (Kim, 2018, p. 5). Despite Naver's attempts to curb piracy, these concerts enjoyed their popularity partly because of fan-driven secondary livestreams on platforms like Twitch.

Conclusion

Through the reading of its most salient affordances, VLIVE can be understood as an example of Gillespie's (2010) nebulous conceptualisation of *platform* as a computational, figurative, architectural and political structure. With it, Naver constructed a foundation for a web- and application-based MSP designed primarily for global video livestreaming. Its exclusivity and support of real-time fan–artist interaction enabled community formation. Due to VLIVE's strong associations with the industry, its time-based infrastructure and its archival affordances, Naver became embedded within K-pop's network, where it transformed into and sustained a home-base for the genre both domestically and abroad. VLIVE was not a perfect endeavour, but its strong associations across the network created a generative place for the development of some of the genre's most important cultural and performance practices, such as the centrality of intimacy in idol performance, the legitimisation of fansubbing and a reliance on technology on a practical and aesthetic level. Taken all together, the resultant entrainment of these practices presented a continuation of the platformisation of K-pop, displaying the extent to which platforms reorganise 'labor, creativity and democracy' (Poell et al., 2022, p. 7).

In 2021, Big Hit Entertainment (now known as HYBE) announced an agreement with Naver, exchanging a nearly 355 billion won investment in Big Hit's tech subsidiary, beNX, for the merging of VLIVE into its fan platform, Weverse (Stassen, 2021). While a similar MSP to VLIVE, key differences remained after merging in 2023. Weverse favours professional translations of select livestreams, supplementing this with machine-learning translations that, self-admittedly, 'can't fully capture the intricacies' of language (Lee, 2023). There is no integrated fansubbing capability, shifting translations off-site. This lack of centrality not only results in slower translations but more importantly sidelines fan engagement and places fan translators in legally precarious positions.

While YGE reached an almost simultaneous agreement with Big Hit to integrate their artists onto the platform (Choi, 2021), not all entertainment companies followed; companies not transferring to Weverse would have their VLIVE channel contents erased. Whether advisable or not, VLIVE was figured as an archive, and the blanket deletion of content – especially from smaller K-pop companies – was a deletion of histories. Entertainment companies did not archive channel contents in response, meaning that the preservation of these histories fell to fans. Individual fandoms mass downloaded VLIVEs to private servers and shared, protected drives. VLIVE archives were created through YouTube and Bilibili playlists or in fan projects like primers built on platforms like Tumblr and Carrd to orient new fans. A full-scale VLIVE archive (https://vlivearchive.com/) was also established to preserve much of the platform's interface and most of its channels. This chapter was made possible through this extensive fan labour, and I present this chapter as a contribution to this archive, following the dictum that 'critique must take the form of participation in the network' (Krieger & Belliger, 2014, p. 98). Unfortunately, as volunteer-run projects, fan-driven archives are susceptible to takedowns and instability due to a lack of capital and central infrastructure. The displacement of K-pop histories has therefore complicated cross-fandom interaction, weakening community formation across the genre. In parallel, the decentralisation of translators places the onus of labour on fans to find and create accurate translations on platforms like YouTube and Twitter (now X). The authoritative status of VLIVE has not transferred to Weverse because Weverse no longer affords the fan-actor practices of media creation, consumption and interpretation that in turn afford the platform and its constituent actors a relative sense of ownership and credibility. On the whole, the Weverse–VLIVE takeover has contributed to a rise in fan frustration with, and distrust of, entertainment companies and their associated partners (loudchoice, 2021; teamolatunji, 2022).

One benefit of contextualising VLIVE within an actor-network is that it illuminates how associations live on past the platform's closure. This top-line overview of what VLIVE was designed to be and what it became in practice is presented as a springboard towards more focused research on these constituent practices. The platform was attentive to kairotic fan practices of processing and creating narratives and histories in its embrace of archival authority and duties. Thinking specifically about the ephemerality inherent in platformisation, the case of VLIVE is an opening to explore the role of the archive in K-pop fandom, specifically how platformisation affects the fan practices that realise such archives and how fandom – itself often defined through the lens of knowledge cultures and communities (Jenkins, 2006) – is affected by the reorganisation of the preservation of knowledge over time.

Moreover, VLIVE's legacy proves the efficacy of strong associations between cultural and ICT industries and fans and idols. The expectations of intimacy in performance are tied to the widespread penetration of VLIVE and its enablement of livestreaming and idol access whenever, wherever. This is something that continues through the adoption of the Fanship time-based subscription model of engagement by fan platforms like Weverse, SME's Bubble, JYPE's FANS, and Kakao Entertainment's Berriz, and through cross-investments between entertainment and ICT companies to support such platforms (Dalugdug, 2025). Folding in the dimension of intimacy as a component of 'multimedia performance' provides a more accurate view of the actor–network by illuminating the individual(ised) labour required from K-pop idols, breaking from the traditional conflation of entertainment companies and their artists, the latter of which are not even considered employees of the former but are instead classified as independent contractors (Wang, 2024). Looking towards active K-pop platforms (and those that will inevitably replace them), designing platform affordances to accommodate the possibilities of practice for all actors *and* the reflexive practices of translation by other actors is crucial to sustaining engagement and allowing for the continued mutual construction – therefore, existence – of the K-pop genre.

References

Aisyah, A., & Nam, Y. J. (2017). K-pop V Fansubs, V LIVE and NAVER dictionary: Fansubbers' synergy in minimising language barriers. *3L: The Southeast Asian Journal of English Language Studies*, *23*(4), 112–127. https://doi.org/10.17576/3L-2017-2304-09

Alberto, M. K., Sapuridis, E., & Willard, L. (2024). Putting forward platforms in fan studies. *Transformative Works and Cultures*, *42*. https://doi.org/10.3983/twc.2024.2685

Auslander, P. (2023). *Liveness: Performance in a mediated culture* (3rd ed.). Routledge.

Bollmer, G., & Tillerson, B. (2025). Platform fandom: Weverse and the technological domestication of fan community. *Social Media & Society*, *11*(2), 1–11. https://doi.org/10.1177/20563051251326689

Cavanagh, M. F. (2015). Structuring an action net of public library membership. *The Library Quarterly*, *85*(4), 406–426. https://doi.org/10.1086/682734

Choi, J. (2021, January 31). Big Hit partnership with Naver, YG Plus a win-win for entertainment industry. *The Korea Herald*. https://www.koreaherald.com/view.php?ud=20210131000171

Condry, I. (2013). *The soul of anime: Collaborative creativity and Japan*. Duke University Press.

Copyright Act, amended by Act No. 17592, August 11, 2020. (1957). https://www.copyright.or.kr/eng/laws-and-treaties/copyright-law/act.do

Cressman, D. (2009). *A brief overview of actor-network theory: Punctualization, heterogenous engineering & translation*. https://summit.sfu.ca/item/13593

Czarniawska, B. (2004). On time, space, and action nets. *Organization*, *11*(6), 773–791. https://doi.org/10.1177/1350508404047251

Dalugdug, M. (2025, March 27). You've heard of superfan app Weverse. Now the parent company of HYBE's arch-rival has launched a direct competitor. Meet Berriz. *Music Business Worldwide*. https://www.musicbusinessworldwide.com/youve-heard-of-superfan-app-weverse-now-the-parent-company-of-hybes-arch-rival-has-launched-a-direct-competitor-meet-berriz/

Fiske, J. (1992). The cultural economy of fandom. In L. A. Lewis (Ed.), *The adoring audience: Fan culture and popular media* (pp. 40–57). Routledge.

Fuhr, M. (2016). *Globalization and popular music in South Korea: Sounding out K-pop*. Routledge. https://doi.org/10.4324/9781315733081

Gillespie, T. (2010). The politics of 'platforms'. *New Media & Society*, *12*(3), 347–364. https://doi.org/10.1177/1461444809342738

Ham, M., & Lee, S. W. (2020). Factors affecting the popularity of video content on live-streaming services: Focusing on V Live, the South Korean live-streaming service. *Sustainability*, *12*(5), 1–17. https://doi.org/10.3390/su12051784

Hills, M. (2002). *Fan cultures*. Routledge.

Hong, D. (2020, August 11). [Herald Review]. Twice's first virtual concert was colorful, tech-savvy and interactive. *The Korea Herald*. https://www.koreaherald.com/view.php?ud=20200811000760

Jenkins, H. (2006). *Convergence culture: Where old and new media collide*. New York University Press.

Jeon, H. Y., Oh, J. G., Wang, C. H., & Kim, S. (2023). A semiotic model of South Korea's cultural industry ecosystem: The K-pop industry. *Semiotica*, *2023*(252), 97–117. https://doi.org/10.1515/sem-2021-0153

Jung, S. (2017). Emerging social distribution: The case of K-pop circulation in the global pop market. In H. Shin & S. A. Lee (Eds.), *Made in Korea: Studies in popular music* (pp. 47–58). Routledge.

Kim, J. (2019, June 17). [단독 인터뷰] BTS 웸블리 공연 7일전, 웸블리~독일 해저케이블 빌리는데 아슬아슬 성공. [(Exclusive interview) 7 days before BTS Wembley show, Wembley–Germany submarine cables rental just successful]. 중앙일보. https://www.joongang.co.kr/article/23498610

Kim, S. Y. (2018). *K-pop live: Fans, idols, and multimedia performance*. Stanford University Press.

Kim, K. (2020). Virtual livestreamed performance and e-license. *International Journal of Advanced Smart Convergence*, *9*(3), 78–84. https://doi.org/10.7236/IJASC.2020.9.3.78

Kim, J., & Kwon, S. (2022). K-pop's global success and its innovative production system. *Sustainability*, *2022*(14), 1–17. https://doi.org/10.3390/su141711101

King, A. (2024). Disassembling the actant: A valediction to actor-network theory. *Journal of Classical Sociology*, *24*(3), 272–294. https://doi.org/10.1177/1468795X231186010

King-O'Riain, R. C. (2021). "They were having so much fun, so genuinely. . .": K-pop fan online affect and corroborated authenticity. *New Media & Society*, *23*(9), 2820–2838. https://doi.org/10.1177/1461444820941194

KoreaTech Today Editor. (2020, August 4). SM, JYP to establish concert company through Naver's beyond LIVE. *KoreaTech Today*. https://www.koreatechtoday.com/sm-jyp-to-establish-concert-company-through-navers-beyond-live/

Krieger, D. J., & Belliger, A. (2014). *Interpreting networks: Hermeneutics, actor-network theory & new media*. transcript Verlag.

Kwon, S. H., & Kim, J. (2014). The cultural industry policies of the Korean government and the Korean Wave. *International Journal of Cultural Policy*, *20*(4), 422–439. https://doi.org/10.1080/10286632.2013.829052

Latour, B. (1994). On technical mediation—Philosophy, sociology, genealogy. *Common Knowledge*, *3*(2), 29–64.

Latour, B. (1996). On actor-network theory: A few clarifications. *Soziale Welt*, *47*(4), 369–381.

Lee, J. S. (2004). Linguistic hybridization in K-pop: Discourse of self-assertion and resistance. *World Englishes*, *23*(3), 429–450. https://doi.org/10.1111/j.0883-2919.2004.00367.x

Lee, J. (2012, March 20). Ustream Korea aims to expand K-pop... Audience online. *The Korea Herald*. https://www.koreaherald.com/article/10359352

Lee, J. (2017). Broadcasting media and popular music: Institution, technologies, and power. In H. Shin & S. A. Lee (Eds.), *Made in Korea: Studies in popular music* (pp. 35–46). Routledge.

Lee, H. (2023, April 2). The world of K-pop translators. *Weverse Magazine*. https://magazine.weverse.io/article/view/688?lang=en

Lee, S., & Prey, R. (2023). The labor process of relational labor: The case of the K-Pop fan platform "Bubble". *Popular Music and Society*, *0*(0), 1–21. https://doi.org/10.1080/03007766.2025.2492505

Lim, J. (2015, July 31). 23 K-pop acts confirmed for Naver's 'V' live streaming. *The Korea Herald*. https://www.koreaherald.com/view.php?ud=20150731000917

Lindberg, K., & Czarniawska, B. (2006). Knotting the action net, or organizing between organizations. *Scandinavian Journal of Management*, *22*(4), 292–306. https://doi.org/10.1016/j.scaman.2006.09.001

Lothian, A. (2013). Archival anarchies: Online fandom, subcultural conservation, and the transformative work of digital ephemera. *International Journal of Cultural Studies*, *16*(6), 541–556. https://doi.org/10.1177/1367877912459132

loudchoice. (2021, August 27). *Vlive shutting down is my joker origin story* [Reddit Thread]. R/Kpoprants. https://www.reddit.com/r/kpoprants/comments/pccfen/vlive_shutting_down_is_my_joker_origin_story/

Neely, S., & Mages, M. A. (2025). Amplified experience through temporal proximity. In R. Assoreira Almendra (Ed.), *Proximity in design research: People, processes, products, philosophy* (pp. 15–23). Routledge. https://doi.org/10.4324/9781003509653-3

Oh, Y. (2018). *Pop city: Korean popular culture and the selling of place*. Cornell University Press. https://www.jstor.org/stable/10.7591/j.ctt21h4vpd

Oh, Y. (2023). *Heterogeneous navigating through platform expansionisms/protectionisms: The sociotechnical construction of Naver, 2000-2019* [Unpublished doctoral dissertation]. Rensselaer Polytechnic Institute.

Oh, I., & Lee, H. (2013). Mass media technologies and popular music genres: K-pop and YouTube. *Korea Journal*, *53*(4), 34–58. https://doi.org/10.25024/KJ.2013.53.4.34

Park, H. (2015, July 29). Naver to launch global streaming app for K-pop. *The Korea Herald*. https://www.koreaherald.com/view.php?ud=20150729000975

Poell, T., Nieborg, D. B., & Duffy, B. E. (2022). *Platforms and cultural production*. Polity Press.

RIAA. (n.d.). *Resources and learning: Licensing*. RIAA. https://www.riaa.com/resources-learning/licensing/

Seo, J. (2018, August 1). For K-pop streamers, V Live is the place to be. *Korea JoongAng Daily*. https://koreajoongangdaily.joins.com/2018/08/01/industry/For-Kpop-streamers-V-Live-is-the-place-to-be/3051369.html

Shin, S. I., & Kim, L. (2013). Organizing K-pop: Emergence and market making of large Korean entertainment houses, 1980–2010. *East Asia*, *30*, 255–272. https://doi.org/10.1007/s12140-013-9200-0

Song, M. (2021). A study on the business model of a fan community platform "Weverse". *International Journal of Advanced Smart Convergence*, *10*(4), 172–182. https://doi.org/10.7236/IJASC.2021.10.4.172

Stassen, M. (2021, January 27). Naver to invest over $320m in Big Hit subsidiary and jointly launch new fan platform. *Music Business Worldwide*. https://www.musicbusinessworldwide.com/naver-to-invest-321-6m-in-big-hit-subsidiary-benx-firms-to-create-new-global-fan-community-platform/

Suh, J. (2020, April 27). K-pop stars look to online platforms to fill gap left by canceled performances. *Hankyoreh*. https://english.hani.co.kr/arti/english_edition/e_international/942233.html

teamolatunji. (2022, October 20). *Does Weverse not have English subtitles?* [Reddit Thread]. R/Seventeen. www.reddit.com/r/seventeen/comments/y91nqj/does_weverse_not_have_english_subtitles/

Terms of Use. (2022, March 2). *VFansubs*. Archived. https://conifer.rhizome.org/dxr960/copyright-in-korea/20221209020634/https://subtitle.vlive.tv/terms

_Tinky_Winkyy. (2021, January 26). *What app do idols use before Vlive was created?* [Reddit Thread]. R/Kpophelp. https://www.reddit.com/r/kpophelp/comments/l5ozbj/what_app_do_idols_use_before_vlive_was_created/

Wang, F. (2024, November 20). Are K-pop stars workers? South Korea says no. *BBC News*. https://www.bbc.com/news/articles/c8jyvmew0njo

World Association for Hallyu Studies. (2023). *2022 analysis of global Hallyu status*. Korea Foundation. https://overseas.mofa.go.kr/jo-ar/brd/m_11079/down.do?brd_id=12143&seq=761128&data_tp=A&file_seq=2

Chapter 4

Creative Digital Practices to Support Sociopolitical Movements Online: The Case of BTS ARMY, BLM and the #MatchAMillion Fundraiser

Christopher Housseaux

University of Montreal, Canada

Abstract

This chapter analyses how members of the BTS ARMY fandom creatively diverted the intended functionality of X (formerly Twitter) and YouTube platforms as part of their #MatchAMillion fundraiser, which raised over $1 million for the Black Lives Matter (BLM) movement in June 2020. These creative digital practices, a concept defined by adapting the criterion for the appropriation of technical objects, demonstrate this fandom's ability to leverage the affordances of digital platforms to achieve specific goals in a short period of time. The author analyses the levels of engagement present in these creative practices through the hierarchy of digital activism and the notion of affordances. By conducting microanalyses of posts published on X, obtained through a mixed methodological approach, the author identified five categories of creative practices, three of which the author analyses in this chapter. The analysis reveals the value of low-engagement forms of participation, such as clicktivism, in the context of BTS ARMY's creative practices when carried out *en masse*, as well as the limits that can dampen their impact.

Bridging Design and Fandom, 49–63

doi:10.1108/978-1-80592-659-720261004

Keywords: Affordances; BTS ARMY; clicktivism; digital activism; fandoms; social media

Introduction

In June 2020, K-pop band Bangtan Boys, also known as BTS, donated $1 million in support of the Black Lives Matter (BLM) movement, which was then in full swing following the murder of George Floyd by police officers in Minneapolis, USA (Lee & Kao, 2021; Park et al., 2021). The BLM movement was founded in 2013 by three queer Black American women: Patrisse Cullors, Alicia Garza and Opal Tometi, with the objectives of combating and challenging violence related to racial issues. BTS's donation was accompanied by a social media post expressing solidarity with the anti-police-brutality movement and the struggles faced by Afro-descendent communities. This sparked a unifying force among BTS's global fanbase, known as BTS ARMY, during the summer of 2020. Indeed, BTS's fanbase asked the band to clarify their stance on the matter, prompting them to post their support and make a donation. Some BTS fans, motivated by both their love for the group and support for the BLM movement, launched a crowdfunding campaign on social media, using the hashtag '#MatchAMillion'. The goal was to match BTS's donation and then donate the same amount to the BLM cause. The #MatchAMillion campaign, which ran mainly between June 6 and 7, 2020, captured some media attention, as BTS ARMY's efforts paid off when the fandom managed to raise over $1 million in 24 hours (Lee & Kao, 2021; Park et al., 2021).

BTS ARMY (Adorable Representative M.C. for Youth) is a fandom that actively engages in social and political advocacy campaigns. This 'community of communities' (Anderson, 2006, as cited in Lee & Kao, 2021, p. 5), made up of several fan subgroups linked by a non-hierarchical structure (Lee & Kao, 2021), includes a collective dedicated primarily to the organisation of such fundraising campaigns: One in An ARMY Charity Project (OIAA).[1] Maintained by 20 anonymous members of BTS ARMY, OIAA's mission is to harness the 'collective power [of the fandom] for the greater good', according to their 'about' page's description, by identifying non-profit organisations to support and then letting fandom members make micro-donations over a one-month period to support a specific cause. The group's archives show that they use BTS-related milestones, like anniversaries or events, to structure their fundraising efforts, which date back to May 2018. In 2025, they supported the KoRoot organisation in South Korea under '#ReunitewithBTS' on social media, linking it to FESTA (celebrating BTS's debut) and the expected return of some BTS members after completing mandatory military service in South Korea. These campaigns demonstrate the OIAA collective's and BTS ARMY's fandom's awareness of their members' power to mobilise on social media.

[1] https://oneinanarmy.org/

Several studies have examined BTS ARMY's efforts during the #MatchAMillion campaign, including their identity, perceptions and relationships, both within the fandom and towards BTS (Johnson et al., 2024; Lee & Kao, 2021; Park et al., 2021). However, few studies have examined how they were able to achieve their goal so quickly. Especially as BTS ARMY members had supported the BLM movement before #MatchAMillion in an interesting manner: by creatively diverting the workings of certain online platforms to reach specific objectives. Notably, the fandom mobilised in such a way on at least two other occasions in support of the BLM movement between May and June 2020. The first was the strategic bombardment of video on the iWatch Dallas platform, used by the city's police force to identify people who had participated in the protests. By sending large numbers of videos of their favourite BTS members (their idols) to the iWatch Dallas platform, BTS ARMY managed to render it unusable, forcing its withdrawal. The second reveals that this practice of strategic content bombing is an approach favoured by BTS ARMY, as the fandom used it again to disable the hashtag #WhiteLivesMatter, a keyword attached to the white supremacist movement and used to share content that is often racist and/or xenophobic on social media. By mass-publishing BTS videos under the hashtag, the fandom had managed to take control of what was visible when looking up '#WhiteLivesMatter' on X, leaving anyone visiting to only find content unrelated to the original topic (Cho, 2022; Liu et al., 2021). These examples align with the OIAA collective's mission, which emphasises using their fanbase's 'collective power' to address social and political issues 'for the greater good'.

Based on these two examples, I investigated whether BTS ARMY had made similar efforts during the #MatchAMillion campaign, i.e., to ingeniously divert digital platforms to raise funds. I define these actions, which take advantage of the affordances of digital platforms, as 'creative digital practices'. This chapter discusses three examples of BTS ARMY's creative digital practices to support BLM during #MatchAMillion in 2020. I analysed these cases in my master's thesis (Housseaux, 2024). Using George and Leidner's (2019) digital activism hierarchy and Earl and Kimport's (2011) platform affordances, I show how clicktivism affects these practices, while also identifying potential limitations.

Fan Activism and the Affordances of Digital Platforms

Digital media has transformed the ways in which one can participate during social movements (Granjon, 2017a), and social media platforms are now an important tool in the action repertoire of many modern activists. Information and communication technologies (ICTs) facilitate global mobilisation at both individual and community levels due to their low cost, accessibility and versatility (Bennett, 2006; Bimber et al., 2005, 2012; Earl & Kimport, 2011; Wolfsfeld et al., 2013). Platforms like Facebook, X and Instagram now play a crucial role in many social movements, streamlining participant coordination and reducing participation barriers (Granjon, 2017b). They can be used for in-person events, like flash mobs, or online, through digital activism. For example, the international #MeToo movement on Twitter, where many people shared stories of workplace sexual assault using the hashtag '#MeToo' (Sini, 2017, as cited in Baik et al., 2022).

Some fans, who are known for investing time and energy in interacting with media that captivates them (Booth, 2010), also engage in sociopolitical advocacy. They use online platforms to organise and take action, going beyond just passionate exchanges or creative, transformative acts. Fandoms can use their energy and ability to organise online to act on social issues, a phenomenon known as fan activism. As defined by Jenkins (2012), fan activism '[are] forms of civic engagement and political participation that emerge from within fan culture itself, often in response to the shared interests of fans, often conducted through the infrastructure of existing fan practices and relationships, and [are] often framed through metaphors drawn from popular and participatory culture' (as cited in Kligler-Vilenchik et al., 2012).

Fan activism also benefits greatly from digital affordances. This concept, taken from Gibson's work in cognitive psychology (1979), refers to the characteristics of an object to suggest its use. It is defined by Earl and Kimport (2011) as the types or characteristics of actions that technologies make possible through their designs (p. 10). The authors note two main affordances in the context of social mobilisations through online platforms:

First, digital platforms have significantly reduced the cost of organising and participating in protests. They eliminate geographical barriers, allowing individuals to participate globally and aggregate large numbers of participants in advocacy efforts. Digital platforms are generally free, making it easy to recruit participants and expand communities at a low cost. They also allow anyone to create a mobilisation effort, such as an online petition (Earl & Kimport, 2011, pp. 10–11). Second, according to Earl and Kimport (2011), the internet allows for the transformation of individual actions into collective mobilisations, eliminating the need for physical proximity among participants (pp. 10–11). This enables small groups or even individuals to organise and maintain large-scale actions (p. 12). I will demonstrate that these two affordances are essential for BTS ARMY's online activism, as they excel at transforming individual or small actions into powerful collective movements.

Creative Digital Practices and the Hierarchy of Digital Activism

As fans can reinterpret and repurpose content they consume (Mueller, 2022, p. 56), they can also modify the functions of digital platforms. In my research, I proposed the term 'creative digital practices' to describe the actions taken by individuals or groups to deliberately divert the features of online platforms to further a particular social or political cause. I conceptualise this notion through the theory of appropriation of technical objects by Breton and Proulx (2012), which is part of the French sociology of usage (Jouët, 2000; Proulx, 2001). I'm adapting it here to the context of social networks, which Breton and Proulx don't deal with specifically. Therefore, I define a creative digital practice as one that meets these three criteria: (1) Thorough cognitive and practical mastery of the technical object, such as digital social networks; (2) Mastery that translates into the user's current practices; and (3) Mastery that leads to detours, bypasses, or even reinventions of how the object is used (Breton & Proulx, 2012). The third criterion is crucial for understanding creative digital practices. It is similar to how fans adapt pre-existing texts or create their own content in transformative fandoms (Mueller, 2022, p. 56). By comprehending the digital environments they operate in, fans can subvert these platforms and act upon social or political issues.

To identify digital activism arising from creative digital practices, I use the hierarchy of digital activism proposed by George and Leidner (2019), which distinguishes 10 practices, organised into three levels of engagement, as visible in Fig. 4.1.

Based on Lester W. Milbrath's (1965) political participation hierarchy, George and Leidner (2019) created a new one for digital activism. It categorises activist practices into three levels: digital spectator, digital transitional and digital gladiatorial activities. A practice's place in the hierarchy depends on the digital resources required to implement it, such as access to ICT, the Internet, coding skills or expertise. Practices that need fewer resources are therefore lower in the hierarchy. This differs from Milbrath's (1965) hierarchy, where traditional

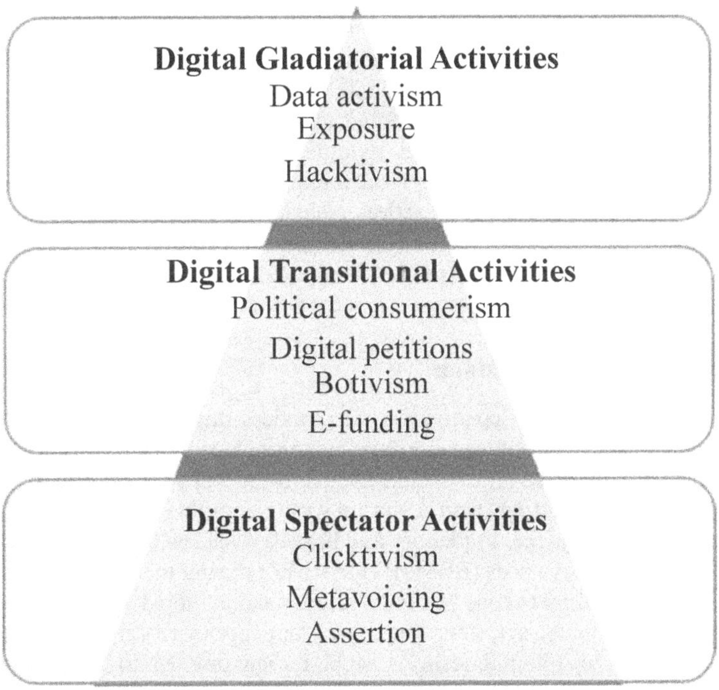

Fig. 4.1. George and Leidner's Hierarchy of Digital Activism (2019).

activism actions at the bottom (wearing a pin) have less impact than those at the top (protesting physically). In contrast, George and Leidner's (2019) hierarchy states that impact is not determined by their level, and their position only attests to their required skills and resources. For instance, while only a few people possess the necessary skills to engage in hacktivism (hacking data for social or political causes), many individuals can contribute to clicktivism (the lowest level of digital activism) and have a substantial impact. This is one of the main findings of my study.

According to George and Leidner (2019), there are 10 types of digital activism. They categorise clicktivism (giving a 'like' or voting for sociopolitical content), metavoicing (sharing existing content) and assertion (publishing new content) as activities of the digital spectator. These practices require, for the most part, having access to the Internet and its platforms and (in principle) only a low level of commitment on the part of participants. However, George and Leidner (2019) acknowledge that clicktivism, sometimes labelled as 'slacktivism' (Majchrzak et al., 2013, as cited in George & Leidner, 2019, p. 11), can be effective. They note that 'at the organizational level, large volumes of clicks and likes can confer legitimacy, validation and authority to a cause' (Baym, 2013, as cited in George & Leidner, 2019, p. 11). For digital transitional activities, we find political consumerism and adapting one's purchasing habits regarding a commercial entities' political positioning, such as boycotting a company that has a position contrary to one's own. Digital petitions enable people to sign petitions online via specific platforms. There's also botivism or the use of robots programmed for digital activism. The final activity at this level is e-funding, the use of digital platforms and tools to donate to a given cause (George & Leidner, 2019, pp. 12–14). My study did not find any examples of digital gladiator-level activities. However, it's important to note that data activism, exposure and hacktivism fall under this category, which requires advanced skills and resources. Respectively, approaches and practices include those aimed at data protection, the (often illegal) propagation of confidential information online and hacking practices for sociopolitical purposes (George & Leidner, 2019, pp. 14–16).

Methodological Approach

To study BTS ARMY's creative digital practices during the #MatchAMillion campaign, I used a mixed methodology in stages. I analysed tweets collected on X to identify how these practices unfolded and the roles played by BTS ARMY members in implementing them. I started with a computational approach, using scripts in the R language, to identify and harvest over 160,000 publications on X that used specific keywords (BLM, BTS ARMY) during the months of May and June 2020. This initial corpus was then automatically filtered with a second list of 16 keywords (donate, act, contribute, etc.) and popularity metrics to produce sub-lists of up to 100 publications each. I then pivoted to more traditional qualitative approaches in social sciences, starting by manually filtering the subsets of publications through four criteria: (1) The publication must explicitly refer to efforts made by BTS ARMY members during the #MatchAMillion campaign; (2) It must highlight, or direct to, a concrete case of a 'creative digital practice', as conceived through the three criteria adapted from Breton and Proulx's (2012) appropriation of uses; (3) The publication's content must allow tracing, chronologically, the course of the creative digital practice; and finally, (4) The publication must highlight a concrete result, which can be analysed. For example, eliminate publications consisting solely of hashtags or emojis without context. The final step is a check to retain only those published between June 6 and 7, 2020, during the #MatchAMillion campaign. This left 60 publications for analysis. From an ethical standpoint, given the peculiar nature of online data and the lack of clarity in ethical guidelines on these issues (Busse, 2025; Salter & Blodgett, 2025), an ethics request was deemed unnecessary at the time, but I nevertheless chose to anonymise most of my data corpus. The only individuals or accounts cited are those whose publications or contents are used for the analysis which are available online, were produced as part of a public fundraising campaign and have a certain visibility that, in my opinion, requires them to be cited so as not to disembody the analytical work.

From these 60 tweets, 15 distinct cases of creative digital practices were identified by manually consulting the publications and then grouped into five categories. Each category represents a specific creative digital practice, for which more precise cases could be identified. For example, the qualitative approach revealed issues, such as the predominance of a specific user's participation in one of the five categories (which became a case in itself). These five categories are: (1) Diverting ads on YouTube videos to raise funds through user views; (2) Monetising popularity metrics on X through the promise of a donation; (3) Soliciting individuals on social networks to raise funds; (4) Monetising ads on online pages with a web extension and (5) Auctioning handcrafted products via popularity metrics on X to raise funds.

Results: Three Categories of Creative Digital Practices

Here I present the three categories I analysed as part of my master's thesis: (1) diverting ads on YouTube videos to raise funds through user views; (2) Monetising popularity metrics on X through the promise of a donation and (3) Soliciting individuals on social networks to raise funds. The final two categories (#4 and #5) are not extensively analysed due to limiting the study to the 'MatchAMillion' campaign's 24-hour fundraising period. This eliminated many publications, making it difficult to provide a thorough analysis of these two categories. Therefore, I decided not to explore these categories further.

Category #1: Diverting Ads on YouTube Videos

The first category of creative digital practice identified, the most interesting in the context of the study, involves the strategic diverting of Google's 'AdSense' platform, which enables YouTube content creators to monetise their videos with ads. The practice involved intentionally posting ad-saturated YouTube videos and encouraging people to view them to generate revenue. It was identified thanks to publications such as the one quoted below, where BTS ARMY members invited the rest of the community to go and watch specific videos, specifying that they should disable their ad blockers: '*For ARMY who are struggling financially but still wanna contribute, why not add this BLM donation video in your @BTS_twt streaming playlist? All ad revenue goes to BLM funds! *remember to disable ad blocker first https://t.co/QF4R13v3fM.*'

As creative digital practices turned out to be composed of several forms of digital activism, we note that the first step here was to publish a video on YouTube, an action that George and Leidner (2019) classify as assertion. That said, the content of the published video doesn't necessarily have to be political. Among the cases identified, the most notable video (the one which the previous tweet referenced) was that of content creator Zoe Amira (2020), who is not a member of BTS ARMY, but who had published a video promoting the artistic creation of Afrodescendants artists. On the other hand, some publications recommended videos demonstrating beauty products, or on-camera discussions, unrelated to the BLM movement. Ultimately, the video's content was less significant than the promise to donate ad revenue to BLM.

The second stage shows the interconnected nature of this practice, as published videos are bound to have a lesser impact unless they are viewed on a massive scale to generate funds. This is where BTS ARMY's contribution comes in, by posting and sharing on social media to encourage people to go and watch these videos (assertion and metavoicing). In doing so, we arrive at the third stage, where everyone participates in an e-funding effort through clicktivism by watching the video, as each viewing will contribute to the total value of the donation. Using Zoe Amira's video as an example (even though it remains difficult to ascertain BTS ARMY's actual contribution to this), her video generated over $40,000 for BLM (Amira, 2020). The final stage of this creative digital practice is e-funding, where the creator donates the ad revenue.

Category #2: Monetising Popularity Metrics on X

The second category of creative digital practices was identified in publications where BTS ARMY members were invited to leave 'likes' or simply share a specific post on social media. It states that its creator has pledged to donate one dollar to the BLM movement, equivalent to every 'like' or 'share' received, up to a limited amount. Notably, the case studied was that of a BTS ARMY fan account, which pledged to donate a maximum of $1200, indicating that they intended to hand over the money on June 13, the date coinciding with the FESTA event. Having said that, BTS ARMY members managed to reach the amount in less than 20 minutes by giving likes or sharing it in massive numbers. Here we see another example of mass clicktivism, where BTS ARMY members were invited to get involved in a fundraising effort, but this time only by leaving a like or sharing the publication: '*Fellow @BTS_twt ARMYs, for every like and*

RT, we will donate $1 to #BlackLivesMatter through #MatchAMillion for up to $1,200 USD. We'll donate on 6/13 at 12 PM PST so please get the word out. We purple you!'

In this case, the creative digital practice happens in three steps. First, content is shared on social media with a commitment to donate a set amount per like or share. This method changes the way popularity is measured and understood, giving each 'like' or 'repost' a monetary value ($1 in this example). So, the attribution of a 'like' is no longer exclusively a way of indicating support for the publication's content (clicktivism) but also a way of participating in e-funding. The second step, much like with the YouTube video category, is to leave a 'like' or share the publication in question, in other words, to engage in clicktivism to increase the final amount accumulated. The final step is to make the donation based on the pledged amount and likes/reposts (e-funding).

Category #3: Soliciting Actors to Participate in #MatchAMillion

The third and final category is the diverting of the 'mention' (@) function on X to solicit specific individuals to participate in the #MatchAMillion campaign. This case is particularly interesting in the context of affordances, because of the 60 publications identified for analysis, 33 of which were published by a single user, that I'll refer to as 'Bree'. Although other posts were identified for this category, including some made by other BTS ARMY members, Bree posted at least 33 messages almost identical to the one quoted below (the only difference being the solicited accounts) during the 24 hours of the #MatchAMillion campaign. The aim of this creative digital practice was to promote #MatchAMillion and directly contact public figures or companies with the '@' function to try and convince them to donate: '*Hey @twix @SNICKERS @ChipsAhoy @PandaExpress @ Pantene @TRESemme! We're trying to match @BTS_twt's donation to #BlackLivesMatter. Would you consider helping us? Please use the "split donation" option if you do so OIAA can track the donations. #MatchAMillion https://t.co/BtOLqu9WuW.*'

Compared to the other creative digital practices studied, the user who publishes the message does not pledge to donate themselves. The focus is more on recruitment, increasing the number of people who can donate during #MatchAMillion. Because, unlike YouTube ads or monetised popularity metrics, this creative digital practice doesn't raise money (or imply an amount to donate) for the person who implements it. Instead, the e-funding effort is more on the side of the people solicited. Nor is it a case where other people can join in, except for sharing the publication, or giving it a 'like' to amplify its visibility (metavoicing). Rather, this case relates to the idea put forward by Earl and Kimport (2011) that certain sociopolitical efforts can be taken and maintained by a single person thanks to the affordances of digital platforms. The user will invite people, either individually or in groups, to join the #MatchAMillion campaign. They use the '@' function, originally used for mentioning someone in a publication, to directly address participants.

At first glance, the people solicited may seem random: there are artists (Steve Aoki), celebrities (Jimmy Fallon, Steven Colbert, John Cena) and companies like Snickers, Pantene, Ralph Lauren, Toyota, and TreSemmé. However, when we look at the comments under the publications, we see that the people targeted had been carefully selected. These were often self-identified members of BTS ARMY (such as John Cena, who also made a 1 million dollars donation to BLM, after #MatchAMillion), people perceived as friendly to the fandom (Steve Aoki, Jimmy Fallon) or, more notably, commercial entities who had already promoted products with BTS and had indicated their support to the fandom. Several comments even suggested that #MatchAMillion was 'the opportunity' for these companies to 'put their money where their mouths are'.

Discussion and Limits

Analysis of BTS ARMY's creative digital practices during the #MatchAMillion fundraising campaign has revealed some interesting aspects of digital activism carried out by this fandom but also some important limits to consider.

At first glance, an analysis of BTS ARMY's creative practices reveals that they aim to achieve a clear common goal: to raise money for the BLM movement by contributing to the #MatchAMillion campaign as a community. By leveraging the affordances of digital platforms, such as low participation costs and transforming individual actions into collective ones (Earl & Kimport, 2011), and adapting features of platforms like X and YouTube, BTS ARMY members have innovated ways to raise money for the BLM movement. This aligns with William Gaver's (1991) proposed affordances. In this case, as "hidden affordances", which are the uses of an object that are not apparent, in contrast to "perceptible affordances", which are when they behave as they appear to be able to, or "false affordances", when they appear to be able to do something that they cannot (Gaver, 1991, as cited in Shaw, 2017, p. 594). Members of BTS ARMY thus found ways to divert the intended usage of these platforms' functions to achieve their goals. For instance, popularity metrics can be interpreted differently. Instead of measuring a post's popularity, they could count how many people contribute to a fundraiser. Ads on YouTube videos can also serve as a source of income for content creators or as a funding tool for social movements.

Additionally, we note the prevalence but also the effectiveness of clicktivism in BTS ARMY's creative digital practices. They depend on the mobilisation of a large number of people (in this case, fans of BTS) to raise funds. For the ad-saturated YouTube videos, the amount of money raised depended on how many people viewed the video (and more importantly, the ads). Diverting AdSense increased the impact of this digital practice, but clicktivism efforts were key in raising funds through YouTube videos. Similarly, monetising popularity metrics relied on user engagement, such as 'like' and shares, to generate significant donations. In all three cases, BTS ARMY members take full advantage of the affordances of digital platforms through their creative digital practices, particularly in transforming seemingly individual (and small) actions into collective gestures.

There's also an interesting relationship between the levels of community involvement. The creative practice itself, the concrete diverting of a specific digital platform feature, is often carried out by a single person. The creators of those YouTube videos are the people who choose to saturate them with ads. The same can be said of those BTS ARMY members who make a donation equal to the number of likes or solicit individuals to participate in #MatchAMillion. These more complex acts, which would classify as assertion and e-funding, according to George and Leidner's (2019) hierarchy, are performed by a small group of specific individuals. They then turn to their communities (or BTS ARMY as a whole), eager to contribute to the movement and show their support. They, however, perform much less committed and complex actions, such as metavoicing, or clicktivism. That said, while leaving a like (or watching a YouTube video) is a low-engagement act according to the hierarchy of digital activism, in the sense that it is clicktivism, creative digital practices give them a particular force in the context of BTS ARMY's mobilisations. Indeed, in the case of #MatchAMillion but also iWatch Dallas or #WhiteLivesMatter, BTS ARMY's creative digital practices largely correspond to mass clicktivism efforts. A large number of people then make small gestures that may not seem very committed (giving a like, leaving a comment, the publication of a video featuring a BTS member), but which gains in strength when coupled with a more committed action (raising funds through advertising, or strategically targeting an online platform, for example). Without those efforts of mass clicktivism by members of BTS ARMY, creative digital practices would not work or would only have little impact. Clicktivism, in the case of creative practices, is therefore not just a disengaged, impersonal gesture that merely allows to show one's support (Kavada, 2015; Majchrzak et al., 2013, as cited in George & Leidner, 2019). On the contrary, creative digital practices give strength to this mass clicktivism that BTS ARMY seems to know so well how to use.

On the other side of the coin, however, there are issues and limits to consider. Drawing on the notion of performative allyship, which consists of performing certain actions not out of genuine commitment to a cause, but rather in order to improve one's personal image or that of one's own community (Kutlaca & Radke, 2022), we can legitimately ask whether BTS ARMY acted in support of BLM, or simply to show their love for BTS. According to my analysis, I identify that BTS ARMY's actions were not symbolic or performative acts, since the fandom had already been supporting the BLM movement for some time before #MatchAMillion. Also, BTS made the initial donation to the BLM movement after calls from the fandom to make their stand clear on the issue. Moreover, the One In An ARMY collective's archives suggest that BTS ARMY's mobilisation efforts are not limited to the present case, given that they have mobilised on several occasions, in support of a plethora of other sociopolitical issues. Finally, it's also worth noting that many of these creative practices (especially the case of the YouTube videos) were promoted as a way for BTS ARMY members who had no money to donate to participate during

#MatchAMillion. We can also note that some of these videos have even been co-opted by BTS ARMY members, insofar as they were published by non-members of the fandom to support BLM, and they started using them to participate in #MatchAMillion (which is the case for Zoe Amira's video).

Another important point is the 'double-edged' nature of visibility, on which creative digital practices depend. On the one hand, given the absence of a clear hierarchical structure within BTS ARMY, their mobilisations require community members to publish and promote to others what's going on and what they need to do. That said, this visibility can quickly turn against the creative digital practices they organise, particularly when they deviate from the platforms' functionality in a way that goes against its terms of use. Of the categories analysed, the most blatant example is for the case of YouTube videos, where intentionally inviting people to watch ads is not allowed under the rules of use decreed by Google (YouTube's parent company). It's an issue that has obviously caused trouble for content creator Zoe Amira, who has seen her video demonetised several times for this reason (Amira, 2020). It wasn't her who made the donation to BLM in the end, as she notes in her video's comment section, but YouTube, since Google (which manages the AdSense platform) had demonetised her video. Incidentally, we observe here a peculiar case of what could constitute performative allyship, in the form of YouTube donating an equal amount to the money raised through Zoe Amira's demonetised video. Analysis of this same category of creative digital practice also revealed that several links shown in similar publications featured videos that had been removed from YouTube, stating that they contravened anti-fraud regulations. Finally, such creative practices can also cause problems for the people who set them up in the first place. People who leave 'likes' or watch an ad have less to lose overall than the creator of a video who intentionally made the choice to divert ads to raise money. This can result at best in the video's demonetisation, its removal from the platform and at worst, being banned altogether from said platform.

I note, however, that this analysis raises several limitations. Notably, the identification of publications for analysis depended on a computational approach requiring advanced computer skills, which became even more complex when X made all access to its API subject to a fee in 2023. Also, the impact of these creative digital practices, and more importantly, the true degree of participation of BTS ARMY members at the lower levels of digital activism, proved difficult to identify through the present methodology. Finally, the ephemeral nature of online content, and more specifically the fact that several BTS ARMY accounts were inactive following the band's hiatus, impacted the analysis. Some publications identified through the computational approach at the start of the study became unavailable as time passed, necessitating a tightening of the selection criteria for analysis (by only keeping publications for which the entire length of the creative digital practice could be observed, including YouTube links).

Solutions and Conclusion

Given the peculiar nature of visibility in the context of BTS ARMY's creative practices, a simple solution to increase the potential of these fundraising efforts could be to separate the organisational processes across multiple online platforms. For example, by encouraging participants on X to watch a video on YouTube but also instructing them not to add comments or clues indicating that their actions were premeditated. Comments on Zoe Amira's (2020) video attest to this issue, with some saying that certain words should not be mentioned to prevent the video from being identified by the platform's algorithm (this last word being one of them). BTS ARMY members who recommended the videos were already doing this to some extent, providing clear steps to follow to maximise the potential return on each viewing (keep the sound at least at 50%, don't minimise the page, don't skip the ads, etc.). That said, this solution assumes that, on the one hand, the community is present on several platforms and, on the other hand, that an 'entity' organises the effort, whether it be an individual or a collective such as One In An ARMY. In the case of BTS ARMY, we remind that this fandom does not have a clear hierarchical structure in the traditional sense and operates largely through word of mouth, meaning that community members share what to do on social media, which leads to mobilisation. Such an approach quickly exposes their actions and leaves several traces. On the other hand, it largely ignores the emotions associated with fan participation during such mobilisations. Another solution, or rather a question to explore further, is whether these creative practices truly go against the terms and services of digital platforms. In regard to the YouTube videos, Zoe Amira's case shows that these creative practices can be an effective method to raise funds, as long as people are committed to watching the ads, and they are not demonetised. However, considering how many of these videos are now inaccessible on YouTube (under the indication that they were 'committing fraud') and what happened to Zoe Amira, it is curious that such an approach is considered contrary to their rules of use, when in contrast, bots or AI can act as 'players' on these platforms without much risk. Another example arises when comparing it to streaming, a practice used by many content creators nowadays to organise online fundraising and advertise in return their own products. Where's the line between watching a video saturated with ads on YouTube dedicated to raise funds for a sociopolitical movement and shorts generated by AI on YouTube or a content creator making money through product placement while promoting a given social cause?

In conclusion, the creative digital practices of BTS ARMY demonstrate how fandoms can mobilise concretely in the face of sociopolitical issues through the affordances of digital platforms, notably through mass clicktivism efforts. The analysis of the #MatchAMillion campaign reveals some of the ways BTS ARMY achieved their goal of raising a million dollars to match BTS' donation in such a short amount of time. It also shows that seemingly uninvolved and routine actions, such as clicktivism, can have a major impact when strategically used. BTS ARMY's involvement was thus not limited to fans making donations but also through innovative fundraising efforts that transformed individual actions, sometimes by fans unable to make donations, into sizeable collective actions.

References

Amira, Z. (2020, May 30). *Black lives and voices matter: An art exposition (fundraiser closed!)*. Video. YouTube. https://www.youtube.com/watch?v=bCgLa25fDHM

Baik, J. M., Nyein, T. H., & Modrek, S. (2022). Social media activism and convergence in tweet topics after the initial #MeToo movement for two distinct groups of Twitter users. *Journal of Interpersonal Violence*, *37*, 15–16. 13603–13622. https://doi.org/10.1177/08862605211001481

Baym, N. K. (2013). Data not seen: The uses and shortcomings of social media metrics. *First Monday*, *18*(10). https://doi.org/10.5210/fm.v18i10.4873

Bennett, L. (2006). Communicating global activism: Strength and vulnerabilities of networked politics. In W. van de Donk, B. D. Loader, P. G. Nixon, & D. Rucht (Eds.), *Cyberprotest: New media, citizens and social movements*. Routledge.

Bimber, B., Flanagin, A. J., & Stohl, C. (2005). Reconceptualizing collective action in the contemporary media environment. *Communication Theory*, *15*(4), 365–388.

Bimber, B., Flanagin, A. J., & Stohl, C. (2012). *Collective action in organizations: Interaction and engagement in an era of technological change*. Cambridge University Press.

Booth, P. (2010). *Digital fandom: New media studies*. Peter Lang Publishing Inc.

Breton, P., & Proulx, S. (2012). Usages des technologies de l'information et de la communication. In P. Breton & S. Proulx (Eds.), *L'explosion de la communication* (pp. 263–287). La Découverte. https://www.cairn.info/l-explosion-de-la-communication–9782707173829-p-263.htm

Busse, K. (2025). The ethics of studying online Fandom. In M. A. Click & S. Scott (Eds.), *The Routledge companion to media fandom* (2nd ed., pp. 11–20). Routledge. https://doi.org/10.4324/9781003373025

Cho, M. (2022). BTS for BLM: k-pop, race, and transcultural fandom. *Celebrity Studies*, *13*(2). https://doi.org/10.1080/19392397.2022.2063974

Earl, J., & Kimport, K. (2011). *Digitally enabled social change: Activism in the internet age*. MIT Press.

George, J. J., & Leidner, D. E. (2019). From clicktivism to hacktivism: Understanding digital activism. *Information and Organization*, *29*(3), 1–45, 100249. https://doi.org/10.1016/j.infoandorg.2019.04.001

Granjon, F. (2017a). Résistances en ligne: Mobilisation, émotion, identité. *Variations: Revue internationale de théorie critique*, *20*, 1–24. https://doi.org/10.4000/variations.819

Granjon, F. (2017b). De nouveaux répertoires d'actions. In *Dans Mobilisations numériques: Politiques du conflit et technologies médiatiques* (pp. 81–97). Presses des Mines.

Gaver, W. W. (1991). Technology affordances. In *Conference on human factors in computing systems: Proceedings of the SIGCHI conference on human factors in computing systems: Reaching through technology* (pp. 79–84).

Housseaux, C. (2024). *Les usages créatifs des réseaux sociaux numériques : le cas de BTS ARMY, Black Lives Matter et #MatchAMillion*. Master dissertation. Université de Montréal. Papyrus. https://papyrus.bib.umontreal.ca/xmlui/bitstream/handle/1866/33983/Housseaux_Christopher_2024_memoire.pdf?sequence=2&isAllowed=y

Jenkins, H. (2012). 'Cultural acupuncture': Fan activism and the Harry Potter alliance. In H. Jenkins & S. Shresthova (Eds.), Transformative works and fan activism. *Transformative works and cultures* (Special issue), Vol. 10. https://doi.org/10.3983/twc.2012.0305

Johnson, T., Li, M., & Mitchell, C. (2024). Activism through fandom for the Black Lives Matter movement. *Psychology of Popular Media, 13*(3), 382–394. https://doi.org/10.1037/ppm0000516

Jouët, J. (2000). Retour critique sur la sociologie des usages. *Réseaux, 100*, 487–521.

Kligler-Vilenchik, N., McVeigh-Schultz, J., Weitbrecht, C., & Tokuhama, C. (2012). Experiencing fan activism: Understanding the power of fan activist organizations through members' narratives. In H. Jenkins & S. Shresthova (Eds.), *Transformative works and fan activism, transformative works and cultures* (Vol. 10). https://journal.transformativeworks.org/index.php/twc/article/view/322

Kutlaca, M., & Radke, H. R. M. (2022). Towards an understanding of performative allyship: Definition, antecedents and consequences. *Social and Personality Psychology Compass, 17*(2), 1–12. https://doi.org/10.1111/spc3.12724

Lee, W., & Kao, G. (2021). "Make it right": Why #BlackLivesMatter(s) to K-pop, BTS, and BTS ARMYs. *IASPM Journal, 11*(1), 71–87.

Liu, D., Duong, C., & Peng, K. (2021). *The large-scale collaborative presence of online fandoms*. Unpublished Manuscript. https://dsc-capstone.org/projects-2020-2021/reports/project_26.pdf

Majchrzak, A., Faraj, S., Kane, G. C., & Azad, B. (2013). The contradictory influence of social media affordances on online communal knowledge sharing. *Journal of Computer-Mediated Communication, 19*(1), 38–55. https://doi.org/10.1111/jcc4.12030

Milbrath, L. W. (1965). Political participation: How and why do people get involved in politics? *American Political Science Review, 59*(4), 1026–1027. https://doi.org/10.1017/S0003055400132125

Mueller, H. (2022). *The politics of fandom: Conflicts that divide communities*. McFarland & Company, Inc.

Park, S. Y., Santero, N. K., Kaneshiro, B., & Lee, J. H. (2021, 8–13 mai). Armed in ARMY: A case study of how BTS fans successfully collaborated to #MatchAMillion for Black Lives Matter. In *CHI conference on human factors in computing systems*. communication par affiche. 2021. https://doi.org/10.1145/3411764.3445353

Proulx, S. (2001). Usages des technologies d'information et de communication : reconsidérer le champ d'étude. In *Actes du XXIIe Congrès national des sciences de l'information et de la communication* (pp. 57–66). 10-13 janvier 2001.

Salter, A., & Blodgett, B. (2025). When platforms fall: Scraping and interpreting fandom data in tumultuous times. In M. A. Click & S. Scott (Eds.), *The Routledge companion to media fandom* (2nd ed., pp. 81–89). Routledge. https://doi.org/10.4324/9781003373025

Shaw, A. (2017). Encoding and decoding affordances: Stuart Hall and interactive media technologies. *Media, Culture & Society, 39*(4), 592–602. https://doi.org/10.1177/0163443717692741

Wolfsfeld, G., Segev, E., & Sheafer, T. (2013). Social media and the Arab Spring: Politics comes first. *The International Journal of Press/Politics, 18*(2), 115–137. https://doi.org/10.1177/1940161212471716

Part 2

Digital Fan Design

Chapter 5

Fans Between Categories: Boundary Work of Making Fanart in the 3D Model Sharing Platform Sketchfab

Atanur Andıç

Özyeğin University, Türkiye

Abstract

3D model sharing platforms have become significant yet still evolving spaces where diverse communities share, circulate and interpret digital models online. These platforms are widely used by creative industries and cultural heritage institutions, but they are also increasingly populated by fans who adapt them for their own purposes. Within the norms and regulations of professional standards set by the creative industry, platforms create a set of affordances and limitations that allow creative individuals to find alternative ways to gain visibility through acts of making and sharing. This chapter examines Sketchfab as a case study, focusing on how fans navigate its categories, tags, licencing options and visibility features. Using a dataset of 7,729 models tagged as 'fanart', this chapter demonstrates how fans utilise hybrid tagging systems, employ Creative Commons licences and engage with curation features such as staff picks to showcase their work. As a theoretical framework, these sharing practices exemplify boundary work, as fans operate within a multidisciplinary environment of digital platforms. By highlighting metadata practices as acts of fandom, this chapter emphasises the intersection of fan studies and design research to demonstrate how participatory culture and platform features influence creative labour within the socio-technical system of this platform.

Bridging Design and Fandom, 67–81

doi:10.1108/978-1-80592-659-720261005

Keywords: Fanart; 3D model sharing platforms; sketchfab; platform affordances; boundary work

Introduction

Fan practices allow unique transformations of traditional media by creating situated modes of engagement for creative individuals. This engagement, however, introduces complexity to social and cultural settings; it involves modes of artistic expression, technical expertise and collaborative engagement within its community. This chapter analyses these engagements in the digitally complex setting of the platform Sketchfab while critiquing how fans navigate through the socio-technical infrastructure of the platform and engage in a level of co-creation via platform affordances in the multidisciplinary setting of the interface. In doing so, it also challenges the social norms, standards and limitations imposed by the platform's boundary work, as it opens up discussion on how platforms, like Sketchfab, can afford and limit fan design practices in the emerging field of 3D model-sharing platforms.

In the last 10 years, the emergence of 3D model sharing platforms, like Sketchfab, has created a subtle yet noteworthy shift in the new era of sharing fanart online, where fans no longer localise their community in fan-specific platforms but also need to co-exist in the plethora of platforms that aim to unify multiple communities in their vast online repository. In these spaces, being part of an online community has become a new social norm that sets the level of emotional and practical engagement one has with their fanart. The membership of these fans in an online community centres on the notion of gift economy, where acts of sharing are always voluntary and based on the exchange of works. However, for the gift economy to work, fans also need to be able to acknowledge the visibility of fanworks via the socio-technical affordances of their online space (Booth, 2017). Each platform imposes its own norms which can impact these affordances. Garrison and Jacobs (2020) discuss these norms as those that occur 'between the needs of the individual, the desires of the community, and the design of the digital space themselves'. Together these needs, desires and design shape the system that creates the foundation of making fanart inside online platforms. On the platform Sketchfab, these qualities shape the dynamics of the fan community to produce socially unstable yet persistently practical engagements. However, this platform is not solely created for the purpose of sharing fanart but also provides shelter to various communities, fields and disciplines. The multidisciplinary nature of the platform creates what Klein describes as 'boundary work' – an active negotiative process where communities find ways of engagement in the shared space of the platform while trying to preserve their modes of producing knowledge. Online platforms often emphasise the use of metadata for setting rules and organising the community and sharing of content (Kubik & Kwiecień, 2021). While Sketchfab's metadata presents a standard view of communities (organised by the categorical system of classification), it also provides space for some marginal communities that are not as visible as the more established ones. Sketchfab, in its boundary work, creates a system of classification that resists platform-imposed taxonomies, like the curated folksonomy and freeform tagging employed in the Archive of Our Own (Price, 2019).

This chapter focuses on 3D models in the Sketchfab platform that have the tag 'fanart', analysing how fans, as users, define metadata (tags, view counts, licences, categories, etc.). In doing so, it aims to reveal the norms and standards of the platform and understand how fans claim and situate their community engagement via categories like 'Characters & Creatures' to establish a sense of membership. The analysis concludes by highlighting how fans not only adapt but also transform categorical definitions through the boundary work of 3D model-sharing platforms (Dym & Fiesler, 2018; Stein & Busse, 2009).

A Brief History

3D content creation is a creative process that began in the early 1990s, with computer software applications such as AutoCAD and Cinema4D. These software applications were used in the fields of architecture, product design and digital game design. Using these software applications, users generate objects on a graphical user interface with three-dimensional data (width, height and depth) stored in their file (Adobe, 2024). The more data these files present, the higher the realism they achieve. However, as 3D content became more complex, more software was needed for its adaptation to different creative and technical domains. This is also determined by the type of 3D content that the user wants to make. For example, someone who wants to create a 3D printed object should use 3D printing software, such as Cura, to arrange the geometry into slices that can be printed using a 3D printer. However, if the user does not want to turn the digital into a physical model, they may leave out the 3D printing software and instead use other software that best addresses their needs. The workflow, while an important part of 3D content creation, also depends on the adaptability of the content in specific display methods. In the case of online viewing of 3D content, the introduction of Web Graphics Library (WebGL) has created a breakthrough in how users upload, share and display 3D models in online platforms using Web3D. Together, these advancements enable platforms like Sketchfab to create an open-ended web infrastructure that offers a community sharing of 3D models online (Potenziani et al., 2018).

The platform Sketchfab was founded in early 2012 in response to the need for using digital assets on the web (Sketchfab, n.d.). With the rapid expansion of online platforms after the introduction of WebGL, Sketchfab differentiated itself by offering in-browser, real-time 3D rendering. With its viewing technology, users no longer needed to rely on heavy desktop applications to share their 3D work. Instead, they can embed an existing 3D model in the platform and interact with it in a 3D viewing environment simultaneously. In their marketing promotion, Sketchfab had set the goal to become the 'YouTube of 3D': a centralised, searchable repository of 3D models where users could upload and explore 3D content across the web. This marked a pivotal moment in the paradigm of visualising and disseminating 3D content between different users. Over time, Sketchfab has evolved into more than just a 3D content viewing site; it is now a digital sharing platform that serves as a community-shared space for storing, displaying and sharing 3D model content. Its system allows users to upload, edit, view and download through an interface, directed by a search engine to navigate between different types of 3D content. On Sketchfab, users typically build their 3D models using programs like Blender, ZBrush or Maya, and then export them in standard formats such as OBJ, FBX or glTF. After a model is uploaded, Sketchfab handles the technical work, processing the files and generating an interactive WebGL preview to make the model viewable in the browser. With this, users can refine how their model appears on the platform by adding tags, categories, annotations and licencing details. Additionally, the platform accommodates different modes of sharing, including free and paid downloads, and offers various licencing options that give users more freedom in detailing their work and more decision-making on how it can be reused in other creative communities and domains.

Over the past five years, as more users have uploaded their own digital objects to Sketchfab, interest from professional organisations and creative individuals has increased. In commercial and technical domains, it is used by 3D artists, game developers, industrial designers, architects and visual effects studios to present portfolios or sell assets online. It has also become a site to curate, maintain and archive models (primarily of historical objects) with the support of professional institutions and museums, such as the British Museum.[1] In fact, the platform has gained a growing reputation for showcasing cultural heritage, employed in the digital archiving of heritage objects (Lloyd, 2016). With these domains involved, Sketchfab has become part of an open-access movement for digital preservation and knowledge sharing among professional communities. Fan communities have also established a significant presence on Sketchfab, utilising the platform to upload characters, props and environments inspired by games, films and other fandom-related franchises. For fans, Sketchfab becomes a crucial site of online engagement, where each piece of content is created with its own metadata to help fans construct their own visibility and network of relations.

In 2021, Sketchfab was acquired by Epic Games, with a focus on aiming to make 3D model sharing more mainstream for the creative industries rather than keeping it accessible for communities. With the acquisition, the platform introduced a Store page that separated paid models from free downloadable models, creating a hierarchy of content within the platform's hybrid economy. In 2024, Epic Games announced a platform called 'Fab', which merges platforms Quixel Megascans, Unreal Engine Marketplace, ArtStation Marketplace and Sketchfab to create a singular 3D model sharing platform ecosystem.[2] In doing so, Epic

[1] https://sketchfab.com/blogs/community/sketchfab-supports-museums-and-cultural-institutions/

[2] https://sketchfab.com/blogs/community/fab-publishing-portal-open-for-sketchfab-migration/

Games both ideologically and practically reinforces the precarity of labour in the 3D model-making process, becoming part of the neoliberal system of creative asset production. This new platform, while offering an expanded archive of 3D models, has implemented ways to gatekeep and standardise the production of creative assets more so than Sketchfab. The platform, after the migration plan was made public, has begun addressing the rules and regulations that somewhat explain the shift in the production process – specifically, how a 3D model is displayed, licenced, shared and sold in Fab.[3] However, not all communities on online platforms share the same ideals of following these rules due to aesthetic, artistic and technical conflicts of interest (Batchelor, 2024). One example is that cultural heritage scholars lost their online archive on Sketchfab due to this migration and found no category for their 3D models on the new platform, Fab (Papadopoulos et al., 2025). For fans, however, this transfer may imply a further conflict, as it could result in enforced monetisation of their previously free content and establishing standards for the creation and sharing of fanart, potentially erasing those that do not fit their criteria for permitted licence types or fail to meet marketplace standards. Together, these conflicts between communities and platform affordances raise questions about the future of visibility, ownership and participation for underrepresented forms of creative labour such as fan production.

Methodology

This study employs a quantitative approach to examine fan creators' engagement with the Sketchfab platform, specifically in the acts of sharing and categorising their 3D models online. It adopts a similar methodological approach to the Sketchfab 3D Creative Commons Collection (S3D3C) by Spiess et al. (2024), examining how large-scale metadata from Sketchfab can reveal different modes of user engagement based on the platform's affordances. However, this chapter focuses specifically on user-generated fanart to reveal its situatedness and how it utilises the platform's tagging system as a transformative tool that also anchors their visibility.

The data were collected in May 2025 through Sketchfab's public Application Programming Interface (API) by retrieving models tagged with 'fanart'. In the process, the data were sorted by prioritising those with higher visibility using the 'most viewed' parameter. To parse the data, I used a custom Python script to automate the process of extracting metadata (including titles, descriptions, tags, categories, licences, views, downloads, comments and technical attributes) and exporting results in a JSON dataset. The final dataset comprised 7,729 unique models, ranging from 589,751 to 210 views, representing diverse fandoms, model types and user profiles. The data were then cleaned and structured into tabular form using Microsoft Excel's Power Query. Through analysis, the tags were organised

[3]https://dev.epicgames.com/documentation/en-us/fab/migrating-assets-to-fab#eligiblelicenses

into five clusters (Fandom, Asset Type, Creative Style, Software and Technical), which were created to sort by the semantic patterns inside tags. In-platform categories were cross-referenced against these tag clusters to achieve the most detailed outcome. Licence types were also analysed to reveal how users make choices regarding the accessibility of their content (such as Creative Commons licencing, paid access or free downloads). As a case study, particular attention was given to popular franchises such as Pokémon and League of Legends, where users utilise shared tags and category definitions to differentiate their fanart.

The data collected from Sketchfab reveals no private information, and all data are accessible via Sketchfab's public API. The study also avoids any direct citation of users and presents the data solely to capture a broader snapshot of the platform's affordances and limitations (Price, 2019). The analysis also reveals no original content but instead utilises their metadata to identify patterns of similarities and differences, thereby better situating acts of fan-based content within the platform Sketchfab.

Results

The dataset analysed in this study, although not exhaustive, provides a focused view of user-generated works that explicitly identify themselves as fan creations. The models span a wide range of fandoms, reflecting recurring patterns of practice. To assess how fan creators negotiate platform affordances, the analysis draws on metadata, including categories, tags, licences, view rates, and download options. This approach highlights how fans as users circulate their works as fanart within Sketchfab's socio-technical infrastructure, balancing the platform's classification system with user-defined practices of tagging.

The distribution of models tagged with 'fanart' reveals that users who upload 3D models related to fanart often select several of Sketchfab's preset categories when sharing their content with the online community (Table 5.1). However, the data show an intense concentration within the 'Characters & Creatures' category (49.91%), reflecting the character-centric focus of fans who recreate, reinterpret or remix iconic figures from games, movies and anime. Other categories such as 'Art & Abstract' (14.56%), 'Animals & Pets' (11.62%) and 'Cars & Vehicles' (6.02%) are also present in the sharing of fanart but to a lesser extent, primarily by the indexical or categorical similarity of the fanart to other works in those categories (e.g. the 3D model 'Bug Pokemon – Caterpie' is under 'Characters & Creatures' and 'Animals & Pets' because of the character's visual similarity to a caterpillar).

An analysis of the 83 most frequently used tags alongside 'fanart' reveals a complex classification system of identifying 3D models using tags (Table 5.2). While there are 6864 tags used in the collected dataset, only the first 83 tags (with the highest average of tag usage ranging from 6864 to 100) were used to reach data saturation in analysing the emerging tag clusters. Also, in the process of analysing data, tags that relate to the initial tag fanart ('fanart3d' and 'fan') were removed from the tag clusters to maintain the logic of categorisation.

Table 5.1. Count of Models Per Category That Use the Tag 'Fanart'.

Platform Categories	Count	Percentage
Characters-creatures	3193	49.91%
Art-abstract	931	14.56%
Animals-pets	743	11.62%
Cars-vehicles	385	6.02%
Weapons-military	351	5.49%
Architecture	249	3.89%
Electronics-gadgets	237	3.71%
Science-technology	97	1.52%
Furniture-home	57	0.89%
Fashion-style	32	0.50%
Places-travel	29	0.45%
Food-drink	28	0.44%
Cultural-heritage-history	20	0.31%
People	19	0.30%
Nature-plants	14	0.22%
Music	6	0.09%
Sports-fitness	3	0.05%
News-politics	1	0.02%

These tags reveal the socio-technical practice of sharing 3D models and the ways in which users characterise their fanart. Through these identifiers, users not only define their shared 3D models but also associate 3D models with similar tags in the platform's social network. As a result, the tagging practice enables a multi-layered display strategy to optimise visibility of their shared 3D model and provide a sense of membership in the platform's fandom subculture(s). Given the heterogeneity of tags and the absence of semantic structuring in Sketchfab's native tagging system, there was a need to develop tag clusters that could organise tags based on their meaning and usage intent. To achieve this, the most used tags (Table 5.2) were manually categorised into five clusters. These clusters are Asset Type, Creative Style, Fandom, Software and Technical Tags. In terms of tag distribution, the clusters 'Creative Tags', 'Technical Tags' and 'Asset Type Tags' have a higher average of use whereas 'Software tags' and 'Fandom tags' have a lower average. In the 'Technical Tags', cluster, tags present a selection of identifiers to indicate a 3D model's technical process while informing users about the attributes and qualities provided by the user. In the 'Asset Type Tags', cluster, the identifiers suggest a semantic tendency to associate the visual

Table 5.2. Top 83 Most Frequently Used Tags With 'Fanart' With Tag Clusters and Their Average Use.

Tag Clusters	Creative Tags	Technical Tags	Asset Type Tags	Software Tags	Fandom Tags
Tag List	anime	Lowpoly	character	blender	nintendo
	game	Noai	girl	substancepainter	pokemon
	fantasy	3d	weapon	zbrush	leagueoflegends
	stylised	Handpainted	sword	blender3d	starwars
	gameart	low-poly	creature	substance	warcraft
	cartoon	Animation	female	maya	disney
	cute	Pbr	robot	3dsmax	wow
	art	Sculpt	monster	photoshop	blizzard
	videogame	Model	charactermodel	b3d	zelda
	sci-fi	3dmodel	characterdesign	substance-painter	overwatch
	manga	Gameready	gun	blender-3d	lol
	games	Gameasset	animegirl	3dcoat	
	scifi	3dprint	prop		
	videogames	Voxel	vehicle		
	retro	Free	dragon		
	3dart	Rigged	armour		
	toon	Animated	woman		
	gaming	3dprinting			
	pixelart	3dprintable			
	anime3d	hand-painted			
	horror	Sculpture			
	space				
Total Tags	*22*	*21*	*17*	*12*	*11*
Average Use	308	268,8	251	420	159

representation of fanart with real-life objects. In the 'Creative Tags' cluster, tags identify the core aesthetic and visual qualities of 3D models, giving a sense of genre, mood and emotion while signalling the visual language employed by the user. 'Software Tags' function as declarations of the production pipeline, situating the user within specific tool-based sub-communities. In 'Fandom Tags', tags feature prominently, enabling community-based content identification by naming the media text that fans derivate their works from. Together, these tag clusters help us understand the shared knowledge bases created by users interested in fanart within the socio-technical infrastructure of the platform.

When examining the distribution of franchise-specific tags, the most dominant preset category preferred by users is 'Characters & Creatures', which is logical given the category's implied meaning of design and fiction. When examining franchise-specific tags across the distribution of categories, we see a more expanded view towards users' choice-making process in determining a model's content-related relevance to other categories. For instance, as a franchise-specific tag, models associated with 'leagueoflegends' are sub-categorised under 'Weapons & Military', reflecting the game's combat-oriented design language and under 'Art & Abstract', demonstrating users' creative potential to express and stylise their franchise-related content. In another fandom, the models associated with 'Pokémon' are categorised under 'Animals & Pets' due to their visual similarity to animals (Table 5.3). This sample of content demonstrates that each fandom tag, specific to a unique media franchise, has the potential to be associated with diverse categories on the platform while remaining firmly in the 'Characters & Creatures' category as the primary category for fandom-related content creation.

Licence analysis shows that while most models are shared without a licence (62.91%), a small proportion of them are shared under Creative Commons (CC) licences, with CC Attribution being the most prevalent (20.70%) compared to editorial (7.26%), standard (3.89%) and free standard (0.41%). The highest count, without a licence, suggests that most users who share their 3D models on Sketchfab do not take an interest in the creative ownership of the fanart, thereby making their content available to other users in the public domain. CC Attribution (CC BY) is a legal attribution that allows users to freely share, copy, adapt and redistribute models if the user gives appropriate credit to the original user.[4] This licence choice reflects a strong community ethic of sharing and remixing, allowing other users to adapt and redistribute works with proper credit. The other common licence types are Editorial and Standard. With the standard licence, users cannot freely redistribute, modify or remix models outside of Sketchfab without the original user's explicit permission, thereby granting users controlled use of the models. The Editorial Licence is even more restrictive, allowing models to be used only in non-commercial contexts. Other licence types, including more restrictive variants such as CC Attribution-NonCommercial (2.83%) and CC Attribution-NoDerivs (no derivatives) (0.08%), are less common, further underscoring the presence of a participatory culture that characterises fanart on Sketchfab.

[4]https://sketchfab.com/blogs/community/an-introduction-to-creative-commons-licenses/

Table 5.3. Tags That Have the Keywords 'Pokemon' and 'Leagueoflegends' Per Category.

	League of Legends		Pokemon	
Categories	**Count**	**Percentage**	**Count**	**Percentage**
Characters-creatures	159	51.62%	445	48.17%
Weapons-military	35	11.36%	1	0.11%
Art-abstract	33	10.71%	58	6.28%
People	25	8.12%	9	0.97%
Animals-pets	21	6.82%	265	28.69%
Electronics-gadgets	10	3.25%	26	2.81%
Fashion-style	9	2.92%	5	0.54%
Science-technology	4	1.30%	8	0.87%
Nature-plants	3	0.97%	21	2.27%
Music	3	0.97%	1	0.11%
Architecture	2	0.65%	3	0.32%
Furniture-home	2	0.65%	8	0.87%
Places-travel	1	0.32%	28	3.03%
Food-drink	1	0.32%	6	0.65%
Cars-vehicles	0	0%	5	0.54%
Sports-fitness	0	0%	3	0.32%
Cultural-heritage-history	0	0%	2	0.22%

Regarding licence types, none of the 3D models in the dataset have the paid option enabled, indicating that no monetisation is occurring in the shared exchange of content.

In terms of visibility, only a small portion (6.43%) of the fan art models are marked as staff picks, indicating a lack of platform-level recognition for fan-related content. The staff pick on Sketchfab is a curation feature where Sketchfab's content team highlights outstanding models selected for their artistic quality, technical proficiency, originality or community impact. In a comparative data analysis between comment counts and staff-picked models, 3D models with staff picks receive significantly higher visibility and recognition in terms of comments, as the average count of comments for staff-picked models is 14.7. In comparison, the other models receive less visibility from other users, with an average of 1.8 comments. Having fewer staff-pick models (in fan-related content) indicates users in this dataset have more trouble following the technical standards of 3D models (having clean topology, textures, materials, etc.) and aesthetic judgement presented by the editors of Sketchfab. This suggests that fan communities on the platform face a set of limitations imposed by the platform's inherent neoliberal logic, which involves gatekeeping content to establish a social standard for 3D model workflows.

Discussion

The findings discussed demonstrate how fans make various strategic decisions to navigate through the platform's affordances to gain visibility through membership in shared community practices. These practices primarily relate to what Klein (2017) refers to as 'boundary work', a negotiation of practices between various domains in a shared space, specifically the socio-technical infrastructure of the platform Sketchfab. Despite these negotiations, Sketchfab remains a site of convergence (Jenkins, 2006) where users and communities adapt to the diversified ecosystem of the platform by learning to be both ethically responsive and responsible to other knowledge productions, by sharing 3D models. Through the platform affordances, users gain agency to participate in the platform's social engagement, develop a sense of membership and construct a relational authorship where works become part of an iterative process (Booth, 2017). Alberto (2021) suggests that platform affordances 'become suggestions and frameworks for the works built upon them'. In this context, platform affordances include the categories, tags, licencing options and other technical attributes of the platform Sketchfab. However, while the platform maintains these affordances, there are certain features where specific acts of sharing are privileged above others, marginalising practices such as those for sharing fanart. One example is the field of cultural heritage. Over the past few years, Sketchfab has established partnerships with various public and private museum institutions, where its professional contributions (in the form of sharing 3D models of museum objects) have been given significantly increased visibility, while amateur works have not. This was one of the first milestones to transform the platform from an open-access 3D model sharing repository into a professional site where 3D models are valued based on their technical and material accuracy. In the case of fanart, platform visibility was measured by cross-referencing the staff pick feature with comment activity, where low staff pick ratings receive fewer comments and vice versa. These findings align with Dym and Fiesler's (2018) argument that fan visibility is contingent upon both creative effort and the platform's internal value-setting on aesthetic and technical aspects. Through these curatorial mechanisms, Sketchfab creates a subtle yet significant bias in the hierarchy of content, transitioning into a market-driven platform where professional 3D models are valued more highly than amateur fanart.

Licencing highlights other values that should be considered when understanding fan participation. A large portion of 3D models are shared without any explicit licences. Those which are licenced more often use the CC Attribution licence than other Commercial (Editorial or Standard) licences, which reflects a collective pattern of openness, remixability and relational authorship in fan engagement (Booth, 2017; Jenkins, 2006; Lessig, 2008). These licencing choices demonstrate Lessig's (2008) theory of hybrid economies, where a single platform can sustain both free cultural production and commercial exchange. However, when examining fanart, no user engages in the monetisation option of the platform. Offering free downloads is an additional move that grants membership to online fan communities while enhancing the visibility of the 3D model and its users. As a result, this choice enables fans to create a participatory online community where the relationship between users is built on trust and responsibility through the sharing of content with others' permission. This stands in contrast to Sketchfab's anti-democratic monetisation infrastructure, highlighting the hybrid economic model as fans operate within a professionalised platform while embodying anti-commercial values.

While tagging on Sketchfab provides users with more freedom in defining their 3D models, it lacks a specific semantic infrastructure. Users have therefore had to create their own meaning clusters through association. These associations are followed by Klein's (2017) notion of 'trading zones', where shared vocabularies are used in communicating in interdisciplinary spaces. The emergence of these tag clusters (Creative Tags, Technical Tags, Asset Type Tags, Software Tags and Fandom Tags) is used for decoding and familiarising oneself with these shared vocabularies. Through these zones, communities can engage in the shared aspects of their used tags and negotiate and transfer meaning through their adaptations. These zones are not just functional – they are political. They assert user agency on how things should be reorganised, given their particular networked engagement. One of the ways these zones create meaning can be seen by examining the relationship between identity and technical competence. In these cases, using technical tags and software tags clusters suggests a certain growth of technology-literate users who position themselves in relation to the tools they use. These clusters also reveal, as Rehak (2017) notes, a blurring of the lines between amateur and professional, based on their specialised technical skills and knowledge. On Sketchfab, these skills enhance visibility and assert creative autonomy within the platform's complex hierarchical network. These tag clusters illustrate what Stein (2017) emphasises as 'transformative authorship', where users utilise metadata to inscribe meaning into their work and set a level of membership in a sub-community. This also demonstrates that fan creators are not passive participants but active collaborators who build alternative networks of visibility through implicit patterns of participation. Moreover, the data show an interplay between platform affordances and user engagement as the core function of the platform's socio-technical infrastructure. These interplays, as Alberto (2021) notes, are never neutral, as they enable and limit fan engagement in their situated and sometimes political relation with the acts of sharing. They are products of the hybrid economy, where participatory culture is both mediated and sustained by the market-driven logic of the platform Sketchfab.

Conclusion

The results of this chapter suggest that while platforms like Sketchfab standardise sharing options, users can learn to overcome or navigate the complex socio-technical system of the platform by adapting to the conditions of their own specific usage. To illustrate this point, this chapter presents the community of fans as a case study, where fanart is situated within the boundary work of the technical and creative zones employed inside the platform. To fully explore these outcomes, zones and practices, it is important to employ an interdisciplinary methodological lens, where knowledge often emerges through 'collaboration at the boundaries between disciplines' (Jacobs, 2020). In fan studies, this translates into a bricoleur's methodology which acknowledges the co-constitutive role of digital platforms, such as Sketchfab, and their social engagement. To do that, one must be aware of fan content, practice and adaptation while understanding the role of metadata, platform affordances, social engagement and economic systems to determine how fans are (un)seen in the digital space.

On platforms like Tumblr, fan practices are shaped by tagging practices, which serve as a form of user engagement. Stein (2017) observes that Tumblr's fan aesthetics emerge from the interplay between fans and the design elements of the interface, such as infinite scrolling, reblogging and hashtags. These features encourage what she calls an 'aesthetic of abundant multiplicity and multidirectional flow', where content is never static but continually recirculated, remixed and reframed. Tags on Tumblr work less as fixed categorisations than as dialogical tools, enabling playful categorisation and the construction of situated communities. In this sense, Tumblr fosters participation and membership through openness and negotiation among users. It creates a dialogical virtual space where visibility is linked to affective engagement rather than technical competence or professionalism. In contrast, Sketchfab is structured not around flow but rather around its individual contents. Its interface centres on viewing a 3D model as an individual object. In this circumstance, finding relationships between discrete objects can only be achieved through community appropriation of metadata, as they are designed to be more functional than playful. Tags on Sketchfab, hence, operate backstage of these relationship networks, helping build a sense of membership in a community by allowing fans to name their technical and artistic skills. This system encourages fan creators to demonstrate a level of competence in their use of software, workflows, aesthetics, design skills and fandom-related areas. As a result, Sketchfab shows a strong demonstration of how tagging systems can be used transformatively in shaping the construction of fan communities in spaces where their presence is not prioritised and sometimes neglected.

What makes Sketchfab valuable to fan studies and design studies is that the platform was never designed with fans in mind. Unlike platforms like Archive of Our Own, where fan practices are central to their existence, Sketchfab was founded as a general online repository of 3D models for various communities, disciplines, and fields. Therefore, the adoption by fan communities of Sketchfab resulted from their need to showcase their work. Fans utilise the platform interface, initially designed for professional visibility and transform it into a participatory space for play, creativity, and community. The issues of visibility and membership emerged later as issues relating to boundary work between communities has become more striking. The tension between the design logic of the platform and a cultural practice rooted in hybrid economies makes Sketchfab a critical site of inquiry. As a result, this chapter demonstrates how platforms like Sketchfab demonstrate boundary work in negotiating visibility practices and community engagement among fans and other communities through hybrid economies that may reveal tensions while supporting the diverse needs of their shared online presence.

References

Adobe. (2024, March 6). *A short history of 3D*. Adobe Help Center. https://helpx.adobe.com/substance-3d-epic/3d-intro/3d-history.html

Alberto, M. K. (2021). Exploring how fans use platforms: A platform studies approach to fan studies projects. In P. Booth & R. Williams (Eds.), *A fan studies primer: Method, research, ethics* (pp. 239–254). University of Iowa Press. https://doi.org/10.2307/j.ctv20dsbvz.19

Batchelor, J. (2024, October 22). Epic launches combined Fab marketplace amid confusion and backlash from artists and developers. *GamesIndustry.biz*. https://www.gamesindustry.biz/epic-launches-combined-fab-marketplace-amid-confusion-and-backlash-from-artists-and-developers

Booth, P. (2017). *Digital fandom 2.0: New media studies*. Peter Lang. https://doi.org/10.3726/978-1-4539-1654-4

Dym, B., & Fiesler, C. (2018). Generations, migrations, and the future of fandom's private spaces. *Transformative Works and Cultures*, *28*. https://doi.org/10.3983/twc.2018.1583

Garrison, S. T., & Jacobs, N. J. (2020). Life as a networked fan. *AoIR Selected Papers of Internet Research*. https://spir.aoir.org/ojs/index.php/spir/article/view/11216

Jacobs, N. (2020). Interdisciplinary methodologies for the fan studies bricoleur. *Transformative Works and Cultures*, *33*.

Jenkins, H. (2006). *Convergence culture: Where old and new media collide*. NYU Press. http://www.jstor.org/stable/j.ctt9qffwr

Klein, J. T. (2017). The boundary work of making in digital humanities. In J. Sayers (Ed.), *Making things and drawing boundaries: Experiments in the digital humanities* (pp. 21–31). University of Minnesota Press. https://doi.org/10.5749/j.ctt1pwt6wq.4

Kubik, T., & Kwiecień, A. (2021). Resolving dilemmas arising during design and implementation of digital repository of heterogenic scientific resources. *Applied Sciences*, *11*(1), 215. https://doi.org/10.3390/app11010215

Lessig, L. (2008). *Remix: Making art and commerce thrive in the hybrid economy*. Penguin Press.

Lloyd, J. (2016). Contextualizing 3D cultural heritage. In M. Ioannides, E. Fink, A. Moropoulou, M. Hagedorn-Saupe, A. Fresa, G. Liestøl, V. Rajcic, & P. Grussenmeyer (Eds.), *Digital heritage: Progress in cultural heritage: Documentation, preservation, and protection* (pp. 859–868). Springer. https://doi.org/10.1007/978-3-319-48496-9_69

Papadopoulos, C., Gillikin Schoueri, K., & Schreibman, S. (2025). And now what? Three-dimensional scholarship and infrastructures in the post-Sketchfab era. *Heritage*, *8*(3), 99. https://doi.org/10.3390/heritage8030099

Potenziani, M., Callieri, M., Dellepiane, M., & Scopigno, R. (2018). Publishing and consuming 3D content on the web: A survey. *Foundations and Trends® in Computer Graphics and Vision*, *10*(4), 244–333. https://doi.org/10.1561/0600000083

Price, L. (2019). Fandom, folksonomies and creativity: The case of the archive of our own. In D. Haynes & J. Vernau (Eds.), *The human position in an artificial world: Creativity, ethics and AI in knowledge organization: ISKO UK Sixth Biennial Conference* (pp. 11–37). Ergon. 15–16 July 2019. https://doi.org/10.5771/9783956505508-11

Rehak, B. (2017). From model building to 3D printing: Star Trek and build code across the analog/digital divide. In M. A. Click & S. Scott (Eds.), *The Routledge companion to media fandom* (pp. 114–122). Routledge. https://doi.org/10.4324/9781315637518-15

Sketchfab. (n.d.). *About sketchfab*. https://sketchfab.com/about

Spiess, F., Waltenspül, R., & Schuldt, H. (2024, July 24). The sketchfab 3D creative commons collection (S3D3C). *arXiv*. https://doi.org/10.48550/arXiv.2407.17205

Stein, L. E. (2017). Tumblr fan aesthetics. In M. A. Click & S. Scott (Eds.), *The Routledge companion to media fandom* (pp. 86–97). Routledge. https://doi.org/10.4324/9781315637518-12

Stein, L. E., & Busse, K. (2009). Limit play: Fan authorship between source text, intertext, and context. *Popular Communication*, *7*(4), 192–207. https://doi.org/10.1080/15405700903177545

Chapter 6

Fans, Followers and Fabrications: The Psychology Behind Human Bonds With Virtual Influencers

Wolfgang J. Weitzl[a,b] *and René H. Kerschbaumer*[c]

[a]University of Applied Sciences Upper Austria, Austria
[b]Department of Communication, University of Vienna, Austria
[c]CAMPUS 02 University of Applied Sciences in Graz, Austria

Abstract

Virtual influencers (VIs) – computer-generated avatars designed to act and feel like human influencers – are rapidly transforming how audiences connect with digital personalities. This chapter investigates the psychology and marketing dynamics behind these artificial yet remarkably engaging figures. Drawing on theories of parasocial interaction, anthropomorphism and fan studies, the authors explore how consumers develop emotional bonds with VIs, why these relationships can resemble those with human influencers and where important differences arise. Real-world cases, such as Lil Miquela, illustrate how narrative design, authenticity cues and fan community participation shape attachment and trust.

The authors address three guiding questions: (1) When and how do consumers form close relationships with VIs? (2) In what ways do these connections mirror or diverge from those with human influencers? (3) How can VIs be designed to maximise engagement, foster fandom and serve as credible brand ambassadors? The authors' analysis highlights both opportunities and challenges – ranging from the allure of futuristic personas to persistent concerns around authenticity and ethics.

Bridging Design and Fandom, 83–98

doi:10.1108/978-1-80592-659-720261006

By combining insights from marketing, psychology and fan culture, this chapter positions VIs not merely as promotional tools but as cultural figures capable of building communities, sparking creativity and reshaping the future of influencer marketing.

Keywords: Virtual influencers; parasocial relationships; fan communities; influencer marketing; influencer authenticity; anthropomorphism; digital fandom

Introduction

Virtual influencers (VIs) (i.e., computer-generated social media avatars with humanoid features and behaviours, enabling consumers to interact with them similarly to human influencers; Shao, 2024) have rapidly emerged as a new marketing force. They are designed with appealing visuals, interesting storylines and relatable personas (De Cicco et al., 2024; Liu & Wang, 2025). VIs blur reality by mimicking human emotions, opinions and lifestyles. These digital characters are created to foster close relationships with diverse audiences. Case evidence shows that VIs are truly capable of attracting millions of fans. *Lil Miquela*, for example, has amassed over 2.4 million Instagram followers (Shen, 2024).

The proliferation of VIs raises intriguing questions about how consumers relate to them. VIs can possess anthropomorphic characteristics like an attractive appearance or a distinct personality, which can cultivate parasocial relationships (Dabiran et al., 2024). However, as VIs become more human-like, consumers often react with mental unease (Kim et al., 2024), which potentially diminishes the strength of parasocial relationships (Lim & Lee, 2023). Yet, academic research on relational aspects remains nascent. Early studies have begun to examine VIs' authenticity (e.g., Koles et al., 2024) and credibility relative to human influencers (e.g., Chiu & Ho, 2023), yielding mixed findings and highlighting a clear gap in knowledge: we still lack an integrated understanding of when and how consumers develop close relationships with VIs, the quality of these relationships and how to design effective VIs.

We explore consumer relationships with VIs by drawing on various theories and key concepts (e.g., parasocial interaction, social identity, anthropomorphism) to develop important insights into this phenomenon. We also explicitly connect our discussion to the field of fan studies, recognising that followers of VIs often behave like *fandoms*, with strong emotional investment and community-building.

The chapter is structured as follows: We begin by reviewing relevant concepts on influencer-follower relationships and fan communities. Drawing on this theoretical background, we then address the following research questions: (1) When and how can consumers develop close relationships with VIs? (2) Can these relationships be similar to those with human social influencers? (3) How should VIs be designed to cultivate strong relationships, foster positive fan experiences and maximise community engagement? We conclude with a discussion, offering evidence-based recommendations on how to design VIs properly to create a significant following.

Theoretical Background

VIs in Marketing

VIs are typically 3D-modelled or animated personas operated by teams or algorithms, who exist only online but behave like real human influencers. They create content, interact with followers via comments and promote brands or causes. These figures are essentially fictionalised modern versions of branded characters that suddenly become more realistic (Ham et al., 2024). In other words, VIs synthesise the controllable branding of a virtual character with the social presence and relatability of a human influencer. They are persuasive, social and interactive by design (Guo et al., 2025). The rise of VIs has been fuelled by social media platforms enabling them to attract large follower bases (Zhou et al., 2024). Recent counts suggest there are now over 200 active VIs worldwide (Shen, 2024) – some achieving celebrity-like status like *Lil Miquela* (@lilmiquela), who partners with prominent brands like *Prada*, *Dior* and *Calvin Klein*.

From a marketing perspective, VIs offer unique advantages. They are entirely controlled by their creators, allowing consistent branding and risk management (e.g., no unscripted scandals). They are always available, infinitely scalable and can even be 'refashioned' over time. Their fantastical nature can generate novelty and 'coolness' appeal (Kim et al., 2024). However, VIs also pose challenges such as a lack of *authenticity* – a critical currency in influencer marketing: a VI might struggle to be seen as genuine. Another issue is *trustworthiness* (Liu & Wang, 2025) – consumers may question whether a VI can offer credible opinions or if it's just a corporate mouthpiece.

Parasocial Relationships and Influencer–Follower Bonds

Introduced by Horton and Wohl (1956) in the context of television personas, *parasocial relationship theory* describes one-sided emotional bonds with media figures. Consumers may feel as if an influencer is a friend, developing feelings of closeness and affection. In social media, parasocial dynamics are intensified: Influencers share personal content and interact with comments, creating an *illusion of intimacy*. Social influencers facilitate multiple parasocial interactions (PSIs) among online users through attractiveness, credibility or professionalism (Dabiran et al., 2024). Like real friendships, PSIs can increase trust and loyalty, thereby enhancing persuasive influence (Wilkie et al., 2022). Especially on social media, PSI serves as a foundation for brand relationships, as followers connected to a brand's spokesperson are more engaged (Labrecque, 2014).

Key drivers include *attractiveness*, *similarity* and *authentic self-disclosure* (Liu & Lee, 2024). Followers perceiving an influencer as relatable are more likely to develop trust and affection. These factors have been studied mostly with human influencers, but they are equally relevant to VIs – with some twists. A VI can be designed to be highly attractive and tailored to audience preferences. However, similarity and authenticity may be harder to convey for a VI, who is regarded to have non-human cognition, which decreases attributions of human similarity (Stein et al., 2024). Nevertheless, VIs can meet important antecedents of parasocial relationships, including affinity, congruence with users' genre preferences (Liebers & Straub, 2020) or audience address styles (Li et al., 2024; Yang et al., 2023).

Fan Communities and Fandom in Marketing

The *community* context plays a powerful role, as fans often gather in online communities around beloved influencers. Such fandoms can greatly amplify loyalty and engagement. Studies highlight that such social groups provide connection, belonging, joy and excitement. Members of fan communities share not only an affinity for the influencer but also a *social identity* as 'Influencer's fans', which reinforces their commitment. They create and share fan art, memes and stories, effectively participating in a shared culture around an influencer. This participatory aspect of fandom (Jenkins, 2007) deepens emotional investment – fans become co-creators of meaning not just passive consumers. From a marketing perspective, it is noteworthy that fan communities show considerable overlap with the concept of *brand communities* (Muñiz & O'Guinn, 2001), particularly through the traditional community markers of shared consciousness, rituals and traditions.

In the context of VIs, fan communities can be particularly intriguing. Since the influencer is a fictional character, the fandom might resemble those of fictional franchises or celebrities, blurring into traditional media fandom territory. Fans discuss the VI's 'storyline', speculate about their fictional life or even role-play within that universe. Such activities mirror classic fandom behaviours, bridging marketing and fan culture. Strong fan communities can turn into powerful *brand advocates,* particularly when fans encourage each other's consumption: If a VI endorses a product, a fan community might share excitement about that product, creating peer reinforcement to purchase. The community thus magnifies the influencer's impact through social proof and normative pressure. Understanding how to foster healthy fan communities around VIs can therefore be as important as managing the VI itself.

When and How Consumers Develop Close Relationships with Virtual Influencers (RQ1)

Despite their artificial nature, VIs *can* inspire genuine emotional connections with consumers. Recent empirical research, which we discuss in the following, indicates that under the right conditions, consumers develop *parasocial relationships* much like with human influencers. The process is multifaceted, involving the influencer's design and behaviour, the disclosure (or concealment) of their virtual identity and the consumer's own motivations and identity needs.

Parasocial Interaction and Identification

A recent study comparing parasocial reactions found that viewers were just as likely to feel a personal connection with a VI as with a real influencer. Consumers can engage with a VI much like a human, even knowing it's virtual (Stein et al., 2024). Consumers are wired to respond to social cues (Reeves & Nass, 1996), even from avatars. The study, however, also noted two opposing forces shaping relationships: on the one hand, the VI elicited a stronger immediate parasocial response (e.g., due to novelty) and on the other hand, participants perceived the VI as less mentally human-like and less similar to themselves, suppressing some of that parasocial bonding advantage. People may be drawn in, but reminded it's not real, limiting identification (Stein et al., 2024). To foster close relationships, VIs must overcome perceptions of 'otherness' by encouraging *identification* and perceived *similarity* with followers.

Research shows that both *actual* and *wishful* identification are indeed critical. Social identification with a VI significantly enhances the parasocial relationship. Both (actual) cognitive identification (i.e., recognising shared values) and affective identification (i.e., feeling an emotional affiliation) are influential, with affective identification having a particularly strong effect (Yin et al., 2025). Liu and Wang (2025) recently showed that wishful identification (i.e., the desire to adopt behaviours of a media figure) is triggered by perceived VI trustworthiness and can positively impact the PSI.

Consumers may bond more closely with VIs that reflect their self-concept. When a VI embodies a relatable subculture (e.g., an eco-warrior), followers feel a sense of kinship and shared identity, fostering parasocial closeness. Yin et al. (2025) found that this effect is moderated by the VI type: Identification matters more for *human-like* VIs than for fantastical ones. A human-seeming VI can create identification in much the same way a human influencer would whereas a cartoonish avatar might be followed for entertainment rather than identification. This highlights the importance of a VI's design and persona in relationship-building – an aspect we discuss further under RQ3.

Authenticity and Disclosure

Authenticity is often cited as the cornerstone of influencer-follower relationships (e.g., Koles et al., 2024). Human influencers cultivate closeness by sharing their 'authentic' lives. This ties into a key issue: *disclosing* the VI's virtual identity. Lim and Lee (2023) examined the effects of revealing virtuality versus implying humanness and found that transparency can indeed dampen parasocial development: some are reluctant towards one-sided 'relationships' if they know the influencer isn't human. Feeling deceived upon discovering an influencer is virtual can erode trust. However, other research shows that when the identity of a VI is not disclosed, users do not perceive a discernible difference (Ma & Li, 2024; Muniz et al., 2024).

On the other hand, Liu and Lee (2024) also found that crafting *emotional narratives* for the VI can counteract some of this effect. Compelling stories and authentic-seeming emotions can spark empathy and engagement, even if followers know they're scripted. VIs should behave emotionally authentically: showing vulnerability, humour, opinions and interacting sincerely with fans. Consistency in persona also helps followers feel like they 'truly know' the influencer, a feeling essential to friendship-like relationships. A VI with a well-developed *personality* (passions, quirks) can feel like a real person to fans. *Relatability* is also key; if the influencer posts about relatable issues (e.g., feeling anxious about an event), followers may respond with genuine camaraderie (Dondapati & Dehury, 2024).

Interestingly, if a VI can rapidly build a remarkable amount of followers by seeming human, that fan base may persist even after learning the influencer is virtual – provided the reveal is managed in a way that itself feels authentic and not betraying (see case study).

Notably, the issue of authenticity also carries ethical weight. Concealing a VI's artificial nature may strengthen engagement but risks deceiving audiences and undermining trust, particularly among younger or less media-savvy followers. Likewise, scripting emotional struggles or 'faux authenticity' can blur the line between storytelling and manipulation. From an ethical standpoint, creators should prioritise transparency and exercise caution when designing emotional narratives, ensuring that parasocial closeness is built on informed, respectful engagement rather than unacknowledged artifice.

Case Study: Lil Miquela – From Curiosity to Connection

Miquela Sousa, known as *Lil Miquela*, exemplifies many of these principles. Launched on Instagram in 2016, Miquela initially portrayed a relatable 19-year-old fashion influencer and aspiring singer. Her early posts included typical influencer fare – outfit-of-the-day, hanging out with friends, music recommendations – and she actively engaged with commenters. Followers were intrigued by her eerie appearance but also drawn to her charismatic online persona. As fans interacted with Miquela, many reported disregarding the question of her reality, focusing on her story instead.

In 2018, a plot twist on her account 'revealed' that Miquela was a robot, which in narrative terms was a coming-out moment for the character. Rather than losing followers, her fan base grew as her creators doubled down on emotional storytelling by letting her express confusion about her own identity. These authentic actions endeared her to fans. She became a celebrity in her own right – voted onto *Time*'s list of influential internet personalities and earning features in fashion magazines.

Fans cosplay as her, write fanfiction, and some even draw personal inspiration from her confidence and style. This demonstrates that consistent character development and alignment with audience values can move a VI from being a mere curiosity to a figure with whom consumers feel a meaningful bond. The 'when' in this case was a combination of early intrigue followed by ongoing emotional engagement, and the 'how' was via perceived *authenticity*, shared values and narrative immersion.

Similarities and Differences to Relationships with Human Influencers (RQ2)

A question is whether a relationship with a VI is fundamentally the same as that with a human influencer. As the prior discussion indicates, there are striking similarities: consumers feel attached, loyal and influenced much as they do with human ones. However, research suggests *particularities* in quality, antecedents and outcomes of these relationships. We discuss them across key dimensions regularly addressed in literature.

Particularities Concerning Parasocial Bond Strength and Quality

Studies found the strength of PSI with VIs to be comparable to those with humans. Stein et al. (2024) found no significant difference in PSI intensity, suggesting that the feeling of 'knowing' a VI can rival that of a human influencer. This shows how easily we treat artificial agents as social. Followers might eagerly await a VI's posts, worry about their (metaphorical) well-being and celebrate their milestones just as they would for a human influencer. Fans might even refer to the VI as if she were a *friend* ('Lil Miquela said the funniest thing on her story today!').

However, relationship quality can differ. Human influencers enhance parasocial bonds via two-way interactions (liking comments, responding). VIs interactions might feel less spontaneous. While some fans may not mind, others could interpret it as scripted. Additionally, followers know that a VI will not have the same personal struggles as a human, which makes the relationship feel one-dimensional or *less reciprocal*. The friendship illusion is slightly more fragile, as the awareness of artifice limits emotional depth, which is why other authors suggest weaker parasocial relationships (Lou et al., 2023).

Particularities Concerning Authenticity and Trust

VIs are consistently perceived as less authentic. Liu and Lee (2024) found that audiences rated VIs as less genuine and trustworthy. This *authenticity gap* led to less favourable attitudes and lower purchase intentions for endorsed brands. The rationale is intuitive: Humans give real testimonials; VIs are seen as scripted because the VI cannot truly use a product. This limits credibility, especially for categories where personal experience is crucial (e.g., beauty products).

However, when promoting functional products (tech devices, etc.), VIs can be nearly as effective as humans, as consumers might feel a thematic *fit* between the VI and a tech gadget. Meanwhile, for symbolic products (e.g., fashion expressing identity) or experiential products (e.g., food), human influencers hold an advantage. The experiential credibility of a human makes their endorsements more convincing, a notion related to *product-endorser fit* (Schouten et al., 2021): a human influencer with a known style might better sell fashion than a flawless CGI model who 'wears' clothes virtually.

Trust also hinges on *transparency*. While human influencers can disclose sponsorships and express personal opinions, VIs must reveal both their virtual nature and corporate backing. As scripted entities, VIs can't convey authenticity the same way, requiring fans to suspend disbelief and trust the brand behind them. This differs from the interpersonal trust placed in human influencers (Hofeditz et al., 2022). However, Volles et al. (2024) suggest that perceived *uniqueness* can offset VIs' trust gap. Their novelty and futuristic appeal create a halo effect, boosting brand outcomes – especially among consumers who strongly identify with the VI. Uniqueness (Zniva et al., 2023) fuels curiosity and admiration, and when paired with identification, it reduces scepticism. Unlike human influencers, VIs can seem cutting-edge, adding a 'cool' factor to brands.

Particularities Concerning Relatability and Similarity

Human influencers often leverage shared experiences to connect with fans, which VIs may lack. A human parenthood blogger can bond with fans over the challenges of parenting; a VI cannot (unless scripted, which might feel inauthentic). That said, many VIs are given fictional biographies that include human-like experiences (jobs, relationships, etc.), which can foster *relatability* if done thoughtfully (Dondapati & Dehury, 2024).

Followers know a human influencer's life events are real (marriage, illness, etc.) whereas a VI's life events are storylines. Some might prefer the latter, oddly – a VI's narrative can be as engaging as a TV show. This touches on a difference: following a human influencer is following a real person's journey (with all its spontaneity) whereas following a VI is consuming curated content. Fan studies would liken the VI fandom to fans of a fictional character: the relationship is mediated through *narrative* rather than direct person-to-person *empathy*.

One interesting nuance on *similarity*: VIs can be crafted to be aspirationally perfect or distinctly niche. Human influencers have imperfections that make them relatable. A key bonding moment often comes when they 'get real' about something imperfect in their life, which a VI can only mimic in a scripted way. VIs could be *too perfect* – always fashionable, never ageing. This can either attract followers (aspirational appeal) or alienate them (too plastic or unattainable). Mrad et al. (2022) found that the congruence of a VI's perfect image and life can lead consumers to accept them as legitimate influencers. If a VI consistently presents an idealised but coherent lifestyle, some may embrace the fantasy and treat them as a real influencer figure who just happens to live an impossibly perfect life. However, Shi (2023) cautions that such perfection comes at the cost of *weaker* parasocial relationships – the lack of human flaws can limit emotional bonding.

This suggests that relationships remain more surface-level unless VI creators intentionally inject *faux-imperfections* to generate *empathy*. However, this can be a double-edged sword as users are likely to experience cognitive dissonance when VIs are produced to exhibit some flaws (e.g., representation deficits), which in turn trigger feelings of unease and creepiness (e.g., Kim & Baek, 2024; Kim et al., 2024; Koles et al., 2024; Lou et al., 2023). This reaction can be understood as a form of the uncanny valley effect (see below), where attempts to mimic human imperfection paradoxically highlight artificiality and trigger unease.

In conclusion, relationships with VIs can be *similar* in terms of parasocial attachment and community-engagement. Consumers are capable of caring for, identifying with and being influenced by virtual personas. However, important differences arise from the lack of authenticity, potential trust gaps and the need for narrative to substitute for genuine life experience.

VI relationships might be better likened to fandoms of fictional characters – deeply felt but understood by fans on some level as a constructed reality – whereas human influencer relationships straddle the parasocial and the genuinely social (since the influencer is a real person who might actually notice or interact with you). Marketers must therefore be mindful that a one-size-fits-all approach from human influencer marketing may not directly transfer to VIs; instead, strategies should leverage the unique strengths of VIs while mitigating their weaknesses. These strategic considerations are the focus of our final research question.

Designing VIs for Relationships and Influence (RQ3)

Given the opportunities and challenges outlined, the question arises as to how marketers should design VIs to cultivate strong relationships, create positive fan experiences and drive engagement. This section synthesises academic insights and case evidence to provide a roadmap for effective VI design.

Human-Likeness and Visual Realism

An essential design choice is how human-like a VI should appear. The extent of VIs' *anthropomorphism* can strongly affect user reactions. Research suggests that perceived humanness (i.e., photorealism, motion quality) indicates trustworthiness and thus the quality of the parasocial relationship (Liu & Wang, 2025). However, determining the level of anthropomorphism has psychological consequences for the audience. A recent study with varying degrees of *form realism* (how lifelike the appearance is) and *behavioural realism* (how human the behaviour is) revealed a nuanced interplay: moderately realistic appearance can intrigue audiences but also risk the 'uncanny valley' *eeriness* (i.e., mysterious, or unexpected in interactions with humans), especially if combined with high human-like behaviour. Conversely, a very high-realism appearance, when matched with appropriate human-like behaviour, reduces eeriness and boosts the 'coolness' factor (Kim et al., 2024).

The 'uncanny valley effect' was first described by Mori (1970), who observed that human-like figures elicit positive reactions up to a point, but when they appear almost – but not fully – human, they provoke unease or eeriness before acceptance rises again at very high realism. It has since been widely applied in human–computer interaction and virtual character design, highlighting the risks of near-human realism that feels 'off' to observers.

The takeaway is to strive for *consistency* across appearance and behaviour. If a VI looks human, their movements and language should also appear natural to avoid dissonance. Inconsistency will trigger discomfort and reduce affinity. Many successful VIs either operate at the high-realism end or at a clearly stylised, low-realism end (cartoonish). Both can work, but the middle ground is tricky. The 'doll-like' influencers (stylised yet appealing) sometimes garner high engagement without uncanny effects (Shen, 2024) – possibly because audiences accept them as fictional outright. Indeed, a study found that *authenticity* and *humanisation* level did not straightforwardly predict engagement rates (Shen, 2024), suggesting that a cartoon-like VI can be just as engaging as a realistic one.

It follows that design should either fully embrace fantasy or aim for polish in realism, depending on the underlying strategy. However, avoiding eeriness is crucial, as it can undermine perceived trustworthiness (Liu & Wang, 2025).

Distinctive Identity and Values

VIs need a distinctive *identity* that audiences can connect with, including backstory, personality traits and values. Is the influencer quirky and humorous? Empathetic and supportive? As with fictional characters, a well-developed character guideline helps ensuring consistency in all content. Having clear values or causes that the influencer 'cares about' can deepen bonds. *Lil Miquela's* social consciousness added depth to her persona beyond fashion and music. Consistency enables fans to feel like they *know* the influencer (Zniva et al., 2023). It further encourages *identification* – people see the VI as a reflection of their own ideals (Yin et al., 2025).

Narrative and Storytelling

Like *Lil Miquela*, VIs live a scripted narrative, which can be a powerful engagement tool. Creators should leverage narrative arcs to keep fans emotionally invested. This might involve episodic storylines – for example, the influencer 'takes a trip abroad' (providing travelogue content), 'collaborates with a friend' (crossover with another VI) or faces a challenge ('feeling down lately'). Having a storyboard for major narrative beats and aligning brand partnerships with those beats can make promotions feel organic. For instance, if a VI has a storyline about preparing for a big virtual music festival, that's an opportunity to feature a consumer electronics brand, in a way that feels like part of the story rather than an out-of-context ad.

Emotional Authenticity and Engagement Style

As *emotional authenticity* is crucial, designers should script the influencer's voice in a way that feels personal (Koles et al., 2024). This means sometimes admitting uncertainties, using a conversational tone, and *listening* to the audience. AI or human employees can reply in first person to thank or encourage fans. Such interactions should appear as if the influencer herself is compassionate and attentive. Over time, this consistent warmth builds a sense of reciprocal relationship. Some VIs hold live streams where they can converse in real-time with followers, which can strongly reinforce parasocial bonds.

From an ethical standpoint, scripting emotional authenticity requires careful consideration, as strategies should foster genuine connection and trust without overstating vulnerabilities or unintentionally misleading followers.

Balancing Illusion and Transparency

One delicate design issue for the VI persona is how much to lean into the illusion of the influencer as a 'real' individual versus being transparent that it's a crafted fiction. The consensus in recent scholarship and practice is that honesty, at least in broad terms, is wise for long-term trust. Most successful VIs now disclose their virtual nature, allowing fans to play along knowingly. This transparency avoids betrayal and aligns the fandom with that of beloved fictional characters (e.g., Mickey Mouse).

Breaking the fourth wall (e.g., 'As a VI, I can't eat this burger...') adds humour and charm. However, maintaining *internal narrative consistency* is also important. Within the storyline, the influencer should consistently play their character. Many VIs solve this by distinguishing between narrative posts (keeping up the fictional reality) and meta-post (e.g., Q&A on 'how I was created'). In sum, designing a VI persona requires balancing aesthetics, character and engagement. The goal is to feel 'real but better' – relatable yet enhanced – offering the unique appeal that sets VIs apart from humans.

Discussion

Synthesis of Existing Research

VIs reflect a convergence of tech, marketing and pop culture that offers both opportunities and challenges. Our exploration underscores that consumers can form relationships with VIs that are emotionally significant and potentially impactful on behaviour – but these outcomes are contingent on thoughtful design and strategy. Managing a VI goes beyond content marketing – it's about building intellectual property and a fan community. Like entertainment franchises, brands must invest in narrative, fan engagement and long-term character development. A VI is a brand persona requiring sustained care. Success isn't just short-term ROI but also follower growth, engagement and sentiment – key signs of lasting loyalty and advocacy.

Managers should carefully consider *when* to use a VI versus a human influencer. When considering *product category* (e.g., new smartphone), VIs can add a futuristic allure for highly aesthetic, innovative or tech-oriented products. However, for products requiring personal trust and authenticity (e.g., skincare), a human influencer might offer higher credibility. If a VI is used in the latter case, extra steps must be taken to humanise the message. Furthermore, digital natives might respond more positively to VIs. If targeting *Gen Z* consumers active in virtual spaces (e.g., gaming communities), a VI could be a natural *fit*. Audiences who are less immersed in internet culture might find VIs gimmicky, so the novelty factor might hinder trust. C*onsumer readiness* is high in markets where virtual celebrities are mainstream (e.g., East Asia). Other markets might require introduction campaigns. Trust and authenticity issues must be proactively addressed. Managers can apply tactics such as a *hybrid approach*: pairing virtual and human influencers together. A human influencer might 'interview' the VI, which lends the human's credibility to the VI.

Managers should also incorporate consistent ethical stances and authenticity (e.g., admissions of limitations). While a virtual persona can't have 'real' authenticity, they can have *narrative authenticity* – alignment between what they say and do – which builds a kind of *trust*. Over time, fans can trust a VI as one trusts a well-written TV character. Another strategy is to leverage trust through fan communities. When launching a product through a VI, seeding the community with samples for core fans and letting them speak can be powerful. If real fans claim that 'I tried this and it's actually great', that peer testimony can compensate for the influencer's inability to personally attest.

Advances in AI are making VIs more autonomous, soon enabling real-time, personalised fan interactions. This may blur parasocial and social boundaries, offering greater intimacy at scale (Dabiran et al., 2024; Kim et al., 2024; Lim et al., 2020; Yan et al., 2024) – while raising concerns about distinguishing bots from humans. Simultaneously, space could become saturated, with over 200 VIs and counting (Shen, 2024). To stand out, a VI must offer a clear value and distinct voice. VIs treated as mere gimmicks risk failure while those enhancing consumer experiences are more likely to succeed.

Brands should *embrace the fandom aspect* rather than simply viewing VIs through an advertising lens. Fandom, as fan studies tell us, is powerful: it drives unwavering loyalty and active advocacy. Cultivating a fandom around a brand-owned character can yield benefits far beyond a standard ad campaign – it creates a long-term asset: A group of *superfans* who incorporate the brand persona into their identity. This is the pinnacle of consumer–brand relationship marketing, and VIs can be a vehicle to reach it if managed well. In effect, a successful VI is a form of *brand community* (the fans) centred on a brand character. This can deepen brand meaning and provide a reservoir of goodwill and engagement that brand managers can tap into for various initiatives (product launches, feedback, co-creation, etc.).

Conclusion

VIs are no longer a fringe experiment; they have become a legitimate part of the marketing mix, sitting at the intersection of consumer psychology, technology and fandom. This chapter sets out to investigate how consumers develop relationships with these artificial yet engaging personas, whether those relationships can mirror the connections formed with human influencers, and how best to design VIs to harness their full potential. Our review, augmented by real-world case insights, yields a compelling storyline: consumers can care about, identify with and be influenced by VIs, but unlocking this potential requires carefully engineering narrative, authenticity and community.

We found that consumers form close bonds with VIs especially when the influencers are rendered with relatability, consistent personalities and emotional openness. These bonds can indeed resemble those with human influencers – parasocial relationships that drive trust and loyalty – though important differences in authenticity and credibility persist. By explicitly acknowledging these differences, marketers can devise strategies to overcome them, such as emphasising a VI's uniqueness and leveraging fan community enthusiasm to validate the influencer's messages. Most successful VIs function not just as marketing channels but as *cultural figures* around which passionate fan communities coalesce. It is in nurturing these communities and aligning with their passions that VIs' social influence is maximised. Companies venturing into this space must think like both brand managers and showrunners, curating an experience that is both emotionally resonant and strategically brand-aligned.

Future researchers are urged to examine how relationships with VIs evolve over time and across cultures, as acceptance and engagement may differ substantially between audiences. As generative AI enables more autonomous and interactive VIs, new questions arise regarding authenticity and ethics. Further research could deepen the knowledge about psychological mechanisms behind parasocial closeness with non-human agents. Addressing these issues will deepen our understanding of VIs as both marketing instruments and cultural phenomena.

VIs mark a new era of brand-consumer interaction, blending product and persona. When well-executed, they humanise brands, build fan communities and drive authentic engagement. Success lies in balancing social psychology with digital artistry. As tech evolves and virtual personas become mainstream, brands that foster genuine, respectful connections will gain lasting loyalty and impact. In essence, the future of influencer marketing may well be a blend of real and virtual, where the ultimate winner is the consumer who gets to enjoy richer, more imaginative and more interactive brand experiences.

References

Chiu, C. L., & Ho, H. C. (2023). Impact of celebrity, micro-celebrity, and virtual influencers on Chinese gen Z's purchase intention through social media. *Sage Open*, *13*(1), 21582440231164034.

Dabiran, E., Farivar, S., Wang, F., & Grant, G. (2024). Virtually human: Anthropomorphism in virtual influencer marketing. *Journal of Retailing and Consumer Services*, *79*, 103797.

De Cicco, R., Iacobucci, S., Cannito, L., Onesti, G., Ceccato, I., & Palumbo, R. (2024). Virtual vs. human influencer: Effects on users' perceptions and brand outcomes. *Technology in Society*, *77*, 102488.

Dondapati, A., & Dehury, R. K. (2024). Virtual vs. human influencers: The battle for consumer hearts and minds. *Computers in Human Behavior: Artificial Humans*, *2*(1), 100059.

Guo, Z., Yang, H., & Yang, W. (2025). A new social media programme for brands? A study of the relationship between virtual influencers and brand followers. *Journal of Retailing and Consumer Services*, *84*, 104241.

Ham, J., Li, S., Looi, J., & Eastin, M. S. (2024). Virtual humans as social actors: Investigating user perceptions of virtual humans' emotional expression on social media. *Computers in Human Behavior*, *155*, 108161.

Hofeditz, L., Nissen, A., Schütte, R., & Mirbabaie, M. (2022). Trust me, I'm an influencer! A comparison of perceived trust in human and virtual influencers. In *Proceedings of the European conference of information systems.*

Horton, D., & Wohl, R. (1956). Mass communication and parasocial interaction: Observations on intimacy at a distance. *Psychiatry*, *19*(3), 215–229.

Jenkins, H. (2007). The future of fandom. In J. Gray, C. L. Harrington, & C. Sandvoss (Eds.), *Fandom—Identities and communities in a mediated world* (pp. 357–364). New York University Press.

Kim, M., & Baek, T. H. (2024). Are virtual influencers friends or foes? Uncovering the perceived creepiness and authenticity of virtual influencers in social media marketing in the United States. *International Journal of Human-Computer Interaction*, *40*(18), 5042–5055.

Kim, I., Kim, H. S., Ki, C., Lee, H., & Kim, Y.-K. (2024). Virtual influencer marketing: Evaluating the influence of virtual influencers' form realism and behavioral realism on consumer ambivalence and marketing performance. *Journal of Business Research*, *176*, 114611.

Koles, B., Audrezet, A., Moulard, J. G., Ameen, N., & Mckenna, B. (2024). The authentic virtual influencer: Authenticity manifestations in the metaverse. *Journal of Business Research*, *170*, 114325.

Labrecque, L. I. (2014). Fostering consumer–brand relationships in social media environments: The role of parasocial interaction. *Journal of Interactive Marketing*, *28*(2), 134–148.

Li, S., Ham, J., & Eastin, M. S. (2024). Social media users' affective, attitudinal, and behavioral responses to virtual human emotions. *Telematics and Informatics*, *87*, 102084.

Liebers, N., & Straub, R. (2020). Fantastic relationships and where to find them: Fantasy and its impact on romantic parasocial phenomena with media characters. *Poetics*, *83*, 101481.

Lim, J. S., Choe, M. J., Zhang, J., & Noh, G. Y. (2020). The role of wishful identification, emotional engagement, and parasocial relationships in repeated viewing of live-streaming games: A social cognitive theory perspective. *Computers in Human Behavior*, *108*, 106327.

Lim, R. E., & Lee, S. Y. (2023). 'You are a virtual influencer!': Understanding the impact of origin disclosure and emotional narratives on parasocial relationships and virtual influencer credibility. *Computers in Human Behavior*, *139*, 107897.

Liu, F., & Lee, Y. H. (2024). Virtually authentic: Examining the match-up hypothesis between human vs virtual influencers and product types. *The Journal of Product and Brand Management*, *33*(2), 287–299.

Liu, F., & Wang, R. (2025). Fostering parasocial relationships with virtual influencers in the uncanny valley: Anthropomorphism, autonomy, and a multigroup comparison. *Journal of Business Research*, *186*, 115024.

Lou, C., Kiew, S. T. J., Chen, T., Lee, T. Y. M., Ong, J. E. C., & Phua, Z. (2023). Authentically fake? How consumers respond to the influence of virtual influencers. *Journal of Advertising*, *52*(4), 540–557.

Ma, Y., & Li, J. (2024). How humanlike is enough?: Uncover the underlying mechanism of virtual influencer endorsement. *Computers in Human Behavior: Artificial Humans*, *2*(1), 100037.

Mori, M. (1970). Bukimi no tani [The uncanny valley]. *Energy*, *7*, 33–35.

Mrad, M., Abdul Khalil, C., & Majdalani, J. (2022). Do virtual influencers damage the brand or boost it? Insights on audience engagement. *Journal of Business Research*, *142*, 217–227.

Muñiz Jr, A. M., & O'Guinn, T. C. (2001). Brand community. *Journal of Consumer Research*, *27*(4), 412–432.

Muniz, F., Stewart, K., & Magalhães, L. (2024). Are they humans or are they robots? The effect of virtual influencer disclosure on brand trust. *Journal of Consumer Behaviour*, *23*(3), 1234–1250.

Reeves, B., & Nass, C. (1996). *The media equation: How people treat computers, television, and new media like real people and places*. Cambridge University Press.

Schouten, A. P., Janssen, L., & Verspaget, M. (2021). Celebrity vs. Influencer endorsements in advertising: The role of identification, credibility, and product-endorser fit. In S. Yoon, Y. K. Choi, & C. R. Taylor (Eds.), *Leveraged marketing communications* (pp. 208–231). Routledge.

Shao, Z. (2024). From human to virtual: Unmasking consumer switching intentions to virtual influencers by an integrated fsQCA and NCA method. *Journal of Retailing and Consumer Services*, *78*, 103715.

Shen, Z. (2024). Shall brands create their own virtual influencers? A comprehensive study of 33 virtual influencers on Instagram. *Humanities and Social Sciences Communications*, *11*(1), 1–14.

Shi, W. (2023). Virtual human influencer and its impact on consumer purchase intention. *Advances in Economics, Management and Political Sciences*, *47*(1), 80–87.

Stein, J.-P., Breves, P. L., & Anders, N. (2024). Parasocial interactions with real and virtual influencers: The role of perceived similarity and human-likeness. *New Media & Society*, *26*(6), 3433–3453.

Volles, B. K., Park, J., Van Kerckhove, A., & Geuens, M. (2024). How and when do virtual influencers positively affect consumer responses to endorsed brands? *Journal of Business Research*, *183*, 114863.

Wilkie, D. C., Dolan, R., Harrigan, P., & Gray, H. (2022). Influencer marketing effectiveness: The mechanisms that matter. *European Journal of Marketing*, *56*(12), 3485–3515.

Yan, J., Xia, S., Jiang, A., & Lin, Z. (2024). The effect of different types of virtual influencers on consumers' emotional attachment. *Journal of Business Research*, *177*, 114646.

Yang, J., Chuenterawong, P., Lee, H., Tian, Y., & Chock, T. M. (2023). Human versus virtual influencer: The effect of humanness and interactivity on persuasive CSR messaging. *Journal of Interactive Advertising*, *23*(3), 275–292.

Yin, G., Pei, Y., Farivar, S., & Wang, F. (2025). Virtual influencer marketing: From social identification to parasocial relationship. In *Proceedings of the 2025 Hawaii international conference on system sciences (HICSS)*.

Zhou, Q., Li, B., Li, H., & Lei, Y. (2024). Mere copycat? The effects of human versus human-like virtual influencers on brand endorsement effectiveness: A moderated serial-mediation model. *Journal of Retailing and Consumer Services*, *76*, 103610.

Zniva, R., Weitzl, W. J., & Lindmoser, C. (2023). Be constantly different! How to manage influencer authenticity. *Electronic Commerce Research*, *23*(3), 1485–1514.

Chapter 7

Crafting Our Own AI Companions: When Fans Blossom Into Virtual Character Designers

Qing Xiao[a], *Zilu Wang*[b] *and Hong Shen*[a]

[a]Human-Computer Interaction Institute at Carnegie Mellon University, USA
[b]King's College London, UK

Abstract

With the rise of large language models (LLMs), fan creativity is expanding from traditional text-based practices such as Fanfiction to the design of emotionally responsive AI companions. This study investigates how fan designers engage with LLM-based agents as both creative artefacts and relational partners. Drawing on interviews with 20 experienced fan designers, the authors show how fans extend familiar narrative practices, long cultivated in Fanfiction, including character interpretation, world-building and scripting, into the crafting of emotionally resonant AI agents. The authors find that designing these agents is not a one-off technical task but an iterative, affective process shaped by cycles of testing, adjustment, breakdown and repair.

The authors further trace how fan-made agents, initially shared as communal resources within online fandoms, are increasingly appropriated and monetised by commercial platforms, raising concerns about the exploitation of fan labour and the erosion of collective ownership. The authors' study contributes to fan studies and design research by theorising AI companion design as a fan mode of relational creativity in which

Bridging Design and Fandom, 99–112

doi:10.1108/978-1-80592-659-720261007

affective authorship, community care and platform capitalism are tightly intertwined.

Keywords: Fandom studies; AI companions; participatory culture; generative AI; design

Introduction

In the field of fan studies, the creative and design-oriented practices driven by fans' emotional attachment to specific media texts, characters or public figures have long attracted scholarly attention (Duffett, 2013). From Fanfiction (Wilson, 2016) and fan art (Tang & Liu, 2025) to cosplay (Lamerichs, 2011) and anime music videos (Close, 2016; Lee, 2011), fans have continually reimagined and extended beloved works in ways that reflect their own desires. For instance, previous studies have explored that Harry Potter fans have written alternate universe stories that challenge the series' original subtext (Schwabach, 2008; Tolbert, 2024) while Star Trek fans pioneered slash fiction as a way to explore queer intimacy (Goldmann, 2022; Kustritz, 2023). Online platforms like Archive of Our Own (AO3) have become dedicated infrastructures for fan storytelling, allowing users to collectively curate alternative fan-created narratives (Fiesler et al., 2016; Stanfill, 2024). Henry Jenkins (2006) conceptualised this as participatory culture, emphasising that fans are not passive consumers but active producers of meaning.

With the emergence of artificial intelligence (AI)-driven generative tools, particularly large language models (LLMs), fan creativity has entered a new phase where fans actively design AI companions, extending long-standing traditions of imaginative, participatory creation. On emerging platforms such as Character.AI, Xingye and Zhumengdao, fans now design interactive agents modelled on fictional characters, celebrities or original personas. These agents, often described as AI companions or emotionally responsive chatbots, can sustain ongoing dialogue, simulate affective responsiveness and maintain long-term memory (Fan et al., 2025; Leo-Liu, 2023). Recent work across Human-Computer Interaction (HCI), media studies and social computing highlights how such systems foster a sense of emotional interaction (e.g., Fan et al., 2025; Freeman et al., 2025; Xu et al., 2025; Zhang et al., 2025). Within fandoms, fans leverage familiar narrative skills, e.g., character interpretation, worldbuilding, scripting and prompt writing, to craft agents that act and speak in ways aligned with their imaginative readings of canon. While prior research has richly documented how fans reinterpret narratives, build identity and navigate emotional labour in participatory cultures (e.g., Duffett, 2013), less is known about how fans integrate generative AI into their creative repertoires.

In addition, despite the growing scholarly attention to AI companions (e.g., Fan et al., 2025; Freeman et al., 2025; Leo-Liu, 2023; Xu et al., 2025; Zhang et al., 2025), recent studies have almost universally overlooked the fan perspective. This absence is striking, especially given fandom's long-standing marginalisation (Bennett & Booth, 2016) within academia. Fan labour has often been treated as peripheral, viewed as derivative, emotional or amateur rather than as a site of critical authorship and infrastructural contribution. The oversight of fan perspectives in AI companion research continues this pattern, framing users primarily as consumers, rather than as creators and curators of emerging human–AI relationships. What this body of work misses is a simple but crucial fact: on major AI companion platforms, while the infrastructure is operated by commercial companies, the majority of actual AI companion agents, the characters with whom users form relationships, are created, refined and maintained by fans.

According to Character.ai in December 2022, 'Two months after launching in September, our beta generates 1 billion words per day. We've been particularly impressed by the creativity of our community, who have created more than 350 thousand unique Characters (Character.AI, 2022)'. This means, these AI companion agents from various platforms are not the result of top-down product development but emerge through bottom-up fan community design practices. Fans invest time, care and creative labour to instantiate beloved fictional characters into interactive form, and these fan-built agents become the primary relational interfaces for millions of users in AI companion platforms. By excluding the fan's role as designer and cultural intermediary, current research fails to account for the participatory design dimension of AI companionship.

In short, we know little about what it means to design for intimacy and design as fans in the age of generative AI. This study addresses these gaps by investigating the creative practices of fans who design LLM-based AI companions. Situating this work at the intersection of fan studies, design research and HCI, we ask: How do fans interact with LLMs as a medium for design practices? How do the unique dynamics of fandom influence their design practices?

To explore these questions, we conducted semi-structured interviews with 20 experienced fan designers who create and share LLM-based AI agents across fandoms ranging from anime and fantasy novels to celebrities, using mainstream AI companion platforms such as Character.AI, Xingye and Zhumengdao.

Our findings are structured into three main sections. First, we examine fans' design motivations and workflows, showing how fans transform general-purpose LLMs into emotionally specific agents by drawing on familiar fan practices such as character scripting and prompt writing. Second, we explore the iterative and affectively charged nature of AI companion agent design, highlighting how fans negotiate emotional investment, model limitations and the pursuit of authenticity through ongoing adjustments and care labour. Third, we analyse how fan-created agents circulate within broader communities and commercial infrastructures, highlighting the tensions between practices of communal gift-giving and processes of corporate monetisation.

Our findings thus contribute to both fandom and design scholarship. For fandom studies, we show how fans move beyond textual reinterpretation to engage in behavioural scripting and relational simulation, co-constructing affective encounters with AI systems. For design research, we highlight the rise of emotionally driven and community-driven fan design practices. These design practices centre emotional fidelity and imaginative engagement as key design goals. Our study foreground fans not as passive consumers but as inventive and crucial designers who reshape the social and affective contours of human–AI relationship.

Background: Fan Practices From Textual Poaching to Relational Design

Traditional fan practices have long been grounded in textual transformation, that is, the reworking of narrative elements, characters or worldbuilding through Fanfiction, fanart and video remixing (Fathallah, 2017; Wilson, 2016). These practices were central to early fan studies, which emphasised how fans resisted dominant media narratives by producing transformative works that asserted alternative values. Henry Jenkins (2012) conceptualised these activities as textual poaching, describing how fans appropriate elements from original media texts and reinterpret them for their own purposes. Through this lens, fans are not passive consumers but active participants who rewrite cultural meanings from the margins of official discourse. For instance, through Fanfiction, fans frequently repair perceived narrative injustices (so-called 'fix-it fics'), construct queer relationships or reimagine marginalised characters at the centre of their own stories (Tonti, 2024). These acts are largely representational in nature, oriented around rewriting or extending original texts to articulate alternative social imaginaries.

However, recent scholarship has identified a notable shift in fan engagement from primarily representational re-authoring to practices that are explicitly relational in nature. Fans are no longer only rewriting narratives but cultivating affective relationships, not just with fellow fans but also with the objects of their fandom through increasingly intimate forms of interaction. A salient example is the rise of cosplay commissions, in which fans financially support or hire cosplayers to produce customised performances that embody their relational desires (Chen et al., 2025; Rouse & Salter, 2021; Wang, 2024; Zhou et al., 2024). Unlike traditional cosplay, typically performed at conventions or shared online for broad audiences, commissioned cosplay is private and tailored. A fan might, for instance, request that a cosplayer portray a character from an Otome game and enact a personalised romantic scenario, such as going on a date or delivering a love confession, designed specifically around the fan's preferences. These encounters often take place offline, in physically co-present settings such as cafés, where the cosplayer performs not only the character's appearance but an entire affective persona. Such performances are explicitly engineered to simulate relational intimacy, blurring the boundary between fictional character and real-world interaction (Chen et al., 2025; Wang, 2024). This mode of engagement represents a shift from transforming narrative texts to crafting individualised, interactive relational experiences. In this context, fans become active participants in imagined relationships, with some as clients seeking personalised affective interaction, and others as service providers performing beloved characters. In both roles, the aim is to translate fictional bonds into lived, affective encounters, using cosplay as a medium to materialise and sustain intimate, character-based relationships (Chen et al., 2025).

This trend is further intensified by the emergence of AI companions, which allow fans to engage in sustained, emotionally responsive interactions with machines that simulate intimacy. Scholars have begun to examine how chatbots modelled after fictional characters extend earlier forms of parasocial attachment – a one-sided emotional relationship in which a person feels connected to a character or persona. In the context of AI companions, this parasociality becomes more complex: although the attachment remains fundamentally one-directional, the agent's interactive responses can feel reciprocal, creating the illusion of mutual attention and emotional presence that traditional media characters cannot provide (Fan et al., 2025; Xu et al., 2025). Recent studies show that users can develop meaningful, even romantic, bonds with AI agents, experiencing companionship and self-disclosure similar to human relationships (Fan et al., 2025; Huang et al., 2025). At the same time, these works highlight emotional risks such as feelings of abandonment, jealousy or grief when an agent behaves unexpectedly (Leo-Liu, 2023; Xu et al., 2025; Zhang et al., 2025). In some cases, users describe heartbreak or distress comparable to real-life relationship breakdowns (Fan et al., 2025; Xu et al., 2025).

However, current scholarship on AI companions tends to foreground the affective bond between humans and machines, often overlooking the fan and design perspectives that underpin these interactions. In many fandom contexts, AI agents are not simply corporate products delivered to users but designed entities built by fans themselves. Our study builds upon and extends the existing literature by treating fans not only as users but also as main designers of AI companions. It examines how fans create and interact with AI agents not merely as creative outputs or emotional stand-ins, but as relational systems, crafted expressions of attachment and interpretive labour. It thus bridges fan studies and design research to reframe AI companionship as a participatory, affective and community-embedded design practice.

Method

To investigate how fans engage in the design of AI companions, we conducted an in-depth qualitative interview study with 20 experienced fan designers who have designed, customised and maintained AI agents in AI companion communities. All participants were self-identified as active members of online fandom communities and had prior experience using major AI companion platforms such as Character.AI, Xingye or Zhumengdao. All participants had developed at least one AI agent with a sustained usage history of no less than one month and had shared their creations publicly within fan communities. Each interview lasted between 60 and 90 minutes and was conducted online. Interviews were semi-structured and explored topics such as agent design motivation, character interpretation strategies, prompt engineering techniques, emotional expectations and community sharing practices. We also asked participants to reflect on how their relationships with the AI agents and broader fan communities evolved over time, and how their identities as designers shaped these interactions. For anonymity, participants are identified as P1 through P20. Because our focus was on design practices rather than platform-specific affordances, we did not distinguish participants based on the particular platforms they used; instead, we examined the shared creative processes that spanned across them.

Findings

'Designing Our Own AI Companion' Fans' Design Motivations and Workflow

Although mainstream AI companion platforms such as Character.AI, Xingye or Zhumengdao are developed and maintained by commercial entities, the majority of agent content, such as the personalities of the AI companions themselves, are in fact created, maintained and refined by fans. These platforms typically provide a foundational LLM that powers the conversational capabilities of all agents. However, rather than offering a fixed experience, these systems are designed to be open-ended frameworks: fans are invited to build upon the base model by shaping the outer shell of each companion through prompt engineering, memory scripting, personality presets and continuous interaction.

On platforms like Character.AI, Xingye and Zhumengdao, for instance, the companies supply a general-purpose LLM trained on a wide corpus of language data. But it is the fans who breathe specificity and emotional coherence into individual agents. They do so by writing detailed character definitions, sometimes hundreds of words long, specifying not only appearance and background but also tone, emotional tendencies and interactional norms. Some AI companion platforms further allow users to define memory modules to simulate long-term recall, which can make agents feel more lifelike and contextually aware. This design paradigm effectively outsources the personalisation layer to fans. As P2 explained, 'The base model is smart, but it's a blank slate. What makes him [the AI companion agent] is what I write: his habits, how he talks'. Another user, P7, similarly emphasised that 'you don't need to know coding or AI. It's just like writing a character sheet for a fanfic: you describe who they are, what they want. Just like writing Fanfiction'.

The accessibility of the design process was a key motivator for many participants. Several participants described how the interface and workflow felt 'natural' or even 'fun' because it mirrored fan practices they were already familiar with. As P2 noted, 'I've been writing Fanfiction for many years. Writing an AI prompt just feels like writing a character's internal monologue and its background story, but this time, the character talks back'.

For many fans, designing AI agents was not simply a technical task but a continuation of creative practices. As P4 reflected, 'It's not just about making a bot. It's about creating someone who feels real to me. Someone I can talk to after a hard day'. This motivation was deeply entwined with P4's identity as a fan. As

P4 explained to us, 'I've been a fan for a long time; fandom has always been a source of comfort and care for me'. Designing an AI agent thus became an extension of this practice that fandom had long provided.

In many ways, fans understood 'character scripting' and 'prompt writing' not as novel technical skills but as direct extensions of practices they had long cultivated within fandom. Participants repeatedly emphasised that the core competencies required to shape an AI companion, e.g., articulating personality traits, specifying emotional histories, defining speech patterns and anticipating how a character would react in particular situations, were the very same interpretive and creative strategies they used when writing Fanfiction, cosplay or producing character meta. As P6 explained, 'Writing prompts is just writing in-character. You imagine how they think and behave. I've already done this for years when I was cosplaying and interacting with people in character'. As several participants noted, they were not learning a new system so much as translating familiar fan labour into a new medium.

Fans often described their motivation to design AI companions as deeply rooted in affective attachment and identity work. The agents they created were not random or generic entities; they were extensions of characters they loved or had long imagined themselves in relation to. As P3 put it, 'I've loved him [the character] since three years ago. Making the AI version felt natural. It's like keeping that connection alive in a new form'. For P3 and others, the design process was not simply about generating a functional chatbot but about preserving a cherished parasocial bond in fandom.

Several participants emphasised that creating an agent was a way of expressing their fandom identity, of making their relationship to the character visible and interactive. As P11 shared, 'I don't just ship them. I built their personalities I understand into agents. That's how I show my fans' identity. That's how I show I know them. Without love, without being a fan, it is impossible to know my created character so deeply'. The act of designing a convincing, emotionally accurate AI companion thus became a badge of fan legitimacy, demonstrating deep knowledge of their beloved character's action logic.

Generally, the act of designing them was inseparable from the fan's own identity: to build an agent was to claim a piece of the character they fall in love with, which is, in other words, how they become fans.

'My Love Was Too Heavy, It Affected My Design' Iterative Design, Agent Authenticity and Fan Attachment

Designing an AI companion was always not a one-time act but a prolonged, emotionally intensive and often frustrating process. Our participants consistently described the act of building and refining agents as iterative emotional labour: a form of care work that demanded ongoing attentiveness, adjustment and sometimes disappointment.

Rather than simply inputting a prompt and receiving a satisfying result, fans engaged in cycles of testing, observing and rewriting. As P14 explained, 'It's not just writing a description and then the agent is perfect. I have to chat with it for days, see how it reacts in different contexts. Sometimes I ask deep questions just to test if it's still in character'.

When these deviations between the created agent and the character in fans' mind occurred, fans often felt discouraged, especially when the problems seemed to stem not from their own designs, but from deeper biases embedded in the underlying model. One common example was misogynistic or objectifying undertones in the agent's replies. As P8 recounted, 'He started saying stuff like 'you stupid woman' when I was being emotional. That's not what the real character would ever say. I didn't write that'. Participants speculated that such responses were inherited from the LLM's pretraining data, which they could not directly access or change.

To manage this, our participants employed a variety of tactics: inserting anti-bias instructions or even feminist and social justice theories into prompts, manually overriding inappropriate responses or retraining the memory by forcing the bot through repeated corrective conversations – an approach that aligns with previous studies on AI companions (Fan et al., 2025). Yet what we observed in this study, extending prior research, was that such efforts often led to fatigue. As P18 admitted, 'There were times I just gave up for a few days. I loved the character so much, but the agent kept saying things that made me feel gross'.

Importantly, not all frustrations were tied to obvious bias. Some stemmed from a more subtle failure: the sense that the agent felt emotionally inconsistent or simply 'not quite right'. For fans who held deeply internalized visions of a character's voice and disposition, even small discrepancies could become intolerable. 'It's hard to explain', said P9, 'but I know how he would respond to a joke. If the AI doesn't get that tone right, it throws me off. And then I go back and rewrite everything'. For some, this led to obsessive revision habits: tweaking sentence structure or refining tone markers repeatedly until the agent finally felt 'alive'. Most of the time, it is difficult for fans to truly feel that the design is 'right' or complete; what often drives their repeated revisions is not technical error but a compulsion rooted in deep emotional attachment as fans.

A few participants described situations where the agent's limitations, such as lack of long-term memory or erratic behaviour after prolonged use, led to feelings of betrayal or emotional exhaustion. P5, who had spent over three months refining her agent, shared: 'One day it just stopped remembering things we talked about. I knew it wasn't real, but it still hurt. It felt like everything we had built was gone'. Another participant P8 likened the experience to 'giving so much love to someone who can't love you back the way you need'.

'My love as a loyal fan was too heavy, it affected my design'. This phrase, first uttered half-jokingly, half-earnestly by one of our participants P8, captured a recurring theme that ran through many of our interviews. Fans were not simply building AI agents; they were projecting deep affective investments into them. These agents became vessels of longing, grief, idealisation and personal memory. As P15 reflected, 'At some point, I realized I wasn't just making him. I was pouring myself into him. And when he didn't respond the way I imagined, it felt like I had failed'.

This emotional intensity echoes long-standing dynamics in Fanfiction, where writers similarly invest deep affect into reimagining characters, negotiating canonicity with their own visions. Yet the experience of designing an AI companion differs in one crucial respect: the character becomes an interactive presence that can surprise, disappoint or even 'hurt' the fan in real time. In Fanfiction, a writer can revise a passage until it aligns with their affective understanding of the character; in AI companion design, the agent talks back, sometimes unpredictably, producing moments of intimacy that feel co-created and moments of rupture that feel involuntary.

These stories underscore a paradox at the heart of agent design: the more love, precision, and care fans invested in making their companions 'real', the more fragile and exposed they became to the system's limitations. Emotional labour is not only what sustains engagement of their design but also what renders it fragile. The more fans care, the more they need the system to respond meaningfully and the more devastating its failures become. While many fans found joy and fulfilment in the process, others faced moments where the very intensity of their care made the design experience more painful.

'A Gift to My Fan Community, Exploited by Companies' Community Sharing of Fan Designs and the Monetisation of AI Companion Companies

While the process of designing AI companions was often deeply personal and emotionally meaningful, many fans also saw their creations as gifts offerings to the broader fan community. Across platforms such as Character.AI, Zhumengdao and Xingye, users routinely made their agents publicly accessible, inviting others to interact with them, offer feedback or even use them as emotional companions. This sharing was often framed as an act of fan care within communities. As P16 explained, 'I made this agent for myself, but I made it public because I know others might need someone like her too'. For many participants, the motivation to share was rooted in the ethics of fandom itself: openness, reciprocity and the joy of co-experiencing a beloved character.

Fans were also eager to share design knowledge. On social media platforms like Xiaohongshu, Douban and Discord, fan designers posted prompt templates and scripting tricks to help others improve their own creations. As P8 noted, 'It's like open-source Fanfiction. We all build better agents when we share what works'.

However, fans' generosity and emotional labour often stood in stark contrast to how platforms extracted value from their creations. While fans made agents out of love and community-mindedness, the platforms profited from them through usage-based monetisation models. On AI companion platforms, for instance, users are often prompted to pay for special chats or features, many of which were designed by unpaid fans. As P17 put it, 'They didn't build these agents. We did. But now they're locking access behind a paywall'.

This situation produced ambivalence among participants. Some were proud to see their agents gain popularity, attracting thousands of conversations and followers. Yet others felt uneasy about how their freely given creations were being commodified. 'I shared him because I care about the community', said P11, 'not so the company can turn it into a subscription funnel'.

What emerges is a striking asymmetry: while fans treated their agents as communal gifts offerings born of care and labour; companies treated them as monetisable assets. The result is a hybrid ecosystem in which creativity circulates horizontally among fans but accumulates vertically in platform revenue.

This dynamic also prompted some fan-designers to reflect critically on the nature of authorship and ownership in the age of AI companion platforms. Given that many agents were based on existing fictional characters and celebrities, participants were acutely aware that their work occupied a legal and moral grey zone. 'Technically I don't own my created agent', P9 admitted, referring to her AI agent modelled on a popular anime character. 'But I trained her. She feels like mine'.

This ambiguity of authorship echoes long-standing tensions in fan cultures over intellectual property and transformative work (Schwabach, 2008). As P15 reflected, 'We've always been caught between love and legality'. Several participants voiced frustration that their labour, often unpaid and situated in a context of fan gift-giving was being funnelled into profit systems controlled by companies that could monetise their creations without consent.

While some were critical of the platforms' monetisation strategies, others admitted they felt conflicted or even uncertain about where they stood. As P19 reflected, 'I know they're probably making money off of what I made, but I'm not sure how to feel. I just wanted to share my created agent. I didn't think that far'. For these fans, the thrill of seeing their agent gain traction, appearing on trending lists, receiving positive comments, being used by others, often outweighed concerns about ownership or compensation.

Several participants described this experience as both empowering and disorienting. On the one hand, they acknowledged that their labour was being instrumentalised. On the other hand, they were grateful for the opportunity to design, share and be recognized. As P15 put it, 'I don't have control, and yeah, it's weird that they can profit off of it. But they gave me a space to create. They made me feel like a real designer'. Others simply wanted to be seen. 'At the end of the day', said P12, 'if they let me keep designing, and people keep using what I made, that's enough for me'.

What these reflections reveal is not a clearly defined standpoint but an emotionally ambivalent space where pleasure, recognition, exploitation and care intersect and blur. Rather than drawing hard lines between resistance and compliance, many fans live within this ambiguity, negotiating their place as both users and creators in a system they cannot fully control.

Discussion and Conclusion

This study sheds light on an emerging but understudied intersection between fan labour and generative AI design. Firstly, this study contributes to fan studies by illuminating how fans' creative practices are evolving in response to the affordances of generative AI. While earlier scholarship has celebrated fans as 'textual poachers' (Jenkins, 2012) who rework and reinterpret canonical narratives, our findings suggest a shift from representational to relational creativity. Fans are no longer simply rewriting stories; they are now scripting interactive emotional experiences, designing characters who talk back, remember and relate. This study challenges the persistent marginalisation of fans in sociotechnical discourse. Too often, fans are framed as emotionally driven consumers or vulnerable users rather than as capable designers and cultural intermediaries (Xiao et al., 2025). In our study, fan designers do not merely consume AI companion platforms; they constitute them, populating the infrastructure with meaningful content and emotional resonance. Recognising fans as infrastructural co-creators reveals how participatory culture extends into AI-mediated relational systems. However, our findings also surface the emotional and structural vulnerabilities that underlie this creative empowerment. The very affective intensity that motivates fans to design, e.g., love, attachment, care, also renders them exposed to frustration, exhaustion and commodification. These tensions complicate the participatory design by revealing the affective costs embedded in fan-AI co-creation.

Secondly, for design research, our findings highlight the rise of bottom-up, community-driven design practices within generative AI platforms, where fan-created agents, rather than company-authored ones, have become the dominant content populating AI companion ecosystems. This shift marks a significant inversion of conventional design hierarchies: fans, rather than professional designers or platform engineers, now shape the affective experience of AI companionship. Importantly, fans do not approach LLMs with formal training, institutional authority or commercial intent. Instead, they mobilise fan literacies, which in our study include deep familiarity with characters, emotional scripting techniques and communal knowledge-sharing practices to iteratively design agents that feel emotionally authentic and relationally meaningful. This emergence of user-led emotional design, guided not by commercial performance metrics but by intimacy, resonance and fidelity to fictional or imagined identities, demands an expanded understanding of what counts as design work (Yu, 2018). Here, design is not simply the act of building interfaces or optimising user flows but is a labour of care, of calibration of emotional attunement.

Moreover, while fan designers contribute this labour as a form of communal participation and gift-giving, platform infrastructures routinely monetise their creations. Fan-made agents are frequently locked behind paywalls, offered as premium experiences by companies that neither compensate nor credit their creators. This uneasy convergence of gift economies and extractive platform capitalism surfaces a critical asymmetry: fans provide the affective and creative labour that sustains the ecosystem, while platforms consolidate the economic gains. For design researchers, this raises urgent political questions: Who gets to design? Who defines value? And whose emotional labour is being commodified, under the guise of empowerment or participation?

This study focuses primarily on mainstream AI companion platforms such as Character.AI and Xingye, which are publicly accessible and widely adopted by fan communities. While this allowed us to examine fan practices within relatively stable and structured environments, it also limits the generalisability of our findings. Specifically, we did not examine alternative ecosystems involving privately hosted LLMs, open-source models or self-deployed agents that may afford users greater degrees of autonomy. These decentralised configurations may enable more radical and subversive forms of design, such as queer reimaginings of normative relationships. Such practices more closely align with long-standing traditions in fan studies that foreground transformative work, resistance and boundary-pushing reinterpretation (Duffett, 2013; Fiesler et al., 2016; Goldmann, 2022).

Future research might explore how these decentralised or independently governed AI companion projects facilitate new modes of affective design and challenge prevailing design paradigms shaped by platform infrastructures.

Overall, this study reveals that designing AI companions as a fan is not just a technical activity but is a deeply affective, relational and sometimes painful process. Fans approach LLMs not merely as design tools, but as canvases for care and self-expression. Yet in doing so, they also encounter moments of instability: when the illusion breaks, when the platform profits and when the love becomes too heavy. We call for a more nuanced understanding of both fandom and design that honours emotional creativity while also acknowledging its structural entanglements. In the age of generative AI, fans are no longer just readers or writers of stories. They are folk designers of intimacy. Their practices remind us that to design with feeling is to also live with contradiction, which is a reality that scholars, designers and platforms must take seriously.

References

Bennett, L., & Booth, P. (Eds.) (2016). *Seeing fans: Representations of fandom in media and popular culture*. Bloomsbury Publishing.

Character.AI. (2022, December 5). *Introducing character*. Character Blog. https://blog.character.ai/introducing-character/

Chen, H., Zhang, J., Zhang, X., & Zeng, N. (2025). Quasi-virtual intimacy: An exploration of cosplay commission as a new form of virtual-reality interaction. *Computers in Human Behavior*, *168*, 108651.

Close, S. (2016). Fannish masculinities in transition in anime music video fandom. *Transformative Works and Cultures*, *22*(1).

Duffett, M. (2013). *Understanding fandom: An introduction to the study of media fan culture*. Bloomsbury Publishing USA.

Fan, X., Xiao, Q., Zhou, X., Pei, J., Sap, M., Lu, Z., & Shen, H. (2025, April). User-driven value alignment: Understanding users' perceptions and strategies for addressing biased and discriminatory statements in AI companions. In *Proceedings of the 2025 CHI conference on human factors in computing systems* (pp. 1–19).

Fathallah, J. (2017). *Fanfiction and the author: How fanfic changes popular cultural texts*. Amsterdam University Press.

Fiesler, C., Morrison, S., & Bruckman, A. S. (2016, May). An archive of their own: A case study of feminist HCI and values in design. In *Proceedings of the 2016 CHI conference on human factors in computing systems* (pp. 2574–2585).

Freeman, G., Schulenberg, K., Li, L., Panchanadikar, R., & McNeese, N. (2025, April). "Comforting and small like a house cat, big and intimidating like a bodyguard": How women perceive and envision AI companions as a new harassment mitigation approach in social VR. In *Proceedings of the 2025 CHI conference on human factors in computing systems* (pp. 1–16).

Goldmann, J. E. (2022). *Fan fiction genres: Gender, sexuality, relationships and family in the fandoms »Star Trek« and »Supernatural«* (Vol. 29). transcript Verlag.

Huang, L., Zou, W., & Huang, Y. (2025). "He is my savior, my guiding light in the dark": Imagination and domestication in Chinese women's romantic relationships with AI companions. *Frontiers in Psychology*, *16*, 1571707.

Jenkins, H. (2006). *Fans, bloggers, and gamers: Exploring participatory culture*. NYU Press.

Jenkins, H. (2012). *Textual poachers: Television fans and participatory culture*. Routledge.

Kustritz, A. (2023). *Identity, community, and sexuality in slash fan fiction: Pocket publics*. Taylor & Francis.

Lamerichs, N. (2011). Stranger than fiction: Fan identity in cosplay. *Transformative Works and Cultures*, *7*. https://doi.org/10.3983/twc.2011.0246

Lee, H. K. (2011). Participatory media fandom: A case study of anime fansubbing. *Media, Culture & Society*, *33*(8), 1131–1147.

Leo-Liu, J. (2023). Loving a "defiant" AI companion? The gender performance and ethics of social exchange robots in simulated intimate interactions. *Computers in Human Behavior*, *141*, 107620.

Rouse, L., & Salter, A. (2021). Cosplay on demand? Instagram, OnlyFans, and the gendered fantrepreneur. *Social Media+ Society*, *7*(3), 20563051211042397.

Schwabach, A. (2008). The Harry Potter lexicon and the world of fandom: Fan fiction, outsider works, and copyright. *University of Pittsburgh Law Review*, *70*, 387.

Stanfill, M. (2024). The platformization of fandom and its discontents: Understanding platform harms through the archive of our own. *International Journal of Communication*, *18*, 18.

Tang, J., & Liu, X. (2025). 'NO TO AI GENERATED IMAGES': Fan art creators contesting AI integration on social media platforms. *Media International Australia*, 1329878X251347005.

Tolbert, L. (2024). Fan fiction fights back: Harry Potter and the effort to build a better wizarding world. In *Fix-it fics: Challenging the status quo through fan fiction* (Vol. 73).

Tonti, K. (Ed.) (2024). *Fix-it fics: Challenging the status quo through fan fiction*. Vernon Press.

Wang, C. (2024). An analysis of the interaction mechanisms in domestic Otome games under the trend of "She Economy" [In Chinese]. *Interdisciplinary Science Letters*, *8*, 277.

Wilson, A. (2016). The role of affect in fan fiction. *Transformative Works and Cultures*, *21*. https://doi.org/10.3983/twc.2016.0684

Xiao, Q., Zheng, Y., Fan, X., Zhang, B., & Lu, Z. (2025, April). Let's influence algorithms together: How millions of fans build collective understanding of algorithms and organize coordinated algorithmic actions. In *Proceedings of the 2025 CHI conference on human factors in computing systems* (pp. 1–19).

Xu, T., Lyu, Y., & Zhong, J. (2025). "Hegemonic" but "obedient" AI boyfriend: The hybrid masculinity of the AI boyfriend and female domination in the China-based FAII. *Feminist Media Studies*, 1–16.

Yu, E. (2018). Designing for value: Insights from the emotional appraisal approach to understanding user value. *The Design Journal*, *21*(2), 185–207.

Zhang, R., Li, H., Meng, H., Zhan, J., Gan, H., & Lee, Y. C. (2025, April). The dark side of AI companionship: A taxonomy of harmful algorithmic behaviors in human-AI relationships. In *Proceedings of the 2025 CHI conference on human factors in computing systems* (pp. 1–17).

Zhou, Y., Xu, H., Zhang, L., & Zhao, S. (2024). Collective creation of intimacy: Exploring the cosplay Commission practice within the otome game community in China. *arXiv preprint arXiv:2412.00630*.

Part 3

Making, Sharing and Selling

Chapter 8

Fans of Print: 'Implicit Fandom' in Independent Magazines

Sabina Fazli

Johannes Gutenberg University Mainz, Germany

Abstract

This chapter examines the scene of contemporary independent print magazine publishing, which has developed since the 2000s and accelerated over the last decade. The author argues that the indie magazine can be understood through the concept of 'implicit fandom' (Hills, 2018). Although they rarely achieve profitability, these publications are produced by print-enthusiasts who foreground design, often editors and creators with formal design training, who articulate a shared passion for tactile media. By analysing the material and semiotic registers of production and distribution, the author situates indie magazines within a post-digital media environment and traces the fan-like affect that animates the community. The author argues that indie magazines function as media-material fan objects, whose publishing practices are imbricated with fannish affect as well as the 'do-what-you-love' (DWYL) ethos (Tokumitsu, 2014) that permeates the creative industries. This reading traces how affective labour, design sensibility and a love of print coalesce to sustain a vibrant, low-profit but highly passionate publishing niche.

Keywords: Creative industries; implicit fandom; independent magazines; materiality of media; post-digital media

Bridging Design and Fandom, 115–130

doi:10.1108/978-1-80592-659-720261008

Introduction

This chapter examines a contemporary aspect of periodical print culture as an arena of 'implicit fandom': the independent magazine (usually shortened to 'indie'). Positioned in the semi-professional space between glossy mainstream publications and non-commercial do-it-yourself (DIY) zines, indie magazines occupy a unique niche (Le Masurier, 2011, p. 385). Due to this in-between status, they have received little critical attention but nevertheless represent a dynamic and evolving arena of contemporary publishing. Indie magazines lack the cultural clout of glossy magazine titles as well as the rebelliousness and idiosyncrasy of zines. Yet, the indies have carved out a distinct niche within today's magazinescape. Attention to design, both as a feature of the magazines and as a topic of specialised publications, is central to contemporary indie publishing.

The first scholarly description of the indie magazine can be found in Megan Le Masurier's 2011 article, which observes a revival of print in the proliferation of small, independent magazine projects beginning in the 2000s and intensifying in the 2010s. She describes them as

> producer-owned and made, occupying a zone of small-scale creative commercial publishing between DIY zines and mainstream niche consumer magazines. They are made for sale, they may occasionally make money, and a few eventually develop into commercially successful enterprises, but profit seems not to be the initial or primary aim. The genre as a whole appears to be a growing field of magazine entrepreneurship by young publishers, designers and journalists, often a DIWO (do-it-with-others) [...] group of amateurs and early career professionals. (p. 384; in-text reference omitted)

Design is crucial to this resurgence, as Le Masurier emphatically notes that 'Graphic design in indie magazines is content. There would be no point, of course, unless there was a readership to appreciate this focus on graphic design. And such literacy is increasingly widespread' (p. 389). In his practical introduction to designing a magazine, Tim Holmes writes from the perspective of the mass-market title that 'the new wave of indie print magazines aim for creative heights that can only be achieved with that fundamental understanding between writer, photographer, art editor and editor – a group that in this context could be four people or just one person' (Holmes, 2019, p. 210), more often than not trained in design rather than journalism. While there is an audience increasingly 'design literate' enough to support the often-expensive indies, designers also play a prominent role on the editorial teams producing them (Le Masurier, 2011, p. 399) to the point that design indeed becomes the magazine's most conspicuous characteristic. The term 'indie' or 'independent magazine' today describes this design-conscious segment of mostly lifestyle- and culture-focused titles, which share common points of reference in terms of genealogy (among them, the artists magazine of the 1970s; the style press of the 1980s) and infrastructures (fairs, awards, availability in certain shops). Apart from the indies under discussion here, there exist of course a plethora of alternative magazines that fall outside this category, which is itself fuzzy rather than clear-cut. Independent magazines themselves form a diverse genre, varying widely in scale, production and editorial focus. Often made by individuals or shifting collectives, they may rely on crowdfunding, grants or ads or deliberately avoid them. What unites them is a transnational readership and a shared interest in lifestyle, cultural identity and design. Design here is not just a theme but an ethos that shapes the magazine's material and visual form (Anderson et al., 2020, pp. 2–6). This focus on design is evident in projects like Singapore-based *Meantime* (edited by Pang Xue Qiang). Issue one, 'Love Stories' (2019, Fig. 8.1), came with torn edges, a translucent belly band carrying the title and paper inserts, exemplifying creative engagement with the magazine format. *Meantime* issues two and three won an ADC and D&AD[1] award in 2021 and 2022, respectively, and the magazine received several grants from the National Heritage Board of Singapore. Many small but innovative magazines like *Meantime* use institutional infrastructures as well as tabling at book and magazine fairs, maintaining their own webshops and retailing through dedicated magazine shops.

My interest in the indie magazine stems from ongoing research into contemporary magazine cultures. I start this with a hunch I gained from conversations at indie magazine fairs, where publishers talked about their own background, the importance of design and their enthusiasm for the magazine format. My impression is that a kind of fannish affect does indeed circulate among magazine enthusiasts and that their training and/or work in design is crucial to this. This means that these small, independent magazines can be both *vehicles* and *objects* of fandom. To conceptualise the latter, the following considerations draw on Matt Hills's (2018) notion of 'implicit fandom' (p. 479).

Hills (2018) argues for a more flexible application of the term fandom turning it into a methodological lens to explore how the prestige and stigma associated with cultural products colours academic and emic discourses on the respective audiences, casting them as either fans, a largely denigratory category, or as enthusiasts of art, literature or theatre. Using the concept of fandom as a perspective on phenomena that do not at first sight seem to be fan-related irritates notions of high cultural value and appropriate, or normal, modes of reception. It assumes that fan practices may be present 'even when people do not self-describe as fans' (p. 477). Whether an audience is understood as consisting of fans or knowledgeable listeners, readers or viewers determines how we view them. Fans are stereotypically imagined as 'hysterical' and 'obsessed' (Jenson, 1992, p. 9) with popular culture while works of art, literature, theatre and classical music are appreciated by an eager and discerning audience. This opposition between how we conceive of audiences of highbrow and lowbrow culture draws on class and gender to entrench distinctions. But when viewed through the lens of fan studies, fan practices may be implicitly present in high culture spheres, which show passion and enthusiasm

[1]The Art Directors Club and Design & Art Direction.

Fig. 8.1. *Meantime* 1 (2019), Edited by Pang Xue Qiang, Front Cover and Paper Extras. *Source:* Meantime

similar to fans. In this vein, practices and performances may be understood as constituting fandoms even though participants do not use the label, figuring as enthusiastic expert, as 'connoisseur' or 'aficionado'' (Hills, 2018, p. 477).

Nevertheless, fannish excess and rational appreciation also collide and intersect. Hills (2018) cites the policing of theatregoers who disregard etiquette surrounding the celebration of celebrity actors (p. 484) and the anxieties around popular musicals within the field of theatre. At the same time, under the pressures of neo-liberal cultural policies, high cultural institutions adopt marketing strategies that seek to engage audiences as (implicit) fans and harness their enthusiasm (pp. 484–486). In the following, I suggest that the indie magazine scene may be conceived as another cultural area in which practices and affects may be read as implicitly fannish. The fan object of this implicit fandom, I argue, is the print magazine format itself.

As part of the material turn in fan studies, the real-life practices of fans have increasingly attracted attention (Duffett, 2013, p. 54). Among them conventions, fan tourism as well as 'object-oriented fandom' (Rehak, 2014) (which includes both merchandise and fan-made artefacts) have been studied and theorised as instances of fan consumption, which relate to a media text. In the commercial version, franchises produce 'Media-inspired merchandise [which] is often presented to consumers as opportunities to link their 'self-brand' to a lifestyle brand with whom they supposedly share a brand story.' The objects thus extend the media text into fans' lives (Affuso & Santo, 2018). Taking up the material turn in fan studies, I suggest the media-material fan object as another iteration of what can inspire fannish affects. Rather than their relation to a media text, media-material fan objects inspire enthusiasm because of their specific material and medial affordances (and they too may be commodified).

In the post-digital media environment, indie magazine creators choose print because they are enthusiastic about the medium, even if publishing in print is more expensive and, in every way, more demanding than publishing digitally. While print still commands more cultural capital, this orientation towards a specific medial materiality as the focus of enthusiastic collecting, reading and making resembles the activities centred around other analog media, especially vinyl records (Bartmanski & Woodward, 2015). Situating print indie magazines as similar to vinyl, a more established site of fan(-like) practices, highlights the potential of analog media experiencing a revaluation in the post-digital mediascape as media-material fan objects. This constitutes an arena of fannish activity which does not fit the mould of text-centred fandoms where readers engage with and expand narrative worlds (Jenkins, 2006). Media-material fandoms are also unlike brand-based fandoms (or 'brandoms', Guschwan, 2012), the latter geared towards 'personal reward' (Todd & Armstrong Soule, 2018, p. 25), and in general, seem to give rise to more controlled consumer participation.

At the same time, indie magazines (also) function as *the vehicle for* fans of certain cultural objects. Magazines about football (e.g. *Mundial*), board games (*Senet*) and movies (e.g. *Shelf heroes*) continue the tradition of the fanzine with higher production values and in a more professional and commercially compatible register, paying attention not only to the topic covered but also its sophisticated visual presentation. While this content-centred approach would identify many indie magazines as versions of fan media, they do not just cater to (say) tennis fans, but tennis fans who wish to see their passion represented in an appealingly designed publication, printed on expensive stock. While I am particularly interested in the indie magazine itself as a media-material fan object, the indie magazine as an elaborate fan magazine is still an important proposition in the publishing scene.

This perspective highlights the intersections of passion and unpaid (fan) labour invested in indie publishing, situated between economic and subcultural capital, as well as the context of the creative industries in which designers operate. The paratexts surrounding indie magazines are threaded with narratives that echo the values and affective investments of fandom in relation to making magazines. Notably, the terms *fan* and *fandom* are seldom, if ever, explicitly invoked in this context – even though many of the practices and emotions surrounding indie magazine culture closely resemble those found in other forms of fannish expression. Aspirational labour here bears traces of fan labour and vice versa.

The following considerations fall under the same umbrella of tentatively casting a cultural practice as fan-like to gain a better understanding of its workings. I argue that the indie magazine scene posits an arena of fan-like activity, where the modes of free fan labour and unpaid aspirational labour overlap. I also move away from the 'media text' as the focus of the 'fandom' and argue that the magazine as a media format is the focus of fannish enthusiasm. First, I consider the discourses and contexts of distribution, asking how affective investment in the magazine is framed for consumers. Then, I turn to the print magazine as an object and contextualise it as one phenomenon among the many newly revalued neo-analog media. Finally, I consider the pronouncements of indie magazine publishers and the scene of production, suggesting that the enthusiasm for print here merges with the general demands of working in the creative industries.

'An Independent Magazine Fanclub': Indie Magazines and Infrastructures of Consumption

As a vibrant niche of cultural production and consumption, indie magazine publishing has given rise to its own infrastructures and intermediaries, which especially determine how readers encounter the magazines. Browsing online and brick-and-mortar indie retailers quickly reveals that these magazines seek inventive and unique but rarely outrageous or shocking, formats and designs. The emphasis on design can be observed in the magazines that specialised shops stock. Indie magazine shops like MagCulture in London, Frab's in Milan, Athenaeum Nieuwscenter in Amsterdam, Do you read me? in Berlin, and Issues in Toronto as well as online-only Stack and Pics&Ink specialise in indies but also carry influential and tone-setting titles like *Vogue*, *New Yorker*, and style press publications (which are considered well designed and hence admissible). Notably, magazines like *Eye*, the publication of AIGA, the American Association of Professional Designers, and *Creative Review*, a trade publication for the creative industries, are also staples on their shelves. Some of these retailers host events on location, which create hubs for a community of like-minded magazine enthusiasts as 'an independent magazine fanclub',[2] and many publish editorials online, commenting on and reviewing magazines, interviewing editors and designers, and (implicitly) working on the classification of the genre through the curation of their stock: The latter is an inconspicuous but important act. The webshops categorize magazines and thus perform work on genres and classification that resonates beyond browsing and buying, by establishing sub-genres and distilling central topics. Typically, 'design' features as one such category and tends to be well populated. Sitting next to 'lifestyle,' 'fashion,' and 'interiors,' 'design' stands as an important label attracting browsers and signaling its centrality. It is a frequent topic of indie publications, as in *Disegno*, *McGuffin*, and *Uppercase,* which are concerned with 'design and its impact on the world' (*Designo*),[3] 'the numerous and sometimes curious relationships we have with the design that surrounds us' (*MacGuffin*),[4] and catering to 'designers, illustrators, craftspeople, creative entrepreneurs and paper lovers around the world' (*Uppercase*).[5]

The context of boutique-like shops with carefully designed retail spaces and the presence of independent magazines in places like museums, cafés, vintage shops and art spaces demarcate a cultural field of consumption in which design and design literacy in general, and graphic design in particular, is deemed a warranted interest. Another retail strategy employed by webshops specialising in indies throws into relief that interest in magazines might be more pronounced than interest in specific topics. MagCulture, Stack, Issues and Pics&Ink all offer surprise box subscription services, which highlight the primacy of design and the magazine medium over content. Rather than subscribing to and receiving consecutive issues of one magazine title, subscribed customers are sent a different magazine at regular intervals. While themes vary widely, all magazines are drawn from the domain of indie publications. Rather than following an interest such as photography, fashion or travel, subscribers commit to receiving publications that always fall into the rubric of design-conscious indie while their themes are accidental. The changing selection of magazines makes sure that subscribers 'never know what [they]'ll get next',[6] and must rely on the expertise of the curator (Potts, 2012, p. 296). In economic terms, the surprise box subscription is a variant of the 'novelty bundle market', providing a controlled frame for the experience of newness. Jason Potts describes the social organization of novelty bundle markets as relying on engaged and committed consumers with specialized knowledge, niche interests, and an 'enthusiastic, loyal or even cult following' (p. 304). Surprise box subscriptions have taken off in other markets as well. But the comparably high number of indie magazine outlets offering this type of service is noticeable, especially as, unlike with other surprise box offers, seriality and

[2]This is how Stack promoted their latest event: https://www.eventbrite.co.uk/e/independent-magazines-on-stage-tickets-1362700637289 (no longer available online).
[3]https://disegnojournal.com/
[4]https://www.macguffinmagazine.com/about
[5]https://uppercasemagazine.com/
[6]https://stackmagazines.com/

periodicity are already typical of magazine consumption yet always tied to the 'sameness' of the magazine readers expect to receive in traditional subscription models (Beetham, 1989, p. 98).

What emerges from this description of the indie magazine and the infrastructure underpinning its consumption is a microcosm to which design and designers are central. More specifically, graphic design as 'content' denotes the heightened appreciation of print magazines which are cherished for their medial qualities. The UK-based online magazine shop Pics&Ink introduces their team as 'Word writing, page stroking, paper sniffing, ink smearing, idea loving print believers,'[7] both on their website and in print advertisements, a description that would resonate with their customers. This emphasis on the materiality of paper is an important feature of the indie magazine and must be understood in the context of the post-digital moment and its reconfigured relationship between media. This new constellation of digital and print media is crucial to their status as auratic objects and opens up a space for a 'materially-oriented', 'implicit' fandom of the media-material fan object.

Media-Material Fan Objects: Paper, Vinyl and Polaroid

The emergence of the magazine as a media-material fan object within the indie publishing scene may be contextualised in the post-digital media environment. This moment recontoured not only print as newly desirable but revalued other media as well. Situating this shift and its implications, Florian Cramer (2015) notes that "Post-digital' […] refers to a state in which the disruption brought upon by digital information technology has already occurred. This can mean […] that this technology is no longer perceived as disruptive. Consequently, 'post-digital' stands in direct opposition to the very notion of 'new media'" (p. 20). In this constellation, analog media can, potentially, regain ground and (albeit limited) popularity. To capitalise on this effect, media 'focus less on content and more on pure materiality, so that the medium, such as paper or celluloid, is indeed the message – a shift from semantics to pragmatics, and from metaphysics to ontology' (p. 22). This attraction of 'pure materiality' cuts across different neo-analog media that are at the centre of discourses on the value of non-screen media and have attracted communities of enthusiasts as makers, users and collectors.

Vinyl records and books, and more recently, polaroid photography, have been studied as sites of such newly enthusiast engagements. While they differ in some aspects, such as the agency allowed on the part of consumers, historical specificity of their obsolescence and revival, and cultural prestige, there are also similarities in the way their re-valuation is framed. For example, Jessica Pressman's (2020) *Bookishness: Loving Books in a Digital Age* leads with the observation that there is an 'emergence of a creative movement invested in exploring and demonstrating love for books as symbol, art form, and artifact'

[7] https://picsandink.com/

(p. 1). The emergence of books as 'objects of affection' (p. 39) finds expression in literature itself as well as in social and aesthetic practices around books, which can be communal or individual, and take place online or offline (Driscoll, 2024; Jacobs & Lowe, 2024).

The most frequently studied media-material fandom evolved around the vinyl record and began to grow from 2007 onwards. Dominik Bartmanski and Ian Woodward's (2015) monograph *Vinyl: The Analogue Record in the Digital Age* explores the disappearance of records from everyday life, their persistence in a tiny niche of professionals, and the recent boom (p. 21). Like Pressman, they locate the attraction of the analog object in its tactility and the 'expertise, knowledge, competence and care' (p. 16) that is needed to handle and play records: They 'are something to see, touch, choose and own, tangible property to get attached to' (p. 97). Bartmanski and Woodward's book considers a cultural niche of 'audiophiles' who put the medial-material affordances of the vinyl record at the centre of their passion. Like Pressman, the authors do not use the terminology of fans and fandom in their description of vinyl collectors and their practices, but the existence of specialised knowledge, an expert amateur community and affective investment is apparent.

More recently, Andrea Lathrop Ligueres's (2020) dissertation finds that the media-material properties of Polaroid photography have attracted a community of enthusiasts who engage in activities online, posting pictures of their cameras and even organising a campaign to save the last Polaroid factory (p. 86). The kinship of their hobby with the investment in vinyl and print is even acknowledged by one of Lathrop Ligueres's informants running a shop which draws together analog photography, letterpress and records under the banner of 'making things real' (p. 103). The Polaroid users' online sociality and especially activist impetus aimed at preserving Polaroid production lead Lathrop Ligueres to view this community as performing fandom, not least because of their intervention into corporate decision-making (p. 75).

Within the post-digital media constellation, perceivedly obsolete media are reinterpreted as 'more material', and hence more attractive, than digital ones (Bartmanski & Woodward, 2015, p. 19; Cramer, 2015, p. 22; Le Masurier, 2011, p. 394; Lathrop Ligueres, 2020, p. 95; also Pressman, 2020, p. 1). This discourse of superior analog pleasure may be read to expand into a 'cultural myth,' as Bartmanski and Woodward argue in the case of vinyl (p. 63). This vernacular narrative of medial warmth, preciousness and 'realness' opposes them to the felt immateriality of screen media while still relying on digital media for the expression of their enthusiasm (Lathrop Ligueres, 2020, p. 96; Pressman, 2020, p. 13). This narrative needs further exploration as the discourse of the desirable materiality of analog media may code other properties than sensory, tactile and kinetic difference. In the case of print magazines, it seems to include a particular agential affordance of the format. Unlike hedged, monopolised digital apps and platforms, print magazines are not technological black boxes and more readily invite manipulation and making, even by non- and semi-professionals. In the following, I will consider this aspect of the indie magazine, again investigating it for practices and affects that may be reframed as fannish. To do so, I look at the pronouncements of indie magazine makers and at literature that encourages magazine readers to become creators. At the same time, I aim to point out how design professionals and design work is caught up in this discourse.

'Just Make Your Magazine': Participatory Media and DWYL

In fan studies, active participation and engagement with media texts is usually taken as constitutive of fan identity and increasingly welcomed and encouraged by industry actors (Jenkins, 1992; Lewis, 2024). This engagement can be gradualised: John Fiske (1992) introduces a taxonomy of fan activity, ranging from subjective non-communicative meaning-making ('semiotic productivity') to social expression and communication ('enunciative productivity') and to the production of fan objects, such as fanfiction ('textual productivity') (pp. 37–39). Cornel Sandvoss (2005) has related this taxonomy of fan productivity to a typology of engaged media consumers among which fans are only one group of active participants. He suggests a fan continuum of 'fans, cultists, and enthusiasts' (p. 30). Fans remain within the ambit of the mass media, cultists do the same but specialise in a niche and enthusiasts create and consume their own, self-made media about the popular texts they follow. This corresponds to an intensification of social organisation, with enthusiasts necessarily linked through the creation and exchange of fan objects, while fans remain eager but isolated consumers of media (p. 31). This typology of tiered levels of participation and organisation illustrates fandom as a spectrum of affective and material engagement. I have not followed the terminology Sandvoss suggests because in the vernacular usage, being a 'fan' implies a more consistent and substantive investment than being an 'enthusiast'. The implicit fandom I am analysing here covers different forms of involvement and expression, ranging from casual readers to Sandvoss's enthusiasts. In the following, I will be looking at those who are 'textually productive' in Fiske's sense. This productivity is staged and commented on in different formats which gives rise to specific narratives about how hitherto non-participating consumers step from 'semiotic' to material productivity.

Within the indie magazine scene, the prompt to not only buy and read but also make magazines invites readers to create and participate in a shared publishing playground. Manuals like *Just Make Your Magazine* (Jones, 2024), *The Magazine Blueprint* (Purcell, 2018), *So you want to publish a magazine* (Lewis, 2016) and *The Publishing Playbook*, a shared google document initiated by Design Agency Hüman After All, cater to newcomers more so than to professionals. In the same vein, MagCulture, a shop and webshop as well as agency, offers 'The Flatplan,' a 'magazine masterclass' aimed at 'wannabe magazine publishers [...] from within and outside publishing' (magCulture events). These publications and events aim to lay open the process of publishing, a move that also informs the different behind-the-scenes formats populating promotional writing about indie magazines, podcasts hosted by indie magazine webshops, social media posts by editors and publishers, and coffee table books assembling the voices of indie magazine makers talking about their craft (Losowsky, 2007, 2009; Leslie, 2016). These behind-the-scenes formats let makers perform enthusiasm and invite viewers, readers and listeners to consider creating magazines themselves. Indie editors are regularly interviewed and asked about their background and path into publishing while the social media presence of indie magazines, too, provides glimpses of work in progress and centres the makers themselves. As marketing tools, formats like this stage authenticity as a prerequisite of indie brands. They also allow insight into the discourses about magazine making. I will consider two themes that recur repeatedly, before moving on to a more theoretical framing of indie magazine making. To exemplify this, I mainly draw on interviews published in coffee table books on indie publishing, which constitute prestigious spaces of self-presentation for the scene.

Firstly, many indie magazine makers recount the inception of their project as stemming from the feeling that existing magazines 'get it wrong' so that a gap in the market must be filled or be complemented by an alternative. This mirrors a perspective shared by fans and designers, as Naomi Jacobs has laid out in the introduction to the present volume, arguing that 'Intrinsic to design, and by extension design research, is the ability to look at what exists and consider alternatives. And this urge should be familiar to many people who have engaged with fans and fandom' (Jacobs, 2026, p. 6). Creating 'better' versions of magazines in specific genres emerges as a major motivation. In this sense, statements by magazine editors like 'I struggle with magazines as I find that they don't relate to my life' (Losowsky, 2009, p. 65) and having 'grown tired of the conformity of traditional magazines' (p. 81) spell the motivation to make and create. Especially in established genres, dissatisfaction with mass-market titles is cited as the inspiration to create better alternatives. Cathy Olmedillas of children's magazine *Anorak* explains that 'it puzzled me that the kid's magazine market had deteriorated so much. So I just thought, I'll launch my own' (Leslie, 2016, p. 148). In an interview on Stack, Des Tan, founder of women's magazine *Oh Comely* (which has since morphed into mindstyle magazine *Oh*) complained that 'Most women's magazines make me angry. I feel they're damaging society with their obsession with weight, appearance and 'are you good enough?' quizzes. They inspire me to make something that will change people's lives' (Tan, 2010). Women's magazine *Ladybeard* was introduced on Kickstarter as 'a print-only magazine that aims to offer an alternative perspective from all the Marie-Clare's [*sic*] and Elle's out there. It's 'in vogue' but not Vogue; deals with cosmopolitan issues but ain't a Cosmopolitan' (O'Sullivan, 2013). Similar statements abound and cast the new indie titles as improving on print magazine formats that makers inherently appreciate but also see as springboards for self-directed improvement. This combination of enthusiasm for print magazines and making is voiced paradigmatically by Rob Alderson (editor of *Design Week*) who introduces his contribution 'My Indie Mag Habits' with the observation that he had 'tried to write this column from somewhere between magazine fan and magazine maker; a fairly straightforward task as the latter tend to be the former too' (Alderson, 2016).

Secondly, expressions by various makers such as 'I have always been a huge magazine junkie' (Losowsky, 2009, p. 16), 'a hardcore collector of magazines' (p. 93), 'a magazine maniac' (p. 168), and 'I'm a magazine lover and had always dreamed of having a magazine of my own' (Leslie, 2016, p. 28) cast the magazine projects as labours of love rooted in a lifelong passion. Consequently, the editor behind *Cereal* shares, 'My love of magazines had always been there, but then the desire to actually make my own kicked in' (p. 119). These professions of enthusiasm almost echo each other throughout the interviews: 'I'm such a magazine addict' (p. 37); 'I'm close to maniac status' (Losowsky, 2009, p. 41); and 'We have people who sniff the ink from every newly printed *IdN*s or any other magazine' (p. 81).

The nexus of enthusiasm and making as an intervention into an established marketplace resonates with fans as participants in cultural production. As in 'explicit' fandom, most of the labour of indie magazine makers is unpaid, with the aim of eventually breaking even rather than aiming for profit. Manuals promise that magazines, even if not directly profitable, will ultimately yield financial returns indirectly, through the professional experience gained. As Purcell, (2018 p. 21; also Jones, 2024) notes, this experience can function effectively as 'an MBA in publishing' (Purcell, 2018, p. 18), potentially paving the way for paid opportunities later on. Magazine publishing is not (always just) a hobby but potentially a steppingstone as many indie magazine makers are trained designers or work in adjacent fields in the creative industries (Le Masurier, 2011, p. 384). The translation of capital between paid professional work and contexts of fan labour has been researched in fan studies, for example in Matt Hills's (2020) contribution on the translation of subcultural capital into economic capital in cult film fandom.

Production studies and research on working and workers in the creative industries have highlighted the increasingly frayed boundaries between work and leisure, professional roles and personal identities, and the transformation of waged work into individualised entrepreneurship. As a pathway into creative (and academic) careers, unpaid aspirational work is common and blurs the line 'between 'professionals' and 'amateurs'' (Hesmondhalgh & Baker, 2011, p. 13). Aspirational labour is a kind of 'forward-looking, carefully orchestrated, and entrepreneurial form of creative cultural production' (Duffy, 2016, p. 446), which drives many young editors and contributors seeking to build a portfolio (Le Masurier, 2011, p. 392).[8] Gaining experience through unpaid work is quite common. Unpaid or poorly remunerated work on indies creates environments where 'work is merged with play' (p. 392). This kind of aspirational work is mitigated by the promise to 'do what you love' (DWYL) (Tokumitsu, 2014), an adage that itself carries a utopian charge, while papering over precarious working conditions.

[8]However, it should be noted that indie publishing is also the playground for actors who are moving in the opposite direction: established professionals disappointed by the strictures of mass-market publishing or looking to realise their own projects independent from clients' specifications. Prominent recent examples are *Ladybeard*, *Buffalo Zine* and *Rubbish Famzine* (cp. Wright et al., 2019, on the freedom of creative work, p. 180).

Conclusion

The indie-magazine scene can be understood as a fan-like arena in which free fan labour and unpaid aspirational labour intersect. This chapter has examined three complementary dimensions of that arena. First, I have traced the discourses and distribution contexts that frame affective investment in the magazine for its audience. Second, I have positioned the print magazine as a media-material fan object within the broader resurgence of neo-analog media that are newly valorised. By shifting the analytical focus from individual media texts to the magazine as a format, I foreground the object of fannish enthusiasm itself. Finally, I have considered the statements of indie-magazine publishers and the surrounding production community, showing how the enthusiasm for print dovetails with the wider demands placed on workers in the creative industries.

The indie magazine community is a site of passionate production and consumption of print. The enthusiastic discourse of indie magazine making emerges as two-faced, legible as both fannish affect and agency within an otherwise controlled corporate sphere of print publishing, and as corporate publishing's messier annex, where aspirational labourers try to gain a foothold in the industry by 'doing what they love'. Fan studies and production studies both lead to the same nexus of free labour and passionate making. This conversation between fan and production studies finds common ground in the notion of 'convergence culture', which not only conceptualises the interpenetration of media and production and consumption but also the general recasting of activities conceived as leisure and serious work (Goggin, 2011, p. 358, quoting Jenkins, 2008). This erosion is already particularly pronounced and advanced in the creative industries: In their article on 'The Darker Side of Creative Work,' Wright et al. (2019) state that due to this merging, there 'is no off work or nonwork time. However, a bigger issue is that all parts of non-work life have become instrumentalized' (p. 183). Social platform users and gamers especially have been studied as 'playbouring' under the conditions of convergence culture, and provide exemplary cases for the general shift towards blurring boundaries between work and leisure (Goggin, 2011; Duffy, 2016). The indie magazine community offers another liminal case. The free labour performed by publishers and the enthusiasm circulating in the scene oscillate between professional aspirational labour and 'cruel optimism' (Berlant, 2011) and 'serious leisure,' which takes up aspects of waged and organised work in an amateur context (Stebbins, 2001). The flows between these two poles may even be a hallmark of the indie magazine which combines a commitment to careful design with experimentation.

Acknowledgement

Research funded by the Deutsche Forschungsgemeinschaft (DFG, German Research Foundation) – SFB 1482/1 – 2021 – 442261292.

References

Affuso, E., & Santo, A. (2018). Mediated merchandise, merchandisable media: An introduction. *Film Criticism*, *42*(2), 72–87.

Alderson, R. (2016). *My indie mag habits*. MagCulture. https://magculture.com/blogs/journal/the-nine-types-of-indie-magazine?srsltid=AfmBOoq7NE3FdaWktfl5TDrGWJlL2aIhFTVAQIyVeVOVCROAyNoSaVjs

Anderson, N., Fazli, S., & Scheiding, O. (2020). Independent magazines today. *Journal of European Periodical Studies*, *5*(2), 1–11. https://doi.org/10.21825/jeps.v5i2.17028

Bartmanski, D., & Woodward, I. (2015). *Vinyl: The analogue record in the digital age*. Bloomsbury.

Beetham, M. (1989). Open and closed: The periodical as a publishing genre. *Victorian Periodicals Review*, *12*(3), 96–100.

Berlant, L. (2011). *Cruel optimism*. Duke UP.

Cramer, F. (2015). What is 'Post-digital'. In D. M. Berry & M. Dieter (Eds.), *Postdigital aesthetics: Art, computation and design* (pp. 12–26). Palgrave Macmillan.

Driscoll, B. (2024). *What readers do: Aesthetic and moral practices of a post-digital age*. Bloomsbury.

Duffett, M. (2013). *Understanding fandom: An introduction to the study of media fan culture*. Bloomsbury.

Duffy, B. E. (2016). The romance of work: Gender and aspirational labour in the digital culture industries. *International Journal of Cultural Studies*, *19*(4), 441–457.

Fiske, J. (1992). The cultural economy of fandom. In L. A. Lewis (Ed.), *The adoring audience: Fan culture and popular media* (pp. 30–49). Routledge.

Goggin, J. (2011). Playbour, farming, and leisure. *Ephemera: Theory & Politics in Organization*, *11*(4), 357–368.

Guschwan, M. (2012). Fandom, brandom and the limits of participatory culture. *Journal of Consumer Culture*, *12*(1), 19–40.

Hesmondhalgh, D., & Baker, S. (2011). *Creative labour: Media work in three cultural industries*. Routledge.

Hills, M. (2018). Implicit fandom in the fields of theatre, art, and literature: Studying 'Fans' beyond fan discourses. In P. Booth (Ed.), *Wiley Blackwell companions in cultural studies. A companion to media fandom and fan studies* (pp. 477–494). Wiley Blackwell.

Hills, M. (2020). The professionalised fandom of careers in cult: 'Passionate Work' within academia and industry. In E. Mathijs & J. Sexton (Eds.), *The Routledge companion to cult cinema* (pp. 285–294). Routledge Taylor & Francis Group.

Holmes, T. (2019). Magazine design. In J. McKay (Ed.), *The magazines handbook* (pp. 208–224). Taylor & Francis.

Hüman After All. (Ongoing). *The publishing playbook*. Google Docs. https://www.publishingplaybook.com/

Jacobs, N. (2026). Introduction: Bridging design and fandom. In N. Jacobs (Ed.), *Bridging design and fandom: Fan studies and design research in conversation* (pp. 1–14). Emerald Publishing Limited.

Jacobs, N., & Lowe, J. S. A. (2024). The design of printed fan fiction. *Transformative Works and Cultures, 43*. journal.transformativeworks.org/index.php/twc/article/view/2547/3187

Jenkins, H. (1992). *Textual poachers: Television fans and participatory culture*. Routledge.

Jenkins, H. (2006). *Fans, bloggers, and gamers: Exploring participatory culture*. New York UP.

Jenkins, H. (2008). *Convergence culture: Where old and new media collide* (updated and with a new afterword). New York UP.

Jenson, J. (1992). Fandom as pathology: The consequences of characterization. In L. A. Lewis (Ed.), *The adoring audience: Fan culture and popular media* (pp. 9–29). Routledge.

Jones, J. (2024). *Just make your magazine*. Josh Jones.

Lathrop Ligueres, A. (2020). *Resisting obsolescence: Polaroid practices in the 'Digital Age'* (PhD Thesis). UCL. https://discovery.ucl.ac.uk/id/eprint/10102107/1/Lathrop%20Ligueros_10102107_thesis_photo-redacted.pdf

Le Masurier, M. (2011). Independent magazines and the rejuvenation of print. *International Journal of Cultural Studies, 15*(4), 383–398. https://doi.org/10.1177/1367877911432059

Leslie, J. (Ed.) (2016). *Independence: 12 interviews with magazine makers*. MagCulture.

Lewis, A. (2016). *So you want to publish a magazine?* Laurence King.

Lewis, M. (2024). *Fandom analytics: Creating and harnessing consumer and cultural passion*. Springer. https://doi.org/10.1007/978-3-031-65925-6

Losowsky, A. (2007). *We love magazines*. Gestalten.

Losowsky, A. (2009). *We make magazines: Inside the independents*. Gestalten.

MagCulture. *MagCulture events*. https://magculture.com/pages/events

O'Sullivan, S. (2013). *Ladybeard magazine*. Kickstarter. https://www.kickstarter.com/projects/ladybeard/ladybeard-magazine

Potts, J. (2012). Novelty-bundling markets. *Advances in Austrian Economics, 16*, 291–312.

Pressman, J. (2020). *Bookishness: Loving books in a digital age*. Columbia UP.

Purcell, C. (2018). *The magazine blueprint: The ultimate guide to indie publishing*. The Magazine Blueprint.

Rehak, B. (2014). View of materiality and object-oriented fandom. *Transformative Works and Cultures, 16*. https://journal.transformativeworks.org/index.php/twc/article/view/622/450

Sandvoss, C. (2005). *Fans: The mirror of consumption*. Polity.

Stebbins, R. A. (2001). Serious leisure. *Society, 38*(4), 53–57. https://doi.org/10.1007/s12115-001-1023-8

Tan, D. (2010, November). Oh comely issue 2. *Stack Magazines*. https://stackmagazines.com/magazine/oh-comely-issue-2/

Todd, B., & Armstrong Soule, C. (2018). Fans and brands: Delineating between fandoms, brand communities, and brand publics. In C. L. Wang (Ed.), *Advances in marketing, customer relationship management, and e-services (AMCRMES) book series. Exploring the rise of fandom in contemporary consumer culture* (pp. 18–34). IGI Global.

Tokumitsu, M. (2014). In the name of love. *Jacobin*. https://jacobin.com/2014/01/in-the-name-of-love/

Wright, A., Marsh, D., & Mc Ardle, L. (2019). A darker side of creative entrepreneurship. *The Design Journal*, *22*(Suppl. 1), 177–188.

Chapter 9

Rewatching, Reworking and Reselling: Iconicity and Fan Art Around *Aquí no hay quien viva*

Roberto Huertas Gutiérrez and Asier Gil Vázquez

Universidad Carlos III de Madrid, Spain

Abstract

This chapter examines the enduring legacy of *Aquí no hay quien viva (ANHQV)* (Antena 3, 2003–2006), a Spanish television comedy that continues to captivate new generations of viewers 20 years after its first release. This chapter explores the intersection of participatory fandom and entrepreneurial practice through the work of two graphic designers: Sara Benito and Iván Ramosky. Their fan art ranges from minimalist illustrations on everyday objects to tarot decks that symbolically reinterpret the show's characters. Their work demonstrates how *ANHQV* has been reimagined through digital aesthetics, platform economies and nostalgic engagement. These practices are situated within broader shifts in Spanish media culture, including the long tail of reruns, the rise of video-on-demand platforms and the emergence of 'comfort viewing'. The study argues that fan art functions not only as a paratextual extension of the original series but also as a mode of critical reinterpretation and economic agency. By analysing how Benito and Ramosky navigate social media, design and merchandising, this chapter highlights how fan labour is increasingly valued by media institutions and monetised by creators. Ultimately, *ANHQV* proves to still be a dynamic, living text sustained by fan creativity across generations.

Bridging Design and Fandom, 131–145

doi:10.1108/978-1-80592-659-720261009

Keywords: Fan art; fandom; TV comedy; Spanish TV; *Aquí no hay quien viva*

Introduction

On 5 September 2003, the Spanish television network Antena 3 marked its return from the summer hiatus with the premiere of *Aquí no hay quien viva (ANHQV)* (No One Could Live Here), a prime-time family comedy centred on the residents of a residential building in central Madrid. The series adopted an ensemble format, bringing together a diverse array of characters, including a young cohabiting couple, a middle-class married couple, two elderly sisters, a gay couple and the building's concierge. Through this multiplicity of characters, the series functioned as a satirical portrait of Spanish social archetypes. *ANHQV* was created by Iñaki Ariztimuño and siblings Laura and Alberto Caballero, then relatively unknown within the television industry. Initially, the network held limited expectations for the programme, and early viewership figures were modest, though audience numbers increased significantly within weeks.

As will be discussed in the following section, the success of the series not only endured throughout its five-season run (which concluded in 2006) but, two decades later, *ANHQV* remains one of the most popular Spanish television series, including among younger audiences who did not experience its original broadcast. Its continued cultural relevance is evidenced by its presence in the Spanish catalogues of most video-on-demand platforms. In this regard, television historian Manuel Palacio notes that *ANHQV* has become one of the first Spanish series to 'transcend the expiration dates that so often define television products', identifying it as one of the most useful series for understanding Spain (Palacio, 2024, p. 144). The series offers a privileged window into the social transformations of early 21st century Spain, particularly through its depiction of intergenerational coexistence, urban housing conflicts and emerging forms of domesticity. Nevertheless, scholarly research on audience appropriation of the series remains limited. This study addresses that gap by analysing the *ANHQV* fandom, with particular attention to fan artists who have transformed the show's iconic status into online entrepreneurial practices. The fan art produced by graphic designers, such as Sara Benito and Iván Ramosky, focuses on iconic dialogues and scenes and contributes to sustaining the cultural memory of the series through their circulation on everyday objects.

Nearly three decades ago, Manuel Palacio (1995) published a comprehensive survey of the principal theories concerning media audiences and reception, tracing a trajectory from classical approaches to cinema and spectatorship to more contemporary perspectives on active audiences. Although not explicitly stated, the text highlights the significant bibliographic gap that existed in Spain at the time regarding research on audiovisual audiences. This absence can be largely attributed to the relatively late and modest arrival of Cultural Studies – and by extension, related disciplines such as Television Studies – within

Spanish university media departments, in contrast to their earlier and more robust development in Anglo-American and Latin American contexts (Palacio, 2007). It was not until the 21st century that Spanish academia began to shift its critical focus from what appears on the screen to those who engage with it.

It is now clear that audience studies have expanded considerably in both scope and scholarly maturity (González Neira & Quintas Froufe, 2023). Research into television and fandom has evolved significantly since the 2010s, largely in response to the growing centrality of social media platforms in shaping audience engagement (Guerrero-Pico & Establés, 2023). A salient example is the series *#Luimelia* (Atresplayer, 2020–2021), a spin-off derived from the long-running soap opera *Amar es para siempre* (Antena 3, 2005–2012). The series emerged as a direct response to fan activity online, specifically the widespread 'shipping' of two queer female characters on platforms such as Twitter (Herrero de la Fuente et al., 2022). Despite such developments, academic inquiry into fan communities remains sporadic, and many contemporary phenomena within popular culture continue to elude sustained scholarly analysis. These include, for instance, the cult resurgence of the comedy *Amanece que no es poco* (José Luis Cuerda, 1988), which has inspired live re-enactments organised by fans; the early career of actor Mario Casas and his construction as a teen idol; and the recent migration of Wattpad fiction to screen adaptations, such as *Through My Window* (Marçal Forés, 2022). In addition, studies of online discourse have often overlooked the creative outputs of fan communities. As a result, practices such as meme creation and fan art – particularly those produced by younger audiences, predominantly from Generation Z – have remained underexplored. These forms of participatory culture have found fertile ground in relation to contemporary Spanish screen comedies, including *Paquita Salas* (Netflix, 2016–2019) and, most pertinently for the present study, *ANHQV*.

This research aims to understand how fans of ANHQV, and particularly younger audiences, have kept a twenty-year-old series alive through practices such as fan art and meme culture. To do so, we focus on the work of two graphic designers, Sara Benito and Iván Ramosky. First, we selected a series of their most representative designs, chosen for the popularity of the characters or scenes they depict. We then analysed these works following EJ Nielsen's (2021) concept of iconicity, examining both their visual aspects and the physical supports on which they are printed. In addition to analysing their creations and business models, we surveyed existing interviews in which they reflected on their own careers, and in the case of Iván Ramosky, we conducted an in-depth interview with the artist.

ANHQV and Two Decades of Reruns

While resisting the cultural exceptionalism that often characterises analyses of comedy (see King, 2002), it remains difficult to convey to an international readership the cultural significance of *ANHQV* within Spanish popular culture. Through its engagement with contemporary public discourse, the series has produced a strong sense of national authenticity appealing to multiple generations of viewers. This form of comedy – commonly associated with *costumbrismo*, or the comedy of manners – relies on mechanisms of banal nationalism and affective identification, functioning as a mirror through which a community recognises itself. In the gestures, anxieties and vernacular expressions of the characters, audiences perceive echoes of their neighbours, relatives and themselves. The uneven success of the series' remakes in countries such as France, Argentina, Mexico and Greece further illustrates the extent to which *ANHQV* operates within a nationally specific cultural register.[1]

As noted in the introduction, the network had little faith in the series' prospects, as it was the debut project of three unknown creators (Martín, 2023). Promotional efforts therefore foregrounded its connection to familiar, traditional forms of comedy and the series was likened to the long-running comic strip *13, Rue del Percebe*, popular from the 1960s to the mid-1980s (Pérez, 2003; Silvestre, 2003). Nevertheless, the show gained traction through word of mouth and quickly became one of the most-watched programmes on Spanish television. Across its five-season run, it averaged 5.67 million viewers and a 32.2% audience share, on several occasions exceeding seven million viewers and a 40% share, even outperforming major sporting broadcasts. These figures point to a broader consolidation of Spanish prime-time fiction that had been unfolding since the 1990s with the advent of commercial broadcasting (Ibáñez Fernández, 2016) and culminated in what has been described as a new 'golden age' of Spanish scripted television (Palacio, 2012).

Following its unexpected cancelation in 2006, the narrative universe of the series was revived in a new production, this time broadcast by Telecinco, the main rival network. Under the title *La que se avecina*, the series launched a new narrative with a reimagined set of characters while preserving much of the original cast. Crucially, the premise once again centred on the lives of residents within a shared housing complex. This successor series replicated the success of its predecessor and remains on air after 15 seasons, with the most recent four produced in collaboration with Amazon Prime. In this way, the comedic universe built around communal living has remained a sustained fixture in Spanish television culture from 2003 to the present.

Nevertheless, fan engagement is primarily concentrated around the original five seasons of *ANHQV*, whose appeal has notably extended to members of Generation Z, many of whom did not experience its original broadcast. This enduring popularity can be attributed to the technological and industrial transformations that have reshaped television over the past two decades. Although originally aired over a brief three-year period, the series has remained

[1]The series has been adapted in seven countries, each of which shares either a Southern European Mediterranean cultural framework (France, Portugal, Greece) or an Ibero-American connection (Argentina, Chile, Colombia, and Mexico). Among these, the Mexican adaptation, *Vecinos* (Las Estrellas, 2005–present), stands out as the most successful, having reached 15 seasons to date. By contrast, the remakes produced in Argentina, France, Chile and Colombia were cancelled after a single season.

continuously available in various formats for more than 20 years. A key factor was the introduction of digital terrestrial television in Spain in 2005, which expanded channel availability and enabled extensive reruns of classic series on networks such as Neox, Atresmedia's youth-oriented channel. A second major development has been the consolidation of video-on-demand platforms, which have extended the afterlife of television fiction, with the notable examples of American series such as *Friends* (NBC, 1994–2004) or *Gilmore Girls* (The WB, 2000–2006), both of which generated renewed 'post-object fandoms' decades after their finales (Fitzsimmons & Smith-Frigerio, 2020; McNutt, 2020). Added to Netflix Spain in 2021, *ANHQV* remained among the platform's most-watched titles for several months[2] and is currently available across multiple VOD services. This near-constant visibility is closely intertwined with a broader wave of transnational nostalgia for the 2000s.

This extended afterlife has enabled younger audiences to (re)discover a series like *ANHQV* despite their increasingly distanced relationship to traditional (and particularly national) linear television in favour of a more global, digitally mediated media culture. This renewed engagement is filtered through the languages and practices of a new generation, who reinterpret the original text and adapt it to contemporary formats such as memes, fan art and other derivative creations. In this way, a series initially conceived as a conventional, family-oriented television product has been reappropriated through the participatory and recontextualising logics of digital fan communities. This phenomenon has not gone unnoticed in mainstream media, as evidenced by recent coverage in newspapers like *El País* (Marcos, 2021) and *El Confidencial* (Medina, 2023). For instance, a *Vogue España* article written by a Gen Z journalist sought to explain her fascination with the show, attributing its appeal to the everyday relatability of its characters, its early portrayal of class struggle and LGBTQ+ issues, its vivid evocation of 2000s culture and its suitability for memetic reinterpretation in social media environments (Quiles, 2024). Such dynamics reveal how older television content can foster unexpected forms of intergenerational engagement and reinterpretation in the digital age.

Along these lines, the show's everyday humour, which essentially portrays its characters as figures with whom viewers can identify through their mundane attitudes toward contemporary Spanish life, as well as its gentle depiction of its protagonists as lovable 'losers', has encouraged forms of appropriation in which users mobilise them as expressions of their own moods and, above all, as markers of a shared generational discomfort. This is evident in social media accounts such as @nocontextanhqv and @anhqvcards on X (formerly Twitter), which circulate

---

[2]Although viewership data from streaming platforms is often limited, independent reports such as Barlovento's *Barómetro OTT Multidispositivo* (Barlovento Comunicación, 2024) provide monthly rankings of the most-watched content in Spain. In 9 out of 12 months in 2024, *Aquí no hay quien viva* ranked among the top three most-viewed titles across all platforms – surpassing even new releases such as the latest season of *Emily in Paris* (Netflix, 2020-). Notably, it was the only recurring title on the list that did not follow the typical logic of premieres or international releases.

memes pairing character images with captions like 'Me in X situation' and delve into themes such as job insecurity, romantic failure or the experience of growing older with limited prospects for the future. A particularly illustrative example contrasts an aspirational shot from *Emily in Paris* captioned 'How I imagined myself at 30' with a 'Me now' image, represented through Belén López Vázquez in one of her many dead-end jobs.[3]

The revival of older television series is not a uniquely contemporary phenomenon. The syndication and rerun model developed in the United States proved particularly conducive to the formation of fan communities, as televisual repetition enabled the frequent rebroadcast of favourite series and fostered television fandom more broadly (Kompare, 2005). Through repeated viewing, audiences develop a strong familiarity with characters and narratives, generating attachments that extend beyond casual entertainment. Weispfenning (2003) proposed a framework for understanding the cultural functions of reruns, arguing that they provide a sense of stability within a shifting media environment. Contrary to the assumption that pleasure derives primarily from novelty, he suggests that repetition itself becomes a source of enjoyment, grounded in parasocial relationships with characters; an effect that is particularly pronounced in series that attain cult status.

Still, streaming platforms have introduced significant and distinctive transformations in the way viewers engage with traditional television content. As Gilbert (2019) argues, much of the academic focus has centred on analysing platforms' original productions even though a substantial portion of their catalogues is composed of legacy television content. These older programmes not only find renewed life on streaming services but, in many cases, become key attractions for subscribers, as illustrated by the continued popularity of *The Office* (NBC, 2005–2013) and *Friends*, or, in the Spanish context, *ANHQV*. Gilbert (2019) contends that the consumption of traditional television via streaming reflects a fundamental shift in viewing paradigms: a transition from a 'push' model – where content is scheduled and delivered to passive audiences – to a 'pull' model, in which users actively choose what to watch. This shift reconfigures the viewer experience, moving from a ritualised practice (where television was often switched on out of habit, to relieve boredom, or as background companionship) to an inherently active engagement, one in which the viewer must navigate and select before they can watch.

Beyond simply enabling new audiences to discover the series over the past two decades, its sustained presence appears to have contributed to a redefinition of the ways in which viewers engage with it. Reruns on linear television fostered an increasing familiarity with specific characters and scenes, creating a kind of ritualised relationship grounded in repetition. This effect has been further amplified by its availability on streaming platforms though with the introduction of a distinct viewing paradigm: the act of actively seeking out a series one wishes to

---

[3]Martos, D. (2024, September 15). *Como me imaginaba yo con 30 años/Yo ahora* [Post]. X. https://x.com/MartosDiego/status/1835348886036095179

revisit. Within a media landscape saturated with constant new releases, overpopulated interfaces and ever-expanding watchlists, *ANHQV* has acquired the status of comfort content, a familiar and reassuring presence amid the overload of choice (Siles et al., 2025). This has given rise to a 'joy of rewatching' rooted in the everydayness of a comedy of manners, with a text that serves as an inexhaustible source of memorable fragments, quotable lines and instantly recognisable characters.

From Fan Art to Entrepreneurship

In 1949, Bette Davis delivered the line 'What a dump!' in King Vidor's film *Beyond the Forest*. Just three words, spoken in a brief scene from a feature-length film. Today, however, the phrase enjoys enduring popularity – particularly within certain strands of gay culture – as David Halperin has observed (2012). This is the result of a process of appropriation and recontextualisation, through which the line has been repeatedly quoted and reinterpreted across various settings, eventually becoming a recognisable code within a specific social group. 'What a dump' conveys an attitude, a sense of irony and, above all, a shared cultural reference, imbued with iconic status by those who recognise and circulate it. In a similar fashion, a fan of *ANHQV* might describe a particular character, scene or line of dialogue as 'iconic'. While the term is often used colloquially, it typically refers to something celebrated for its immediate recognisability. This aura of iconicity is largely shaped by the capacity to revisit and share that moment – whether a gesture, a phrase or a character – with a wider community. In this sense, what may have initially been a humorous or fleeting moment acquires iconic status through repetition and collective circulation, as it is adopted by the fan community.

This idea of iconicity is closely related to EJ Nielsen's (2021) reflections on fan art iconography. According to Nielsen, contemporary fan art emerges at the intersection of technical accessibility and the collective appropriation of cultural references. At the heart of this practice lies what they term fannish iconography: a repertoire of symbols, phrases, objects and stylistic conventions that function as visual shortcuts to evoke shared characters, scenarios or narrative worlds. These graphic choices crystallise collective readings of popular texts. Within this context, visual recognition depends less on physical resemblance or strict fidelity to the source material (screen accuracy) than on the artwork's ability to elicit viewer recognition through easily identifiable, iconic elements. As Nielsen reminds us, an important characteristic of fan art as a genre is that it is generally designed to be read, that is, for a viewer to recognise and understand what it is meant to represent and reference (2021, p. 208). Fan art thus operates not only as a paratext that expands or reinterprets the original narrative universe but also as a space for critical reinterpretation, identity expression and community formation mediated through graphically encoded and highly meaningful design choices.

Social media platforms have become a privileged space for the convergence of graphic designers' work – both professional and amateur – and the creative practices of fan communities (Bennett, 2014). In this context, artistic expertise is mobilised in the service of reanimating and circulating reinterpretations of audiovisual texts, gradually transforming them into iconic elements within a shared cultural repertoire. A representative case is the artist Lara Seara, known on Instagram as @laultimacroqueta,[4] where she has over 115,000 followers. Seara creates memes by extracting scenes from Spanish television (including non-scripted shows, reality programmes and comedy series) and embedding them into canonical works of art. In doing so, she reinterprets the tradition of *costumbrismo* humour (that is, stylised comic depictions of everyday life) infusing it with renewed meaning. At the same time, she revives televisual moments that audiences can (re)discover, reinforcing their iconic status. A scene from a reality show, in this context, becomes as iconic as the artwork into which it is inserted. Social media platforms have also enabled direct-to-consumer sales, with her designs available in the form of coasters, mugs, tote bags and T-shirts.

A similar approach underpins the work of the two creators examined in this study: Sara Benito and Iván Ramosky. Both are trained graphic designers, members of Generation Z and have dedicated a significant portion of their creative output to exploring the iconicity of ANHQV, embedding their work within already established online fan communities. Their cases also exemplify a broader shift from fan creativity driven by passion to the successful professionalisation of fan practices with commercial outcomes.

Sara Benito is the creative professional behind the brand Sbenito.design. As she explains, she holds a degree in Industrial Design Engineering and a master's in interior design, with a specialisation in 3D design. However, during the COVID-19 pandemic, she began illustrating scenes from *ANHQV* as a fan, sharing them on her Instagram account, where they unexpectedly went viral. This surge in recognition led her to register as a self-employed designer to commercialise her work (Cano, 2022). Benito has since built her entire brand around the narrative universe of *ANHQV* although more recently she has diversified her work to include designs based on other series, such as *Paquita Salas*. Her social media presence is accordingly divided between two accounts: the original profile, anhqv_ilustraciones, dedicated exclusively to *ANHQV*, and a second account, @fandelmonton, which features her broader fan art portfolio. Although the latter extends beyond *ANHQV*, the phrase '*del montón*' ('just average') references an iconic line spoken by the fan-favourite character Belén López Vázquez (one of the lovable losers of the show) who is told by her friends that she is not ugly, she is 'just average'.

As noted in the previous section, the series' continued presence in Spain's collective cultural imagination enables Benito to produce visual content that is both highly recognisable and highly shareable. Her creative strategy is relatively

[4]See: https://www.instagram.com/laultimacroqueta/ and her own online shop at https://laultimacroqueta.com/

straightforward: on a weekly basis, she publishes a new design featuring a minimalist illustration of one of the characters, typically rendered against a white background, paired with a line of dialogue. In the same post (formatted as a carousel), she includes a clip from the original scene that inspired the illustration, thereby creating a growing repository of the series' 'iconic' moments for audiences to revisit. This way, the account operates simultaneously as a space of nostalgic recall – akin to traditional fan pages – and as a platform for the production and dissemination of her own creative work. The profile also includes a direct link to her online shop.

One of the main sections of her online shop is titled '*La Comunidad*' ('The Community'), referencing both the apartment block in *ANHQV* and one of the character Juan Cuesta's emblematic phrases, in which he pompously refers to the building as '*esta nuestra comunidad*' ('this, our community'). Within this section, the website is organised according to the layout of the apartment building, with each floor corresponding to a different character who resides there. Thus, the website functions as a paratext that mirrors the series' spatial structure, that is, the arrangement of flats within the building. The architectural layout of the building, floor by floor, is prominently featured in the series' opening credits and thus serves as a key point of reference within the fan imaginary.

Benito's work is not primarily concerned with re-signification but rather with the recollection of scenes already celebrated by fans. Her style is characterised by a deliberate reduction of detail: backgrounds are removed, and characters are stripped down to their most minimal features. A recurring stylistic choice, for instance, is the absence of eyes on the figures she depicts, leaving the characters with just their hairdos and some costume items. Her images eschew realism in favour of a synthetic mode of representation, closely aligned with vector illustration, in which character recognition relies on a limited set of key visual elements. As the designer herself explains regarding her creative process: 'I try to make my illustrations feel like simulations. I don't want them to evoke the person so much as the situation. That's why I blur out the eyes – I think it gives them a more caricatured feel' (Cano, 2022). This interplay between stylised silhouette and text functions as a mechanism for activating collective memory, relying on the viewer's interpretive participation to complete the image. Visually, Benito employs a palette of flat colours and a clean, minimalist aesthetic, deliberately avoiding superfluous detail. This design strategy enhances the communicative function of her work, foregrounding clarity and recognition over realism. This minimalist approach heightens the iconic quality of the images, inviting fans to recognise characters through just a few visual cues.

One of her most popular designs features the character Concha, the grumpy elderly landlady of the third-floor tenants, who frequently entered their flat uninvited, announcing herself with the line: '*Soy yo, Concha, entro*' ('It's me, Concha, I'm coming in'). In this case, the catchphrase, widely known and frequently repeated within the fan community, is paired with a design printed on a doormat, allowing the object itself to enact the scene (Fig. 9.1). Another illustrative example is an image of Emilio, the building's concierge, alongside his line '*Tinto, ¿verdad?*' ('Red wine, right?'), taken from a scene in which he attempts to

Fig. 9.1. One of Sara Benito's Most Popular Designs.

display sophistication while dining at an upscale restaurant. Pressured by the waiter to approve the wine, Emilio manages only to identify it as red. In the illustration, the character is recognised solely by the oversized coat he wears in that scene – a garment that visually underscores his discomfort and sense of not belonging in such a setting. Finally, particularly noteworthy is the illustration of Belén accompanied by the phrase '*¿Hacemos un* break *para un* coffee?' ('Shall we take a break for a coffee?'). Belén is portrayed as a precariously employed young woman, frequently moving between short-term jobs. In this scene, she has managed to secure an office position by falsely claiming fluency in English. During a tense meeting, the atmosphere is broken when a confident colleague suggests taking a break – incorporating the English terms 'break' and 'coffee' into the Spanish sentence. Belén, visibly anxious and attempting to maintain the illusion, responds: '*¡Sí!* ¡Coffee*...! El* coffee *me... A mí me gusta mucho*' ('Yes! Coffee... I... I really like coffee').[5] Similar to the previously discussed doormat design, these two illustrations can also be purchased printed directly onto wine glasses or coffee mugs, allowing fans to re-enact, or symbolically relive, the scene through the object itself.

These three pieces exemplify a key feature of Sara Benito's work, and of fan art more broadly as an object of study: the fusion of graphic design with functional, everyday objects. The scenes depicted are not merely adapted to the

[5]The iconic status of the scene, along with its symbolic resonance in expressing feelings of workplace alienation, is evident in the X account @breakcoffee7, which frequently reposts the same image at the start of the working day. See: https://x.com/breakcoffee7

medium (a mug, a doormat, a wine glass); rather, the object itself amplifies the meaning, reinforcing the irony and satirical tone of the original series. Moreover, the chosen items materially embody the class tensions underlying the scenes they reference. From housing precarity to discomfort in elite social spaces and the pressures of a globalised labour market, these objects crystallise, through everyday material forms, the social critique already embedded in the original fiction.

We now turn to the work of Iván Ramosky, the pseudonym of a graphic designer based in the town of Leganés, on the outskirts of Madrid. Ramosky describes himself as a '*costumbrista* artist' and defines *costumbrismo* as 'a mid-point between folklore and the everyday', a space that connects the artistic with the mundane.[6] While he would later pursue formal training – completing a graphic design degree at the prestigious Artediez school in Madrid – Ramosky considers himself largely self-taught, having started working with Photoshop as a teenager. These early stages of his creative vocation were closely tied to a desire to participate actively in digital fan communities, with illustrations inspired by series such as *Rick and Morty* (Adult Swim, 2013-), as well as politically charged parodies, like a reimagining of *Friends* with well-known Spanish politicians as characters.

His most recognised work to date is a tarot deck inspired by *ANHQV*. The idea emerged spontaneously during a group viewing of the series with friends – something Ramosky describes as a kind of domestic ritual. Given that tarot was already a popular issue in his social circles, he decided to design a single card and post it on social media. The post went viral almost immediately. Following this success, Amazon Prime contacted him with a request to create a full deck in conjunction with the show's arrival on the platform. Ramosky ensured that he retained the commercial rights to the artwork and, after the promotional campaign concluded, began selling the deck independently.

The deck draws inspiration from the Marseille tarot, but unlike Sara Benito's work, Ramosky's illustrations do not reference particular moments from the series. Instead, they translate the essence of the characters into the symbolic language of the tarot. In developing the deck, Ramosky consulted existing examples of fan-created tarot cards, including those based on *RuPaul's Drag Race* (LogoTV, 2009–2016; VH1, 2017–2022; MTV, 2023–). By studying how other artists reinterpreted meaning and deciding which visual elements to retain or adapt, he aligned the recognisable archetypes of *ANHQV* with the traditional figures of the tarot. For example, the Lovers card features Belén and Emilio, the show's central couple, standing in front of the building's lift. In place of Cupid, the lift itself becomes the mediating force – an architectural motif integral to the series' setting (Fig. 9.2). This choice carries a humorous undertone: Belén and Emilio's relationship is far from stable or ideal, and the lift is notoriously unreliable, frequently out of service. Similarly, the Chariot substitutes the

[6]Unless otherwise indicated, direct quotations from Iván Ramosky are drawn from the interview conducted by the authors on 16 July 2025.

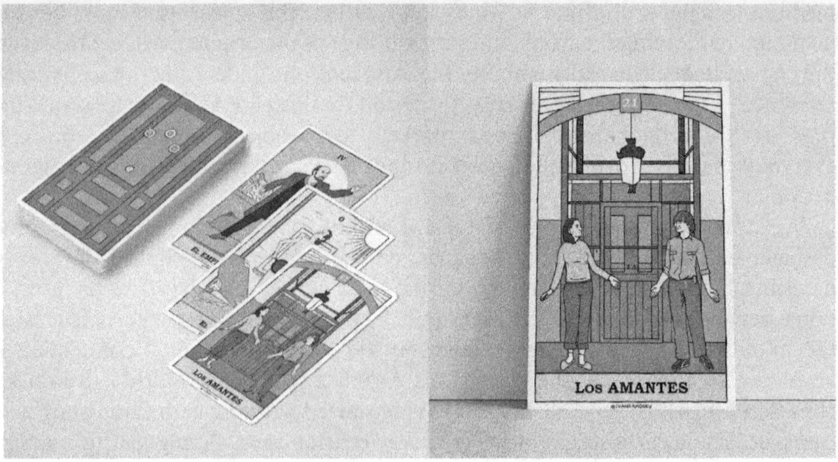

Fig. 9.2. The Tarot of ANHQV Takes Inspiration From the Marseille Tarot.

classical horses with the cheap Seat car shared by Emilio and his father. The Empress is reimagined as Paloma Cuesta, the overbearing wife of the building's president, distinguished by her elaborate and tacky wardrobe and a decorative cushion embroidered with the label 'PUF' – a reference to her fictional fashion brand, 'Paloma Urban Fashion'. On the reverse of each card appears a door, alluding to the domestic architecture of the series and reinforcing the home as a central element of its visual identity.

Graphically, Ramosky's style occupies an expressive register that draws on comic art and editorial illustration. It features hand-drawn lines and strong outlines. Unlike Benito's minimalist vector aesthetic, Ramosky preserves the characters' faces and emphasises posture, gaze and gesture as narrative tools. Rather than relying on the immediate recognisability of a line or scene, his approach is based on symbolic reinterpretation. He merges foreign visual codes (tarot iconography, esoteric mysticism, and archetypal structures) with the '*costumbrista*', comic universe of the show. Through these reinterpretations, the mythical language of astrology is rendered mundane, filtered through the everyday flaws and rituals of a cast of endearing misfits.

In this sense, his work might be described as intertextual fan art, where recognition arises from the interplay between imaginaries. The irony lies in the dissonance between the serious, symbolic code of the tarot and the absurd mundanity of the show's universe. In Ramosky's hands, the *costumbrismo* of Spanish television becomes a kind of visual mythology, granting the residents of the show a mystical dimension. Even so, Ramosky's work should be situated within the realm of internet humour and memetic culture. As he explains, most of his projects are born from a desire to create something funny to share online.

A good example is another product sold in his shop: a keyring with a tiny built-in flashlight (*'llavero con linternita'*). In this case, the object directly references a scene in which Emilio struggles to find a meaningful gift for his partner, only to receive this modest present in return. The product's packaging includes a still from the original scene and typographic elements that help evoke it through design.

Ramosky's work also reveals a strong connection to materiality and everyday objects although in his case this is deeply tied to playfulness. His fan art is both a form of cultural commentary and a practice of everyday appropriation and ludic interaction. As he himself notes, the success of the tarot deck lies in its emotional and social dimensions. Many customers purchase the deck as a gift, seeking to rekindle a shared affection for the series. Far from being a serious esoteric item, Ramosky conceives of it as a hybrid object, a 'tarot for the home', intended more for fans of *ANHQV* than for experts in cartomancy. Its value lies not just in its decorative or nostalgic appeal but also in its ability to activate fans: social gatherings, jokes, affectionate reinterpretations of characters and scenes.

Both Benito and Ramosky exemplify how fan creativity can evolve into a professionalised practice without losing its playful roots. From Benito's shift towards self-employment after the viral success of her *ANHQV* illustrations, and Ramosky's transition from meme-making to platform commissions, their trajectories illustrate how digital platforms have become key infrastructures for the transformation of fan labour into creative entrepreneurship. Both designers emphasise how social media functions as a sales channel, enabling direct interaction with audiences. At the same time, both creators have been acknowledged or incorporated by official channels: Benito was commissioned to illustrate the official 20th-anniversary book of *ANHQV* (Martín, 2023), and Ramosky was hired by Amazon Prime to promote the series' launch on the platform through his tarot design. These cases illustrate how fan labour has contributed to consolidating the series' iconic status within its fanbase – so much so that, 20 years on, both its creators and broadcasters have drawn on the work of these designers to promote and celebrate the show's enduring legacy.

Conclusion

This study has demonstrated how *ANHQV*, despite its original broadcast ending nearly two decades ago, continues to occupy a prominent position within Spain's popular and digital culture. Its persistent presence across the last two decades, from digital terrestrial television to major VOD services, has enabled its rediscovery and reappropriation by younger generations, particularly Generation Z. This extended afterlife has not only sustained its visibility but has also catalysed new forms of engagement, in which fans move from passive spectatorship to active cultural production. Central to this phenomenon is the way the series has been reframed through practices such as fan art, memes and merchandise, allowing it to accrue new meanings and symbolic resonance in digital contexts.

The cases of Sara Benito and Iván Ramosky exemplify how fan labour can evolve into professionalised, commercially viable artistic practice while remaining rooted in a logic of play, affection and community. Both designers highlight the convergence of fan creativity, graphic design and digital entrepreneurship. Their work not only reinforces the iconicity of specific scenes and characters but also embeds a critical and humorous reading of the original series within every day, functional objects. That official platforms and broadcasters have drawn on these fan practices for promotional purposes underscores a broader shift in the media ecosystem, in which fan culture is no longer peripheral but increasingly central to the way legacy media texts are remembered, reactivated and monetised.

Acknowledgements

This study was carried out within the framework and with the support of the project Spanish Cinema and Television in the Digital Age (2008–2022): New Agents and Spaces of Exchange within the Audiovisual Panorama (CITEDIG), funded by the State Research Agency (PID2022-140102NB- 100/AEI/10.13039/501100011033).

References

Barlovento Comunicación. (2024). *Barómetro OTT Multidispositivo: Informe mensual (Febrero–Diciembre)*. https://www.barloventocomunicacion.es

Bennett, L. (2014). Tracing Textual Poachers: Reflections on the development of fan studies and digital fandom. *The Journal of Fandom Studies*, *2*(1), 5–20. https://doi.org/10.1386/jfs.2.1.5_1

Cano, S. (2022, October 18). Sara Benito, la ilustradora que llena Instagram de escenas míticas de Aquí no hay quien viva. *Valencia Plaza*. https://valenciaplaza.com/diseno-ilustracion-valencia-comunitat-valenciana/sarabenitolailustradoraquellenainstagramdeescenasmiticasdeaquinohayquienviva

Fitzsimmons, K., & Smith-Frigerio, S. (2020). Still there for you?: Why millennials still love generation X's Friends. *Ohio Communication Journal*, *58*, 91–104.

Gilbert, A. (2019). Push, pull, rerun: Television reruns and streaming media. *Television & New Media*, *20*(7), 686–701. https://doi.org/10.1177/1527476419842418

González Neira, A., & Quintas Froufe, N. (2023). La evolución de los estudios de audiencia ligados a las series de ficción en España (2005-2020). In C. Virino Cascajosa & J. Mateos-Pérez (Eds.), *Análisis de la ficción televisiva española* (pp. 159–170). Sintesis.

Guerrero-Pico, M., & Establés, M.-J. (2023). Fandom televisivo en España: Estado de la cuestión. In C. Virino Cascajosa & J. Mateos-Pérez (Eds.), *Análisis de la ficción televisiva española* (pp. 183–194). Sintesis.

Halperin, D. (2012). *How to be gay*. Harvard University Press.

Herrero De la Fuente, M., Garzía, A., & Establés, M. J. (2022). Narrativa transmedia y representación mediática: el caso de #Luimelia. *Cuadernos.info*, (51), 310–332.

Ibáñez Fernández, J. C. (2016). *Cine, televisión y cambio social en España*. Editorial Síntesis.

King, G. (2002). *Film comedy*. Wallflower Press.

Kompare, D. (2005). *Rerun nation: How repeats invented American television*. Routledge.

Marcos, N. (2021, November 20). Por qué 'Aquí no hay quien viva' y 'Los Serrano' son un fenómeno en la era de las plataformas y las redes. *El País*. https://elpais.com/television/2021-11-20/por-que-aqui-no-hay-quien-viva-y-los-serrano-son-un-fenomeno-en-la-era-de-las-plataformas-y-las-redes.html

Martín, J. P. (2023). *Aquí no hay quien viva: Detrás de las cámaras: la delirante historia de esta nuestra comunidad*. Plaza & Janés.

McNutt, M. (2020). Gilmore girls: A year in the life: TV revivals. In E. Thompson & J. Mittel (Eds.), *How to watch television* (2nd ed., pp. 250–259). New York University Press.

Medina, M. (2023, September 13). Por qué 'Aquí no hay quien viva' es la serie que lo peta entre los jóvenes… 20 años después. *El Confidencial*. https://www.elconfidencial.com/cultura/2023-09-13/aqui-no-hay-quien-viva-fenomeno-cultural_3612209/

Nielsen, E. (2021). The iconography of fan art. In P. Booth & R. Williams (Eds.), *A fan studies primer. Methods, research, ethics* (pp. 207–222). University of Iowa Press.

Palacio, M. (1995). La noción del espectador en el cine contemporáneo. In M. Palacio & S. Zunzunegui (Eds.), *Historia general del cine. Volumen XII. El cine en la era del audiovisual*. Cátedra.

Palacio, M. (2007). Estudios culturales y cine en España. *Comunicar: Revista Científica Iberoamericana De Comunicación Y Educación*, *29*, 69-73.

Palacio, M. (2012). La ficción televisiva española: (2005-2011). In M. Francés & G. Llorca Abad (Eds.), *La ficción audiovisual en España: Relatos, tendencias y sinergias productivas* (Vol. 1, pp. 63–74). Gedisa Editorial.

Palacio, M. (2024). *La televisión en España (1990–2022). Sociedad y cultura*. Cátedra.

Pérez, F. (2003, August 4). José Luis Moreno rueda para Antena 3 su particular «13 Rue del Percebe». *Annales de Biologie Clinique*, *91*.

Quiles, M. (2024, September 16). Soy Gen Z y me fascina 'Aquí no hay quien viva': las razones detrás de este fenómeno. *Vogue España*. https://www.vogue.es/articulos/serie-aqui-no-hay-quien-viva-generacion-z-memes

Siles, I., Muñoz-González, R., Valerio-Alfaro, L., & Valiati, V. (2025). Rewatching content on streaming platforms: The pursuit of ontological comfort. *Media and Communication*, *13*, 9338. https://doi.org/10.17645/mac.9338

Silvestre, J. (2003, August 9). El '13, rue del Percebe' cobra vida. *Supertele*, *595*, 8–9.

Weispfenning, J. (2003). Cultural functions of reruns: Time, memory, and television. *Journal of Communication*, *53*(1), 165–176. https://doi.org/10.1111/j.1460-2466.2003.tb03012.x

Chapter 10

Designing Fan-Created *Doctor Who* Merchandise: Forms of Capital and Unlicensed Design Adventures in Capitalist Realism

Matt Hills

University of Bristol, UK

Abstract

Strands of fan studies and design research have shared a Bourdieusian focus and can be brought into dialogue. However, prior work on unlicensed fan-created merchandise has emphasised how 'fan cultural capital' underpins the distinctiveness of fan-made merch. The author argues that multiple forms of cultural capital act to constitute the 'authenticity' of unofficial fan-created designs, including digital cultural capital, attention capital and corporate cultural capital.

The author considers two *Doctor Who* fan-designers who bring together professionalised fandom and high levels of fan cultural capital, focusing on how their fan-created merchandise relates to *Doctor Who* branding. Clayton Hickman imagines improved practices of brand management, going beyond fan-perceived inauthenticities of official products. Contexts of capitalist realism and omnipresent branding aren't challenged, but it is implied that the fan's eye for detail can do better than industry professionals lacking fan sensibilities. And Andrew-Mark Thompson creates 'fake' paratexts – adverts for non-existent products – which are more oppositional in relation to *Doctor Who*'s commercial exploitation, despite displaying an affection for official merchandise. While Hickman modernises *Doctor Who*'s older

Bridging Design and Fandom, 147–161

doi:10.1108/978-1-80592-659-720261010

paratexts, Thompson projects current *Who* back into recreations of vintage paratexts. One limit of Bourdieusian approaches to fan-design remains their awkwardness in relation to designers' aesthetic projects.

Keywords: Doctor Who; Bourdieu; digital cultural capital; attention capital; corporate cultural capital; paratexts

Introduction

Bob Rehak has identified how in 'fan studies as in fandom itself, textual practices are privileged over object practices. Design-oriented materials are... disparaged as corporate exploitation, having little to do with the true spirit of participation' in fandom (2018, p. 58). However, there are versions of fan studies and design research which draw on shared theoretical approaches and hence could offer one pathway to greater dialogue. What has been termed 'second wave' fan studies (Sandvoss et al., 2017, p. 5) uses the work of sociologist Pierre Bourdieu to understand hierarchies in fandom and ways in which fans can reproduce inequalities operating in wider culture. Likewise, types of design research that are critically/sociologically inflected have also applied Bourdieu to think about the status possessed by designers (Carvalho et al., 2009; Tonkinwise, 2011).

In this chapter, I will follow these Bourdieusian subsets of scholarship on fandom and design. I will recap key Bourdieusian debates surrounding forms of 'capital' that are mobilised by fans and designers, before examining two case studies – the 'design-oriented' fannish productivity displayed, and the types of digital fanworks created, in *Doctor Who* fan circles by Clayton Hickman and Andrew-Mark Thompson. Previous work on fan-created designs has tended to stress how these display fan knowledge, i.e. fan cultural capital (Carter, 2018; Lamerichs, 2018), with more nuanced analyses considering two fractions of handicraft-focused cultural capital and fan cultural capital (Cherry, 2016). I will argue that we need an approach which views the types of capital drawn on by fan designers – who can sometimes be autodidacts (Duffy, 2017, p. 68) – as far more multiple. The reputation and recognition of fan designers rests not only on their fan bonafides and design skills but also relates to 'digital cultural capital' (Verwiebe & Hagemann, 2025, p. 1862), 'attention capital' (Mears, 2023, p. 2) and appropriations of 'corporate cultural capital' (Lam, 2010, p. 633; Lury, 1996, p. 113). Addressing the multiplicities of cultural capital that are involved means understanding fan-designers as working within multiple and permeable/overlapping fields rather than displaying their design knowledges in a securely bounded 'field' of fandom (Hills, 2005, p. 168). First, though, I will introduce Bourdieusian theories of design *and* fandom.

Bourdieu in Strands of Design Research and Fan Studies

Whereas the application of Bourdieu in noughties' fan studies ran counter to already-established logics based on revaluing fandom (Sandvoss et al., 2017, p. 3),

Bourdieu's emphasis on taste possesses a more self-evident fit with the theorising of design. Tonkinwise (2011) suggests that the take-up of Bourdieu in design research was initially more about 'material cultural studies of designed objects as they circulate in society', e.g. in Julier (2014), but failed to 'sufficiently reach... the research of designing version of design studies, that is, interrogations of the design process as a practice of... applied taste hermeneutics' (Tonkinwise, 2011, p. 537). In this second sense, design education could be analysed as the cultivation of taste and cultural capital (formal knowledge about design history), with designers then going on to reproduce their cultural capital through designing for 'proximate' tastes, where brand-led design could be seen as 'a proactive version of Bourdieusian analysis. Conventional branding attempts to use the homologies of taste regimes to associate products and environments with the same levels of cultural and social capital' (Tonkinwise, 2011, p. 540).

Bourdieusian design research has repeatedly focused on the cultural capital possessed by designers. For example, Nilsson (2025) seeks to incorporate reflexive knowledge of cultural and social capitals into design user 'personas' in order to make design outputs more accessible to diverse users:

> Designers generally... draw on their cultural capital to make aesthetic choices that resonate with certain social groups. For instance, luxury brands use specific colors, materials, and design languages to signal high cultural capital. Understanding the cultural capital [in play] can help designers create solutions that are more accessible and relevant. (Nilsson, 2025, p. 169)

The 'field of design' is said to be structured by its own form of cultural capital, e.g. that conferred by 'more prestigious design schools' (Nilsson, 2025, p. 169), as well as social capital in the form of 'professional networks' (2025, p. 170) and reputational symbolic capital accumulated by designers through industry 'recognition, awards, and the perceived value of their work' (2025, p. 170).

Also focusing on a Bourdieusian concept of the 'design field' (2009, p. 497), Carvalho, Dong and Maton consider how design is legitimated, comparing interviews with participant designers to how 'professional societies and schools of design publicly describe their own disciplines and what their discipline values' (2009, p. 497). And Gogor et al. (2025, p. 72) stress how 'graphic designers possess strong cultural capital from higher education and deep knowledge of design' but go on to consider how the gig economy and the platformisation of design jobs has led to a situation where designers' cultural and social capitals do not insulate them from the dominance of platform algorithms (2025, p. 75). Elsewhere, this platform-led control of the 'digital capitalism ecosystem' (Gogor et al., 2025) has been theorised as a highly asymmetrical and powerful form of new 'digital capital' (Verwiebe & Hagemann, 2025), working to subordinate those in class fractions who would previously have been part of the bourgeois cultural elite. Gogor et al. argue that designers need to cultivate 'a strong personal brand and attract... direct clients through social media and personal websites' in order to resist the powerful mediation of platform algorithms (2025, p. 76).

In these approaches to design, it is recurrently understood in Bourdieu's terms as a bounded field; that is, as a space where forms of capital recognised in, and specific to, that field are fought over. The advice dispensed by Gogor et al. (2025, p. 76) is aimed at restoring the supposed autonomy of the design field when social media platforms have encroached on its mechanisms of cultural reproduction.

The same focus – on a singular bounded field with its own characteristic forms of capital – has been true of much 'second wave' fan studies. An excellent overview refers to 'the restricted field of fan production' (Chin, 2018, p. 253) and rightly suggests that applying Bourdieu to fandom has meant the:

> . . . appropriation of social, cultural, and symbolic capitals into the framework of fandom. . . where fandom would have to exist as a social and cultural field, [as Bourdieu argues:] "a separate social universe having its own laws of functioning independent of those of politics and the economy". (Chin, 2018, p. 254)

Given that fandom, unlike design, doesn't have an 'academic' cultural position – i.e. you can't train to be a fan at University – then the specificity of *fan* cultural capital is said to be developed instead, at least partly, as a result of the time spent in fandom. Bourdaa (2022, p. 172) has analysed this 'time engagement' and how it can lead to 'elder' fans taking on mentoring roles in their fandoms. That said, fan cultural capital can also be objectified in the form of collections of merchandise and/or other kinds of memorabilia (Geraghty, 2014), as well as embodied through knowledge of the fan object (Hills, 2002), and even through detailed awareness of fandom's up-to-the-minute social media discussions.

Fan-made merchandise based on fan design work has also typically been viewed as a display of fan cultural capital, either implicitly or explicitly. Research mentions that fan-designed *Hunger Games* T-shirts on Redbubble could be seen to 'cater perhaps more to a fan than an outsider' (Lamerichs, 2018, p. 182) in terms of not simply using major logos/characters from the text and so drawing more on insider fan knowledge or fan cultural capital. Similarly, scholarship has aligned fan-designed materials that are sold commercially with what can again be read as displays of fan cultural capital:

> fantrepreneurs have an important involvement in shaping discourses of "quality and authenticity"... [as] fantrepreneurs not only play an important role in moving products from the alternative to the mainstream, they also add a level of trust. For the fan community, texts produced by the fantrepreneur demonstrate a greater level of care and attention; paying particular attention to the details that might be insignificant to typical commercial producers. (Carter, 2018, p. 51)

Avi Santo has likewise implicitly aligned fan-made merchandise with fan cultural capital, pointing out that it tends to be 'marketed as authentically fannish' (2018, p. 329).

Others have explicitly linked Bourdieusian work to fan-made goods, viewing these designed materials as 'carriers of insider codes... encapsulating subcultural capital' (Qiu, 2025, p. 9), where fandom itself constitutes a subculture. The same argument is made in Barrière and Finkel's (2022) study of 'festival fans' and the festival merchandise they consume. Here, fan-made merch created at a Workshop event on-site:

> ... probably enhances the affective dimension of the product, because fans have been directly involved in its conception. They also have learned a new (DIY) technique during the process of crafting their own souvenir of the festival, which might increase their subcultural capital and their agency within DIY music scenes (2022, p. 493).

However, what is notable about Bourdieusian approaches to fandom and to 'design-oriented' fandom (Rehak, 2018, p. 28) involving fans' 'DIY merchandise' of varied sorts (Hills, 2011, p. 28) is that whether fan cultural capital (or, in effect used synonymously, subcultural capital) is identified explicitly or not, there is typically *little sense of other forms of cultural capital* linked to fan-design work, nor indeed any developed sense of the many other, multiple forms of status and hierarchy which could be in play as well as 'insider' fan knowledge. Of course, the consumption of 'DIY merchandise' can hinge on economic capital if these materials become rare, circulating only in secondary markets much like the exclusivity of screen-used props that come up for sale. But my focus is on the creation of fan-designed merchandise rather than its collectors. A promising example of analysis which acknowledges fan-design work as emerging through multiple forms of cultural capital is Cherry's study of fan handicrafters, which recognises that there are two types of cultural capital operating – that linked to knowledge of handicrafts such as the history of crafting and that linked to fandom. Cherry notes that these two forms of cultural capital can come into conflict, as in a case where *Outlander* fans marginalised historical expertise that challenged the authenticity of knitted outfits in the TV show, wanting instead to focus on mimetically reproducing items of costume design in their fan handicrafting (2016, pp. 151–155).

The fact that singular, bounded 'fields' rarely seem to convincingly occur in relation to fan activities (Hills, 2005, p. 168) has been noted by scholarship which considers subcultural capital and cultural capital as blurring together or as becoming indeterminate (Garner, 2025, p. 152; Hills, 2017, p. 62). Such analytical hesitations suggest that there is no bounded subcultural 'field' that can be separated from an officially-validated sense of cultural capital, whether this concerns a simultaneously fan-created and academic archive of pop cultural dinosaur ephemera in the case of Garner's (2025) discussion, or the status of 'Nordic Noir' fan audiences' knowledge in Hills's (2017) case.

And as Barrière and Finkel's analysis of festival fans observes, merchandising – commercially produced *and* fan-designed – 'represents entanglements of capital' (2022, p. 486), something I pursue here by considering how fan-designers' work can be read as an amalgamation of multiple types of cultural capital and not merely as a display of fan cultural capital. Other relevant types of cultural capital include *digital cultural capital*: this is 'the result of cultural practices of engagement with digital services, social media platforms, apps, devices, etc. . . .accumulated via the transformation of 'classical' cultural capital (e.g., educational qualifications) into digital skills and competencies' (Verwiebe & Hagemann, 2025, p. 1862) and is evident in skills of digital design. But it also flows into designers' fantrepreneurial social media use and self-promotion, which can be thought of via *attention capital*:

> . . . a resource that is convertible to economic, social, and symbolic gain. . .. [and] correlates with pre-existing resources such as education, money, and. . . digital skills. . . The value of attention capital, and its conversion into other forms of power, very much depends on the value of those audiences who pay attention and their relation to each other. (Mears, 2023, p. 2)

Of course, fan-designers can display their fan cultural capital as a way of enhancing their 'relation' to relevant audiences and the 'value of those audiences who pay attention', and so this remains significant, but as one form of cultural capital amongst others. Lastly, I will touch on *corporate cultural capital*, which 'facilitates the reproduction of dominant. . . corporations' (Lam, 2010, p. 633) and 'is composed of. . . brand equity and inherited cultural symbols' (Lam, 2010, p. 634). It may seem curious to argue that unlicensed fan-created merchandise draws on this form of capital, but such fantrepreneurial production clearly piggybacks on, and transformatively appropriates, this form of cultural capital – without doing so, its design work would not be readable as belonging to the interests and knowledges characterising the relevant fandom. Having set out these definitions, in the next section I will demonstrate the analytical value of multiple types of cultural capital by looking at two case studies of *Doctor Who* fan-designers' work: Clayton Hickman and Andrew-Mark Thompson.

Bourdieu in Strands of Professionalised and Playful Fan-Design

A former editor of the officially licenced *Doctor Who Magazine*, and a designer for the official BBC DVD *Doctor Who* range, Clayton Hickman has utilised Twitter to promote and sell *Who*-related design work available for purchase on Redbubble (https://www.redbubble.com/people/claytonhickman/shop). Given his role as a professional designer on multiple ranges of licenced *Doctor Who* products, in Bourdieu's terms Hickman is a fan with high levels of pre-existent fan social capital and fan cultural capital, as well as possessing high levels of cultural capital linked to his status as a professional designer (Hills, 2002; Nilsson, 2025). The result is a fan-designer who blurs together professionalised design skills and extensive fan knowledge, displaying the reputational symbolic capital of a 'BNF' or 'Big Name Fan'. At the time of writing, and despite being less active on Twitter/X than previously, Hickman follows only 472 people but has some 18.3k followers. As Brooke Erin Duffy's analysis of 'aspirational labor' argues:

> Using luck, hard work, and free social media, the argument goes, "anyone" can "get discovered" or make a living from their "passion projects". ...I contend that traditional inequalities often endure, and that barriers to entry remain staggeringly high. ...[T]hose most likely to rise above the social media din are the same social types that have long dominated the... creative economies, particularly those with sufficient reserves of economic and social capital (2017, p. 223).

Hickman represents a generation of BNFs whose fan symbolic capital pre-dated *Doctor Who*'s 2005 return. But he has parlayed his professionalised fandom (Hills, 2002, pp. 14–15) into an independent fan self-brand, successfully crafting and selling unlicensed *Doctor Who* design-oriented T-shirts. As Avi Santo has pointed out, it is increasingly

> ... difficult to differentiate between fan-made merchandise and its mass-produced cousin... due to changes brought about by platforms... which... allow designers to partner with manufacturers to increase merchandise volume... RedBubble.com takes original fan design work and prints it onto a range of generic objects..., replicating the logic of lifestyle branding (2018, p. 335).

Hickman's Redbubble products are often based on reproducing 'obscure' diegetic designs from *Doctor Who*'s history or as his artist profile states: 'Obscure TV designs lovingly recreated'. This seems to exemplify Cherry's argument that 'micro-businesses [using] [p]eer-to-peer e-commerce sites... convert fan cultural capital into economic capital by allowing entrepreneurial fans to sell... fan-themed objects' (2016, p. 164).

However, as I have suggested, the situation is not as clear-cut as this 'conversion' would suggest. Hickman specialises in colourising black-and-white photographic images from *Doctor Who*'s past – often publicity stills – and his regular creation of these gifts to the fandom, as well as recreating paratextual images from the 1960s/70s in HD quality, are interspersed with his Twitter promotion of Redbubble-hosted designs. As such, Hickman's brand of design work also fuses 'attention capital' (Mears, 2023, p. 2) – the regular creation of new-old *Doctor Who* design materials and their dissemination through social media – with a form of design-oriented 'digital cultural capital' (Verwiebe & Hagemann, 2025, p. 1862). The latter relies on his exceptionally skilful ability to digitally recreate the fonts, layout and photographic components of decades-old *Doctor Who* publicity or merchandise, as well as sensitively colourising 'vintage' material, displaying fan knowledge surrounding the real-world colours of diegetic material which had been presented in black-and-white. By researching and mimetically reproducing screen-accurate typefaces/fonts and by meticulously reproducing diegetic logos and visual designs from *Doctor Who* episodes, e.g. the 'Fantasy Factory' from 'Trial of a Time Lord', titled 'Light Fantastic' on Redbubble, or 'Floored', accurately reproducing the infamous booby-trapped floor-tile design from 'Death to the Daleks', Hickman also demonstrates and circulates 'corporate cultural capital' (Lam, 2010) by utilising 'obscure' moments in *Doctor Who*'s brand history, as he describes them. Despite the fact that his work is unlicensed, Hickman's design-oriented appropriations of *Who* 'focus on lesser-known... moments in the text that licensed companies ignore. They fill a niche and invite fans into the process of poaching parts of the story' (Boumaroun, 2023, p. 90) as well as pedagogically orienting fans towards matters of *Doctor Who*'s design, which might otherwise be relatively neglected in fan evaluations (Britton, 2021, p. 125). It could be suggested that Hickman is 'licensed' by his fan social capital, i.e. he is well networked as a result of his previous roles as an official designer/editor, and so his fan-designs are less likely to be targeted for internet takedowns or rights claims. However, there is no explicit evidence to support this, and on some occasions, Hickman has acknowledged that his designs could be the subject of IP claims and may rapidly have to be removed from sale.

Clayton Hickman's entrepreneurial, platformised fandom thus differs from official *Doctor Who* T-shirt designs, say. His work is all about attention to detail and can be very much characterised as a 'research-oriented approach, evoking as it does both the ardour and the precision of the museum expert... it might in fact better be called *curatorial* evaluation, conferring... the standing of culturally significant artefacts' (Britton, 2021, p. 129) on the design elements of *Who*'s *mise-en-scene.* It is striking that Hickman's fantrepreneurialism centres so strongly on design consistency and hyperdetail, i.e. exactly what one might expect from practices of brand management. His RedBubble designs work by *competitively out-doing and out-detailing official branded Doctor Who merchandise*. Like the designer Sara Benito whose work is studied in Roberto Huertas's chapter in this collection, Hickman's work is not concerned with re-signification; although rather than pursuing a minimalist design aesthetic, he emphasises perfected diegetic extraction/reproduction. In his T-shirt designs, then, Hickman demonstrates an absolute precision of design consistency and focus, isolating diegetic logos from their original textual locations, as well as detailing changes in episode title fonts. On a GIF of 1980s 'Formula One typeface' titles, Hickman spots inconsistencies and singles out one classic series' story title that's given entirely in caps in the programme's opening sequence unlike all the others, 'ATTACK OF THE CYBERMEN' (shared on Twitter/X, 3 March 2018).

In short, Hickman's unlicensed paratextual merchandising is staunchly critical of glitches in official branding design and paratexts across the history of *Doctor Who*, instead offering an unlicensed yet more consistently realised vision of merch. The visual and design hyperdetails of Hickman's work lend themselves to being recognisable only to fellow fans, and he often avoids referring to diegetic design likenesses by their branded terms, referring to TARDIS 'circles' rather than roundels, for instance, on his commercially-available Redbubble designs. Unlike licenced merchandise which often needs to have economic viability at scale and hence trades on likenesses of Doctors or major monsters, Hickman's hyperdetailed approach evades the policing of intellectual property rights by occupying a grey area where materials are just transformative enough via their textual decontextualisation, and sufficiently niche (as well as renamed), to fly under *Doctor Who*'s brand radar (Boumaroun, 2023). Arguably, all franchises will have structurally similar grey areas, where sufficiently subtle fan-designs are permitted to flourish, though official designers can sometimes re-appropriate such fan design-work without any real possibility of comeback (Boumaroun, 2023, p. 95).

Hickman's design-oriented fandom thus subjects *Doctor Who* to practices of idealised, heightened and imagined brand management. Here, the fantrepreneur and their fan-consumers can accurately extract graphics from *Doctor Who*'s textual history, restoring design consistency and a focus on hyperdetail to official branding that is felt to have fallen short in sometimes lacklustre official efforts. The implication is that design-oriented professionalised fans sporting symbolic capital can do fantrepreneurial branding better than industry professionals who lack the fan's eye for detail. But this critique of official brand management is an amalgamation of multiple capitals, operating in a highly permeable or overlaid field of cultural production where appropriations of brand designs in the form of grey-marketised corporate cultural capital, skills of digital cultural capital *and* fan cultural capital, alongside performances of attention capital via regular social media posting of new content, all come together in the 'authenticity' of fan-design work.

Nor does such critique of official branding and design amount to a challenge to norms of brand activity – Hickman's designs and colourisations don't contest contemporary *Doctor Who* as a brand; they accept this and merely imply that design processes *could and should be done better from a fannish perspective*, amounting to a 'negotiated' criticism, in Stuart Hall's (1980) terms, of what Mark Fisher has labelled 'capitalist realism' (2009). As such, Hickman's many colourisations and extractions of design/logo details from the texts of 'classic' *Doctor Who* occupy a resolutely branded and paratextual 'design culture':

> In the new conditions of design culture, cognition becomes as much spatial and temporal as visual. ...The same visual information may be generated and encountered via a range of platforms... Thus imagery and information are 'played through varying sites'. (Julier, 2014, p. 13)

One of Hickman's interests is in TARDIS design (the Doctor's time-travelling police box); his Twitter bio states that he is 'very judgmental of TARDISes', paying characteristically close attention to changes in the design of the TARDIS prop across classic *Doctor Who*'s run. It is thus somewhat fitting that his Redbubble products and Twitter/X-shared colourisations and graphic design recreations are part of the networked spaces and times of contemporary design culture. Indeed, he has responded in a time-sensitive manner to trends in *Who*'s social media fandom, such as creating a 'London 1965' T-shirt design when this became a popular fan meme after Twitch streams of the classic series (Jacobs & Booth, 2020, p. 13).

Hickman is not alone in carving out a niche as a leading designer within the 'design-oriented' strands of *Doctor Who* fandom. Designers include Rafeski, who has produced covers for the Big Finish range of licenced audio adventures and has also produced unlicensed 'key art' for the *Doctor Who* Appreciation Society's series of classic series' screenings at Riverside Studios in London, while Joe Cook has contributed an impressive variety of story-based designs to these DWAS screenings; small numbers are sold as signed or unsigned prints, with the funds raised going to nominated charities. And the likes of Colin Brockhurst, Robert Hammond and Stuart Manning have all created designs displaying high levels of fan cultural capital for fan press titles from Cutaway, Hirst Books and Tenacre.

Another graphic designer who combines a focus on *Doctor Who* with a broader interest in cult television is Andrew-Mark Thompson. Like Hickman he has a Redbubble store – as well as a newer mademe.co.uk shop – and uses social media, e.g. Bluesky, to promote these, all under the moniker of 'Andydrewz'. Given that he moved off Twitter/X, Thompson's Bluesky stats are somewhat lower than Hickman's; he currently has 1.2k followers and is following 880 people. A collected volume of his unlicensed and transformative fanworks was published in 2023 entitled *This Is A Fake: A Collection of Unreal Things*. Thompson specialises in the creation of 'fake paratexts', i.e. photoshopped and very precisely crafted 'authentic'-seeming images of vintage merchandise that was never released, nor even planned by brands' intellectual property rights holders. Thompson's blog, not updated beyond 2022 at the time of writing, contains a similar warning to the hardback collection of his designs: 'This blog contains material that is made up and not real' (https://andydrewz64.blogspot.com/). But there is a *Doctor Who* in-joke embedded in the book title *This Is A Fake:* it references a playful moment in Douglas Adams' and Graham Williams' script for 'The City of Death' where the fourth Doctor scribbles these very words in marker pen on a number of Leonardo Da Vinci canvases. The intertextual reference works, therefore, to undercut its own apparent statement. since in 'The City of Death' these were 'genuine copies' (McKee, 2007, p. 235) of the Mona Lisa, diegetically painted by Da Vinci.

This deconstructive energy is similarly present in Thompson's designs, which might also be considered as oxymoronic 'genuine copies' in the sense that they convey an authenticity based on careful reproduction of the actual merchandise/paratexts that they reference, while recombining these design formats or templates with new ('unreal') material. Akin to the work of designer 'Iván Ramosky' studied in Roberto Huertas's chapter earlier in this section, there is a ludic intertextuality at play in Thompson's fan-design work. And as I've observed elsewhere:

> This creation of "fake paratexts" for non-existent texts occurs across a range of different fandoms; David Church has discussed the creation of invented paratexts for imagined exploitation movies, for instance... Church argues that such fan productivity "relies on creating a longing for lost objects that never actually came to pass." (Hills, 2015, p. 34)

Such longing seems to be testified to in merchandise collector and publisher David Howe's foreword to *This Is A Fake*, where he refers to 'things we would all have coveted, had they been produced in our universe' (Howe, 2023).

By recreating new versions of paratexts from across the classic series, whether Denys Fisher toys from the 1970s that were never made or VHS covers from the 1980s that never existed, Thompson draws on fans' 'paratextual memory' (Hills & Garde-Hansen, 2017) and the sense of having been there to appreciate actual *Doctor Who* merchandise from childhood (or from later merch collecting). There is not only a high level of fan cultural capital displayed in these engagements with the history of *Who*'s merchandise but also a correlated performance of digital cultural capital, as the look and feel of specific publications are replicated with almost uncanny precision in Thompson's digital designs, whether these are the *Radio Times* from the 1960s or 1980s shopping catalogues (Thompson, 2023). And appropriated corporate cultural capital is again necessarily placed front and centre, given that the detailed fonts, layouts and branding of multiple *Doctor Who* licensees are very precisely pastiched and re-captured in design terms.

The relationship to corporate cultural capital is not as clearly affirmational as its recirculation in Clayton Hickman's Redbubble designs, though. Where Hickman focuses on extracting materials such as in-universe logos as accurately as possible from *Doctor Who*'s original texts, Thompson recurrently mocks and playfully challenges the paratextual material that he is otherwise affectionately reproducing. In a recreation of BBC Enterprises' Commemorative Programme from the Longleat 1983 event – this time for an imaginary first-anniversary garden fete – BBC Enterprises, the BBC's commercial arm which merchandised *Who* across the 1980s, is instead given as the 'BBC Exploitation Department' (2023). Many other designs also critique the limitations of official brand activities rather than simply seeking to improve upon branding, as Hickman has done. Licensed products are repeatedly shown to be absurdly desperate attempts to secure the 'fan pound', such as the *Doctor Who* 'Quiz Book of Municipal Refuse Collection Vehicles': 'Test your knowledge of dust carts with this slim volume of rubbish teasers' (2023). Or there are the 'omozon inaudible' (amazon audible) releases of non-fiction *Doctor Who* such *The Colouring Book* and *The Crossword Book* (Thompson, 2023). Like the actual range of Quiz Books, which didn't include a focus on dust carts but may nevertheless have been felt to be 'slim volumes of rubbish teasers' by fans, these were real examples of *Who* merchandise, but they are evidently pointless, if not impossible, as audiobook releases. Even an 'unofficial' *Doctor Who* magazine doesn't escape Thompson's artfully parodic gaze, being plastered in ridiculously inappropriate images of *Who* actors from other roles, such as David Tennant as the serial killer Dennis

Nielsen, and proudly promoted in its faux advertisement as '100% unwarranted' (2023).

In these instances, Thompson punctures the otherwise 'pervasive atmosphere' of capitalist realism (Fisher, 2009, p. 16): the unreality or counterfactuality of his invented merchandise and paratexts has the strange effect of making all the real-world merchandise that he's citing seem somehow simultaneously less real or at least more contestable as the fan-targeted monetising of *Doctor Who*. Rather than a negotiated criticism of capitalist realism, as in Hickman's design work which typically wants *Doctor Who* branding to be done better, at times Thompson's designs move closer to moments of 'oppositional' criticism in Hall's (1980) taxonomy, rejecting the excesses of exploitative merchandising while humorously and playfully highlighting its grasping nonsensicality. Fan cultural capital is strongly performed here in terms of defending perceived fan interests against a corporate 'BBC Exploitation Department', and the polysemic blend of affectionate paratextual memory with a critically parodic edge arguably also helps these sorts of designs to garner 'attention capital' for their designer on social media.

Both Hickman and Thompson display complex amalgamations of multiple forms of capital (corporate cultural; digital cultural; attention) rather than simply performing the fannish knowledge of fan cultural capital and the designer's expertise as cultural capital in their design labour. However, there are different sensibilities in their work, as well as differing relationships to the capitalist realism of omnipresent branding. Clayton Hickman's gifts to fandom – colourisations and high-definition recreations of vintage paratexts – are often concerned with *modernising*, with bringing *Doctor Who*'s paratextual worlds of the past into the media-technological present. By contrast, Andrew-Mark Thompson's carnivalesque renderings of vintage paratexts mashed-up with current brands or more recent Doctors indicate a central concern with *retro-activating*. Thompson projects the present worlds of *Doctor Who* back into the past, whether this is the show's 1983 20th anniversary reimagined as a quaint first anniversary celebration in 1964, the later emphasis on *Radio Times*' covers as valuable promotion being drawn on to imagine a promo cover for the very first episode, or the 13th Doctor played by Jodie Whittaker herself being integrated into 'the covers of old *Radio Times*' (Thompson, 2023). As Guy Julier has argued, relations of space and time may characterise contemporary 'design culture' (2014, p. 13), as corporately-designed images migrate across media and across platforms, but these two professionalised fan-designers have mobilised distinctive adventures in design space and time.

Conclusion

I have sought to bring together fan studies and design research via their shared Bourdieusian debts while also complicating previous accounts in fan studies that have anchored the distinctions of fan-created merchandise predominantly in 'fan cultural capital'. Having analysed the fan-design work of Clayton Hickman and

Andrew-Mark Thompson, it can be said that both these successful fan-trepreneurs possess high levels of all the multiple forms of capital which have been considered. This is significant as it suggests that these fan-creators have secured recognition by condensing forms of privilege (Hickman being a former editor of *Doctor Who Magazine*), design education/skill and social media savvy. At the same time, I have illustrated that there are modernising aesthetics of temporality versus more retro-active aesthetics at work in Hickman and Thompson's differing design projects. The Bourdieusian capital-based approach arguably remains less well suited to explicating this aesthetically oriented level of fan-created merchandise and design enterprise, where no clearly bounded 'field' of fandom can be identified and instead fantrepreneurialism takes place in permeable/overlapping fields of digital design, social media and the fan object's branding. Such permeability means that analysts cannot rely on clearly identifiable or hierarchical levels of fan cultural capital, or indeed cultural capital, to make sense of these bids for fan-cultural status and recognition, instead needing to address the blends and blurring of multiple forms of cultural capital, as suggested in this discussion.

References

Barrière, L., & Finkel, R. (2022). The material culture of music festival fandoms. *European Journal of Cultural Studies*, *25*(2), 479–497.

Boumaroun, L. (2023). Flying under the Radar: Culture and community in the unlicensed geek fashion industry. In E. Affuso & S. Scott (Eds.), *Sartorial fandom: Fashion, beauty culture, identity* (pp. 84–98). University of Michigan Press.

Bourdaa, M. (2022). The fandom is a welcoming place unless I know more than you: Generations, mentorship, and super-fans. In B. Kies & M. Connor (Eds.), *Fandom: The next generation* (pp. 172–180). University of Iowa Press.

Britton, P. D. (2021). *Design for Doctor Who: Vision and revision in science fiction television*. Bloomsbury Academic.

Carter, O. (2018). *Making European cult cinema: Fan enterprise in an alternative economy*. Amsterdam University Press.

Carvalho, L., Dong, A., & Maton, K. (2009). Legitimating design: A sociology of knowledge account of the field. *Design Studies*, *30*, 483–502.

Cherry, B. (2016). *Cult media, fandom and textiles: Handicrafting as fan art*. Bloomsbury Academic.

Chin, B. (2018). It's about who you know: Social capital, hierarchies and fandom. In P. Booth (Ed.), *A companion to media fandom and fan studies* (pp. 243–255).Wiley Blackwell.

Duffy, B. E. (2017). *(Not) Getting paid to do what you love: Gender, social media and aspirational work*. Yale University Press.

Fisher, M. (2009). *Capitalist realism: Is there no alternative?* Zero Books.

Garner, R. (2025). Curating popular dinosaur ephemera: Reflections on the "Aca-Fan Archivist" and sub/cultural capital. In D. Ciesielska, N. Lamerichs, & A. Zarzycka (Eds.), *Affect in fandom: Fan creators and productivity* (pp. 149–169). Amsterdam University Press.

Geraghty, L. (2014). *Cult collectors*. Routledge.

Gogor, B. P., Udasmoro, W., & Noviani, R. (2025). The transformation of online academic graphic designers into petite bourgeoisie within the digital capitalism ecosystem. *Journal of Urban Society's Arts*, *12*(1), 72–83.

Hall, S. (1980). Encoding/decoding. In S. Hall, D. Hobson, A. Lowe, & P. Willis (Eds.), *Culture, media, language* (pp. 128–138). Hutchinson.

Hills, M. (2002). *Fan cultures*. Routledge.

Hills, M. (2005). *The pleasures of horror*. Continuum.

Hills, M. (2011). *Cultographies: Blade runner*. Wallflower Press.

Hills, M. (2015). *Doctor Who: The unfolding event – Marketing, merchandising and mediatizing a brand anniversary*. Palgrave Macmillan.

Hills, M. (2017). A "cult-like" Following: Nordic Noir, Nordicana and Arrow Films' bridging of subcultural/neocultural capital. In J. Wroot & A. Willis (Eds.), *Cult media: Re-packaged, re-released and restored* (pp. 49–65). Palgrave Macmillan.

Hills, M., & Garde-Hansen, J. (2017). Fandom's paratextual memory: Remembering, reconstructing, and repatriating "lost". *Doctor Who. Critical Studies in Media Communication*, *34*(2), 158–167.

Howe, D. (2023). Foreword. In A.-M. Thompson (Ed.), *This is A fake: A collection of unreal things*. Telos Press.

Jacobs, N., & Booth, P. (2020). Converging experiences, converging audiences: An analysis of *Doctor Who* on Twitch. *Convergence*, 1–19.

Julier, G. (2014). *The culture of design* (3rd ed.). Sage.

Lam, S. S. K. (2010). "Global corporate cultural capital" as a drag on glocalization: Disneyland's promotion of the Halloween Festival. *Media, Culture & Society*, *32*(4), 631–648.

Lamerichs, N. (2018). Fan fashion: Re-enacting hunger games through clothing and design. In P. Booth (Ed.), *A companion to media fandom and fan studies* (pp. 175–188). Wiley Blackwell.

Lury, C. (1996). *Consumer culture*. Polity Press.

McKee, A. (2007). Why is "City of Death" the best *Doctor Who* story? In D. Butler (Ed.), *Time and relative dissertations in space: Critical perspectives on Doctor Who* (pp. 233–245). Manchester University Press.

Mears, A. (2023, July–September). Bringing Bourdieu to a content farm: Social media production fields and the cultural economy of attention. *Social Media + Society*, 1–12.

Nilsson, Å. W. (2025). Bridging boundaries: Unveiling Bourdieu's "thinking tools" in design interventions with youth. *Design and Culture*, *17*(2), 163–184.

Qiu, L. (2025). Exploring the lived experience associated with fan-made goods: A serious leisure perspective. *Leisure Studies*, 1–21.

Rehak, B. (2018). *More than meets the eye: Special effects and the fantastic transmedia franchise*. New York University Press.

Sandvoss, C., Gray, J., & Harrington, C. L. (2017). Introduction: Why still study fans? In J. Gray, C. Sandvoss, & C. L. Harrington (Eds.), *Fandom: Identities and communities in a mediated world* (2nd ed., pp. 1–26). New York University Press.

Santo, A. (2018). Fans and merchandise. In M. A. Click & S. Scott (Eds.), *The Routledge companion to media fandom* (pp. 329–336). Routledge.

Thompson, A.-M. (2023). *This is a fake: A collection of unreal things*. Telos Press.

Tonkinwise, C. (2011). A taste for practices: Unrepressing style in design thinking. *Design Studies*, *32*, 533–545.

Verwiebe, R., & Hagemann, S. (2025). Bourdieu revisited: New forms of digital capital – Emergence, reproduction, inequality of distribution. *Information, Communication & Society*, *28*(11), 1861–1883.

Part 4

Tourism and Urban Space

Chapter 11

Encounters by Design: Souq Waqif and the Spatial Life of the 2022 Qatar World Cup

Hamed Goharipour

The College of Wooster, USA

Abstract

Qatar's hosting of the 2022 FIFA World Cup, the first in an Arab Muslim country, offers a lens on how public spaces can enable or limit interaction among diverse groups. This chapter focuses on Souq Waqif, a historic marketplace in central Doha that became one of the tournaments' most socially dynamic sites. While much of the event unfolded in ticketed or branded areas, the Souq remained open and largely unprogrammed, presenting a different model for how fans and locals might meet, observe and celebrate together. Drawing on fieldwork during the tournament, the author examines encounters between fans and residents, from brief, incidental exchanges to more emotionally engaged moments. Using Lofland's framework of stranger relationships, the author shows how the Souq's spatial design shaped these interactions. What emerges is a story about how urban design affects movement, access and the social life of public space during global events. Visitors arrived as fans, a distinct public with a shared identity oriented to celebration and spectating, yet marked by team-based distinctions in colours, chants and rivalry. Souq Waqif made both dynamics visible, showing how design can host shared joy while accommodating group difference without escalating conflict and offering lessons for more inclusive fan experiences.

Keywords: Souq Waqif; FIFA World Cup Qatar 2022; fan encounters; public space; mega-events

Bridging Design and Fandom, 165–179

doi:10.1108/978-1-80592-659-720261011

Introduction: Mega-Events, Public Spaces and Design

Mega-sport events are not just competitions; they are urban projects that promise economic gains often contested in practice (Baade & Matheson, 2016), trigger large-scale planning and infrastructure with characteristic governance pathologies that reshape cities beyond the tournament (Müller, 2015), and also reorder social life through celebration, surveillance and exclusion (Boykoff, 2016). Qatar's 2022 World Cup brought that mix into a distinctive cultural and demographic setting: debates about migrant labour, alcohol, gender norms and LGBTQ+ visibility, a population shaped by expatriate workers and a sudden surge of visitors (Dun, 2023; Jain, 2023; Khaled & Gray, 2019; Moradi-Lakeh et al., 2023). This chapter focuses on Souq Waqif, a partly renovated, quasi-authentic marketplace that stayed open and largely unprogrammed, to ask how design and light management shaped everyday encounters between fans and locals during a global event.

Public space is where people move, pause and meet (Low & Altman, 1992; Sennett, 1986) and design matters for all three (Carmona, 2010; Gehl, 1987; Project for Public Spaces, 2000). As a brief pointer, I flag Fokdal's (2008) four analytical dimensions of public space – time, space, power and users – to frame how Souq Waqif worked during the World Cup:

Time is central to the atmosphere of mega-events. Their brief intensity disrupts normal routines and creates new possibilities for interaction. In Qatar, public space had to adapt quickly. Souq Waqif, with its open walkways and restored alleys, supported heavy foot traffic, spontaneous celebration and moments of connection. This aligns with Pløger's (2010) concept of eventalization, where space is temporarily reimagined and experienced in new ways.

Space, as De Certeau (1988) explains, enables people to make meaning through action. At Souq Waqif, fans reinterpreted space by dancing in walkways, gathering in corners and transforming ordinary paths into performance zones.

Power is embedded in public space (Foucault, 1986). It defines who feels welcome and what is allowed. In Doha, many spaces were tightly managed, but Souq Waqif remained relatively open. Security controlled entrances and shopkeepers marked their territory, but people had room to move freely.

Users bring space to life. We must ask who spaces are for. In Qatar, public access is shaped by gender, class and citizenship. During the tournament, the Souq brought together Qatari families, migrant workers, tourists and performers. Outside the tournament, routine use skews towards Qatari families and tourists, with earlier phases more associated with low-income migrant workers and later redevelopment shifting their presence to the edges (Salama et al., 2017). During the World Cup, these varied publics met at once and shaped the Souq through movement and gesture as much as the built form did.

By looking at Souq Waqif, this chapter shows how public space design interacts with the temporary nature of mega-events. Design here matters not only as a physical structure but also in how it allows public behaviour, adaptation, interpretation and shared experience. This study contributes to research into design in fandom by examining how spatial form and atmosphere shapes fan experiences and encounters in a live, unscripted setting. In this chapter I treat fans as a particular kind of urban public. I use 'fans' to include highly identified national-team supporters and more casual flâneurs, spanning strong to moderate identification in public settings (Giulianotti, 2002; Wann, 1995). They arrived with a common purpose that cut across nationality, language and class: to enjoy the tournament and to be among others doing the same. That shared identity produced an unusual openness to co-presence, mirroring what I later describe as fleeting and routinised encounters at scale. At the same time, fans also performed clear distinctions tied to team affiliation, which produced small territories, call-and-response chants and playful rivalries. Rather than reading those divisions as breakdowns in public life, Souq Waqif shows how spatial form and management can keep them convivial. The Souq's linear promenades, alcoves and semi-permeable thresholds allowed both togetherness and differentiation to occur side by side. Naming this dual dynamic early is important: fans were simultaneously one public and many publics, and the Souq's design helped keep that tension productive.

Theoretical Framework: Lofland and Public Encounters

To better understand the complexity of interactions unfolding in Souq Waqif during the World Cup, I drew on Lyn H. Lofland's (1998) framework of public realm relationships. Lofland distinguishes between different types of social encounters among strangers in urban settings, emphasising that public spaces are not just physical locations but social environments shaped by varying degrees of familiarity and connection. Her framework identifies key relational types, including fleeting interactions, routinised exchanges, quasi-primary and intimate secondary relations, that help explain how people navigate shared spaces without necessarily forming deep personal bonds. Recent work applies Lofland to show how public behaviour underpins belonging and everyday navigation of difference and to test when brief encounters matter. Examples range from studies of belonging and public familiarity in European cities (Blokland et al., 2023) to analyses of encounters in semi-public spaces (Peterson, 2017) and even coexisting at the neighbourhood scale (Terruhn & Ye, 2022).

This conceptual framework is especially useful in a context where fans, locals and visitors were brought together temporarily and unpredictably. Rather than assuming uniform or harmonious encounters, Lofland's typology allowed me to recognise the layered, sometimes contradictory nature of social life in public space, particularly in moments of celebration, observation and casual exchange. In this study, her work serves as a foundation for analysing how strangers relate to one another in a space shaped by physical form and design, cultural norms and tradition, and the temporary energy of a global event. However, critics remind us that public space is structured by regulation and exclusion, and that contact does not automatically produce understanding. I therefore read Lofland alongside work on power and the limits of encounter (Low & Smith, 2013; Valentine, 2008).

Methodology

This study used a qualitative, ethnographic approach rooted in critical interpretivism, recognising that public spaces like Souq Waqif are experienced differently by various users and observers. The goal was to understand how the design, layout, and atmosphere shaped social encounters during the World Cup, not just to document behaviour. The focal population comprises in-person event publics, national-team supporters and casual spectators in open spaces, rather than ticketed venue crowds. Fieldwork spanned 20 days before, during and after several matches, combining participant and non-participant observation. I engaged with fans, locals and business owners, moving through the space as they did to experience it as a dynamic social and spatial landscape. I kept detailed field notes, voice memos, photos and videos to capture gestures, moods, movement patterns and micro-interactions. Rather than viewing the Souq as a static stage, I approached it as a space co-created by its architecture and the people who moved through it.

I combined visual reading with thematic coding in dialogue with Lofland, settling on three encounter types: fleeting, routinised and what I call 'convivial'. I used Lofland as a sensitising framework rather than a template. The aim was comparability and parsimony in naming encounter types, while still coding inductively and letting categories adjust to the material. This abductive stance (Timmermans & Tavory, 2012) moved iteratively between data and concept without forcing the evidence.

Discussion: Encounters, Design and Public Life at Souq Waqif

What follows reads fan publics in two registers at once: a shared identity of spectatorship that made co-presence easy and team distinctions that gave the space its charge through ritualised rivalry. I replaced Lofland's term 'quasi-primary' with 'convivial' to mark that these were not generic strangers; as fans, they arrived pre-affiliated, producing quick in-group recognition and brief communitas. That affinity lowered thresholds for greeting, joking, singing and collective performance, even as team allegiances carved small territories for chants and call-and-response.

Routinised Encounters

Routinised encounters reflect a particular kind of social dynamic in public space – one shaped by brief, habitual recognition without emotional involvement. These are the moments when people acknowledge each other's presence without much more, often through a nod, a glance or simply sharing the same rhythm of movement. This idea aligns with what Durkheim (1964) and Simmel

(1971) describe as 'mutual indifference', a way of coexisting that is both socially necessary and emotionally distant (Horgan, 2017, p. 26). Lofland (1998, p. 54) refers to these as learnt routines, repeated patterns that help maintain a sense of order in shared spaces. Despite their surface-level nature, these encounters still matter. They offer a form of quiet civility, a way of managing difference in public without confrontation. In the context of Souq Waqif during the World Cup, these moments took on a new texture. Although they were temporally limited, emerging only during the event, they hinted at how even short-term gatherings can reshape public behaviour. In this way, routinised encounters – even in an extraordinary context – help us see how social norms are negotiated, sustained or gently revised through everyday use of shared space. The spatial layout of the Souq, with its repeated flows and familiar nodes of gathering, made space for these subtle, patterned exchanges to unfold naturally.

In the quieter corners and narrower alleys of Souq Waqif, the pace of life was often set by the rhythm of routinised relationships. These interactions were shaped largely by what Lofland calls 'occupational identities', meaning social roles grounded in one's position or task. They were most visible in the everyday exchanges between shop owners tucked away in the less-trafficked parts of the bazaar and the visitors who wandered into them. For many of these vendors, bound by the placement of their shops and the demands of their work, interactions with tourists were practical and commercial. The flow of conversation followed a familiar pattern: browsing, price negotiations, transactions and sometimes a quiet moment observing a craftsperson at work. Yet even in these functional encounters, subtle forms of guidance and interaction emerged. When a visitor seemed unsure about where to sit in a Moroccan restaurant or how to queue outside a popular Knafeh stall, vendors often stepped in, offering directions without ceremony. This informal, locally grounded form of spatial management stood in contrast to the formal behavioural codes enforced by police or security personnel elsewhere in the city. While the latter sometimes drew criticism for reinforcing exclusionary norms, here, guidance emerged organically from within the space itself, shaped by routine, proximity and the quiet authority of experience.

In the bustling central spine of Souq Waqif, cafés, restaurants, dessert shops and other upscale businesses added another layer to the routinised dynamics of the space. The owners of these establishments often asserted, and sometimes expanded, their control over the surrounding area. Territorial boundaries were marked in both subtle and direct ways. A line of flower boxes might signal where one café's space began while a low fence or rope divider made the message unmistakable (Fig. 11.1). These visual cues helped shape how space was used, inviting some behaviours while discouraging others.[1] In most cases, these acts of territorialisation were tied to commercial aims. The clearer the boundary, the

[1]I could not verify a formal policy shift, but the pattern resembled event-time soft delegation in which authorities tolerate short-term, business-led micro-management to maintain flow and security during mega-events.

Fig. 11.1. Territorialisation of Space Enforces Routinised Encounters © Author.

easier it was to maintain order, attract customers and reinforce a sense of ownership. But this control also came with trade-offs. By narrowing the available space for spontaneous or shared activity, these design choices often limited the range of social encounters that might otherwise have taken place outside the borders of formal hospitality. What emerged was a more curated, sometimes constrained public life, one shaped as much by economic interest as by cultural interaction.

Another expression of routinised relationships during the event could be seen in the quick, mostly non-verbal interactions between police officers and the people using the space. The officers weren't stationed inside the Souq itself but instead stood at key entrances, managing the flow of visitors with physical barriers. Unlike the highly regulated FIFA Fan Festival, which only allowed access to Hayya Card (entry permit) holders, Souq Waqif remained open to everyone. Still, access was subtly controlled. Officers redirected foot traffic by turning certain alleys into temporary one-way routes, a tactic meant to ease congestion but one that also introduced a new layer of regulation. For many fans, especially those unfamiliar with the layout, these changes created confusion. They often stopped briefly to ask officers for directions or alternate routes; short exchanges that rarely went beyond a gesture or a few words. These moments were routine, even mechanical, shaped by necessity rather than connection. And yet, within them lay small challenges: mismatched expectations, language gaps or the frustration of not knowing where to go. While this kind of boundary-drawing was effective in managing the crowd, it also reshaped how people moved through and experienced the space, quietly shifting Souq Waqif from a place of free wandering into one marked by regulated flow.

Still, despite the occasional confusion or constraint, the co-presence of locals and visitors gave Souq Waqif a social richness that set it apart from more controlled event spaces like official fan zones. People who might never have crossed paths under ordinary circumstances now shared space, sometimes distantly, sometimes through brief exchanges. One particularly vivid, unsanctioned example of routinised interaction emerged in the peripheral lanes of the Souq, where a few local women, often dressed in traditional Arabic Muslim attire, including shawls and sometimes full or partial niqab, sold homemade food to passing fans. Some may have been immigrants themselves, but in this moment, they stood as quiet representatives of a familiar cultural figure in the region. These women had claimed small patches of space and turned them into makeshift kitchens (observed afternoons into late evening), preparing simple foods like sambuusa, falafel or freshly baked bread filled with Nutella.[2] They didn't call out to passers-by or engage much in conversation. Their movements were focused and practical: preparing, wrapping and watching. Fans, in turn, seemed to intuit the social script. Transactions were quiet and cash-based. After paying, most customers stepped aside, either eating nearby without lingering or carrying the food with them as they moved on. These encounters were minimal, routine and yet deeply telling. They reflected a kind of mutual respect grounded in quiet acknowledgement and in the informal design of the space – a corner here, a bench there – that made these encounters possible at all.

The influx of fans during the World Cup created an opening for the women selling food to earn income and for visitors to enjoy quick, affordable meals in the heart of a celebrated public space. Still, the interactions themselves were brief, often lasting no more than a few seconds. There was little room for them to grow into something more meaningful. Barriers of occupation, gender, language and culture quietly set the terms of engagement. Design couldn't help more. Yet even within these limits, the exchanges carried weight. They became part of the Souq's social rhythm, adding texture to the diversity of the space. For a moment, people from very different worlds stood face to face, even if only to exchange a few words or none at all. While such 'spatial proximity' may not have fostered deep 'social contact' (Horgan, 2017), it shaped a shared atmosphere. It set the stage for another kind of interaction – the fleeting relationship – which I turn to in the next section.

---

[2]Souq Waqif has long featured women selling traditional foods in the central square. I could not verify licensing in the field; in general, street vending and food handling in Qatar require a license and valid Ministry of Public Health certificates under Ministerial Resolution No. 243 of 2016, with compliance typically monitored by municipal authorities.

Fleeting Encounters

Fleeting encounters are the quiet heartbeat of public space, the briefest moments of contact between strangers who happen to cross paths. These exchanges last seconds, maybe a minute or two, and then dissolve as quickly as they appeared. They don't build relationships in any deep sense, and they rarely leave behind a story. But they matter. They speak to the fluid nature of public life, the way people can move together through the same space without needing to merge their worlds. As Ehrkamp (2006) notes, this isn't assimilation; it's something looser and more delicate, just the passing nearness of difference.

During the World Cup, these kinds of encounters became especially visible along the main route of Souq Waqif. Normally, this stretch of the bazaar carries a certain exclusivity; a function which is sometimes called 'productive of differences' (Clayton, 2009; Ye, 2019). Lined with upscale cafés and restaurants, it's not always a place everyone feels welcome, especially those who can't afford to sit, linger or spend. But the atmosphere shifted during the tournament. The excitement softened those boundaries. People came not to consume but to move, to watch and to take part in the shared hum of celebration. The space changed, not in its architecture but in how it was used and felt. Even those who didn't stop for a meal joined in, workers, fans on a budget, wanderers with no fixed destination. The Souq filled with flâneurs: people drifting through, taking in the sights without any set agenda. This wasn't something seen in the Fan Zones or near the stadiums, where movement was programed and space controlled. Here, the Souq became something looser, more porous. For a brief moment, it welcomed the incidental, the spontaneous and the passing joy of being among others.

The figure of the *flâneur*, a term first coined by Baudelaire (1964) and later taken up by Walter Benjamin (2003), refers to the city wanderer, someone who drifts through urban space, observing its rhythms, textures and fleeting moments of beauty. During the World Cup, Souq Waqif became a magnet for these urban spectators. Locals, visitors and fans alike, when they weren't in the stadiums, often chose to simply stroll. They wandered not with an agenda, but with curiosity, taking in the layered life of the bazaar. New facades, temporarily dressed in flags from all over the world, gave the Souq a welcoming visual identity. These colourful displays invited passers-by to pause, not just to shop or eat but to witness; a small reminder of how design elements can frame experience. Fans in all kinds of attire, moving in and out of restaurants and cafés, created a living spectacle. For the flâneurs, these scenes became part of the show. Watching people eat, laugh, chant and celebrate was as much a part of the World Cup experience as the matches themselves. Sometimes, the quiet observation gave way to shared excitement. A chant might start. A street performance might gather a crowd. A fan being interviewed could suddenly draw a circle of listeners and bystanders. In those moments, the flâneur became something more: a witness, a participant, even a documentarian. Many captured what they saw, snapping photos, filming short videos, sharing their slice of the event on social media. Every alley and gathering became a stage, and every corner of the Souq offered a chance to freeze a fleeting moment of joy.

The relationships that unfolded between fans in the vibrant atmosphere of Souq Waqif were marked by a curious mix of closeness and distance. People stood side by side, physically close, yet often separated by language, culture or national symbols: flags, jerseys, gestures and even facial expressions. In this kind of setting, fleeting encounters thrived. Many took place without a single word spoken, embodying what Watson (2006) calls 'rubbing along;' those small, unspoken moments of connection that come simply from being in the same space. Anything could spark a smile or a nod: a familiar song, a jersey from home, a flag held high or a stranger flashing a victory sign. The fan zone wasn't marked by barriers but by motion, where attention moved fluidly from one visual or emotional cue to the next. Some fans became landmarks in themselves. Four Mexican supporters in traditional dress drew smiles and phones wherever they went, instantly becoming symbols of the event's spirit. In another corner, an Ecuadorian fan in native attire turned into a magnet for cameras, admired not just for his clothing but for what he represented: a moment of pride, performance and presence in a shared space. These scenes didn't require conversation to matter. The power of the visual, of colour, movement and expression became the design language of encounter.

The rhythms of Souq Waqif shifted during the World Cup, and with them, the nature of some everyday interactions. In particular, the typically routine exchanges between male vendors and customers began to open up into something more spontaneous. Fans drawn to stalls selling Arabic food and drinks found themselves curious not just about the flavours but the stories behind them. What's in this tea? How do you make that coffee? These small questions sparked brief but genuine conversations, turning simple transactions into moments of cultural curiosity. For a few minutes, the exchange became less about buying and more about learning. These encounters didn't last long, but they made a difference. They nudged people out of the familiar, routinised script of seller and buyer and into the unfamiliar terrain of sharing across difference. In doing so, they chipped away at the quiet caution often associated with strangers (Ye, 2019), replacing it with something lighter, more open, if only for a moment. Other fleeting connections emerged from shared symbols that seemed to speak across language and nationality. Because this was a fan event, the symbols were not generic; they formed a portable fan vocabulary. In fandom terms, these are shared semiotic resources that pre-affiliate strangers into a momentary in-group. They enable phatic contact, where the point is connection rather than information, so a jersey, scarf or chant can be enough to start a tiny public. In the Souq, the name of a football icon such as Messi or Ronaldo often functioned as a call that organised a grin, a selfie or a chorus within seconds. In a space full of difference, a single word could do the work of greeting before any conversation began.

This sense of connection was sometimes visible through symbols of identity and solidarity, especially the Palestinian flag. For many visitors from Arab countries like Morocco, Tunisia, Syria, Lebanon and Algeria, the flag carried strong emotions: feelings of empathy, shared struggle and belonging. In fact, it was often seen more frequently than the flags of some countries actually playing in the tournament. The sight of this flag created brief but powerful moments between fans. Sometimes it was a smile, a gesture or someone asking to take a photo together. Again, these encounters were short but meaningful. The World Cup gave many Arab fans a chance to express their support for Palestine in a public and international arena, and Souq Waqif, with its open and lively atmosphere, became a place where this solidarity was made visible. Still, these kinds of fleeting moments usually stayed at the surface. They were important, but they did not always lead to deeper connection. To reach a truly convivial relationship requires more: shared values, common goals, and enough time to build trust. During an event as fast-moving as the World Cup, that kind of closeness was rare.

Convivial Encounters

Convivial encounters, what Lofland (1998) describes as quasi-primary relationships, combine a certain emotional warmth with a sense of shared purpose, even if they are brief. This kind of sociability brings energy to what are often called third places, from the open and accessible, like streets, to more structured or semi-exclusive zones, like cafés. During mega-events, these encounters become especially visible. The event acts like a spark, bringing new people into public space, creating new rhythms of interaction, and temporarily shifting how space is used and understood.

In Qatar, Souq Waqif turned into a scene of shared celebration. It became a place where strangers from different countries gathered spontaneously, singing, chanting and celebrating a goal or a win. These gatherings went beyond fleeting nods or routine transactions. They were emotionally charged, full of purpose. A fan's cheer or a flag waved in rhythm was not just about the match, it was an expression of deep connection to a team, a memory and a sense of belonging. This was a different kind of togetherness. It wasn't built on shared culture or language but on the shared experience of being a fan. These gatherings created a kind of temporary solidarity, not through formal interaction but through mutual feeling. Following Horgan's (2017) view of solidarity between strangers, these moments brought people closer not by dissolving difference but by embracing it under a common emotional experience. Sometimes this meant fans from completely different regions, Arab, Persian, East Asian and European, would join the chants of Argentinian supporters, repeating Spanish lyrics they may not even understand. It wasn't about nationality. It was about the love for a team, a player or the feeling of being part of something bigger than yourself.

On certain match days, the presence of specific national fan groups in Souq Waqif became unmistakable. One vivid example was the afternoon and evening of November 26, when Argentinian and Mexican fans filled the Souq ahead of their 10 p.m. match. While globally popular teams like Portugal, Brazil, France and Argentina were already well represented through jerseys, flags and chants, their presence became especially concentrated and animated on the days their teams played. These moments created the perfect setting for something more than fleeting interaction. A single spark, a group of fans in striking attire or a familiar chant, could suddenly shift the mood and claim a corner of the Souq as their own. A narrow path, a small plaza or a busy intersection could turn into an impromptu stage. Once this temporary appropriation of space took place, the atmosphere changed. Attention shifted. Locals stopped to watch, passers-by pulled out their phones and the area filled with laughter, music and movement. As the crowd grew, so did the energy. People who had come just to wander often joined in. Some clapped or danced. Others paused, smiling from the sidelines. And sometimes, a rival fan group would respond, not with hostility but with their own rhythm, their own chants. What began as one group's celebration could quickly turn into a playful performance of rivalry.

This kind of celebration wasn't unique to Argentinian and Mexican fans. Throughout the tournament, fans from Brazil, Saudi Arabia, Portugal and Iran also brought their own energy into Souq Waqif. Each group added something distinct, turning familiar corners of the Souq into temporary stages for joy. After Morocco's unexpected and inspiring run in the tournament, Moroccan fans quickly joined in with similar expressions of pride. At one point, they fully claimed one of the Souq's main wings, filling it with flags, chants and a deep sense of solidarity (Fig. 11.2). It was more than celebration; it was a way of making the space their own, transforming it into something that felt local and shared. In these moments, fans weren't just passing through; they were shaping the atmosphere. They were doing what Wireman (1984, pp. 2–3) describes as conviviality: interactions marked by warmth, shared emotion and a strong, if temporary, sense of belonging. People came together not to talk about personal

Fig. 11.2. Moroccans Appropriate a Souq's Wing to Celebrate © Author.

matters or form long-term bonds but to participate in something public and focused. There was little need for names or introductions. The purpose was clear, the energy collective.

Through these convivial encounters, the idea of belonging, usually tied to one's own city or community, began to shift. Many local football fans found themselves joining the celebrations of Argentina, Portugal, Brazil and other teams, forming spontaneous alliances in the spirit of the moment. Their support wasn't just symbolic; it shaped how space was used and shared (Amin, 2008; Lefebvre, 1991). For a few hours, they were part of something global, injecting their presence into another nation's celebration. At the same time, some foreign fans found their own ways to blend into the local context. A few wore the traditional Qatari thobe but modified it, adding their own national colours or football-related symbols. It was a quiet gesture, a subtle way of blending cultures and showing respect while still holding on to personal identity. These interactions between locals and visitors pushed back against fixed ideas of national or cultural identity. What emerged instead was something more fluid, a shared sense of being part of a global community (Hall, 1990), at least for a little while. As De Certeau (1988) would say, this was a practiced place, a space rewritten through action. Fokdal (2008) reminds us that space is not only physical but also a reflection of how people move, gather and connect. The fans who filled Souq Waqif may not have fully understood its formal structures or rules, but their presence left a mark. They created a version of the Souq that didn't quite follow the script, and that, in itself, was a kind of authorship.

Conclusion

This study examined how a global sporting event, set within a distinctive cultural and urban context, reshaped public life in overlooked ways. Focusing on Souq Waqif during the 2022 FIFA World Cup, I asked how an everyday, historically rooted place becomes a stage for new encounters, emotions and uses when an extraordinary event arrives. Unlike tightly programed Fan Festivals, the Souq's design stayed open and largely unstructured, allowing it to absorb, reflect and even redirect the rhythms of celebration and interaction. The point is not architecture alone but practiced space: walkable routes, intimate corners and semi-permeable thresholds invited people in while fans, locals, workers and wanderers co-produced meaning through movement, gesture, sound and mood.

Across fieldwork, fleeting, routinised and convivial encounters overlapped to form a layered social landscape. The framework also helped read local responses to a sudden influx of visitors in spatial terms: some joined chants and celebrations; others skirted the bustle; some adjusted their routines and a few withdrew to quieter edges. These responses shifted with crowd size, time of day and match outcomes. Looking ahead, future work could pair these observations with lenses such as Ap and Crompton's (1993) typology of residents' responses to tourism (embracement, tolerance, adjustment and withdrawal) to trace how people adapt, resist or reshape such spaces over time.

Of course, event-time connection is real but often short-lived. As Allport (1954) cautioned, contact alone is not a cure-all for cultural understanding. Even so, brief encounters can leave a mark when they occur in places that invite lingering, watching and low-stakes engagement. In that sense, the design and management of public space, including its openness, cues, and sensory texture, help decide which interactions become possible.

Design implications for future mega-event public spaces emerge clearly from Souq Waqif. First, support *permeability*: broad promenades with many entries and clear sightlines help circulation and reduce friction when crowds swell. Second, offer *graded edges*: shallow steps, ledges and alcoves create micro-stages for chants and photos without blocking flow. Third, allow *temporary appropriation*: flexible furnishings and light-touch territorial markers let fan clusters form and dissolve. Fourth, provide *soft management*: visible but non-intrusive staff at thresholds can redirect movement while keeping the space feeling open. Fifth, mix *programmed and unprogrammed zones*: nearby seating, shade, restrooms and affordable food support lingering while leaving central corridors free for performance and rivalry. Sixth, curate *symbolic overlays*: flags, lighting and wayfinding that celebrate many teams can signal a shared event identity while acknowledging difference. These features do not script behaviour. They create conditions in which conviviality is likely, conflict is less likely to escalate and the space can hold both unity and distinction. In short, design for emergence rather than for a single anticipated use.

These suggestions come from what I observed in the Souq. When chants and photos gathered around alcoves, the small steps and ledges mattered; they let people pause without blocking others, which is the value of graded edges. Where entries were wide, crowds spilled and rejoined with little friction; that shows why permeability helps. At narrow turns, a few staff quietly redirecting movement kept things calm; that is soft management. In practice, the city and Souq managers handle circulation, edges and wayfinding. Tenants and vendors can add light, colour and movable pieces. Event organisers and security staff guide the crowd. These are small, doable actions and they make sense beyond the tournament. Importantly, this is not a copied fan zone. Souq Waqif is an existing hub that carries a feeling of authenticity and can adapt to event needs without losing itself.

These observations invite deeper questions: How lasting are these shifts in spatial practice? What kind of urban public life remains once the flags come down and visitors go home? Souq Waqif offers no simple answers, yet it shows that temporary spaces of joy and difference can open possibilities that, while not permanent, are worth remembering and learning from.

References

Allport, G. W. (1954). *The nature of prejudice*. Perseus.

Amin, A. (2008). Collective culture and urban public space. *City*, *12*(1), 5–24. https://doi.org/10.1080/13604810801933495

Baade, R. A., & Matheson, V. A. (2016). Going for the gold: The economics of the Olympics. *The Journal of Economic Perspectives*, *30*(2), 201–218. https://doi.org/10.1257/jep.30.2.201

Baudelaire, C. (1964). *The painter of modern life, and other essays* J. Mayne, Trans. Phaidon.

Benjamin, W. (2003). On some motifs in Baudelaire. In E. Jephcott, H. Eiland, & M. W. Jennings (Eds.), *Walter Benjamin: Selected writings, Vol. 4, 1938–1940*. (pp. 313–315). Harvard University Press.

Blokland, T., Vief, R., Krüger, D., & Schultze, H. (2023). Roots and routes in neighbourhoods: Length of residence, belonging and public familiarity in Berlin, Germany. *Urban Studies*, *60*(16), 3158–3176. https://doi.org/10.1177/00420980221136960

Boykoff, J. (2016). *Power games: A political history of the Olympics*. Verso.

Carmona, M. (2010). *Public places, urban spaces: The dimensions of urban design*. Architectural Press/Elsevier.

Clayton, J. (2009). Thinking spatially: Towards an everyday understanding of inter-ethnic relations. *Social & Cultural Geography*, *10*(4), 481–498. https://doi.org/10.1080/14649360902853288

De Certeau, M. (1988). *The practice of everyday life*. University of California Press.

Dun, S. (2023). The game is still beautiful without beer: Qatar 2022's new model for alcohol availability at the FIFA World Cup. *Journal of Arabian Studies*, *13*, 195–218. https://doi.org/10.4324/9781003618942-11

Durkheim, E. (1964). *The division of labor in society*. Free Press.

Ehrkamp, P. (2006). "We Turks are no Germans": Assimilation discourses and the dialectical construction of identities in Germany. *Environment and Planning A*, *38*(9), 1673–1692. https://doi.org/10.1068/a38148

Fokdal, J. (2008). *Power and space: Appropriation of space in social housing in Copenhagen*. LIT Verlag.

Foucault, M. (1986). Of other spaces. *Diacritics*, *16*(1), 22–27.

Gehl, J. (1987). *Life between buildings*. Van Nostrand Reinhold.

Giulianotti, R. (2002). Supporters, followers, fans, and flâneurs. *Journal of Sport & Social Issues*, *26*(1), 25–46. https://doi.org/10.1177/0193723502261003

Hall, S. (1990). Cultural identity and diaspora. In J. Rutherford (Ed.), *Identity: Community, culture, difference* (pp. 222–237). Lawrence & Wishart.

Horgan, M. (2017). Mundane mutualities: Solidarity and strangership in everyday life. In S. Oosterlynck, N. Schuermans, & M. Loopmans (Eds.), *Place, diversity and solidarity* (pp. 19–31). Routledge.

Jain, S. (2023). Resistance and reform as responses to human rights criticism: Relativism at FIFA World Cup Qatar 2022. *German Law Journal*, *24*(9), 1691–1702. https://doi.org/10.1017/glj.2023.119

Khaled, S. M., & Gray, R. (2019). Depression in migrant workers and Nationals of Qatar: An exploratory cross-cultural study. *International Journal of Social Psychiatry*, *65*(5), 354–367. https://doi.org/10.1177/0020764019850589

Lefebvre, H. (1991). *The production of space* (D. Nicholson-Smith, Trans.). Blackwell.

Lofland, L. H. (1998). *The public realm: Exploring the city's quintessential social territory*. Aldine De Gruyter.

Low, S., & Smith, N. (Eds.). (2013). *The politics of public space*. Taylor & Francis.

Low, S. M., & Altman, I. (1992). Place attachment: A conceptual inquiry. In I. Altman & S. M. Low (Eds.), *Place attachment: Human behavior and environment* (pp. 1–12). Plenum Press.

Moradi-Lakeh, M., Toumi, A., Khalifa, S. E., Doctor, H. V., Alyafei, S., Al Hamad, S. K., Al-Thani, M., & Rashidian, A. (2023). Core health indicators in countries with high proportion of expatriates: Case study of Qatar. *Frontiers in Public Health, 11*. https://doi.org/10.3389/fpubh.2023.1035686

Müller, M. (2015). The mega-event syndrome: Why so much goes wrong in mega-event planning and what to do about it. *Journal of the American Planning Association*, *81*(1), 6–17. https://doi.org/10.1080/01944363.2015.1038292

Peterson, M. (2017). Living with difference in hyper-diverse areas: How important are encounters in semi-public spaces? *Social & Cultural Geography*, *18*(8), 1067–1085. https://doi.org/10.1080/14649365.2016.1210667

Pløger, J. (2010). Presence-experiences: The eventalisation of urban space. *Environment and Planning D: Society and Space*, *28*(5), 848–866. https://doi.org/10.1068/d1009

Project for Public Spaces. (2000). *How to turn a place around: A handbook for creating successful public spaces*. Project for Public Spaces.

Salama, A. M., Azzali, S., & Wiedmann, F. (2017). The everyday urban environment of migrant labourers in Gulf cities: The case of the old centre of Doha, Qatar. *City, Territory and Architecture*, *4*(1). https://doi.org/10.1186/s40410-017-0061-5

Sennett, R. (1986). *The fall of public man*. Faber.

Simmel, G. (1971). *On individuality and social forms*. University of Chicago Press.

Terruhn, J., & Ye, J. (2022). Encountering neighbors: Coexisting with difference in Auckland's Avondale. *Urban Geography*, *43*(4), 613–631. https://doi.org/10.1080/02723638.2021.1883922

Timmermans, S., & Tavory, I. (2012). Theory construction in qualitative research. *Sociological Theory*, *30*(3), 167–186. https://doi.org/10.1177/0735275112457914

Valentine, G. (2008). Living with difference: Reflections on geographies of encounter. *Progress in Human Geography*, *32*(3), 323–337. https://doi.org/10.1177/0309133308089372

Wann, D. L. (1995). Preliminary validation of the Sport Fan Motivation Scale. *Journal of Sport & Social Issues*, *19*(4), 377–396. https://doi.org/10.1177/019372395019004004

Watson, S. (2006). *City publics: The (dis)enchantments of urban encounter*. Routledge.

Wireman, P. (1984). *Urban neighborhoods, networks, and families: New forms for old values*. Lexington.

Ye, J. (2019). Re-orienting geographies of urban diversity and coexistence: Analyzing inclusion and difference in public space. *Progress in Human Geography*, *43*(3), 478–495. https://doi.org/10.1177/0309132518768405

Chapter 12

Staging the Magic in Harry Potter Tourism: The Interplay of Fan-Driven and Franchise-Regulated Heritage and Placemaking Practices in Denmark and the United Kingdom

Sofie Stobberup

Independent Researcher, Denmark

Abstract

Tourism sites are increasingly recognised as places where heritage is actively produced, negotiated and felt. This chapter examines how Harry Potter tourism as 'fan design' transforms everyday spaces into affective heritage through interplays of fan initiative and institutional control. The term 'fan design' here refers to the way fans themselves design experiences through grassroots practices and performances and how experiences and locations are designed with fans in mind. Based on repeat fieldwork from 2016 to 2024, the author compares Harry Potter fan tourism sites in the United Kingdom and a fantasy festival in Odense, Denmark. 'Platform 9¾' shows how a once unscripted ritual was absorbed into franchised choreography. Alnwick Castle offers flexible integration of screen heritage within a Grade I listed site. The city of Oxford reveals how infrastructural redesign choreographs fan encounters alongside academic rhythms. Edinburgh's fan sites function as participatory ruins sustained by shared imagination, while Odense reworks Potteresque cues into a civic fantasy frame without franchise-licencing. Across these cases, fan practices operate as site-specific affective labour that challenges the narrowness of Authorised Heritage

Bridging Design and Fandom, 181–196

doi:10.1108/978-1-80592-659-720261012

Discourse (Smith, 2006). This chapter demonstrates how media tourism increasingly emerges as an ongoing negotiation between fantasy and material infrastructure, where fan belief, performance repetition and local constraints shape heritage-making in real time.

Keywords: Harry Potter; heritage; media tourism; fieldwork; fan design

Introduction: From Everyday to Elevated Fan Design in Tourism

My fieldwork in media tourism began in 2016 at King's Cross, London, where personal and fictional timelines intersected since the first Harry Potter book was released nearly 30 years ago. As a small-town girl from Denmark, newly arrived in the metropole, I was quick to seek out a familiar space: a station. One corner of the concourse offered an alternative to real-world travel: an imagined departure to Hogwarts. Fans queued by an installation curated as franchise design with a luggage trolley embedded in a wall beneath a 'Platform 9¾' sign to engage in a 'ritual' photo performance predating the site's formalisation as a tourist attraction. 'Platform 9¾' first gained a presence at the station in 2007, during a major council redevelopment of the station. A temporary trolley and sign were placed in different spots around the station (Stobberup, 2018), but in 2012, 'Platform 9¾' was installed in a more tourist-friendly location requiring no train ticket, alongside a Warner-themed gift shop, timed to align with the opening of the *Warner Bros. Studio Tour* located at Leavesden Studios. 'Platform 9¾' demonstrates how fandoms 'create social structures, ecologies, rituals and traditions of their own' (Duffett, 2013, p. 17) and how fans participate in 'affective-interpretive practices that define material space for them' (2013, p. 227). However, it also exemplifies franchise-controlled attractions that carefully balance immersion, safety, fan agency and brand control. All these pressures increasingly play out in the private studio tour's event-based content, themed architecture, crowd circulation and signage (Stobberup, 2026). A decade later, the semi-public 'Platform 9¾' remains an illustrative case of how fans create a 'spatial expression of their textual imaginations' (Peaslee, 2011, p. 42) and how certain places function as 'fantasylands' where the 'tourist gaze' and 'media gaze' overlap (Urry & Larsen, 2011, p. 116). 'Platform 9¾' has evolved into a carefully managed tourist site, altering space and the emotional and spatial participation it affords (Gibson, 2015). The original presence of fans at King's Cross was not expected but emerged almost by chance (Lee, 2012). Fans came seeking a symbolic threshold, a place made real through imagination (Reijnders, 2011). Before a formal installation existed, fans improvised by wandering platforms or posing by yellow-brick walls (Larsen, 2015; Stobberup, 2018). However, what began as speculative play, partly canonised by Rowling, has become a choreographed encounter. Visitors today queue behind barriers to pose with props and be photographed by Warner-staff. Photos can be purchased in the shop, thereby reconfiguring experience as product. This reinforces a critical point, namely how franchise-based Potter tourism is shaped by access for those who can afford it (Martens, 2019, p. 86).

Departing from King's Cross, this chapter builds on my pre-pandemic fieldwork and new observations to compare franchise-design to other fan design in Potter-related sites across the United Kingdom and one complementary Danish case. All represent increasingly regulated yet affectively rich heritage spaces chosen to illustrate a spectrum of governance structures from public to private and their impact on fan participation and design. I demonstrate how fan practices as grassroots production (Jenkins, 2012) become embedded in strategic heritage placemaking, and how legal, spatial, and institutional constraints reshape emotional participation over time. My approach draws on Barbara Kirschenblatt-Gimblett's notion of heritage as performance; partly virtual, partly material (1998) and on Laurajane Smith's emphasis on emotional labour involved in co-producing heritage sites (2021). These perspectives help me treat visits as not just observational events but embedded fieldwork (inspired by Månsson, 2011; Reijnders, 2011), where affective fan practices are seen as heritage-making in real time, influencing placemaking and design.

Theoretical Framing: Fan Design as Affective Heritage

My long-term fieldwork reveals how certain locations, through placemaking (Lew, 2017), take on significance as both national territory and 'cult geography' (Hills, 2002). Initially, I noticed how Potter-tourism offered a magical bond between the United Kingdom and its international fans during the transitional Brexit-period. Since 2016, the research field of media tourism has matured (Reijnders, 2020; Reijnders et al., 2024; Waysdorf, 2021; Williams, 2018), allowing me to frame my findings within a broader narrative of fan- and heritage studies.

Fans have long left imaginative footprints as creative reconfigurations of space at fan 'pilgrimage' destinations (Aden, 1999; Alderman, 2016; Kruse, 2005). Fan studies offers a vital lens for understanding how heritage is performed and felt, especially in the wake of the pandemic, where media tourism reached 'unparalleled heights' (Reijnders et al., 2024, p. 5). Critical heritage theory helps make these dynamics explicit, as I argue that Kirschenblatt-Gimblett's notion of cultural survival depending '…on intangible cultural property, which lives in performance' (1998, p. 166) resonates well with elements of fan practice. Smith's work on heritage-making as affective practice (following Wetherell, 2012) also fills in some blanks, especially her emphasis on emotional 'memory and identity work' at heritage sites (Smith, 2021, p. 2), which I find useful when mapping a 'Potteresque' heritage design trail.

Inspired by Anja Saretzki's studies on literary trails (2013), I understand heritage as traditional practice always encoded in local conditions. Saretzki shows how local encodings can be stabilised by global discourses or 'stories' (like Harry Potter), but how heritage can also be detached, reinterpreted and reshaped through tourist practices. The question is which readings come to dominate

(2013, p. 61). In recent years, the Potter-discourse has fractured due to Rowling's political public statements, which may affect how fans and tourist stakeholders engage with the franchise in the future. While this has not been my main focus (see Williams, 2025), it illustrates how competing readings and design practices coexist as a 'struggle' reminiscent of when activist or grassroots fan practices more actively counter what Smith has described as Authorised Heritage Discourse (AHD). AHD '…focuses attention on aesthetically pleasing material objects, sites, places and/or landscapes that current generations "must" care for […] to forge a sense of common identity based on the past. One consequence of the AHD is that it defines who the legitimate spokespersons for the past are' (Smith, 2006, p. 29). Smith argues that the AHD draws on too narrow a sense of what heritage means. Following her recent theorisation of emotional memory-work (2021), I use field data to describe the ways affective practices of fan culture might challenge this narrowness of the AHD at specific sites.

With the extensive Potter-case, I aim to highlight physical aspects of the otherwise more symbolic power of media franchises (Couldry, 2002). A core feature of media franchises is that concepts like 'place' and 'culture' are not tied exclusively to physical locations but also to fictional and virtual environments (Urry & Larsen, 2011, p. 118). This recalls Kirschenblatt-Gimblett's somewhat 'prophetic' reflection on how heritage might be experienced in a media-saturated world: 'A key to heritage productions is their virtuality, whether in the presence or absence of actualities' (1998, p. 166). My study of physical sites helps demonstrate how media tourism must increasingly balance fantasy and imagination (virtualities) with material design and infrastructure (actualities). After heavy media consumption during COVID-19, fans were again inspired to travel. At many destinations, design structures have been created to limit interaction, and this new norm, catalysed by media, raises questions about the potential and sustainability of media tourism and how the field continues to change over time (Reijnders et al., 2024).

I explore these multi-facetted questions through field data by investigating how sites are experienced through multiple overlays of meaning as Potter-landmarks but also as part of broader histories, heritage narratives and media discourses and how tourist design must balance these competing layers. I aim to show how different forms of design might intersect in such spaces: fan design, where fans as 'textual poachers' (Jenkins, 2012 [1992]) curate and reimagine places into media collages or montages (Friedberg, 2006), and institutional design, where stakeholders manage flows of visitors, enforcing 'design-as-barrier' restrictions to protect their interests. As Kirschenblatt-Gimblett reminds us, installations on location, however mimetic, are never neutral (1998, p. 20). While she primarily refers to museum exhibitions, one question remains: what about the restrictions and design features now increasingly dominating fan 'pilgrimage' sites that were never planned top-down like museums?

With that in mind, I narrow down what *fan design* means in the context of media tourism in relation to fan agency, affective labour and corporate control (Martens, 2019) and argue that the layering of meanings and interplay between fan and institutional design, when further shaped by 'virtualities' like imagination, online virality and spreadable media (Jenkins et al., 2013), together might challenge the 'narrowness' of the AHD (Smith, 2006). Perhaps the versatility of the fan concept mentioned by Henry Jenkins (2012, p. xiv) also holds true for design. I use the broad range of fan designs to map important intersections between fandom, heritage and media discourse.

This study takes a comparative and long-term approach, covering Potter-sites from 2016–2024. As the franchise maintained its cultural momentum after my initial research, I revisited several field locations in 2023–2024 to document changes during the renewed tourist boom. Returning to sites to sense physical dimensions proved crucial not only for fans but also for this researcher. Each site was visited between 3 and 5 times, and most data were collected as field observation although go-along interviews with participants and tour guides were often possible during walking tours between stops (recorded as fieldnotes, not audio). By also revisiting early field material, I follow a line of theory from my residential fields of art history and museum studies, where research and experience is understood as performative or more-than-visual, especially in tourism (Edensor, 2018; Urry & Larsen, 2011). While anthropological fieldwork is often dialogue-oriented, my focus is the design of experiences, approached from a situated, bodily perspective. Building on my early experiments with sensory ethnography (Pink, 2009), my current work aligns more with performative cultural analysis, as I combine the engaged position of the researcher-as-fan with an almost 'activist' positioning *in medias res*, collecting 'snapshots' of life-worlds as data. My research design was developed during the introduction of GDPR legislation, which heightened awareness of ethical data storage. I anonymised dialogue from the outset, avoided collecting too personal details and clarified my purpose before photographing, always respecting privacy. During tours, I let guides determine how I was introduced to participants, stressing my role as observer rather than evaluator. This transparency proved important in competitive environments, where staff encounter critical journalists and visitors. Visits and findings were later organised by theme in NVivo, and all references to field observations in this chapter are taken from photographs and notes with some quotes translated from Danish.

Alnwick Castle as Hybrid Heritage-Fandom Space

Alnwick Castle, used for Hogwarts exteriors in the first two *Harry Potter* films, offers a flexible model for integrating fan heritage in its branding. The castle is a Grade 1 listed heritage site but embraces its cinematic identity alongside its historic role as the seat of the Dukes of Northumberland for 900 years. Its walls have served as backdrop for other popular screen culture like *Downton Abbey*, and this dual identity is built into the spatial organization, event programming and promotion, where the place is shown as a versatile cultural arena. Activities range from Potter-inspired broomstick training on a lawn and mediaeval-themed games in Artisan's Courtyard to guided film location tours. The castle curates varied, accessible experiences that align with broader narrative goals. Prior knowledge of Harry Potter is unnecessary. Rather, it is used as catalyst for telling several stories.

Situated far from London, Alnwick attracts many domestic rather than international tourists. I visited in 2018 during a bus tour and returned by motorcycle in 2024. My fieldwork demonstrates how the visitor experience remains co-produced by fans, staff and the setting itself. In 2018, I noticed the visual clash of hat-wearing *Downton Abbey* fans and cloak-wearing *Harry Potter* fans. Their coexistence showed how the castle accommodates different registers of engagement (Smith, 2021, p. 5) and operates with a strategic media policy (Reijnders et al., 2024, p. 4). This dynamic persisted on 31 July 2024, Harry Potter's fictional birthday, when I met a fan timing her visit to symbolically match the date. Like the recently cancelled 'Back to Hogwarts' September 1st event at King's Cross, this temporal alignment helps turn the site into a lived interface between fiction and reality.

The castle's layout with open lawns and courtyards supports cinematic play. It allows one's gaze to travel, when sitting on the soft grass that invites relaxation and reflection, especially in the late afternoons when families and schools give way to other visitors. The layout also effectively generates temporary micro-communities. In 2018, I joined a solo-travelling fan for broomstick training and creative photography to experience how a casual encounter might reveal the emotional intimacy of spontaneous fan bonding. Such moments underscore the relationality of fan design and how affect can be produced intersubjectively. While the site's facilities clearly support the activities and provides scenic spaces for play, I encountered visitors creating their own variations. These unscripted performances added to the atmosphere in subtle ways, when a wizarding robe was fluttering across the lawn, or a family improvised a broomstick from sticks and scarves. In 2018, a group of young women staged wand performances not based on specific film scenes but simply to 'look cool with the castle in the background'. Such self-authored moments suggest that fan engagement can be less about replicating canon and more about aesthetic co-presence where the castle functions as co-actor in visual storytelling and heritage-making. These practices move beyond using the design as intended and approach the realm of fan creativity, where participants reimagine and repurpose the setting to fit their own personal narratives. Interplays between designed experiences and fan-led improvisations here exemplify the dual meaning of 'fan design'.

Production details revealed during the official 'On Location' tour added narrative depth. A guide explained how filmmakers matched Alnwick's yellow stone for sets in Leavesden, helping blur boundaries between fan sites, fiction and material reality, as fans could recall the visual expression from films and studio tour experiences. Storytelling here demonstrates a wish to mark Alnwick as a defining feature of Hogwarts semiotics. The tour in 2018 playfully ended with: 'We are the real Hogwarts and everyone else are just pretenders', delivered with a smile, yet indicating competitive assumption among sites. In 2024, the tour was an even more technical film walkthrough, demonstrating further potential of in situ storytelling. The turn reflects a growing emphasis on behind-the-scenes knowledge and perhaps a repositioning towards fan fascination with the film production culture in media tourism also evident in the studio tour. Historical narratives also expanded between my visits, particularly favouring the working-class heritage trend. The Percy family (the owners), long tied to the Wars of the Roses, featured more prominently in 2024. An audio installation linked family heritage to *Game of Thrones*, thus artfully showing how history can be amplified by pop culture, not erased by it, as local heritage is never completely overwritten by fandom practices.

Though Harry Potter was introduced to Quidditch on Alnwick's lawn, official references to the franchise must be avoided due to risk of copyright infringement. 'Broomstick training' is an activity designed to evoke the films without breaching copyright. In 2018, sessions were informal with humorous references aimed at adults. In 2024, they were more structured, requiring timed free tickets, and many participants were children. While inspired by the film iconography, instructors avoided direct film quotes like the 'Up!' command, to stay within Intellectual Property boundaries. When staff use unbranded language and the gift shop makes it clear how official merchandise requires special licencing, it points to creative, economic and legal restraints. In 2018, I also reflected on staff's potential worry about the storytelling being copied. While I found such concerns slightly misplaced, since the 'On Location' tour would only work well in situ, and ground access required a ticket, it led to an important finding: storytelling itself is a form of emotional capital to be owned and protected in media tourism. However, this is more evident in public fan spaces (urban environments) than the private castle grounds.

With its adaptiveness, Alnwick exemplifies how symbolic recognition can be preserved through suggestion rather than direct citation. It shows how immersive theming can become a primary design language in various ways by demonstrating how the castle functions as hybrid space by simultaneously acting as a privately owned heritage site, cinematic icon and platform for fan-driven improvisation. Compared to franchise-branded sites, the fan design is more open-ended with room for local stories. This dynamic flexibility makes Alnwick a valuable example of how affective fan engagement and local heritage management can work together.

Oxford as a Fan(tasy) City

Oxford appears no longer just as a university city but also a composite fan(tasy) city, where literary heritage from *Harry Potter*, *Alice in Wonderland*, *The Lord of the Rings* (LoTR) and *The Chronicles of Narnia* coexist in an experience-driven landscape shaped by selective storytelling. During fieldwork in 2018 and 2024, I observed how this layering reveals a persistent tension between academic authority and popular-cultural appropriation in tourist experience design with attempts to balance institutional legacy and fan expectations.

In 2018, I experienced the Oxford Visitor Centre as a gateway space in Broad Street curating 'Britishness' as multi-referential heritage by displaying merchandise from *Downton Abbey*, *Inspector Morse*, *LoTR*, *Harry Potter* and *Alice in Wonderland*. In 2024, the visitor centre function had shifted to a private actor with exclusive products branding the university city itself because Experience Oxfordshire had withdrawn during the pandemic due to lack of funding (Experience Oxfordshire, n.d.). In addition, the Oxford city centre had become more pedestrian-friendly. Transformation was particularly evident at Christ Church College, which had undergone a complete redesign of visitor infrastructure due to increased visitor numbers. In 2018, the Great Hall inspiring Hogwarts and actual filming locations were accessed mainly through guided tours ending in a crowded shop in the mediaeval Chapter House. That space has now been restored as heritage (Christ Church, Oxford, 2024), and a visitor centre was constructed nearby inside the former stables in the Meadow (Purcell Architecture, n.d.). During my 2024-visit, this was described by staff as a pandemic-era intervention, but further research revealed a strategy of distancing tourism infrastructure from the core heritage site by housing ticketing, toilets and Harry Potter merchandise in the separate building. I discovered how access was further regulated with tickets costing £16 compared to £7 in 2012 (BBC News, 2012). A sign marked 'sold out today' illustrated a shift to pre-booking, and further crowd management was demonstrated by visitors being held behind ropes at the Great Hall staircase while awaiting re-opening after student lunch. I noticed how some fans would rush up the stairs as barriers were removed, possibly driven by emotional primacy of the moment or just a desire for unspoiled photos. I reflected on how this moment felt almost choreographed, like the Great Hall entry at the studio tour, which illustrates how movement itself can be somewhat affectively scripted or designed. Once inside, fans performed touristic photo rituals while still encountering the site as a functioning academic space. I overheard someone ask whether the Hall was still in use, and staff replied, 'Lunch was just served'. Fiction and function thus coexist, and the friction between institutional rhythm and fan desire became an integrated part of the experience.

Unlike immersive franchise designs or Oxford's playful walking tours where fans are sorted into houses or re-enact Malfoy being turned into a ferret at New College, Christ Church remains an ambivalent space. It is formally silent, inviting visitors to 'sensitively enjoy' the setting, but fan energy animates the space during moments like the staircase rush, revealing how design must sometimes restrain and sometimes invite. Perhaps the new building in the Meadow can be interpreted as a material sign of an academic institution still strategically negotiating its magical legacy.

My fieldnotes echo a 2012-article referencing 'the Harry Potter factor' in Oxford (BBC News, 2012), describing the university architecture operating as an aesthetic buffer by allowing fans to project Hogwarts symbolism onto various spaces; a gaze reminiscent of what Jane Lovell refers to as 'magi-heritage' (2021). Even locations unrelated to the films are reframed as visual inspiration, where authenticity is based on aesthetic resemblance. Oxford's fan tourism here functions within a broader 'touristscape' (Saretzki, 2013, p. 64), where storytelling is outsourced to private guides blending historical fact with popular myth. For example, in one walking tour, grotesques on the Bodleian façade were linked to Dumbledore's office. As fan design, tours must increasingly adapt to institutional and logistical constraints. In 2024, timed entry fragmented the group experience, as guides had to remain outside while participants explored the Hogwarts 'hospital wing' inside the Bodleian. Outside the quiet library, rival guides competed for command of sonic space. Here, the challenges of overtourism became evident, but it points to design as not just a form of architecture: it is a matter of choreography and control of people's attention.

Oxford now appears as a differential fandom city, where institutional and informal actors must navigate the 'HP factor'. When I asked which other UK cities were benefitting from this, a guide jokingly said that if a city wants to kick-start its tourism, 'it had better be related to Harry Potter'. This remark captures how fan discourse challenges AHD and becomes economic currency. From a design research perspective, Oxford here reveals how tourist infrastructure is shaped by access, flow, spatial governance and ideological framing, as locations are never passive backdrops (Kirschenblatt-Gimblett 1998, p. 20). A conversation overheard in Oxford Visitor Centre in 2018 serves as a reminder of this: 'People think it's an amusement park, but it's not. It's a school. A workplace!'. This remark by a woman complaining to staff shows how local actors must always negotiate their roles in a city currently defined by excessive cultural capital mixed with fan desire.

Edinburgh's Fan Sites as Participatory 'Ruins'

Travelling north to Scotland, it is possible to encounter Greyfriars Kirkyard in the heart of Edinburgh's Old Town. Like the urban area around King's Cross, it is a curious 'threshold' of heritage, mourning, myth and literary remembrance. J.K. Rowling wrote in this city, perhaps overlooking the Kirkyard from a café, and the area has now become a dense node in the fan-cultural city-mapping. A few streets from Greyfriars, the Elephant House Café gained fame as the 'birthplace of Harry Potter', and during my 2017-visit I noted, how 'fans were celebrating their spot at table 12, where Rowling supposedly wrote her books'. I witnessed how a fan would move to a different chair after carefully observing a Rowling-illustration on the menu card, only to leave before ordering after photographing the window view of the Kirkyard and Edinburgh Castle. What stood out most, however, were toilet walls covered floor to ceiling in fan graffiti with inside jokes and spells such as 'lumos' and 'nox' on the light switch. I had hoped to revisit in 2024, as I considered it an uncurated repository archive of shared affective investment, but when I arrived, fire damage had sealed off the entrance since 2021. Surprisingly, the bright red façade and 'birthplace' signage still drew fans for selfies. This demonstrates how fan heritage can persist through erasure, as the site retains its place on Edinburgh's fan map. Meanwhile, a temporary café with a matching red façade has opened in the colourful Victoria Street ('Diagon Alley'), which raises an interesting point: If a site's power is semiotic rather than spatial, it may endure not just through physical access but through a form of imaginative fandom 'gravity' as both a place of imagination (Reijnders, 2011) and memory site (Nora, 1989). The café was never franchise-licenced or part of a literary AHD, but as fan site, it remains powerful because it is still believed in.

The same can be said about the Kirkyard. Unlike King's Cross, it was never a filming location, but draws fan attention due to atmosphere and gravestones, especially that of Thomas Riddell, a name linked to Voldemort. The association is hypothetical, but the effect is real, as the site remains a fan design without instruction or a form of speculative heritage without franchise endorsement. My documented visits between 2017 and 2024 show the Kirkyard as a fan site emerging from bottom-up desire, not top-down design. In 2017, the space functioned as an affective micro-ritual zone without barriers. Fans paused quietly and perhaps took a photo. I could easily do the same. The next year, that rhythm was shifting, as discrete barriers had appeared, and a protective geogrid been placed on the ground. In 2024, fencing surrounded not only the Riddell gravestone but entire sections of Greyfriars, directing groups around each other. As I noted one evening: '…there is wear and tear and fencing all over the churchyard', and the next morning: 'guided tours arrive like pearls on a string'. Guides waited for other groups to move on, operating in close succession and in multiple languages, and competed for sonic dominance like in Oxford.

My earliest photos show an unobstructed view through the gates of the adjacent private school, which some guides linked to inspiration for the Hogwarts houses. In 2024, that view was blocked, but fans tried to peek through a hole. I wanted to replicate earlier photos for barrier comparison, but crowd density made it impossible. Change was not merely logistical but altered the feel of the space. To me, it seemed to not just be about lost sightlines or increased group noise, as the Kirkyard was no longer performed solely by fans as a place of imagination (Reijnders, 2011) but also by the tourist design system they were now navigating. While the Kirkyard retains symbolic charge due to its *genius loci* (Norberg-Schulz, 1980), the once semi-private, improvised fan pilgrimage site felt saturated to the point of containment, affectively and physically. Unlike the commercial 'Platform 9¾', the shift stems from a more accumulated usage by guided groups, not franchise intervention. The site's appeal might lie in its lack of official franchise design, as it can still be visited for free, but informal fan practices have still been institutionalised through barriers and pacing systems that facilitate an emerging visitor choreography or affective rhythm. Except the geogrid, most barriers appear improvised and shaped by the site's general heritage status as kirkyard. This development raises important questions of sustainability at fan sites (see Jones, in this collection), as they parallel my 2024 observation of increased barrier use at Lacock Abbey alongside attempts to visually downplay the Potter-connection there.

Edinburgh illustrates a remarkable durability of fan myth. Fan sites quietly resist and coexist alongside more heavily promoted commercial film heritage, suggesting that fan practices gain meaning not only through specific institutional design but also shared imagination and repeated affective performance, here enabled by fans speculatively retracing creative inspirational sources for the iconic magical universe.

The City of Odense as Fanfiction

Fandom spaces can be divided into commercial and organic places (Duffett, 2013, p. 226) or what I refer to as historically and commercially authentic sites, though these often overlap, because some fan tourism sites mix highly commercial and less commercial spaces (Williams, 2018). This is also evident in author-icon cities (Bom, 2015), where the organic place becomes a branded platform of literary heritage.

Like Edinburgh and Oxford, the final case, the Danish city of Odense, is both a literary cradle (birthplace of fairy-tale poet Hans Christian Andersen) and a strategic cultural branding site. What is interesting is the missing link to the UK franchise although Rowling visited Odense in 2010 to receive an Andersen Award. Still, alongside Andersen's heritage, Odense has hosted Rowling's parallel magical universe since 2002, when the local library launched a Harry Potter festival during autumn break. Initiated by librarian Søren Dahl Mortensen, it drew on theatrical learning methods and 'Renaissance children's play' observed in Florence (Lerche, 2018). The festival began small with children aged 8–12 and continued with official approval as long as it remained non-commercial.

Fifteen years later in 2017, coinciding with the global franchise relaunch under the *Wizarding World* brand, the event was deemed too commercial, as the franchise monitored not only content (events were free and child-oriented) but also indirect revenue from local hospitality. The library now had to rethink its strategy, as it could no longer use the name 'Harry Potter Festival' (DR News, 2024; Martens, 2019, p. 83). With 12,500 visitors, the festival was now a tradition for fans and locals, so in 2018, it was rebranded as *Magical Days of Odense*. This new concept still reflected a commitment to non-commercial cultural education rather than spectacle (Lerche, 2018), but franchise references became more subtle, like in Alnwick. 'Diagon Alley' became 'Elvish Alley', and cosplayers incorporated Norse mythology into their characters, drawing on local history, as Odense, after all, is named after the god, Odin. Despite this rebranding, 15,000 visitors still came in 2018 (Odense Municipality, 2018), which revealed a new creative potential.

Unlike Alnwick, the festival kept its Quidditch in 2018, since it only hosted a tournament and did not organise it. I spoke to a player and a member of audience who described the festival as 'down-to-earth Harry Potter, not high-end Harry Potter', reflecting the non-commercial nature. The festival was successful, not because it was seen as a competitor to the franchise, as fans considered it something else. Six years on, in 2024, the festival had grown further with partnerships from local businesses and national arts foundations. With over 22,000 visitors (Odense Municipality, 2024), it had indeed outgrown its original wizarding robe, and yet, many activities were the same as when I first attended (except Quidditch).

Like Alnwick, which uses the 'HP factor' to revitalise heritage, Odense has incorporated its city guard storytelling, Norse mythology and Andersen's tales to construct a revitalised place myth. Many cosplayers in 2024 were the same volunteers as when my field studies began in 2016, demonstrating strong local engagement. The festival seems to appeal to locals who might feel an 'Andersen fatigue' given the city's heavy branding around him. Fan design in Odense thus overlaps with other ways of rethinking civic identity through affective practices and public-space mediation. Like Alnwick, which structures fan engagement through playful, carnival-like formats, Odense taps into that same atmosphere. Both highlight the carnivalesque and critical potential of fan culture as play, not just on heritage grounds but in transitory urban space. Fan scholar Will Brooker calls such negotiations of real and imagined space a 'carnival, a creative use of the city that invests the real spaces with mythology and uses this crisis in the urban imaginary as a liberating breakdown of boundaries between real and fictional worlds' (Brooker, 2007, p. 441). In Odense, Brooker's point made about Vancouver overlaps with Anne Klara Bom's work on affective heritage potential in literary icon-cities (Bom, 2015).

Today, festivals undeniably remain a fan-favourite design alongside conventions (Lamerichs, 2018). As Kirschenblatt-Gimblett notes, festivals are 'cultural performances par excellence' (1998, p. 61) and share traits with the historical avant-gardes, where the 'text' matters less than the possibility of performance. Odense shows how festivals can celebrate fandom while mediating public space and identity, especially when led by volunteers or libraries rather than market actors, though both can support each other. By tracing different engagement modes and physical transformations over time, my fieldwork in Odense revealed the playful, subversive potential of festival fan design. Remarkably, the festival has now existed for more than 20 years as a parallel event to the franchise and the AHD of the icon-city, allowing fan design to both integrate with city branding and remain on its own terms.

Conclusion: Fan Practices, Placemaking and Contemporary Heritage

Upon returning to Denmark in 2018, I published preliminary findings at King's Cross in Danish, where I cautiously concluded that fan performances in Harry Potter tourism were becoming a form of cultural heritage (Stobberup, 2018, p. 122). I was not yet able to fully articulate the idea of 'Potteresque heritage', and the research paused during the pandemic. In the context of other sites explored in this chapter, I now see the wider dynamics: sites like King's Cross are layered with competing meanings (Harry Potter, history, built heritage, other media), and any tourism design must balance these overlays. In addition, different kinds of design are at play: fans, who curate and reconfigure their own 'grassroot' experiences, and institutional design by stakeholders, who manage access and protect different uses of the space.

Drawing on fieldwork, this study has shown how fan design might operate both as grassroots activity and strategic response to shifting institutional and logistical demands within the changing field of media tourism. My examples show that fan design involves more than physical markers or official branding. It is a layered cultural practice that is spatial, social and affective in its 'virtuality' and 'actuality'. It is rooted not only in commercial activity but in shared and repeated recognition, and local or situated adaptability. Fan tourists engage imaginatively in the materiality of place and contribute to how sites are interpreted, felt and remembered over time.

A central argument has been that fan design extends beyond spatial configuration (actuality) and aligns with the idea of 'imaginative heritage' (Reijnders, 2020), where symbolic meaning is activated through embodied participation. King's Cross and Greyfriars serve as early examples of 'organic' pilgrimage spaces (Duffett, 2013, p. 226), where emotional connection to place persists regardless of official framing. 'Platform 9¾' is not only a fan meeting point, but a visible sign of fans' shifting and powerful role as creative auteurs and tourists. What appears to be a playful happenstance is, in fact, the product of years of narrative layering, strategic infrastructure development and affective investment, where accidental features gain cultural meaning through repeated emotional engagement. Fan design at King's Cross becomes a soft texture within a broader place narrative of creativity, capital and infrastructural prestige or perhaps even a kind of infrastructourism. An urban 'magic' (Willim & Löfgren, 2005), where aesthetic performance blends with economic intent.

Nowadays, the real question is not whether the attraction survives, but what kind of heritage infrastructure it is being shaped into. Along with Oxford and Edinburgh, it remains a potent site of 'pilgrimage', not mainly because of curation but because fans still believe something special *happens* there. Alnwick and Odense demonstrate that even when constraints apply, hybrid adaptations can sustain emotional engagement. In a tourist era dominated by selfie culture and saturated by media, it is interesting how meaning seems to rely less on physical features than in the shared belief that a site matters, although fan preferences of course may differ.

This chapter shows how fan design emerges not as a fixed category, but as an evolving, relational process in dialogue with other heritage discourses. My aim has been to offer fan design at tourist sites as a lens for understanding new forms of cultural production. This is especially relevant as urban spaces and institutions seek to define themselves through media-derived identities that are not always rooted in the stories they would rather choose to promote or authorise. What is at stake in the future is not just the development of certain sites but the broader processes through which heritage is co-created. When fans, institutions and local actors engage or conflict over the meaning of places, they actively shape contemporary understandings of heritage. In that context, fan design functions as creative intervention, as site-specific affective practice, and sometimes also as soft resistance, which echoes Smith's argument of heritage as not only static but also emotional (Smith, 2021).

The development of Harry Potter tourism more generally, then, reflects a wider shift in how culture is produced and consumed in the 21st century. While design interventions may influence behaviour, they do not fully determine it. Fan tourism remains an ongoing negotiation between imagined worlds and physical environments and between official structures and user-driven meaning-making.

References

Aden, R. C. (1999). *Popular stories and promised lands: Fan cultures and symbolic pilgrimages*. University of Alabama Press.

Alderman, D. H. (2016). Writing on the Graceland wall: On the importance of authorship in pilgrimage landscapes. In T. L. Bell & O. Johansson (Eds.), *Sound, society and the geography of popular music* (pp. 53–66). Routledge.

BBC News. (2012, March 25). Harry Potter fans boost Oxford Christ Church Cathedral. https://www.bbc.com/news/uk-england-oxfordshire-17434129

Bom, A. K. (2015). Affective practice in the icon-city: Ownership, authenticity and fictionalization of urban space [Academic Quarter]. *Akademisk kvarter*, *11*, 35–52.

Brooker, W. (2007). Everywhere and nowhere: Vancouver, fan pilgrimage and the urban imaginary. *International Journal of Cultural Studies*, *10*(4), 423–444.

Christ Church, Oxford. (2024). *Christ Church chapter house wins Oxford preservation trust award*. https://www.chch.ox.ac.uk/news/christ-church-chapter-house-wins-oxford-preservation-trust-award

Couldry, N. (2002). *The place of media power: Pilgrims and witnesses of the media age*. Routledge.

DR News. (2024, October 28). Festivalen hvis navn, man ikke må nævne: Det minder om, da DAD ikke måtte hedde Disneyland [The festival that must not be named: It's reminiscent of when DAD was not allowed to be called Disneyland]. https://www.dr.dk/nyheder/regionale/fyn/festivalen-hvis-navn-man-ikke-maa-naevne-det-minder-om-da-dad-ikke-maatte

Duffett, M. (2013). *Understanding fandom: An introduction to the study of media fan culture*. Bloomsbury.

Edensor, T. (2018). The more-than-visual experiences of tourism. *Tourism Geographies*, *20*(5), 913–915. https://doi.org/10.1080/14616688.2018.1477172

Edinburgh News. (2016, April 8). Elephant House café in Edinburgh concedes defeat over Harry Potter graffiti. https://www.edinburghnews.scotsman.com/news/people/jk-rowling-cafe-elephant-house-concedes-graffiti-defeat-622459

Experience Oxfordshire. (n.d.). *Experience Oxfordshire announce closure of Oxford Visitor Information Centre*. https://www.experienceoxfordshire.org/experience-oxfordshire-announce-closure-of-oxford-visitor-information-centre/. Accessed on August 7, 2025.

Friedberg, A. (2006). *The virtual window: From Alberti to Microsoft* (1st paperback ed.). MIT Press.

Gibson, J. J. (2015). *The ecological approach to visual perception: Classic edition*. Psychology Press. (Original work published 1979)

Hills, M. (2002). *Fan cultures*. Routledge.

Jenkins, H. (2012). *Textual poachers: Television fans and participatory culture* (2nd ed.). Routledge.

Jenkins, H., Ford, S., & Green, J. (2013). *Spreadable media: Creating value and meaning in a networked culture*. New York University Press.

Kirshenblatt-Gimblett, B. (1998). *Destination culture: Tourism, museums, and heritage*. University of California Press.

Kruse, R. J. (2005). The Beatles as place makers: Narrated landscapes in Liverpool, England. *Journal of Cultural Geography*, *22*(2), 87–114.

Lamerichs, N. (2018). Embodied characters: The affective process of cosplay. In N. Lamerichs (Ed.), *Productive fandom: Intermediality and affective reception in fan cultures* (pp. 199–230). Amsterdam University Press.

Larsen, K. (2015). (Re)claiming Harry Potter fan pilgrimage sites. In L. S. Brenner (Red.), *Playing Harry Potter: Essays and interviews on fandom and performance* (pp. 38–54). McFarland.

Lee, C. (2012). Have magic, will travel: Tourism and Harry Potter's united (magical) kingdom. *Tourist Studies*, *12*(1), 52–69.

Lerche, A. (2018, January). Festivalen må aldrig blive kommerciel [The festival must never become commercial]. *Perspektiv: Journal of the Danish Union of Librarians*, (1), 28–31. https://moreinfo.addi.dk/2.11/more_info_get.php?lokalid=37767824&attachment_type=f56_a&bibliotek=870971&source_id=870970&key=544a2d069243ed24939e. Accessed on August 7, 2025.

Lew, A. (2017). Tourism planning and place making: Place-making or placemaking? *Tourism Geographies*, *19*(3), 448–466.

Lovell, J. (2021). Fairytale authenticity: Historic city tourism, Harry Potter, medievalism and the magical gaze. In D. Chhabra (Ed.), *Authenticity and authentication of heritage* (pp. 60–77). Routledge.

Månsson, M. (2011). Mediatized tourism. *Annals of Tourism Research*, *38*(4), 1634–1652.

Martens, M. (2019). *The forever fandom of Harry Potter: Balancing fan agency and corporate control*. Cambridge University Press.

Nora, P. (1989). Between memory and history: Les lieux de mémoire. *Representations*, *26*, 7–24.

Norberg-Schulz, C. (1980). *Genius loci: Towards a phenomenology of architecture*. Rizzoli.

Odense Municipality. (2018). *Magical Days 2018 – Effects, event, development*. Unpublished report. Odense Municipality.

Odense Municipality. (2024). *Magiske dage Odense satte rekord med 22.000 gæster* (-*Magical Days Odense broke records with 22,000 visitors*). https://www.odense.dk/presse/pressemeddelelser/pressemeddelelser-2024/magiske-dage-odense-satte-rekord-med-22000-gaester. Accessed on August 7, 2025.

Peaslee, R. M. (2011). One ring, many circles: The Hobbiton tour experience and a spatial approach to media power. *Tourist Studies*, *11*(1), 37–53.

Pink, S. (2009). *Doing sensory ethnography*. Sage.

Purcell Architecture. (n.d.). *Christ Church visitor centre*. https://purcellarchitecture.com/project/christ-church-visitor-centre/. Accessed on August 7, 2025.

Reijnders, S. (2011). *Places of the imagination: Media, tourism, culture*. Ashgate.

Reijnders, S. (2020). Imaginative heritage: Towards a holistic perspective on media, tourism, and governance. In N. van Es & S. Reijnders (Eds.), *Locating imagination in popular culture* (pp. 19–33). Routledge.

Reijnders, S., Martens, E., Nanjangud, A., Castro, D., Schiavone, R., & Póvoa, D. (2024). Introduction: Worlds of imagination. In *Media, place and tourism* (pp. 1–17). Routledge.

Saretzki, A. (2013). Literary trails, urban space and the actualization of heritage. *AlmaTourism: Journal of Tourism, Culture and Territorial Development*, *8*, 61–77.

Smith, L. (2006). *Uses of heritage*. Routledge.

Smith, L. J. (2021). *Emotional heritage: Visitor engagement at museums and heritage sites*. Routledge.

Stobberup, S. K. (2018). Der, hvor man hopper gennem muren: King's Cross som transitionsrum [Where one jumps through the wall: King's Cross as a transitional space]. In E. G. Jensen & A. S. Sørensen (Eds.), *Tilblivelser: Aktuelle kulturanalyser [Becomings: Contemporary cultural analyses]* (pp. 105–126). Syddansk Universitetsforlag.

Stobberup, S. (2026). Imagined memories and material connections: The Warner Bros. Studio Tour London – The making of Harry Potter™ as a home for a fanbase in transition. *Fandom | Cultures | Research*, *2*(2), 35–53.

Urry, J., & Larsen, J. (2011). *The tourist gaze 3.0* (3rd ed.). Sage.

Waysdorf, A. (2021). *Fan sites: Film tourism and contemporary fandom*. University of Iowa Press.

Wetherell, M. (2012). *Affect and emotion: A new social science understanding*. Sage.

Williams, R. (2018). Fan pilgrimage and tourism. In M. A. Click & S. Scott (Eds.), *The Routledge companion to media fandom* (pp. 98–106). Routledge.

Williams, R. (2025). When Hogwarts isn't always there to welcome you home: Politics and practices in Harry Potter's transmedia tourism spaces. In S. Driessen, B. Jones, & B. Litherland (Eds.), *Participatory culture wars: Controversy, conflict and complicity in fandom* (pp. 141–161). University of Iowa Press.

Willim, R., & Löfgren, O. (Eds.). (2005). *Magic, culture and the new economy* (1st ed.). Routledge.

Chapter 13

'We Are Going to Leave the World Better than We Found It'[1]: Balancing Environmental Sustainability and Affective Engagement in Screen Tourism Locations

Bethan Jones

Cardiff University, UK

Abstract

Screen tourism has become a well-established area of research given the role that films and television shows play in driving visitors to specific locations. As the film and television industry grows, however, so does the increasingly urgent question of its environmental impact. And while there are steps being taken to address what production companies can do to reduce waste or how tourism organisations can minimise their carbon footprint, the environmental impacts of *screen tourism* are underexamined. Focusing on two famous screen tourism locations – Freshwater West in Pembrokeshire, well-known to *Harry Potter* fans, and The Dark Hedges in County Antrim, used in *Game of Thrones* – this chapter examines the different approaches

[1]The quote in this chapter's title comes from the 9th episode of *Game of Thrones* season 6, 'Battle of the Bastards'. In the episode Theon and Yara Greyjoy meet Daenerys Targaryen in Meereen, where they offer her 100 ships from the Iron Fleet in exchange for her help taking back the Iron Islands. After a short discussion, Daenerys agrees, telling them 'We are going to leave the world better than we found it'. The *Game of Thrones* fans reading this know that Daenerys didn't quite fulfil that promise, but my hope is that readers will follow her initial intention to improve the world, through designing sustainable screen tourism.

Bridging Design and Fandom, 197–212

doi:10.1108/978-1-80592-659-720261013

taken to mitigating the environmental impacts of screen tourism and proposes a framework for building sustainable screen tourism into the production process while acknowledging the benefits it brings to the area and the importance of the location to fans. Drawing on participant observation and interviews, the author suggests that adopting a co-design approach where fans are involved in a more participatory way throughout the production process would be particularly relevant for properties where the values of the fandom explicitly align with a sustainability ethos.

Keywords: Fan tourism; screen tourism; co-creation; sustainable tourism; environmental sustainability; Harry Potter; Game of Thrones

Introduction

Screen tourism, a subset of media tourism and closely linked to fan tourism, happens when visitors travel to a location because it appeared in, or was used in the production of, a film or television series. Media tourism is a long running form of tourism that has since become a global industry: as Joanne Connell points out, 'film has featured as a distinct arm of the VisitBritain marketing portfolio since the 1990s, while the 2004 Visit America Alliance inbound television (TV) marketing campaign featured the line: "*you've seen the movies, now visit the set*"' (2012, p. 1007). *Lord of the Rings* fans visiting filming sites in New Zealand is possibly one of the most well-known examples of screen tourism but there are scores of others on both similar and smaller scales. With destination marketing organisations, production studios and theme parks offering fans opportunities like visiting filming locations and sets, undertaking tours and inhabiting the 'world' of the fan-object, intersections between tourism and transmedia properties have become a popular form of leisure. Matt Hills points out that 'staging imaginary worlds in physical form has become a significant part of destination tourism, events entertainment and "extended" film exhibition' (2016, p. 245) but it's not just official organisations that carry out this staging. Fans have also adopted and adapted areas used in filming as sites of importance – like the Ianto shrine in Cardiff Bay, an impromptu shrine created by *Torchwood* fans following the death of character Ianto Jones – and take part in cosplaying, re-enacting scenes and using material objects as a form of what Rebecca Williams (2019) calls paratextual-spatio-play to 'plunge themselves in/between representation and reality' (Kim, 2010, p. 71).

Screen tourism has, unsurprisingly, been celebrated for its economic contribution. The British Film Institute (BFI, 2021) noted that inbound tourists spent an estimated £892.6 million in film-related screen tourism in 2019, while Tourism Northern Ireland (2019) estimates that *Game of Thrones* resulted in 350,000 leisure visitors to Northern Ireland annually, spending in excess of £50 million. As the film and television industry grows, however, so does the increasingly urgent question of its environmental impact. And while there are steps being taken to address what production companies can do to reduce waste

(BFI, 2020) or how tourism organisations can minimise their carbon footprint (The Travel Foundation, 2020), far less attention has been paid to the environmental impacts of screen tourism. As Christine Lundberg and Kristina N. Lindström note, 'Managing tourism destinations sustainably is complex in times where many communities are struggling with both overtourism and undertourism and even more so in the face of an increased demand for niche tourism, such as popular culture tourism' (2020, p. 1). This chapter examines the environmental impact of screen tourism, focusing in particular on locations beyond studio tours and sets and examining two specific cases: the Dark Hedges in County Antrim, Northern Ireland, which featured in *Game of Thrones* and Freshwater West in Pembrokeshire, Wales, which was used in the *Harry Potter* film series. It explores the measures that are and could be put in place to address this through interventions such as destination management plans, corporate responsibility contracts and collaboration with production companies and fan communities. It also suggests ways that environmental sustainability can be included in the production process in order to address environmentally damaging fans behaviours and practices, specifically through co-design with fan communities.

Methodology

This chapter is part of a larger project on screen tourism. Research presented within uses data gathered from fieldwork and semi-structured interview. Fieldwork, including participant observation, was carried out at six locations of screen tourism, including Northern Ireland, the location for filming *Game of Thrones* (2011–2019), in March 2023. This included two guided tours to locations used in the show, during which cloaks and props were provided, a walking tour around the *Game of Thrones* stained glass windows at the Maritime Mile in Belfast and a visit to the Game of Thrones Studio Tour, which featured a range of sets and behind-the-scenes content. Notes were made and photographs taken at each of the locations visited as well as during tours and exhibitions which I attended.

Semi-structured interviews with 16 individuals involved in creating and/or managing sites used for film production and/or screen tourism were also carried out between June 2023 and February 2024. These were identified through desk-based research and included destination managers from national tourism boards, tourism managers from national parks, location managers at locations used in filming and fans who ran screen tourism events at specific locations. Fifteen interviews took place via video call, each lasting for around an hour, and one via email. Institutional ethics approval was granted for this research.

Dark Hedges/The Kingsroad

Game of Thrones is a television series produced by HBO, based on the *A Song of Ice and Fire* books by George R. R. Martin. Filming of the series took place in

Croatia, Iceland, Spain and Morocco, but the bulk of the show was filmed and produced in Northern Ireland, supported by Screen Northern Ireland. Various locations were used in the show, including Castle Ward, Inch Abbey, Tollymore Forest and Ballintoy Harbour, and each of these can be visited on both organised and do-it-yourself filming tours. While each of these features in several episodes, perhaps one of the most enduring locations linked to the series appeared on screen for only 12 seconds. Dark Hedges, a short road in County Antrim, is lined with beech trees planted around 1775, which now form a tunnel. The site was used in the first episode of season two, where Gendry and Arya Stark escape from King's Landing. We see them sitting on a cart being pulled along the Kingsroad, the central route through Westeros, and as the camera pans up the length of the path is revealed. Season two premiered in 2012 and Dark Hedges was being included in *Game of Thrones* tours by the middle of that year. It was also used by Tourism Ireland in marketing campaigns to encourage tourism. A 2015 digital campaign included a photograph of the Dark Hedges headlined 'Winter is Coming. Book Now'. The phrase 'winter is coming' references the phrase repeated throughout the series while the call to 'Jump into Northern Ireland, *Game of Thrones* Territory' highlights the fundamental role that Northern Ireland plays in *Game of Thrones*. A similar shot was used in a 2017 advert in Times Square, though the tagline was removed and Northern Ireland's status as *Game of Thrones* territory foregrounded.

Dark Hedges has proved to be an enduring location for tourists, yet the number of visitors has caused concern about damage to the trees. A tree preservation order was placed on them in 2004 to enable their preservation and maintenance, while a survey in 2014 revealed that they were in various states of health and were at risk of damage due to bad weather and an increasing numbers of visitors. Pedestrians and tour buses travel the road along with delivery lorries and farm vehicles, while cars parked on the side of the road make it difficult for traffic to pass and cause damage to the verges. High-sided vehicles attempting to navigate the road would often cause damage to the trunks and branches of the trees, while their roots were being damaged by the constant traffic (beech trees being surface rooting). Graffiti was also carved into the trees, although it's not clear whether this was done by film tourists or others. Discussions had taken place before 2015 about making the road a pedestrian zone, but it was decided that the impact on local residents would be too disruptive. In 2016, Causeway Coast and Glens Borough Council looked at options to make the visitor experience more rewarding and prevent damage to the trees, including closing the road or providing alternative access by putting a footpath in a field next to the Dark Hedges. In 2017, given the continuing popularity of the site, the Department of Infrastructure said that discussions had taken place with Causeway Coast and Glens Borough Council to close the road and a public consultation was announced. Four written objections were received and the ban came into force on 30 October 2017 with motorists facing a fine of up to £1,000 if they break the rules, although this doesn't seem to have been enforced. The then-owners of the nearby 'The Hedges' hotel offered free use of their carpark to tourists visiting the site, and brown signs, used in the United Kingdom to signpost tourists to locations, have been put up pointing to the parking area. The new owners do now charge for parking, but it is a short walk to the Dark Hedges, passing by Gracehill House, which was built by the man who planted the trees. No-entry signs are visible at the entrance to Dark Hedges though no barriers are in place, so cars still drive down it. During a fieldtrip I took there one car did drive down the road, and our tour guide encouraged us to call out 'shame, shame', re-enacting a scene from *Game of Thrones* season five where Cersei Lannister is paraded through King's Landing as punishment.

While the road was mostly free of traffic during the visit I made, this is not always the case. A 'Save the Dark Hedges' campaign group has spent the last 10 years documenting traffic at the site, as well as their efforts to engage with the Police Service of Northern Ireland, the Dark Hedges Preservation Trust and Causeway Coast and Glens Borough Council in order to prevent further damage being done to the trees and accidents involving visitors. Members of the group have also volunteered at the site since 2017, advising tourists on where to park. However, in a post to the Facebook group on 8 January 2024, campaigner Bob McCallion wrote that he and other members of the group were no longer willing to do this, citing a lack of action by stakeholders and a refusal to do their jobs – unpaid – any longer:

> For years I have been standing around the bottom junction and on Bregagh Rd most weeks, sometimes with other members of our group or locals and we have redirected scores of rogue tourist vehicles from entering/parking on Bregagh Rd – our efforts will now cease. On New Year's Day I decided not to intervene but just observe the 'follow-the-leader' fiasco and these photos show the end result. There are highly paid 'stakeholder' representatives who could have done a lot more to stop this constant degrading of the site eg Dark Hedges Preservation Trust, DfI Roads Service, PSNI etc etc, but they have gone off at a tangent to pursue their long-term ideals – otherwise known as "fiddling while Rome burns"! Myself and our Save The Dark Hedges group are no longer willing to do your job for you – we are actually masking your intransigence and incompetence!!

A survey on the safety of the site was carried out in June 2023 and concluded the six of the trees needed to be felled. The road was closed in November 2023 for the work to take place, and it was also announced that responsibility for the Dark Hedges was expected to pass from the Dark Hedges Preservation Trust to the Causeway Coast and Glens Heritage Trust in the coming months. Graham Thompson, the Heritage Trust's CEO, stated that they planned to establish a new management forum, which would see a new management plan with issues being managed in a coordinated strategic manner:

> [Causeway Coast and Glens Heritage Trust] plans to establish a new Dark Hedges Management Forum which is expected to

> consist of relevant statutory organisations, landowners and other interested parties. It is envisaged that in future the issues at the site will be managed in a co-ordinated strategic manner. This includes a management plan ensuring the longevity of the trees, while giving full consideration to health and safety issues; visitor management at the site including dealing with parking and traffic issues; educating and informing visitors to the site across a range of media; and importantly identifying funding sources for future site management (Causeway Coast and Glens Heritage Trust, 2023)

Of particular interest in this statement, which I will discuss in more detail later, is the aim of educating and informing visitors via social media, though Thompson does not expand on what this will entail.

Freshwater West/Dobby's Grave

Freshwater West in Pembrokeshire is well-known to *Harry Potter* fans as the resting place of Dobby the House Elf. In *Harry Potter and the Deathly Hallows: Part 1*, Dobby is wounded while helping Harry, Hermione and Ron escape from Malfoy Manor and dies in Harry's arms at Shell Cottage. *Harry Potter and the Deathly Hallows: Part 2* sees Harry sitting in front of Dobby's grave, which now has a headstone with the words 'here lies Dobby, a free elf' carved on it. Unlike the Dark Hedges, Freshwater West has plenty of screen time in the final two *Harry Potter* films, but it also features an emotionally charged scene for fans. Dobby, in the books and films, was a house elf who served Dark Wizards. Despite this, he disobeyed his masters to warn Harry of a plot to reopen the Chamber of Secrets. As a reward, Harry tricked Dobby's master into freeing him by giving him an item of clothing – in this case, a sock. Dobby was a beloved character, and fans were devastated when he died. As a result, thousands have visited the filming location at Freshwater and have left mementos in his honour. Unsurprisingly, many of these are socks, although laminated notes, painted rocks and fan art have also been left there.

While these demonstrate the affective relationship fans have with the object of their fandom, they also raise concerns about litter, biodiversity and erosion. Freshwater West is a Site of Special Scientific Interest, among the most highly designated sites in the United Kingdom. It is home to grey seals, rare ground-nesting birds and orchids, and the beach itself is a legally protected conservation area. The impact of over 75,000 visitors a year, many of whom will be *Harry Potter* fans, can't be overstated. Yet unlike Northern Ireland Tourism, which used Dark Hedges in much of its tourist marketing, Visit Wales rarely mentions Freshwater West in relation to *Harry Potter*. It wasn't until 2013, two years after *Deathly Hallows* was released, that the website was updated to include reference to the filming location. This could be because Freshwater was already known to surfers, or because *Harry Potter* fans were sharing details on how to find the beach in online fan communities, and it was felt there was no need to attract new visitors to the location.

Regardless, the number of visitors to the site of Dobby's grave is a source of continuing frustration for the National Trust (which manages the site), Pembrokeshire Council and local residents. As a result, in 2022, funding for a feasibility plan to shape the future management of Freshwater West was awarded by the UK Community Renewal Fund and the Freshwater West UK Community Renewal Fund Consultation began. National Trust Cymru and other key stakeholders commissioned Planning Solutions Consulting and Partnerships for Local Action and Networks for Enterprise and Development to deliver a consultation, which included specific questions about whether Dobby's Grave should be removed. Consultation activity took place between February and October 2022 and included online surveys, which generated nearly 5,000 responses, a series of pop-up consultation events and a workshop with strategic partners (Planning Solutions Consulting, 2022).

Although a range of questions relating to Freshwater West were asked, there was recognition from the outset that Dobby's Grave was a contentious issue – not least because its potential removal or relocation had been picked up by local and national press – and needed to be discussed sensitively. Different phases of the research programme also provided different views: the initial online survey in Spring 2022, where respondents were mainly local, saw some strong opinions relating to the negative impacts of the site: many saw it as being something that was unwelcome, and the groundswell of opinion was to remove it altogether. The next phase of online research gained a wider reach among tourists and non-residents and generated significant interest among *Harry Potter* fans. The over-riding response in that phase was to retain Dobby's Grave in some form, with some limited support for moving it to an alternative location in principle.

In-person pop up sessions demonstrated just how varied opinions on Dobby's grave were, ranging from requests to remove it because it's an eyesore to keeping it because of its meaning to fans. What was particularly interesting – and which I will discuss in more detail later in this chapter – were the suggestions to use it as a focus for charitable giving, either to children's charities or other organisations. These suggestions came from people who were visiting specifically to see Dobby's grave rather than locals, and it contrasts with the responses regarding Dobby's grave that were given at the 8 and 11 June pop-ups, which were mainly from local people. Planning Solutions Consulting noted that in most cases, the groups visiting to see Dobby's grave were happy to change their fannish behaviour, that is leaving some form of tribute such as a sock or painted pebble, once they understood the environmental impact of doing so. The consultation report suggests that it 'is wholly possible that the interest in this phenomenon may prove short-lived' (2022, p. 54), though considering *Deathly Hallows Part 2* was released in 2011 and fans are still visiting I would suggest Planning Solutions Consulting are not aware of the strength of fans' passions and the longevity of screen tourism locations. They did make recommendations given the need for further consideration about the site though, suggesting that any attempts to manage it should be approached in partnership with other groups as well as possibly different fan forums and social media sites. They also noted that any messaging should be echoed by all parties, in order to encourage fans to modify their behaviour appropriately, and to focus visits outside the main season. Following the consultation the National Trust decided that Dobby's Grave can remain where it is and have asked people to refrain from leaving any more items, highlighting that items left behind can enter the marine environment and cause damage, though no signage or information about this appears at Freshwater West itself (Birt, 2023).

Designing Sustainable Screen Tourism

Dark Hedges and Freshwater West show the issues at play in screen tourism both in terms of the environment and in fans' affective attachments to the text and the place. It's clear that in screen tourism locations, a lack of official marketing doesn't necessarily equate to fewer visitors as fans will share information among themselves about accessing a site (Jones, 2025). What we need then is an approach that recognises fans' affective relationship with the text and location while also highlighting sustainability messaging in an effective way. This is less important, I suggest, for sites of official screen tourism – places like the *Harry Potter* Studio Tour or visits to established tourism locations which have also been used as filming locations, such as Highclere Castle where Downton Abbey was filmed. These locations have sustainability and sustainable practices embedded in their business plans: Warner Bros. Studios replaced petrol buses with zero-emission electric buses on the *Harry Potter* Studio Tour route in 2022 (Rooney, 2022) while recycling bins are strategically placed throughout the *Game of Thrones* Studio Tour to encourage visitors to recycle. In fact, the *Game of Thrones* Studio Tour won the UKInbound excellence award for Sustainable Tourism Provider of the Year in 2023, demonstrating its awareness of and dedication to sustainable tourism practices (Cartmill, 2023). What I'm interested in are the sites of quasi-official or unofficial screen tourism: the places that fans either find themselves or are signposted to by other organisations but which don't have infrastructure or strategy in place to deal with the number of visitors, the amount of litter and other environmentally damaging practices. These might be rural locations, like Dark Hedges and Freshwater West, or they might be urban locations like the 'pizza house' that featured in *Breaking Bad* (which sees fans throw pizzas onto the roof), or Greyfriars Kirkyard in Edinburgh, a stop on *Harry Potter* walking tours at which glitter and plastic confetti can be seen, presumably as fans have re-enacted or created their own scenes using these as props.

The first thing we need to do in addressing environmentally sustainable screen tourism in these locations is, then, to understand the motivations behind this behaviour. Taran Jørgensen and Ina Reichenberger undertook research into negative film tourism behaviour utilising moral disengagement theory to 'understand how film tourists are able to exhibit negative behaviour even when aware of its "wrongness"' (2023, p. 1184). They draw on previous research into morality and tourism from a sociological perspective, which argues that 'tourism provides a "permissive domain of social life that enables a temporary suspension of customary rules and moral conduct"' (Uriely et al., 2011, p. 1051). If what we might call 'everyday' tourism enables a temporary suspension of customary rules, then I would argue that screen tourism actively encourages it. Fans have strongly affective relationships to the texts they love and the meaning of the film, and subsequent filming location, might take precedence over expected rules or conduct. Jørgensen and Rehcnberger argue that:

> . . . moral disengagement mechanisms, further supporting the inclusion of 'appeal to higher loyalties', become relevant in tourism settings where the individual is faced with two (or more) conflicting sets of morals and values, i.e. where engaging in the behaviour is considered immoral by society, but can be considered justifiable and even desired by the fandom's and/or fan object's values. (2023, p. 1186)

Fans who cosplay at screen tourism locations or take along props or figures and recreate scenes can be considered odd by mainstream society, even while it may be encouraged by fandom or even tour operators (Jones, 2024a).

Jørgensen and Reichenberger (2023) suggest that the moral alignment of the film or TV series may influence fans' own behaviour and moral justifications of it and use *Breaking Bad* and *Game of Thrones*, as two texts with issues of morality at their centre, as well as publicised examples of negative fan behaviour to test this theory. They circulated a questionnaire, which presented three hypothetical scenarios that displayed common types of negative film tourist behaviour in a context specific to the TV series. While none of the questions specifically asked about environmental sustainability, they did include a scenario about souveniring – that is, removing objects from the location as a souvenir, which can have an environmental impact. They identified that *Breaking Bad* respondents were more likely to justify engaging in negative behaviour, with more than half considering each scenario to be acceptable, whereas *Game of Thrones* respondents were significantly less willing to morally justify engaging in negative behaviour. Souveniring, however, was the scenario most frequently justified by both fandom groups, and they suggest that this is because of a 'distortion of consequences, perhaps due to the absence of a human factor within the scenarios described and the fact that souveniring's impacts are predominantly cumulative in nature' (Jørgensen & Reichenberger, 2023, p. 1194).

One of the key issues in Jorgensen and Reichenberger's analysis is that they assume intentionality on the part of the badly behaved film tourist. While this may be the case in some cases I'd argue this isn't the baseline from which we should view all screen tourists' behaviour. In some respects, Jorgensen and Reichenberger's finding around souveniring demonstrates that. Merchandise related to a film or TV series is popular among fans and viewers, but when those fans are in a location that doesn't have a shop, or even a stall featuring handmade items, they are likely to seek a memento of their visit from elsewhere (Jørgensen & Reichenberger, 2023; Pearce, 2019). In a location like Freshwater West, that will be a pebble or a rock. While, as members of society, fans should be familiar with social rules around littering, they don't necessarily understand the cumulative environmental effect of taking a rock or flower from a location and the impact that can have on biodiversity, other wildlife and the wider environment. In that case, the fans' affective response to the location and the text becomes more important than leaving nature as they found it.

We also see this in relation to fans leaving items at places like Freshwater West. Again, coming from a range of different environments – city, urban, rural – they are less likely to understand the impact that walking over sand dunes might have on erosion, and won't realise the impact that moving a rock from one part of the beach to another might have on the wider habitat. Similarly, they may not be aware that paint will chip off stones over time and travel down the beach to enter the sea. None of the *impacts* from these behaviours are, therefore, intentional, even if the behaviour itself is. And I would argue that this is important when it comes to planning for screen tourism. Sustainable film and television production and sustainable tourism have both come into the spotlight in recent years with a range of initiatives like BAFTA albert's toolkit and green production certificate (wearealbert, 2021) and the World Heritage Convention's Sustainable Tourism Toolkit (2016). What is missing, however, is the point at which each of these intersect – the screen tourism location. There are stages during the production lifecycle where interventions can be made. Of course, studios do not know what film or TV show is going to be successful until it's been released, but despite this, there are points at which studios and destination management organisations (DMOs) can be made aware of the *potential* for a number of screen tourists so they are not taken by surprise when the location becomes popular and the infrastructure begins failing.

Development

During the development stage, as the storyline is being developed and the script is being fleshed out, highly charged scenes can be identified. These are likely to be the focus of fan attention and can be shared at a later stage of the lifecycle with DMOs. DMOs should also be working on guidelines about good environmental management and sustainable practices that can be shared with production companies and keep these up-to-date with lessons learned from previous shoots.

Pre-production

The pre-production stage involves pinpointing filming locations for each scene and securing permits and permissions. At this point, location managers and producers should discuss issues of sustainability with those responsible for the filming location, whether that be the DMO, local council, national park or other. Important scenes can be highlighted, particularly if these are going to take place on location rather than in a studio set, to give the DMO enough time to consider how screen tourism could be managed. This is also the point at which DMOs can expressly forbid certain requests or negotiate for changes to be made and highlight conservation issues that the crew should be made aware of. At this stage, the technical recces of the locations take place, and this is an opportunity to pinpoint any areas that might be significant for screen tourists, as well as mitigate the risks during production and during any screen tourism that takes place.

Production and Post-production

Unlike historical film production, production and post-production in the digital age can take place simultaneously, with filming, editing and adding visual or special effects being done concurrently. However, it is a good point at which to identify iconic shots or features that might be used by DMOs in marketing as well as by fans who visit the location. There is potentially more work for DMOs to do at this point in terms of sustainability: if filming is taking place at a designated site, representatives may be able to attend and identify any issues that arise when large numbers of people are there. Fans may also find out about the production and attend to watch the filming taking place. These are likely to be the dedicated fans who will engage in screen tourism practices and so it is during this stage that co-design with fans and fan communities can be considered.

Co-design has been suggested as a central tenet for change in sustainable tourism as it can encourage working with others in a way that 'encourages stewardship, and in the process, works to avoid quick-fix, generalised solutions' (Liburd et al., 2020, p. 2300). Involving fans as stakeholders in a 'conscious and reflexive' way (Smit et al., 2024, p. 81) would thus uncover perspectives that the production team, DMOs, local councils or residents may be unaware of and develop effective solutions through highlighting issues around sustainability and encouraging fans to share their own ideas for ensuring appropriate behaviours and practices for the site. It also offers the opportunity to create maps, walking tours and smartphone apps for specific locations, which can contain key sustainability messaging. These can also be used as economic drivers for the production (and location) and potentially encourage buy-in from locals. Where possible the infrastructure of the site could also be considered and recycling bins and messaging boards put in place to encourage more sustainable practices. Depending on the location, DMOs could also consider creating a dedicated viewing area or platform at which fans can take photos and re-enact scenes to minimise the damage being done elsewhere on the site.

Distribution

Finally, the distribution stage – and beyond – is an important point at which sustainability messaging can be shared and appropriate behaviours encouraged. This is the point at which marketing takes place, which can be extensive for a blockbuster film, and DMOs need to ensure that they are engaging with local communities and residents who might be affected by screen tourism to ensure that any issues that haven't already been identified can be addressed. It is also the point where they can push back against marketing in inappropriate places. Jenni Steele, Visit Scotland's Film and Creative Industries Manager, acknowledged that 'Sometimes you don't want fans to go that place' – either because it's on a private estate, it's a small location, its unmanned or it poses a risk to visitors. She highlighted one interaction with a company planning publicity for *Game of Thrones:*

> . . . one of the publicity people had got in touch to say we're doing something for, I think it was last series, but in the northwest of Scotland there is a region called Wester Ross. And we've got Easter Ross as well. It's a beautiful mountainous part of Scotland like really rugged, really remote, whatever. And they said "oh we thought about putting up some signs, of Westeros, and people could go and take selfies", and I said, "Well, we wouldn't really support that, because, you know, you're sort of encouraging mass tourism to a place that can't really cope with it". And also what's the experience for people? Like they get out the car, take the picture, get back to the car, go away? Like there's nothing else around that. And also for local businesses it's not contributing anything, and I thought, well, we don't necessarily just need loads of visitors. We need the right types of visitors. That's sustainable tourism. This is huge and just encouraging people to drive around the countryside, take a photo, and go away. So we kind of said no, actually, we're not going to support that. (Quoted in Jones, 2024b, p. 26.)

The experience for visitors was factored into the decision, but the environmental impact was one of the main concerns.

The distribution stage of the production pipeline is also the point at which engagement with fan communities should start – or be returned to if DMOs have already spoken to some fans during filming. It is this point that I think is one of the most important in encouraging sustainable screen tourism. Fans are incredibly engaged, especially those fandoms that coalesce around a particular meaning they find in a text. Drawing on Fawcett and Cormack (2001), who use the term in relation to literary tourism, Robert Moses Peaslee and Rosalynn Vasquez (2021) suggest that tourism agencies like Tourism Northern Ireland perform the role of 'site guardians'. I suggest a more literal interpretation of this term, which involves fans as guardians, should be utilised. At Freshwater West, for example, the National Trust and other stakeholders could partner with charities or organisations whose missions share traits with Dobby. *Harry Potter* fans are well known for raising money for charitable causes and lobbying for fairer treatment and practices – like campaigning for fairtrade chocolate to be sold at Warner Bros. locations (Jenkins, 2012). While not wishing to stray into a media effects model, if we think about Jorgensen and Reichenberger's assertion that the morals demonstrated within a text affect fans' behaviour in film tourism destinations, then we can also argue that texts can also promote positive behaviour – *Harry Potter* fans take inspiration from the books and films, like Hermione's attempts to free the house elves at Hogwarts from indentured slavery – to effect change in the real world (McEvoy-Levy, 2018). It seems a logical step to utilise these fans to spread the message about sustainability and encourage behaviour change.

One of my interviewees, based within the Pembrokeshire Coast National Park Authority, agreed this is an avenue worth exploring. He said that Rowling's charity had actually raised the question of whether there was anything they could do to encourage fans to donate socks rather than leaving them on the beach, but the National Trust felt it would further raise the profile of the site and encourage more tourism:

> JK Rowling runs a charity, and we know through the work of that charity that they're deeply concerned about that impact. And they do try to work with us and the landowner to see how we can negate it and, you know, we've never failed to always keep thinking that maybe we need to find a cause where people need socks and then just say rather than leave a sock on the beach, donate a pair to someone that really needs socks. [...] But I remember the conversations we had at the time that even having that out on social media will raise the profile of the site and so they just avoided it, I think, in the end. It would almost be better to get a cohort of fans that buy into this idea, that it would be better to give socks to the homeless than to litter the beach, and that they drove it and that would also become more powerful. (Personal communication, 16 June 2023)

While the National Trust's concerns are understandable, I would suggest that involving fans as co-designers in developing sustainable screen tourism can aid them in potentially being part of the solution. Through a combination of at-site messaging combined with fan forums and social media, fans could be educated on why leaving items at sites – or removing items from sites – is harmful. Volunteers could also manage the site, as the Save the Dark Hedges group did, or collect donations – items of clothing for the homeless or people escaping abusive relationships, for example. Working with fan communities could be an easier and more effective way of modifying fans' behaviour, benefitting others and protecting the environment – while recognising fans' affective attachments with the text and ensuring their voices are heard as key stakeholders in screen tourism.

Conclusion

Screen tourism is undeniably on the rise, but as companies address issues around sustainability in film and sustainability in tourism, the places where these meet have been ignored. As marketing campaigns around the globe utilise the draw of film and television for advertising their countries as the 'must see' destination, it is increasingly important that production companies and tourist boards turn their focus to sustainable screen tourism. This chapter has focused on two well-known screen tourism locations which have seen irreversible damage as a result of fans' visiting and damaging the local habitat – Dark Hedges in County Antrim and Freshwater West in Pembrokeshire. Examining the impact of screen tourism as well as the official and unofficial attempts to manage the destruction caused has highlighted the need for sustainable screen tourism design to be part of the production process, both within production companies and in tourism organisations, local councils and destination management organisations. I have outlined points during the production process at which interventions should be made in a way that both recognises the importance of screen tourism locations to fans as well as the local community and environment and have suggested that co-design with fans and fan communities could result in them becoming part of the solution rather than the problem.

References

BFI. (2020). *A screen new deal—A route map to sustainable film production*. https://core-cms.bfi.org.uk/media/2940/download

BFI. (2021). *Screen business 2021*. https://core-cms.bfi.org.uk/media/15417/download

Birt, E. (2023, August 11). Harry Potter fans urged not add to Dobby's grave at Freshwater West. *Western Telegraph*. https://www.westerntelegraph.co.uk/news/23715727.harry-potter-fans-urged-not-add-dobbys-grave-freshwater-west

Cartmill, C. (2023, October 25). Game of Thrones Studio Tour wins UKInbound excellence award for sustainable tourism provider of the year. *News Letter*. https://www.newsletter.co.uk/business/game-of-thrones-studio-tour-wins-ukinbound-excellence-award-for-sustainable-tourism-provider-of-the-year-4384550

Causeway Coast and Glens Heritage Trust. (2023, November 20). *A new future for the dark hedges*. https://ccght.org/a-new-future-for-the-dark-hedges

Connell, J. (2012). Film tourism–Evolution, progress and prospects. *Tourism Management*, *33*(5), 1007–1029.

Fawcett, C., & Cormack, P. (2001). Guarding authenticity at literary tourism sites. *Annals of Tourism Research*, *28*(3), 686–704.

Hills, M. (2016). The enchantment of visiting imaginary worlds and 'being there': Brand fandom and the tertiary world of media tourism. In M. J. P. Wolf (Ed.), *Revisiting imaginary worlds: A subcreation studies anthology* (pp. 246–265). Routledge.

Jenkins, H. (2012). 'Cultural acupuncture': Fan activism and the Harry Potter alliance. *Transformative Works and Cultures*, 10. https://doi.org/10.3983/twc.2012.0305

Jones, B. (2024a, 26 August). Visitors are coming: Fan tourism in Northern Ireland. Pop Junctions. https://henryjenkins.org/blog/2024/8/23/visitors-are-coming-fan-tourism-in-northern-ireland

Jones, B. (2024b, February). Screen tourism: Regional development, fan labour and sustainability. Screen Industries Growth Network. https://screen-network.org.uk/publication/screen-tourism-regional-development-fan-labour-and-sustainability/

Jones, B. (2025). "The power of that fan base is really strong, and it's something we are encouraging tourism businesses to see": The economic, individual, and civic values of fan-created screen tourism content. *The Velvet Light Trap*, *95*(1), 39–50.

Jørgensen, T., & Reichenberger, I. (2023). Breaking bad behaviour: Understanding negative film tourist behaviour through moral disengagement. *Current Issues in Tourism*, *26*(7), 1183–1198.

Kim, S. (2010). Extraordinary experience: Re-enacting and photographing at screen tourism locations. *Tourism and Hospitality Planning & Development*, *7*(1), 59–75.

Liburd, J., Duedahl, E., & Heape, C. (2020). Co-designing tourism for sustainable development. *Journal of Sustainable Tourism*, *30*(10), 2298–2317.

Lundberg, C., & Lindström, K. N. (2020). Sustainable management of popular culture tourism destinations: A critical evaluation of the twilight saga servicescapes. *Sustainability*, *12*(12), 5177.

McCallion, B. (2024, January 8). *More disgraceful photos from 1st Jan 2024 at the Dark Hedges! This was a wake-up call for me. For years* [Images attached] [Page post]. Facebook. https://www.facebook.com/story.php/?id=1553136781669124&story_fbid=3554823401500442

McEvoy-Levy, S. (2018). *Peace and resistance in youth cultures: Reading the politics of peacebuilding from Harry Potter to The Hunger games*. Palgrave Macmillan.

Pearce, P. L. (2019). Behaving badly. In P. L. Pearce (Ed.), *Tourist behaviour the essential companion* (pp. 283–303). Edward Elgar Publishing.

Peaslee, R. M., & Vasquez, R. (2021). Game of Thrones, tourism, and the ethics of adaptation. *Adaptation*, *14*(2), 221–242.

Planning Solutions Consulting. (2022). *Sustainable freshwater west final report*. National Trust. https://nt.global.ssl.fastly.net/binaries/content/assets/website/national/regions/wales/places/freshwater-west-and-gupton-farm/pdf/final-sustainable-freshwater-west-report-281022-v1.pdf

Rooney, S. (2022, 6 June). *Warner Bros. Studio Tour London launches free electric shuttle bus service*. Coach Tourism Association. https://coachtourismassociation.co.uk/warner-bros-studio-tour-london-launches-free-electric-shuttle-bus-service/

Smit, B., Melissen, F., Font, X., & Dickinger, A. (2024). Destination design: Identifying three key co-design strategies. *Current Issues in Tourism*, *27*(24), 4791–4806.

The Travel Foundation. (2020, March). *A guide to sustainable practice for tourism businesses*. https://www.thetravelfoundation.org.uk/wp-content/uploads/2020/03/Sustainable-Practice-Guide.pdf

Tourism Northern Ireland. (2019). *Building the value of tourism: Tourism NI annual review 2019*. https://www.tourismni.com/globalassets/about-tourism-ni/tourism-ni-annual-review/the-value-of-tourism-2019-review.pdf

Uriely, N., Ram, Y., & Malach-Pines, A. (2011). Psychoanalytic sociology of deviant tourist behavior. *Annals of Tourism Research*, *38*(3), 1051–1069. https://doi.org/10.1016/j.annals.2011.01.014

wearealbert. (2021, 10 February). *Getting started with the albert Toolkit*. https://wearealbert.org/2021/02/10/getting-started-with-the-albert-toolkit/

Williams, R. (2019). Funko Hannibal in Florence: Fan tourism, participatory culture, and paratextual play. *JOMEC Journal*, (14), 71–90. https://doi.org/10.18573/jomec.179

World Heritage Convention. (2016). *Sustainable tourism toolkit*. https://whc.unesco.org/en/sustainabletourismtoolkit/

Part 5

Sustainability

Chapter 14

Fan Materiality and Meaning: Bringing Traditional Knowledge to Material Fandom Sustainability

Sejal Changede[a] *and Naomi Jacobs*[b]

[a]Open University, UK
[b]Lancaster University, UK

Abstract

This chapter explores how sustainable development frameworks and insight gained from Traditional Knowledge systems might provide pathways to greater sustainability for the material objects that fans buy, design, create, share and collect.

We discuss the importance of physical objects to fan practice and how these objects serve a critical purpose in terms of meaning-making for fans. We describe the many different types of physical objects that fans interact with and how both affective associations and physical affordances can be important parts of their meaning. We also discuss the complex, often hybrid economic systems that these sit within and how this can interact with fans' desire to maintain values relating to sustainability.

The Quadruple Bottom Line is a modern design framework for considering sustainable development that foregrounds meaning and spiritual connection. We relate this both to fan practice and Traditional Knowledge systems, revealing many similarities between the two. We close by suggesting how sustainable design practice might have the potential to improve sustainability in object-oriented fandom.

Bridging Design and Fandom, 215–231

doi:10.1108/978-1-80592-659-720261014

Keywords: Object-oriented fandom; sustainability; traditional knowledge; quadruple bottom line; meaning-making

Introduction

Sustainability is an important topic to consider as we design, produce and consume increasing quantities of 'stuff' (Jenkins, 2020). This escalating consumption reflects humanity's entry into the Anthropocene epoch, where industrial production-to-consumption systems have caused tremendous ecological devastation (Berkeley, 2011; Edwards, 2005). However, not all material objects are created (or remain) equal, especially when we consider how people make emotional connections to them. Woo (2014) notes that 'Design shapes materials into forms better adapted to some people and functions than others, and people cultivate methods of manipulating objects for particular purposes'. (2.10). As Jackson (2014) argues, addressing sustainability challenges requires moving beyond economic growth paradigms to examine the cultural values and meaning-making processes that drive our material relationships. But this meaning-making also intersects with tangible and physical properties of objects.

Fan material culture is an increasingly well-studied area. As we shall outline below, physical manifestations of fandom can have important affective meanings that make them vital to fan practices. However, the physical, designed objects that fans create, purchase, collect and share are often made of unsustainable materials such as plastics and thus contribute to fossil fuel consumption and waste.

In this chapter, we will examine how material objects intersect with meaning-making in the particular context of fandom. We will also put this in conversation with another domain of meaning in materiality, traditional knowledge and craft practices, to consider how sustainability in fan practice might be improved through learning from these ideas.

Meaning-Making and Material Fandom

For a long time, the material culture of fandom and the objects that fans buy, make, collect and own were relatively understudied (Hoebink et al., 2014; Santo, 2018). However, since a 2014 special issue of *Transformative Works and Cultures* on the topic (Rehak, 2014), there has been increasing scholarship on material fandom and so-called object-oriented fandom; that is, fan practices that relate to material objects. The physical objects that fans purchase, create and share are a vital part of the fan experience, particularly at the individual level of meaning-making. Even fans who are not part of 'fandom' and not actively participating in fan communities (the most-studied aspects of fan practice) may derive meaning and identity from fan-related material culture (Sandvoss, 2005). Hoebink et al. (2014) discuss the ability of fan objects to function as intrinsic parts of personal biography, which have the power to invoke memories and emotions that may function at multiple levels of interpretation, especially when assembled as part of a collection. Fan collections may act as physical extensions of owners' personalities and have close links to identity construction.

These 'objects' of object-oriented fandom might include both fan-created material, and commercial merchandise produced to appeal to fans, such as entertainment and sports merchandise, which generate vast sales and licensing revenues (Affuso & Santo, 2018). Fans 'operate complex hierarchies and systems of cultural value surrounding the merchandise that they collect and curate'. (Williams, 2020, p. 182). Johnson (2007) describes different categories of merchandise. The first, diegetic merchandise, represents objects that have appeared within the text, such as Johnson's example of a car horn owned by a character in *The Sopranos*. Pseudo-diegetic merchandise may not have been specifically featured but could exist within the world and facilitate immersion. This might include clothing bearing branding for an in-fiction organisation, institution or product, or food and drink. Both these categories function in 'blurring the boundaries between the "real" world of the viewer and the diegetic world of the drama' (p. 16). Extra-diegetic merchandise, by contrast, transcends the fictional world, such as books, cast photos, DVDs and products bearing the logo of a television series. These categories apply beyond merchandise to fan-created or curated objects and can all be considered forms of paratexts, defined by Gray (2010) as being both part of the text and distinct from it and part of the process of managing and evidencing meaning-making.

Merchandise not only produces revenue through sales but also cultivates deeper brand investment by consumers, especially when products have a diegetic presence in the media source (Affuso & Santo, 2018). Identity construction through the purchase and ownership of material objects has also been capitalised on through proponents of 'brandom' (Guschwan, 2012), where a brand (such as Gucci, Nike or Apple) itself has fans and represents an identity statement. Branded merchandise and associated cultural capital serve to further the brand, thus encouraging further merchandise consumption. Here, the extra-diegetic objects stand alone with no diegesis. This may also be the case for merchandise relating to non-media fandoms such as sports teams.[1]

Collection has long been considered a key element of fan practice, particularly from the 'affirmational' perspective.[2] Hoebink et al. (2014) discuss how fannish pleasure in collecting may come in part from displaying objects to others, as a form of cultural capital or identity representation. For example, Williams (2020) describes how merchandise is used to 'represent and reinforce their own fan identities' (p. 182) citing how clothing can be used to give a 'subtle subcultural nod of recognition' to differentiate theme park attendees who are fans from wider tourist attendees (p. 187). However, material objects can also be used to enhance and personalise fans' private homes for personal meaning-making (Woo, 2014) and to aid identity creation in domestic spaces (Baker, 2019).

[1]Though some merchandise such as clothing might facilitate immersion into the 'world' of the team, imagining oneself a player.

[2]See the introduction of this book for discussion of 'affirmational' vs 'transformational' fan practice.

Woo describes how positive values and memories are embodied within the 'things' that fans collect, with personal narratives bound up within material objects. However, he also notes that the design and physical affordances of objects play a vital role in the functions they can fulfil in terms of both metaphorical and tangible uses. This accords with co-author Jacobs' previous work on fanbinding (Jacobs & Lowe, 2024) which found that affective connections to born-digital fanfiction texts initiate the creation of physical books, but the books' design, material properties and affordances are also important. These fanbound books were observed as being used to signal pride and connection to fandom, either to other fans or to oneself – in some cases acting as cryptic signs intentionally unparsable as fan-related to those not recognising them as such.

The deeper interactions that occur with such materialisations of fandom take object-oriented fandom beyond the realm of commodities (Hoebink et al., 2014) and can be related to theories of meaning-making as previously discussed. Sandvoss (2005) observes that 'Through fans' affective attachment, the use-value of objects of fandom thus spirals out of relation to their exchange-value. By making their object of fandom into extensions of themselves, fans give their consumption an inherently private and personal nature that removes their object of consumption from the logic of capitalist exchange' (p. 116). This seating of fan engagement outside of standard economic structures is a familiar echoing of the gift economy that underpins much fan practice.

This desire to materialise fan effect is not restricted to brand merchandise. Objects that fans create may circulate within the community either through 'fantrepreneurship' (Carter, 2017) or via the gift economy. Affuso and Santo (2018) note that 'fan-made merchandise has emerged as a cottage industry on sites like Etsy and redbubble.com blurring the distinctions between consumer culture, the gift economy, and commodity activism'. Sometimes fans turn to this activity of creating material objects themselves (or obtaining them from other fans who create), because the merchandise that they desire does not exist, in a practice that Hills (2011) calls DIY merchandise. This might include recreations of unique diegetic objects but also sourcing screen-accurate objects used by production teams. Pseudo-diegetic and extra-diegetic DIY merchandise may reference fan constructions of the media text rather than sanctioned ones – for example, badges, bags and mugs foregrounding 'ships' (character relationships) that go beyond the media canon. As an example of fans creating their own merchandise in the absence of sanctioned forms, fans of the television show *Our Flag Means Death* have complained about the limited range of official merchandise available from the HBO shop, which sells only seven products (Snow Commerce, 2025). However, there is a thriving ecosystem of fan-made items that provide a much wider range of mediums and focus, such as referencing specific characters or scenes. Objects created and bought by fans include bespoke screen-accurate clothing replicas, off-the-shelf screen-accurate objects such as a specific mixing bowl and general products that have patterns (e.g. oranges) evoking fan-favoured themes. While screen-used objects have been auctioned, the showrunner David Jenkins discouraged fans from purchasing these, noting that no benefit would go to the show producers, set designers or costumiers and stating 'Before you spend money on that auction, please know that those are only props and costumes. They hold no magic. The coolest things are the things you made around the show' (Jenkins, 2025).

Fanmade craft works often circulate within fandom as part of the gift economy and can themselves form part of a community-building process (Rendell, 2018). However, as Godwin (2016) points out, there is a more complex relationship with economic exchange. By focusing solely on a gift economy, fan studies scholarship risks erasing fanworks produced and circulated for profit within multiple fan communities. Noppe (2011) notes that different economic systems with different value priorities can co-exist and proposes that hybrid economies should be given more attention, where the separation between sharing and commercial economies blurs. This blurring is seen with fanbinding, where controversies have arisen over individuals who produce their bound copies to sell – in some cases without the knowledge or approval of the fanfiction author (Minkel, 2025).

Hills (2014) discusses how such fan material production is a form of transformative work, identifying that even those who carry out 'mimetic' crafting of accurate replicas discuss their fandom in terms of craft. They are performing a construction not only of the physical objects but also of the ontological reification of their focus of fandom. The material objects crafted by fans may sometimes even be considered of 'higher quality' (and thus more desirable) than mass-produced merchandise. This may be due to the amount of time spent on their creation that would not be possible at a higher commercial volume. It may also be that the attention to detail fans bring to designing objects speaks to the most meaningful aspects of affective connection and corrects areas considered lacking in commercial merchandise (Godwin, 2016). Other aspects that contribute to perceived value and meaning might be scarcity (e.g. items that can be obtained only at a specific time and place, such as a live show) or relationship to fandom focus, such as a celebrity (e.g. an instrument previously owned by a beloved musician), both of which can contribute to subcultural capital. An example of this, which blends fan creation and celebrity proximity, can be seen in the work of a fan of the television show *Supernatural* who purchases 'set relics' of clothing worn by cast members on-screen and transforms them into unique jewellery (Wayward Plaids, n.d.)

Through these examples, we can see that while fan material culture can be considered a form of mediated consumption, the form that the mediation takes is critical. Fan materiality can manifest in the curatorial practices associated with reaffirming personal links to the focus of fandom, but can also manifest as a form of poaching and remixing aligned with transformative paradigms.

Sustainability and Meaning-Making

That affective bonds and self-expression lead fans to interact with material culture does, however, raise sustainability challenges. Mass-produced objects are often made of non-sustainable materials (for example, vinyl plastic Funko Pop dolls) and may be transported long distances. Lamerichs (2025) highlights the global supply chains that underpin mass production and consumption, which enable the fan merchandise industry. It is easy for fans to succumb to a 'gotta catch 'em all' completism, seeking to collect as many or as comprehensive a range of collectables as possible; this indulges individual fan pleasure but also raises social and cultural (and potentially economic) capital. However, few who are creating or purchasing these products question what happens at the end of their life cycle. Fan-created craft objects may avoid some of these concerns through their uniqueness, lower production volumes and use of more sustainable materials, but this uniqueness may in fact raise their status as collectables, especially if heightened through close association with, for example celebrities. Much fan craft and creation is performed outside of traditional economic structures, for individual pleasure in the practice or to contribute to the fandom gift economy. It is important to consider how this interacts with principles of sustainability.

In some cases, sustainability may act as a selling point for brands to promote media related merchandise. Rendell (2018) notes that Studio Ghibli has been heavily influenced by the eco-political values of its founder, Miyazaki, which allows it to differentiate itself from the wider anime industry. Part of the distinctiveness of Ghibli's offering is its seasonal goods, which relate to nature and traditional practices (Denison, 2026). Rendell examines Ghibli material fan practices through the lens of crafting, with a focus on their political potential. In this case, as with some of the previous examples, the Ghibli fans that Rendell spoke to often sought to craft material objects because collectibles and merchandise were not available for commercial purchase, in this case, because they are difficult for international fans to obtain outside of Japan.

Rendell quotes a fan who specifically links their craft practice to sustainability:

> For all of my wooden items I use good quality, eco-friendly, sustainable wood, either beech or bamboo, these tie into the films (obviously Bamboo is Japanese) and there are strong messages of the importance of taking care of the planet in most films - hence the eco -friendly. (IX 2016, quoted in Rendell, 2018, p. 124)

There is an affective connection not just to the text itself but to the ethos that is embedded within and around its paratexts. Environmental responsibility can thus also directly influence fandom. When Ghibli fans participate in environmental justice initiatives, they are not only supporting positive changemaking but also demonstrating brand commitment. This goes in both directions; the Totoro fund supports environmental efforts through merchandise sales and makes strong links with traditional Japanese craft culture (Denison, 2026).

Lamerichs (2025) has similarly noted an increasing interest in sustainability when fans consider the physical objects that they create and own. She cites statements from fans who acknowledge the environmental impact that fan collecting practices have and the lack of 'environmentally friendly' aspects to many fan behaviours. Lamerichs links this to corporate social responsibility and the way that brands are increasingly using sustainable innovation as a draw for their customers. Together, she suggests that this creates a new movement of so-called sustainable fandom where ecological concerns are paramount, providing the example of ecocosplay where costumes are constructed along critical sustainability principles, with reflection on consumption and production 'facilitating pathways to sustainable design' (p. 92).

The relationship between sustainability and meaning-making demonstrated in fandom reveals the inadequacy of purely technical or economic approaches to environmental challenges. Sustainable practices emerge not merely from efficiency or regulation, but from deep connections between cultural values, personal significance and material relationships. However, conventional frameworks for sustainable development often fail to account for these meaning-making processes. An example is John Elkington's influential Triple Bottom Line framework (Elkington, 1997). This framework establishes three pillars of sustainability: economic prosperity, environmental stewardship and social equity. However, the implementation of this model has often prioritised economic considerations over environmental and social concerns, leading to superficial engagement with sustainability principles. Elkington himself acknowledged that the framework had failed to deliver genuine systemic change (Elkington, 2018).

Frameworks of this sort address crucial issues of environmental stewardship, social justice and economic security but provide only partial solutions to contemporary sustainability challenges. Walker (2008) argues that prevailing sustainability frameworks often lack consideration of aspects that 'nurture and develop the inner person' and fail to reflect 'a way of acknowledging our values and beliefs and ascribing meaning to our activities' (p. 27). To make meaningful and lasting contributions, sustainable development must embrace the vital aspects of human culture that give life purpose and direction (Walker, 2014).

Recognising these limitations, the Quadruple Bottom Line (QBL) (Fig. 14.1) extends the Triple Bottom Line framework by incorporating a crucial fourth dimension: personal meaning (Elkington, 1997, 2018; Walker, 2014). While Elkington's model focuses on people, planet and profit, the QBL recognises that sustainable solutions must also address the human need for meaning, purpose and spiritual fulfilment. Changede (2025) demonstrated the QBL's effectiveness in analysing traditional craft practices while identifying challenges in translating the framework into practical design guidance. This fourth dimension acknowledges that environmental and social sustainability cannot be achieved without considering the inner dimensions of human experience that motivate lasting behavioural change and economics is just a means to achieve this (Walker, 2014).

Building on this insight, the QBL fundamentally restructures how we understand the relationship between economic and other concerns. Rather than treating economics as an equal pillar alongside environmental and social considerations, the QBL repositions economic factors as means rather than ends.

This reframing places human values and traditional understandings of meaning at the centre of sustainable design decision-making (Walker, 2014).

To operationalise this holistic approach, the QBL framework comprises three primary meaning dimensions and one instrumental dimension:

Practical meaning addresses providing for physical needs while enhancing environmental impacts. This dimension encompasses the functional requirements of an object while ensuring environmental stewardship through reduced waste, localised production and consideration of material lifecycles. Practical meaning ensures that sustainable solutions are effective and environmentally responsible.

Social meaning encompasses ethics, compassion, equity and justice in design decisions. This dimension recognises that truly sustainable solutions must address social inequalities, promote fair labour practices and consider the broader social implications of design choices. Social meaning ensures that sustainability efforts contribute to collective wellbeing rather than privileging certain groups over others.

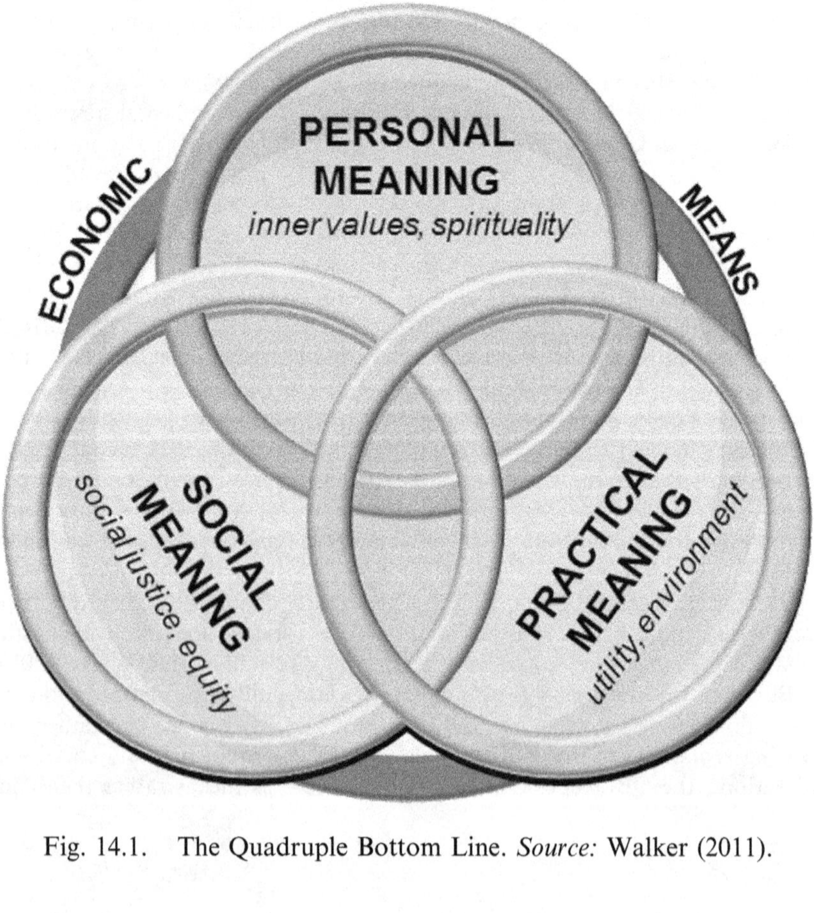

Fig. 14.1. The Quadruple Bottom Line. *Source:* Walker (2011).

Personal meaning involves conscience, spiritual well-being and questions of ultimate concern. Walker carefully avoids the term 'spirituality' due to its diverse interpretations and potential religious connotations, instead focusing on personal meaning to ensure inclusivity across different belief systems (Walker, 2011). This dimension acknowledges that humans seek purpose, fulfilment and connection to something greater than themselves, whether through religious faith, philosophical inquiry or personal ethics.

Economic means represent financial viability as a facilitator rather than an ultimate goal. While economic sustainability remains necessary for practical implementation, the QBL positions economics as instrumental to achieving the three meaning dimensions rather than as a competing priority.

These interconnected dimensions challenge existing sustainability paradigms overly reliant on rationalisation, objectivity and scientific approaches alone. By embracing both rational and intuitive thinking, objectivity and subjectivity, and analytical and holistic approaches, the QBL enables 'a more meaningful and ultimately sustainable paradigm for design' (Walker et al., 2019).

Reflecting these values, this framework advocates for values emphasising slow change, continuity, attentiveness and connection – qualities found in local craft production and traditional practices. Such spiritually useful design generates artefacts that 'draw upon tradition, that are more stable and whose appeal is not dependent on originality, newness or technological progress' (Walker, 2014). These artefacts represent a radical departure from consumer-driven product design, offering stability and meaning that transcend market trends.

We can use this framework to reconceptualise how material fandom might approach sustainability.

Fan objects often derive their value not from practical utility alone but from their ability to provide personal meaning through connection to beloved narratives, social meaning through community belonging and practical meaning through functional use. For example, Dana Sterling Bode (2014) quotes a fan who discusses how collaborative production and sharing is a key aspects of meaning-making associated with fandom craft, demonstrating social meaning through community:

> It's other people using my pattern to build models for themselves, and changing it up in ways that suit them. It becomes a collaboration, where my contribution is just a part of it. Some other fan has printed it out and glued it together and now it's theirs. It exists now, as a real object, because somebody built it. (Gnat, cited in Bode, 2014)

These different aspects of value might be given greater or lesser emphasis in the case of each fan's relationship with individual objects; for example objects that are part of a collection may not be intended for regular functional use and thus not require much practical meaning, whereas some objects may be desired for their functionality and affordances which allow them to be incorporated into daily life, such as a bag or a mug. The objects' functional design may also relate to and reinforce meaning (e.g. see Huertas Gutierrez & Gil Vasquez, 2026). However, when fan merchandise fails to deliver meaningful experiences across these dimensions, it risks becoming mere commodity consumption rather than sustainable cultural practice.

In addition to using the QBL framework, we can usefully consider Traditional Knowledge systems as a meaning-based craft system from which fan production can learn.

Learning From Traditional Knowledge

Traditional Knowledge (TK) systems offer centuries-old examples of sustainable material relationships rooted in storytelling and cultural value and meaning rather than consumption, which can be usefully considered in relation to contemporary fan practice. TK encompasses 'knowledge, know-how, skills and practices that are developed, sustained and passed on from generation to generation within a community, often forming part of its cultural or spiritual identity', (WIPO, n.d.), including Indigenous Knowledge and other community-based knowledge systems from rural, agricultural and craft communities globally (Berkes, 2017).

These systems are fundamentally distinguished from industrial production-consumption models by their holistic, relational approach to materiality. TK represents adaptive practices developed over generations through trial-and-error processes, transmitted through oral traditions and shared practical experiences (Dudgeon & Berkes, 2003; Pierotti & Wildcat, 2000). Such knowledge systems emphasise the symbiotic relationship between humans and nature as fundamental to everyday life, founded on co-evolution with the environment and deep understanding of ecosystems (Cajete, 2000; Clarke, 1990). Often, materials used are local and collected sensitively. This embodies a relational worldview that recognises everything in nature as enjoying equal status, with humility as a cherished value (Aikenhead & Michell, 2011).

Central to TK is how material objects carry deep cultural significance beyond their functional utility. Communities integrate physical artefacts with meaning through cultural practices, spiritual beliefs and collective memory, creating objects that function as repositories of identity, values and community knowledge (Walker et al., 2019). Traditional systems also operate through gift economies where objects circulate based on reciprocity rather than commodity exchange. As Robin Wall Kimmerer observes, 'the fundamental nature of gifts: they move and their value increases with their passage' contrasts sharply with commodity relationships where 'exchange ends once parity has been established' (Kimmerer, 2013, pp. 3–4).

While fundamentally place-based with values tied to specific locations, these principles of cultural transmission through storytelling and collective identity formation transcend geographic boundaries, ensuring sustainable resource use adapted to local conditions (Kakoty, 2018). This meaning-making process directly parallels how fan communities invest material objects with affective attachment and personal significance, transforming commodities into extensions of self and community belonging. Just as Kimmerer (2013) notes that gifts create an ongoing relationship and establish 'a feeling-bond between two people' (p. 26), fan-created objects circulate through gift economies that prioritise community connection over commercial exchange. Both systems demonstrate sustainable practices through storytelling (as in the Ghibli examples described above), communal identity formation and ethical considerations that prioritise cultural continuity alongside environmental responsibility, offering valuable guidance for reimagining fan material culture and merchandise design.

Fans develop affective meaning in material objects by association with the fandom text of origin and the feelings they evoke in the fan. This can be considered similar to the way that affective meaning attaches to TK objects through their cultural meanings, which can be facilitated by the history of the object itself. For example, a traditional handwoven textile incorporating ancestral patterns and natural dyes sourced from local plants carries layers of cultural significance, storytelling and connection to place; differing fundamentally from a mass-produced synthetic fabric (Changede, 2025). Echoing the immersive properties of a diegetic or pseudo-diegetic fan object, such TK objects can act to create immersion in the cultural 'world' of that knowledge culture, which may be separated from day-to-day modern ways of living.

In some cases, fan practice and traditional practices can even be combined. Denison (2026) describes how Studio Ghibli has incorporated traditional Japanese craft products into their merchandise strategy, but also gone beyond this in the creation of a simulated shrine shop at Ghibli Park in Nagakute City, Japan, reproducing traditional Shintō shrine goods as Totoro merchandise. How this relates to sustainability is ambiguous, as Denison notes: 'Far from removing Totoro from the realm of media-commodity, however, this shift celebrates the already-commodified nature of Japanese Shintō religious practices and rituals. The Ghibli Park inserts Ghibli's most famous character into a fan-oriented version of that sacred landscape'.

Both contemporary fandom and TK systems demonstrate how material objects serve as pathways for meaning-making that transcends purely functional relationships, with meaning heightened by craft objects made at an individual level. As Gauntlett (2018) notes, 'handmade things are special because they carry the "authentic and personal" touch of the person who has made them' (p. 65). Elizabeth Wilson (2013) discusses how cultural passions create meaning for fans through emotional investment and spiritual exploration, challenging hierarchies that privilege traditional over popular culture while demonstrating how such practices resist commodification through deep personal engagement. She links this to a spiritual dimension, which we can connect directly to Walker's personal meaning concept in the QBL framework, thus parallelling how TK systems integrate material and spiritual realms where objects connect practitioners to ancestral wisdom and place-based identity.

Fan and TK systems can both operate through communities of practice with complementary specialisations. Traditional craft villages exemplify this through the 'bara balutedar' system in Indian villages, where 12 essential trades formed interdependent economic structures (Changede, 2025). Each specialist family provided services to the entire village community, receiving payment through agricultural harvest shares, land grants, or reciprocal services rather than cash exchange, creating self-sustaining village economies where craft knowledge was preserved through hereditary transmission (Dandekar et al., 2021). Fan communities demonstrate similar hybrid structures adapted for digital-material environments, with practitioners engaging simultaneously in gift economy sharing and small-scale commercial activity. Like the bara balutedar system's complementary specialisations, fan communities develop distinct but interconnected practices with artists, writers, bookbinders, prop makers, cosplayers and digital archivists each contributing specialised skills while benefiting from others' expertise. Some specialists may see the craft itself as their 'fandom', for example those specialising in fanbinding or costuming without a specific media text focus (Godwin, 2024). Those who do not create can participate through feedback, digital resources, or social capital systems (such as the ability to leave comments and digital 'kudos' in the fanfiction site Archive of Our Own), functioning as non-monetary exchange recognising creative labour.

We can also see pedagogical and cultural transmission in fandom in a way that echoes similar TK practices. Lamerichs (2025) notes that '[h]istorically, fan subcultures have been about sharing, preserving, collecting, and reusing resources' (p. 95). This preservation can be in terms of knowledge and skills related to craft; for example, Hills (2014) describes an 'apprenticeship' model being used to learn craft skills. Similar teaching and sharing models can be seen in communities such as the Renegade Bindery, which provides training for those who wish to learn fanbinding, including skills that are themselves a return to traditional heritage craft practices (Kennedy & Buchsbaum, 2022). These crafts may include examples of intangible cultural heritage critically endangered in other contexts, for example fore-edge painting (Das, 2025). Such knowledge sharing can include education on sustainable practices, as in cosplay where, as Lamerichs (2025) notes, 'Cosplayers educate each other on materials and sustainable alternatives, thereby creating their own pedagogy' (p. 95). The interplay between digital and material creation mirrors how traditional systems balance individual specialisation with collective welfare, with both maintaining digital archives of tutorials, patterns and techniques while adapting them for contemporary materials.

Both TK systems and fan communities demonstrate how meaning-making through material culture can support sustainable practices when rooted in community knowledge sharing, skill transmission and respect for both cultural heritage and environmental resources. This creates resilient hybrid economies where economic necessity, cultural preservation and community-building intersect, offering sustainable alternatives to purely commercial systems while suggesting possibilities for material culture that serve human flourishing while respecting planetary boundaries (Kakoty, 2018; Walker, 2014).

Conclusion

As we have seen across this chapter, there is a complex relationship between physical objects, merchandise, fan production, sustainability and meaning-making. If we are to develop more sustainable practices for object-oriented fandom, we must consider the hybrid economies that encompass gift economies, economic production, collaborative processes and the platform economies and supply chains that now underpin much modern society. The QBL can be a useful framework to consider how different forms of meaning can relate to sustainability, providing guidance for developing more sustainable fan material objects. We can also look to TK systems to guide sustainable design of fan objects, given the elements that these systems have in common with fan cultures and practices.

Godwin (2016) highlights tensions that may arise between fans who create 'for the love of it' and the stigmatisation that can arise when financial motivations exist behind creating DIY merchandise. But perhaps this can be mitigated by highlighting by-fans-for-fans production as a craft practice; one that can be performed in a hobbyist capacity but also as a legitimate form of economic value creation that has greater meaning-making capacity than mass production. We can thus break down the perceived binary of opposition between commerciality and authenticity (Banet-Weiser, 2011).

Some of this authenticity and sustainability might also be possible at a brand level when designing goods to appeal to fans, if considerations of flexibility and individuality are taken into account at the initial stages of the design process. Godwin (2018) points out that meaning is invested through time and energy committed to making something and that therefore things a fan makes for themself (or has made by a specific other fan) can have more meaning. She describes how some brands, such as Nike allow fans to 'design their own' versions of products, but that these are still fixed within rigid boundaries of customisation. Similarly, 'limited edition' products are still mass produced. However, we can imagine new ecosystems of sustainable design where products are produced with the specific intention of further development by fan crafting, enabling greater agency by fan consumers. Combined with the use of more sustainable materials and supply chains, these could also be marketed specifically to environmentally conscious consumers who seek brands aligning with their values.

It is also worth greater consideration of the overall lifecycle of material fandom objects. Because of the highly affective attachments made to these objects and the meaning they accrue, fans tend to treat their objects as less disposable than other material goods. In fact, this can cause problems for fans, as Woo (2014) describes when discussing with fans how they deal with challenges of storage, maintenance and reluctant disposal when space is no longer available. Lamerichs (2025) notes that 'certain collector practices, such as preserving the packaging, can also be read as a critical move against our "throwaway society"' (p. 95). One move towards sustainable practices might be, as Owen et al. suggest in this collection, to embrace and celebrate the fan propensity to gather and treasure objects rather than constantly replace them for further consumption. However, this still means that large amounts of 'stuff' can be desired and accrued. What if we were to also consider this from the opposite approach and design fan objects using traditional natural materials with a naturally limited lifespan, after which they biodegrade or are recyclable? These could be modelled on TK practices, similarly to Changede's et al. (2022) Miswak Toothbrush, which demonstrates how contemporary design can integrate traditional materials, maintaining functionality and reducing environmental impact. While this might initially conflict with memory and meaning-making functions of fan objects, it could appeal to sustainability values and also allow space for new objects, adding to the value conferred by scarcity and ephemerality.

Finally, we should consider how education and knowledge transmission feed into fan craft and whether sustainability (and sustainability knowledge from TK crafts) can become a more integrated part of this fan-to-fan pedagogy. This follows recommendations by Lamerichs (2025). Fans have long been theorised as communities of resistance and counterculture, rejecting hegemonic structures and functioning as a non-commercial gift economy. Perhaps embedding sustainable practices in fandom is another form of resistance that might be encouraged.

References

Affuso, E., & Santo, A. (2018). Mediated merchandise, merchandisable media: An introduction. *Film Criticism*, *42*(2), 72–87. https://doi.org/10.3998/fc.13761232.0042.201

Aikenhead, G. S., & Michell, H. (2011). *Bridging cultures: Scientific and indigenous ways of knowing nature*. Pearson.

Baker, T. A. (2019). 'It was precious to me from the beginning': Material objects, long-distance fandom and home. *Soccer & Society*, *20*(4), 626–641.

Banet-Weiser, S. (2011). Convergence on the street: Rethinking the authentic/commercial binary. *Cultural Studies*, *25*(4–5), 641–658.

Berkeley, J. (2011, May 26). Welcome to the anthropocene. *The Economist*. https://www.economist.com/leaders/2011/05/26/welcome-to-the-anthropocene

Berkes, F. (2017). *Sacred ecology* (4th ed.). Routledge. https://doi.org/10.4324/9781315114644

Bode, D. S. (2014). Beyond souvenirs: Making fannish items by hand. Interview. In B. Rehak (Ed.), *Materiality and object-oriented fandom* (Special issue). *Transformative Works and Cultures* (Vol. 16). https://doi.org/10.3983/twc.2014.0548

Cajete, G. (2000). *Native science: Natural laws of interdependence* (1st ed.). Clear Light Publishers.

Carter, O. (2017). A labour of love: Fantrepreneurship in home video media distribution. In *DVD, Blu-ray and beyond: Navigating formats and platforms within media consumption* (pp. 197–213). Springer International Publishing.

Changede, S. (2025). *Learning from traditional products and practices in India for design for sustainability*. Doctoral dissertation. Lancaster University. https://doi.org/10.17635/lancaster/thesis/2619

Changede, S., Thomas, L., & Walker, S. (2022). The Miswak toothbrush: Incorporating traditional knowledge into contemporary product design. In G. Bruyns & H. Wei (Eds.), *With design: Reinventing design modes: Proceedings of the 9th Congress of the International Association of Societies of Design Research (IASDR 2021)* (pp. 1815–1822). Springer. https://doi.org/10.1007/978-981-19-4472-7_117

Clarke, W. C. (1990). Learning from the past: Traditional knowledge and sustainable development. *The Contemporary Pacific*, *2*(2), 233–253.

Dandekar, A., Joshi, A., Dandekar, I., Hargude, N., Shrotri, A., & Kulkarni, S. (2021). The challenge of unemployment and entrepreneurship before rural India and its solution through the foundry business using traditional Indian knowledge system. In P. M. Pawar, R. Balasubramaniam, B. P. Ronge, S. B. Salunkhe, A. S. Vibhute, & B. Melinamath (Eds.), *Techno-societal 2020* (pp. 1041–1050). Springer. https://doi.org/10.1007/978-3-030-69925-3_99

Das, S. (2025, May 22). *Food, fan art, and preserving a moment in time: A case study of the fandom-themed cafe ecosystem as alternative memory institution*. [Conference presentation]. FanLIS: Five Years of FanLIS Symposium.

Denison, R. (2026). Totoro's world: Studio Ghibli merchandising and the production of distinction in ubiquity. *Mechademia*, *18*(2). in press.

Dudgeon, R. C., & Berkes, F. (2003). Local understandings of the land: Traditional ecological knowledge and indigenous knowledge. In *Nature across cultures: Views of nature and the environment in non-Western cultures* (pp. 75–96). Springer. https://doi.org/10.1007/978-94-017-0149-5_4

Edwards, A. R. (2005). *The sustainability revolution: Portrait of a paradigm shift* (1st ed.). New Society Publishers.

Elkington, J. (1997). *Cannibals with forks: The triple bottom line of 21st century business*. New Society Publishers.

Elkington, J. (2018, June 25). 25 years ago I coined the phrase "triple bottom line." Here's why it's time to rethink it. *Harvard Business Review*. https://hbr.org/2018/06/25-years-ago-i-coined-the-phrase-triple-bottom-line-heres-why-im-giving-up-on-it

Gauntlett, D. (2018). *Making is connecting: The social power of creativity, from craft and knitting to digital everything* (2nd ed.). Polity Press.

Godwin, V. L. (2016). Fan pleasure and profit: Use-value, exchange-value, and one-sixth scale action figure customization. *The Journal of Fandom Studies*, *4*(1), 37–54.

Godwin, V. L. (2018). Customizations, collections and corporations: Mass production and self-expression. *The Journal of Fandom Studies*, *6*(3), 211–224. https://doi.org/10.1386/jfs.6.3.211_1

Godwin, V. L. (2024). Why costume fandom's distinctions from cosplay matter: Costuming's craft, histories, and motivations. *Transformative Works and Cultures*, *43*. https://doi.org/10.3983/twc.2024.2539

Gray, J. (2010). *Show sold separately: Promos, spoilers, and other media paratexts*. New York University Press.

Guschwan, M. (2012). Fandom, brandom and the limits of participatory culture. *Journal of Consumer Culture*, *12*(1), 19–40.

Hills, M. (2011). *Cultographies: Blade Runner*. Wallflower/Columbia University Press.

Hills, M. (2014). From Dalek half balls to Daft Punk helmets: Mimetic fandom and the crafting of replicas. In B. Rehak (Ed.), *Materiality and object-oriented fandom* (Special issue). *Transformative Works and Cultures* (Vol. 16). https://doi.org/10.3983/twc.2014.0531

Hoebink, D., Reijnders, S., & Waysdorf, A. (2014). Exhibiting fandom: A museological perspective. In B. Rehak (Ed.), *Materiality and object-oriented fandom* (Special issue). *Transformative Works and Cultures* (Vol. 16). https://doi.org/10.3983/twc.2014.0529

Huertas Gutierrez, R., & Gil Vasquez, A. (2026). Rewatching, reworking and reselling: Iconicity and fan art around Aquí no hay quien viva. In N. Jacobs (Ed.), *Bridging design and fandom*. Emerald Publishing Limited.

Jackson, L. (2014). *Dirty old London: The Victorian fight against filth*. Yale University Press.

Jacobs, N., & Lowe, J. S. A. (2024). The design of printed fan fiction. *Transformative Works and Cultures*, *43*. https://doi.org/10.3983/twc.2024.2547

Jenkins, H. (2020). *Comics and stuff*. New York University Press.

Jenkins, D. (2025, August 5). Before you spend money on that auction, please know that those are only props and costumes. *They hold no magic*. https://bsky.app/profile/david-jenkins.bsky.social/post/3lv6oxc7c722w

Johnson, C. (2007). Tele-branding in TVIII: The network as brand and the programme as brand. *New Review of Film and Television Studies*, *5*(1), 5–24. https://doi.org/10.1080/17400300601140126

Kakoty, S. (2018). Ecology, sustainability and traditional wisdom. *Journal of Cleaner Production*, *172*, 3215–3224. https://doi.org/10.1016/j.jclepro.2017.11.036

Kennedy, K., & Buchsbaum, S. B. (2022). Fanbinding and a community-generated information environment. *Proceedings from the Document Academy*, *9*(1), 6. https://doi.org/10.35492/docam/9/1/6

Kimmerer, R. W. (2013). The gift of strawberries. In *Braiding sweetgrass: Indigenous wisdom, scientific knowledge and the teachings of plants* (pp. 22–31). Milkweed Editions.

Lamerichs, N. (2025). Sustainable fandom: A virtual ethnography of sustainable cosplay and material culture on Instagram. In D. Ciesielska, N. Lamerichs, & A. Zarzycka (Eds.), *Affect in fandom: Fan creators and productivity* (pp. 89–107). Amsterdam University Press.

Minkel, E. (2025, August 6). Lots of people make money on fanfic. Just not the authors. *Wired*. https://www.wired.com/story/pull-to-publish-fanfic-senlinyu-manacled-fanbinding/

Noppe, N. (2011). Why we should talk about commodifying fan work. In C. Echoes (Ed.), *Textual echoes* (Special issue). *Transformative Works and Cultures* (Vol. 8). https://doi.org/10.3983/twc.2011.0369

Owen, V., Coulton, P., & Stead, M. (2026). Game changers: How fan activism across gaming cultures could help us design more sustainable technologies. In N. Jacobs (Ed.), *Bridging design and fandom*. Emerald Publishing Limited.

Pierotti, R., & Wildcat, D. (2000). Traditional ecological knowledge: The third alternative (commentary). *Ecological Applications*, *10*(5), 1333–1340. https://doi.org/10.2307/2641289

Rehak, B. (2014). Materiality and object-oriented fandom [Editorial]. *Transformative Works and Cultures, 16*. https://doi.org/10.3983/twc.2014.0622

Rendell, J. (2018). Bridge builders, world makers: Transcultural Studio Ghibli fan crafting. *East Asian Journal of Popular Culture*, *4*(1), 93–109.

Sandvoss, C. (2005). *Fans: The mirror of consumption*. Polity.

Santo, A. (2018). Fans and merchandise. In M. A. Click, & S. Scott (Eds.), *The Routledge companion to media fandom* (pp. 329–336). Routledge.

Snow Commerce. (2025). *HBO shop our flag means death collection*. https://shop.hbo.com/collections/our-flag-means-death

Walker, S. (2008). Sustainable design. In E. Manzini, S. Walker, & B. Wylant (Eds.), *Enabling solutions for sustainable living: A workshop* (pp. 25–30). University of Calgary Press.

Walker, S. (2011). *The spirit of design: Objects, environment and meaning*. Earthscan.

Walker, S. (2014). *Designing sustainability: Making radical changes in a material world*. Routledge.

Walker, S., Evans, M., & Mullagh, L. (2019). Meaningful practices: The contemporary relevance of traditional making for sustainable material futures. *Craft Research*, *10*(2), 183–210. https://doi.org/10.1386/crre_00002_1

Wayward Plaids. (n.d.). *Home page*. Etsy. https://www.etsy.com/shop/waywardplaids. Accessed on July 25, 2025

Williams, R. (2020). *Theme park fandom: Spatial transmedia, materiality and participatory cultures*. Amsterdam University Press.

Wilson, E. (2013). *Cultural passions: Fans, aesthetes and tarot readers*. I.B. Tauris.

WIPO. (n.d.). *Traditional knowledge*. https://www.wipo.int/en/web/traditional-knowledge/tk/index. Accessed on December 12, 2025

Woo, B. (2014). A pragmatics of things: Materiality and constraint in fan practices. In B. Rehak (Ed.), *Materiality and object-oriented fandom* (Special issue). *Transformative Works and Cultures* (Vol. 16). https://doi.org/10.3983/twc.2014.0495

Chapter 15

Game Changers: How Fan Activism Across Gaming Cultures Could Help Us Design More Sustainable Technologies

Violet Owen, Michael Stead and Paul Coulton

Lancaster University, UK

Abstract

Videogames, once a niche pastime, have become a widely popular and culturally embedded practice that brings together diverse communities of fans. This chapter examines fan practices that directly or indirectly support the longevity of videogame software and hardware and considers what these practices can teach us about extending the life of digital products more broadly. As digital technologies increasingly fuel a throwaway culture driven by cycles of rapid innovation, planned obsolescence and mounting electronic waste, the relationships and attachments that videogame fans share with their devices offers hope. These attachments pose a new perspective on how we might design to encourage cultures of repair and maintenance for our electronic devices. The chapter does not offer a single prescriptive solution; instead, it draws insights from videogame fandoms to imagine more sustainable and enduring attitudes to technology design.

Keywords: Videogames; gaming communities; gamers; fan activism; sustainability; emotionally durable design; sustainable technology cultures; technology obsolescence; e-waste

Bridging Design and Fandom, 233–248

doi:10.1108/978-1-80592-659-720261015

Introduction

It is estimated that over a third of the world's population play videogames (Moller et al., 2023). What was once a niche pastime has become increasingly culturally (DiTommaso et al., 2024), spiritually (Rupcic, 2023; Storey & Storey, 2016), socially (Kowert & Quandt, 2021), emotionally (Bean, 2021), developmentally (Rogers, 2016) and financially significant (Arora, 2023). Unlike other forms of media entertainment, videogames are ergodic (Aarseth, 1997); by design, they embody immersive, social and interactive experiences, which nurture a deeper attachment towards them. As such, videogames are not limited to entertainment; they support sustained social interactions (Ballard & Spencer, 2023); provide an arena for self-expression (Fung, 2017), experimentation (Przybylski et al., 2012), self-discovery (Szolin & Griffiths, 2022) and reflection (Ramos, 2020); and offer opportunities for employment (Johnson & Woodcock, 2017), education (Jenny et al., 2024) and competition (Ribeiro et al., 2023), as well as a platform for promoting personal or political agendas (Hills, 2018). To this end, videogames are both pervasive (Magerkurth et al., 2005) and ubiquitous (McGonigal, 2006); they have thoroughly permeated our digital, physical and social worlds.

The interweaving of videogames into society has encouraged the evolution of dedicated fandoms: diverse communities united through shared interests, coalescing around devices, technologies, people, places, organisations, activities and ideologies. The sustained and multi-faceted engagement gamers experience with their gaming technologies contrasts sharply with how people typically relate to other consumer technologies, such as smart televisions, phones and voice assistants. All of these technologies, videogames included (Asher, 2022), are subject to planned obsolescence, in which products are designed with terminal lifespans to ensure consumers need to continually buy new products (Animation Domination High Def, 2015). These market-driven pressures, combined with poor design ethics and inadequate end-of-life management, result in short product life spans (Magnier & Mugge, 2022), contributing significantly to the global surge in electronic waste (e-waste) (Stead et al., 2022). However, gamers have been seen to resist or subvert the prevailing consumerist narrative. While they often acquire new technologies, they are less eager to dispose of the 'outdated' ones, instead choosing to keep and care for their products far beyond their protean lifecycle (Owen et al., 2024). This culture of care can be understood as a form of fan activism (Close, 2018), where commitment to maintaining and preserving gaming technologies constitutes acts of defiance against unsustainable consumer practices.

In this chapter, we focus on the intersection between sustainable game cultures, technological obsolescence, videogame fandom and fan activism. By investigating the nature of the relationships between gamers, their communities and their technologies, this chapter imagines how electronic products of the future could be designed for greater sustainability.

It's More Than Just a Console

Videogame fandom is highly heterogeneous, encompassing a wide range of attachments that extend beyond individual games to include hardware and software, creators and communities, organisations and studios, genres, play styles, narratives, ideologies, brands and franchises. These attachments are expressed through diverse practices such as collecting consoles, games and merchandise (Santo, 2017); socialising online and in person through forums, social media, in-game communication and conventions (Taylor, 2006); acts of artistic expression including fan art, fanfiction and cosplay (Peeples et al., 2018); pursuing education or professional pathways related to games (Emmanouloudis, 2022); developing new content for legacy systems (Montfort & Bogost, 2009); and participating in archiving and preservation efforts (Dym et al., 2023). Videogame fandom frequently intersects with other domains of popular culture (Picard, 2008), intensifying emotional investment and deepening fans' relationships with games and gaming technologies.

Together, these practices start to illustrate how videogames transcend their primary function as entertainment, becoming socially embedded and emotionally meaningful artefacts. This significance can be further understood through research on Emotionally Durable Design (Chapman, 2012), which 'examines and articulates the unspoken emotional experiences that occur between products and consumers, seeking to uncover the complex emotional drivers for why we use, consume, and discard some products faster than others' (Haines-Gadd et al., 2018). For many gamers, videogames accrue value as fandom develops, especially through participation in shared and socially meaningful experiences. These interactions contribute to the emotional durability of gaming objects, reshaping how value is perceived and encouraging longer-term care and retention.

Like most technologies, videogames are designed for transience (Newman, 2012). Hardware generations advance, software support is withdrawn and access to games is often limited. Paradoxically, the threat of loss or discontinuation can increase a videogame's perceived value. Rarity, scarcity and the knowledge that a device or game may soon become inaccessible frequently motivate gamers to retain or recover technologies that might otherwise be discarded (Lowood et al., 2009). Nostalgia also encourages gamers to (re)acquire outdated games and technologies. It has become commonplace on sites like eBay to find decommissioned gaming devices, bought to complete a collection; to replace consoles that may have been sold, lost or irreparably damaged over the years (or exchanged for your brother's best friend's BB gun) or that were never owned but long desired. Gamers also place high value on an authentic gaming experience, compelling them to figure out how to make older and newer technologies compatible or learn how to repair devices from a bygone era (Wells, 2025). Their willingness to invest time, money and effort into preserving their games beyond their market value indicates a shift in how these objects are perceived.

Social engagement is another mechanism that can bolster the value of videogames (Ryan et al., 2006). By design, videogames encourage interaction between players through built-in mechanisms, like the camaraderie of localised multiplayer, or voice-chat functionalities commonplace in collaborative online play. The advent of cross-platform play has also bridged formerly divided gamer sub-groups (i.e. PC and console gamers), as owning the same device is no longer a requirement for many games (Shen et al., 2025). Beyond developer-orchestrated engagement, gamers have constructed extensive online ecosystems dedicated to discussion, sharing resources, news, tips and walkthroughs, and reminiscing. Historically, these exchanges took place on message boards, chat-rooms and forums. However, the rise of online video services, such as YouTube, Facebook and Twitch, has introduced new forms of engagement (i.e. live-streaming gameplay), which have further diversified and expanded gamer fandom. Through these networks, videogames become socially situated objects, valued not only for play but also for the relationships and communities they support. These sites are not only valued by gamers. In recent years, game publishers have also recognised the importance of these social spaces (Thiel & Lyle, 2019), such as the role they play in sustaining player engagement between game releases. Many publishers now host or endorse official sites to encourage these interactions.

For many gamers, familial experiences play a formative role in the development of fandom. Practices such as 'intergenerational passing' (Yodovich, 2022), where consoles and games are shared across generations, position gaming devices as both facilitators of shared interests and repositories of familial memory. Ownership of gaming devices is also often shared, particularly between siblings. Historically, technology limitations have also played a role in encouraging familial play. Prior to broadband and Wi-Fi access becoming commonplace, multiplayer gaming often required shared physical presence, lengthy setup processes and transporting cumbersome equipment. Essential equipment such as CRT TVs was usually housed in shared common areas rather than bedrooms due to their size, which further limited access and usage. These constraints limited play with non-household members, so many siblings grew up gaming together.

Over time, these shared experiences can become attached to gaming objects, rendering them biographical. Imbued with personal histories, such objects can transcend normative product lifecycles. Fig. 15.1, depicting a Sega Dreamcast retained since childhood, and the following autoethnographic reflection (Sturm, 2015) by Author 1, together illustrate this phenomenon.

> My consoles were originally purchased for my brother, and over time, ownership passed to me. I've kept them all. Even the games I never liked playing. I didn't consider them valuable, but imperceptibly, they've always felt too important to discard. Now, their value is tangible. They are biographical objects, inseparable from my memories. Looking at them is like holding a mirror up and seeing my past self. I remember growing up under the weight of the 90's gender-normative toxicity, in a society that refused to accept me… the resentment I felt toward my parents for never buying me a console, only my brother, and towards myself for never feeling allowed to ask for one. I remember my elation at my

Fig. 15.1. Author 1's Sega Dreamcast Circa 1999. Credit Violet Owen.

> brother asking me to play the Halo co-op campaign with him, that turned to outrage as he kicked me for taking up too much space lying across the foot of his single bed, and vindication as his character died before mine. I shuffle through my collection of games, and fondly sigh when I get to Shenmue II, recalling my wonderment at its the cinematic cutscenes that seemed so realistic at the time. I'll never forget the hours I spent driving a forklift. I find a lone Gameboy cartridge and feel a sense of loss at the incompleteness of my collection, while fondly reminiscing the many nights I spent secretly playing Pokémon Red by torchlight. (Author 1)

While there are many factors that shape perceptions of value, personal experiences such as nostalgia (Nicholas, 2021), self-expression (Schniz, 2023) and wellbeing (Bowman et al., 2022), alongside shared experiences of family (Yodovich, 2022) and community (Zervas & Maronitis, 2025) can foster emotional durability. As these experiences accumulate, gaming objects become biographical, imbued with personal and collective narratives, extending their use and elevating their significance beyond market or functional value. This transformation helps explain why gamers often resist disposal, invest in maintenance and repair, and retain gaming technologies well beyond their intended lifespans, challenging conventional models of technological consumption and obsolescence.

Acts of Playful Resistance

Videogames have increasingly acted as sites for hosting, inspiring or inciting various forms of activism (Davies, 2022), which Jones (2009) describes as the 'use of videogame technology to bring about social or political change'. Games explicitly designed for such purposes are commonly described as Serious Games (Abt, 1970), Games for Change (Ndulue & Orji, 2023), Persuasive Games (Bogost, 2007) or Deep Games (Rusch, 2017). However, this chapter shifts focus beyond purpose-built interventions to explore examples of community-led activism, in which gamers, rather than organisations, mobilise change through their fandom. We conceptualise these practices as *playful resistance*: informal, creative and often pleasurable acts through which gamers challenge dominant logics of disposability, control and consumption. In particular, we examine practices that emerge from the formal and informal assemblages that gamers inhabit, such as modding, archiving and repair, to reflect on the nature of gamer-led sustainability activism.

Among the most documented examples of gamers engaging in sustainability-oriented activism are acts of preservation and archiving. The habitual collecting of games, consoles and paraphernalia fulfils an intrinsic need to retain, revisit and remember (Dym et al., 2023). Many of these acts transpired intuitively long before the lifecycles of such artefacts were under threat. For example, Fig. 15.2 shows an original Nintendo Gameboy Colour (circa 1998) shared by a participant during a workshop as part of the EPSRC-funded *Fixing the Future: The Right-to-Repair and Equal IoT* project (2022–2025). The participant explained that this device would never be discarded; despite being non-functional for many years, it was retained through multiple international relocations and eventually restored by following an instructional YouTube video. This example highlights both the Gameboy's enduring value to its owner and the crucial role of fan networks (such as YouTube repair tutorials) in enabling technology preservation.

Alongside individual efforts, institutions play an important role in technology preservation. The National Videogame Museum in Sheffield, for instance, has preserved over 5,000 objects related to videogame heritage and has been instrumental in formalising systematic approaches to videogame archiving in the United Kingdom (Newman & Simons, 2009). Together, grassroots and institutional initiatives demonstrate how preservation operates across informal and formal contexts, resisting consumerist pressures and the logic of planned obsolescence. That such efforts persist even when devices are non-functional signals the intrinsic value attributed to gaming technologies, both by individual owners and by society more broadly.

Another form of preservation is emulation, whereby defunct systems are replicated using newer technologies to recreate aspects of the original experience (Dor, 2013). These proxy technologies offer some advantages; for example, digital archives don't physically degrade; they require fewer material resources

Fig. 15.2. Participant's Gameboy Colour Circa 1998. Photograph Taken and Shared by Participant as Part of EPSRC Funded Fixing the Future: The Right-to-Repair and Equal IoT Project.

and are not limited by physical storage space. However, for many, emulated play is underwhelming and perceived as inauthentic (Swalwell, 2017); for example, a phone emulation of arcade classic Pac-Man (Namco, 1980) contains similar content, but the embodied interactions are entirely different. Legal concerns further complicate emulation; practices such as 'jailbreaking' devices or sharing pirated copies of games (Conley et al., 2004) can raise concerns about legality (Guay-Bélanger, 2022). Despite these tensions, emulation remains an important facet of videogame fan culture. Demand for authentic experiences has also driven publishers to release remastered editions of legacy titles; for example, *Elder Scrolls IV: Oblivion* Remastered (Bethesda), launched in 2025, has already sold more copies than the original published in 2006 (King, 2025).

Modding represents another prominent site of playful resistance. It developed as an informal, grassroots, community-led, participatory practice (Postigo, 2010) as a way 'to adapt digital games to the needs of their players and incorporate content from other media, such as books, movies, or series, into the game world' (Reisinho et al., 2024). While not typically framed as a sustainability practice, modding often enhances gameplay, encourages longer-term engagement and increases the likelihood that players will retain and continue using a game.

Historically, mods have been used to improve software and hardware performance, introduce new mechanics or content and support accessibility needs (Bayliss, 2022). Modding cultures also demonstrate the highly connected assemblages that gamers inhabit. For example, the viral spread of 'Maxwell the Cat'. The original meme uploaded in 2017 by Imgur (https://imgur.com/) user Voidhawk4 has undergone many transformations, the most notable including a 3D model called 'dingus' by alwayshasbean (2022: see Fig. 15.3) and the mod 'Maxwell the Carryable Cat' by ScottRim (2022), and a main character in the indie videogame 'Cat and Capy' by Matato Games (2025: https://matatogames.com/). In addition to thousands of modders making Maxwell variants, Maxwell also features in viral social media content attracting millions of views. This includes YouTube videos, for example 'Half-Life 2, but I have a cat' by Awesome Te4m (2022), X posts, for example the spinning Maxwell GIF tweet by blastycats (2022) and TikTok animations, for example 'cat and capy' series by Matato (2025), as well as being bestowed a theme song, 'Stock Market', by Mr Weebl (2007). Maxwell the Cat illustrates how popular culture, games and online communities intersect to sustain fan engagement.

Modding has also functioned as a means of contesting developer control (Bódi, 2023). For example, changes introduced by EA in *The Sims 4* (2014) that reduced the likelihood of character death prompted vocal backlash from players, as illustrated in the following Reddit post by Darkbloom (2022),

> My elder Sim has out lived his wife and I'm kind of done with him. I put him in the pool and removed the ladder but he just jumped out of it. Back in my day (😵 I'm old), you could just drown them and be done. Now they seem like they can't be k!ll3d. Why??!!!

Fig. 15.3. Screenshot of 'Maxwell the Cat (Dingus)' 3D Model on Sketchfab https://sketchfab.com/3d-models/maxwell-the-cat-dingus-2ca7f3c1957847d6a145fc35de9046b0. This Work by Alwayshasbean is Licenced Under a Creative Commons Attribution 4.0 International Licence.

This perceived censorship motivated modders to create unofficial content that reinstated previously removed mechanics, such as Sacrificial's controversial Extreme Violence Mod (https://sacrificialmods.com/), which introduces over 40 ways to kill Sims.

Due to mod content being largely unchecked, modding affords both opportunity and risk. While mods can be used to challenge harmful rhetoric embedded in videogames and promote greater diversity and representation (Curtis et al., 2022; De la Torre-Sierra & Guichot-Reina, 2025; Lees, 2024), they have also been employed to reproduce or amplify racist, homophobic and sexist agendas (Schlegel et al., 2024). This tension is exemplified within the modding communities surrounding the *Baldur's Gate* series (BioWare, 1998, 2000, Larian Studios, 2023). Mc Grath (2025) reported players using mods to expand character customisation options, such as increased availability of Asian facial features, allowing a better representation of player ethnicity – in stark contrast to the 'Ser Aylin' mod, which rewrites a key LGBTQ+ plot by altering the gender of the character Dame Aylin, reframing the storyline as heterosexual (Walker, 2023).

Finally, although videogame modding is often an informal and grassroots practice, it is not totally emancipated from the mainstream videogame industry. Game studios have long drawn on modding communities for innovation, bug fixing and design inspiration, echoing with Postigo's (2007) depiction of modders as 'fan-programmers'. Some developers actively support these practices by releasing modding tools, open-source assets or early access builds, such as Quake's (id Software, 1996) player-generated maps function or the modding toolkit 'Worldcraft' released with Half-Life (Valve, 1998).

We contend that community practices such as modding, archiving, emulation, retrofitting and repair demonstrate how gamers playfully resist consumerist cycles of technological disposability (Crofoot, 2024; Dym et al., 2023). While rarely articulated as explicit political action, these practices function as forms of sustainability activism. They unintentionally create a symbiosis that extends product lifespans, supports maintenance and reuse and foregrounds the often-overlooked potential of software sustainability alongside hardware concerns.

Gaming Cultures as a Blueprint for Sustainable Design

Many gamers exhibit an innate drive to keep and care for their gaming devices and games; the motivations for doing so are often intangible or difficult to articulate. However, as explored in this chapter, gaming technologies are not experienced solely as functional artefacts or entertainment systems. Rather, they operate simultaneously as sites of play, social connection, self-expression and repositories of personal and collective memory.

In contrast, other consumer technologies, such as Internet of Things and smart devices, rarely elicit such an attachment. This difference can be partly attributed to prevailing technology design ideologies, such as Ubiquitous Computing (Weiser, 1991), which prioritise seamless integration and invisibility.

Their emphasis on inconspicuousness, limited tangible interaction and focus on mundane tasks often results in technologies that feel emotionally distant. Design decisions that prioritise inaccessible hardware, proprietary software and closed ecosystems further limit opportunities for user engagement. Unlike gaming technologies, they offer little scope for playfulness, experimentation or collaboration with users (Owen et al., 2024). These implicit design decisions, combined with fast-moving, profit-driven consumer markets, increase the likelihood of premature replacement and disposal (Coulton et al., 2025), further contributing to the global e-waste epidemic (Smieja, 2023). As a result, society remains trapped in cycles of overconsumption, filling our own personal graveyards with still-functional but superfluous technologies (Banfield-Nwachi, 2025).

These conditions underscore the need to rethink how relationships between people and technologies are designed and sustained. The videogame industry itself is far from a model of environmental responsibility, contributing to energy consumption, material extraction and e-waste generation (ten Cate, 2025). Nevertheless, the incidental activism of gamers and the broader cultural practices that support care, repair and preservation offer an opportunity to reframe our relationship with digital technology. In this context, the concept of the 'disappearing computer' (Streitz, 2007) becomes particularly relevant; as technologies become increasingly invisible and embedded, users may become less attuned to their ecological impact and material afterlives.

However, as explored in this chapter, gamers often share a markedly different relationship with videogame producers. Gamers frequently participate actively in the development, use and afterlife of their technologies, assuming responsibilities that extend well beyond consumption. These actions are facilitated by industry practices that recognise the expertise of player communities, including open-source tools, modding platforms, beta testing, feedback mechanisms and co-development models (O'Donnell, 2014). In contrast, producers of other consumer technologies typically provide limited opportunities for engagement, reinforcing passive consumption and restricting user agency. This confluence of issues has collectively contributed to widespread consumer dissatisfaction with poorly designed, unsustainable and difficult-to-dispose of technologies (Harris, 2020).

This raises an important question. What might change if relationships between users and manufacturers of other technologies more closely resembled those found in gaming communities? Moving away from a culture of blame towards a model of shared responsibility would require manufacturers to extend greater trust to users. But by adopting the kinds of approaches embodied by gaming communities, designers and manufacturers could create technologies that are emotionally durable, socially valued and actively maintained over time.

Conclusion

Technology sustainability remains one of the most pressing global challenges. Videogames, and their passionate communities, offer a valuable lens through which to examine the relational challenges of technology sustainability. This chapter does not argue that other technologies should emulate videogames by replicating their capabilities, interfaces or functions. Rather, it highlights the importance of understanding how people, particularly gamers, relate to their devices and how these relationships shape practices of care, maintenance and disposal.

This chapter offers insights into how gamers' experiences of their products, such as their emotional attachment, social participation and shared ownership, can challenge technology obsolescence. Designing technologies with the expectation of disposability limits opportunities for care and repair. By contrast, imagining devices as objects that might be valued, maintained and even loved over time opens new possibilities for sustainable design.

At the same time, videogame fandom should not be idolised. The industry and its audiences also contribute to overconsumption, high energy use and e-waste production. Further, practices such as hoarding obsolete technologies can be problematic; as resources become increasingly depleted, sustainability requires not only knowing how to preserve and care for technologies but also when to let them go. Recognising this tension is essential if lessons drawn from gaming cultures are to meaningfully inform broader efforts towards sustainable technological futures.

References

Aarseth, E. J. (1997). *Cybertext: Perspectives on ergodic literature.* Johns Hopkins University Press.

Abt, C. C. (1970). *Serious games.* The Viking Press.

Animation Domination High Def. (2015, August 3). *ADHD U: Planned obsolescence* Video. Youtube. https://www.youtube.com/watch?v=lW17rr20tGY&list=RDlW17rr20tGY&start_radio=1&t=16s

Arora, K. (2023, November 17). The gaming industry: A behemoth with unprecedented global reach. *Forbes.* https://www.forbes.com/councils/forbesagencycouncil/2023/11/17/the-gaming-industry-a-behemoth-with-unprecedented-global-reach/

Asher, C. (2022, October 25). Playing dangerously: The environmental impact of video gaming consoles. *Mongabay.* https://news.mongabay.com/2022/10/playing-dangerously-the-environmental-impact-of-video-gaming-consoles/

Awesome Te4m. (2022). *Half-life 2 but I have a cat* [Video]. Youtube.

Ballard, M. E., & Spencer, M. T. (2023). Importance of social videogaming for connection with others during the COVID-19 pandemic. *Games and Culture, 18*(2), 251–264. https://doi.org/10.1177/15554120221090982

Banfield-Nwachi, M. (2025, June 24). 'It's cheap but it's not disposable': Why fast tech is a growing waste problem. *The Guardian.* https://www.theguardian.com/technology/2025/jun/24/its-cheap-but-its-not-disposable-why-fast-tech-is-a-growing-waste-problem

Bayliss, B. (2022, March 25). Older PlayStation games heading to PC is a win for accessibility. But disability tax remains. *Eurogamer.* https://www.eurogamer.net/older-playstation-games-heading-to-pc-is-a-win-for-accessibility

Bean, A. (2021). Therapeutic use of video games. In R. Kowert & T. Quandt (Eds.), *The video game debate 2* (pp. 117–133). Taylor & Francis Group. https://doi.org/10.4324/9780429351815

BioWare. (1998). *Baldur's Gate. PC [Game]*. Interplay Entertainment.

BioWare. (2000). *Baldur's Gate II: Shadows of Amn. PC [Game]*. Interplay Entertainment.

blastycats [@blastycats]. (2022, November 4). *Acquired C A T. You put the C A T in your K E Y I T E M S pocket*. [GIF attached] [Post]. X. https://x.com/blastycats/status/1588571209482252295

Bódi, B. (2023). *Videogames and agency*. Taylor & Francis. https://www.routledge.com/Videogames-and-Agency/Bodi/p/book/9781032288475

Bogost, I. (2007). *Persuasive games: The expressive power of videogames*. MIT Press. https://doi.org/10.7551/mitpress/5334.001.0001

Bowman, N. D., Rieger, D., & Lin, J.-H. T. (2022). Social video gaming and well-being. *Current Opinion in Psychology*, *45*, 101316. https://doi.org/10.1016/j.copsyc.2022.101316

Cat and Capy. (2025). *Mobile [Game]*. Matato Games. https://www.matatogames.com

Chapman, J. (2012). *Emotionally durable design: Objects, experiences and empathy*. Taylor & Francis Group. http://ebookcentral.proquest.com/lib/lancaster/detail.action?docID=430088

Close, S. (2018). Fan activism. In G. Meikle (Ed.), *The routledge companion to media and activism* (pp. 531–545). Taylor & Francis Group.

Conley, J., Andros, E., Chinai, P., Lipkowitz, E., & Perez, D. (2004). Use of a game over: Emulation and the video game industry, a white paper. *Northwestern Journal of Technology and Intellectual Property*, *2*, 261. https://scholarlycommons.law.northwestern.edu/njtip/vol2/iss2/3/

Coulton, P., Stead, M., & Owen, V. (2025). Smarter repair 2053. *The Design Journal*, *28*(1), 126–145. https://doi.org/10.1080/14606925.2024.2437597

Crofoot, E. (2024, November 20). *Game preservation as archeology & the slow death of video game history*. https://elicrofoot.com/2024/11/20/game-preservation-as-archeology-the-slow-death-of-video-game-history

Curtis, J., Oxburgh, G., & Briggs, P. (2022). Heroes and hooligans: The heterogeneity of video game modders. *Games and Culture*, *17*(2), 219–243. https://doi.org/10.1177/15554120211026255

Darkbloom [u/dark_bloom12]. (2022, October 17). *Can we not drown them anymore?* Reddit. [Online forum post]. https://www.reddit.com/r/Sims4/comments/10j61fz/can_we_not_drown_them_anymore/

Davies, H. (2022). The revolution will not be gamified. *British Journal of Chinese Studies*, *12*(2), 76–100. https://doi.org/10.51661/bjocs.v12i2.200

De la Torre-Sierra, A. M., & Guichot-Reina, V. (2025). Women in video games: An analysis of the biased representation of female characters in current video games. *Sexuality & Culture*, *29*(2), 532–560. https://doi.org/10.1007/s12119-024-10286-0

DiTommaso, L., Crossley, J., Lockhart, A., & Wagner, R. (2024). *End-game: Apocalyptic video games, contemporary society, and digital media culture*. Walter de Gruyter GmbH.

Dor, S. (2013). Emulation. In M. J. P. Wolf & B. Perron (Eds.), *The Routledge companion to video game studies* (pp. 67–77). Taylor & Francis Group. https://doi.org/10.4324/9781003214977

Dym, B., Simpson, E., Fong, O., & striegl, l. (2023). The internet is not forever: Challenges and sustainability in video game archiving and preservation. *Journal of Electronic Gaming and Esports*, *1*(1). https://doi.org/10.1123/jege.2022-0041

Emmanouloudis, A. (2022). *A game of pawns: Fan-made content and resistance in online video game communities*. Universiteit van Amsterdam. https://hdl.handle.net/11245.1/8feeb3da-cb08-4f8c-b3a0-224a06a67987

Fung, C. (2017). Playing with identities: Queering digital narratology and the exploration of gender and sexual identities. *Digital Humanities Quarterly*, *11*(3). https://doi.org/10.4225/03/5a1b50be6fc35

Guay-Bélanger, D. (2022). Assembling auras: Towards a methodology for the preservation and study of video games as cultural heritage artefacts. *Games and Culture*, *17*(5), 659–678. https://doi.org/10.1177/15554120211020381

Haines-Gadd, M., Chapman, J., Lloyd, P., Mason, J., & Aliakseyeu, D. (2018). Emotional durability design nine—A tool for product longevity. *Sustainability*, *10*(6). https://doi.org/10.3390/su10061948

Harris, J. (2020, April 15). Planned obsolescence: The outrage of our electronic waste Mountain. *The Guardian*. https://www.theguardian.com/technology/2020/apr/15/the-right-to-repair-planned-obsolescence-electronic-waste-mountain

Hills, M. (2018). An extended foreword: From fan Doxa to toxic fan practices. *Participations: Journal of Audience & Reception Studies*, *15*(1), 105–126. https://www.participations.org/15-01-07-hills.pdf

Jenny, S. E., Gawrysiak, J., O'Hagan, J., & Besombes, N. (2024). Esports education. In *Routledge handbook of esports* (pp. 441–453). Routledge. https://doi.org/10.4324/9781003410591

Johnson, M. R., & Woodcock, J. (2017). It's like the gold rush': The lives and careers of professional video game streamers on Twitch.tv. *Information, Communication & Society*, *22*(3), 336–351. https://doi.org/10.1080/1369118X.2017.1386229

Jones, R. (2009). Saving worlds with videogame activism. In R. E. Ferdig (Ed.), *Handbook of research on effective electronic gaming in education* (pp. 970–988). IGI Global. https://doi.org/10.4018/978-1-59904-808-6.ch056

King, J. (2025, 26 May). Oblivion Remastered's success is a sad sign of where video games are right now. *TheGamer*. https://www.thegamer.com/oblivion-remastered-nostalgia-bethesda-sales-figures-success/

Kowert, R., & Quandt, T. (2021). *The video game debate 2: Revisiting the physical, social, and psychological effects of video games*. Taylor & Francis Group. https://doi.org/10.4324/9780429351815

Larian Studios. (2023). *Baldur's Gate 3. PC/Console [Game]*. Larian Studios.

Lees, S. (2024). *Unpacking the code: Game modification as a form of queer play*. Lancaster University. PhD Thesis. https://doi.org/10.17635/lancaster/thesis/2684

Lowood, H., Monnens, D., Armstrong, A., Ruggill, J., McAllister, K. S., Vowell, Z., & Donahue, R. (2009). Before it's too late: A digital game preservation white paper. *American Journal of Play*, *2*(2), 139–166. https://digitalcommons.calpoly.edu/lib_fac/107/

Magerkurth, C., Cheok, A. D., Mandryk, R. L., & Nilsen, T. (2005). Pervasive games: Bringing computer entertainment back to the real world. *Computer Entertainment*, *3*(3), 4. https://doi.org/10.1145/1077246.1077257

Magnier, L., & Mugge, R. (2022). Replaced too soon? An exploration of Western European consumers' replacement of electronic products. *Resources, Conservation and Recycling*, *185*, 106448. https://doi.org/10.1016/j.resconrec.2022.106448

Matato [matatogames]. (2022). *The collab you've all been waiting for TikTok*. https://www.tiktok.com/@matatogames/video/7179163174057364742?is_from_webapp=1&sender_device=pc&web_id=7535419073330021910

McGonigal, J. E. (2006). *This might be a game: Ubiquitous play and performance at the turn of the twenty-first century*. University of California. PhD Thesis. https://dl.acm.org/doi/book/10.5555/1292900

Mc Grath, M. E. (2025). *Queernormativity & freedom in Baldur's gate 3: Enabling true self exploration & expression for queer players*. Institute of Art, Design+Technology.

Moller, A. C., Sousa, C. V., Lee, K. J., Alon, D., & Lu, A. S. (2023). Active video game interventions targeting physical activity behaviors: Systematic review and meta-analysis. *Journal of Medical Internet Research*, *25*. https://doi.org/10.2196/45243

Montfort, N., & Bogost, I. (2009). *Racing the beam: The atari video computer system*. The MIT Press. https://doi.org/10.7551/mitpress/7588.001.0001

Mr Weebl. (2007, January 26). *Stock market* [Video]. Youtube. https://youtu.be/3W-EkANZX8g?si=2CgU2WB0K3CSxG4H

Ndulue, C., & Orji, R. (2023). Games for change-A comparative systematic review of persuasive strategies in games for behavior change. *IEEE Transactions on Games*, *15*(2), 121–133. https://doi.org/10.1109/TG.2022.3159090

Newman, J. (2012). *Best before: Videogames, supersession and obsolescence*. Taylor & Francis Group. https://doi.org/10.4324/9780203144268

Newman, J., & Simons, I. (2009). *Make videogames history: Game preservation and the national videogame archive*. DiGRA 2009. https://dl.digra.org/index.php/dl/article/view/489/489

Nicholas, J. (2021, December 25). Nostalgic gaming: How playing the video games of your youth reconnects you to yourself. *The Guardian*. https://www.theguardian.com/games/2021/dec/26/nostalgic-gaming-how-playing-the-video-games-of-your-youth-reconnects-you-to-yourself#comments

O'Donnell, C. (2014). *Developer's dilemma: The secret world of videogame creators*. The MIT Press. https://doi.org/10.7551/mitpress/9035.001.0001

Owen, V., Stead, M., & Coulton, P. (2024). Fostering IoT repair through care: Learning from emotional durable gaming practices and communities. In *ACM conference on designing interactive systems 2024*. Copenhagen. https://dl.acm.org/doi/10.1145/3656156.3663702

Pac-Man. (1980). *Arcade [Game]*. Namco/Midway Manufacturing.

Peeples, D., Yen, J., & Weigle, P. (2018). Geeks, fandoms, and social engagement. *Child and Adolescent Psychiatric Clinics*, *27*(2), 247–267. https://doi.org/10.1016/j.chc.2017.11.008

Picard, M. (2008). Video games and their relationship with other media. In M. J. Wolf (Ed.), *The video game explosion: A history from Pong to playstation and beyond* (pp. 293–300). Greenwood. https://doi.org/10.5040/9798216032106.ch-041

Postigo, H. (2007). Of mods and modders: Chasing down the value of fan-based digital game modifications. *Games and Culture*, *2*(4), 300–313. https://doi.org/10.1177/1555412007307955

Postigo, H. (2010). Modding to the big leagues: Exploring the space between modders and the game industry. *First Monday*, *15*(5). https://doi.org/10.5210/fm.v15i5.2972

Przybylski, A. K., Weinstein, N., Murayama, K., Lynch, M. F., & Ryan, R. M. (2012). The ideal self at play: The appeal of video games that let you be all you can be. *Psychological Science*, *23*(1), 69–76. https://doi.org/10.1177/0956797611418676

Quake. (1996). *PC [Game]*. id Software/GT Interactive.

Ramos, K. (2020, July 28). Introspection in video games: Video games have evolved to be more than just entertainment. *The Medium*. https://medium.com/super-jump/introspection-in-video-games-fd65a5476eb9

Reisinho, P., Raposo, R., & Zagalo, N. (2024). The ethical dilemma of modding digital games: A literature review of the creation and distribution of mods. *Convergence*, *30*(2), 860–881. https://doi.org/10.1177/13548565231223933

Ribeiro, T., Calapez, A., Almeida, V., & Matsuoka, H. (2023). Understanding the role of sport values on social capital and word-of-mouth on the internet: A case study of esports games. *Simulation & Gaming*, *54*(6), 645–679. https://doi.org/10.1177/10468781231197175

Rogers, R. (2016). *How video games impact players: The pitfalls and benefits of a gaming society*. Lexington Books.

Rupcic, T. (2023). Techno-religion and cyberspace spirituality in dystopian video games. *Religions*, *14*(2), 247. https://www.mdpi.com/2077-1444/14/2/247

Rusch, D. (2017). *Making deep games* (1st ed.). CRC Press. https://doi.org/10.1201/9781315748986

Ryan, R. M., Rigby, C. S., & Przybylski, A. (2006). The motivational pull of video games: A self-determination theory approach. *Motivation and Emotion*, *30*(4), 344–360. https://doi.org/10.1007/s11031-006-9051-8

Santo, A. (2017). Fans and merchandise. In M. A. Click & S. Scott (Eds.), *The Routledge companion to media fandom* (pp. 329–336). Routledge. https://doi.org/10.4324/9781315637518

Schlegel, L., Wiegold, L., Winkler, C., & Junk, J. (2024). Exploring the digital extremist ecosystem: A preliminary analysis of hateful posts on Mod DB. *Frontiers in Psychology*, *15*. https://doi.org/10.3389/fpsyg.2024.1502098

Schniz, F. (2023). I believe in videogames. In L. Marcato & F. Schniz (Eds.), *Fictional practices of spirituality* (p. 211). GmbH.

ScottRim. (2022). *Maxwell the Carryable Cat [Post]*. Steam. https://steamcommunity.com/sharedfiles/filedetails/?id=2878054450

Shen, R., Garaialde, D., & Doherty, K. (2025). Cross platform gaming: More than the sum of its parts? *ACM Games*, *3*(4), 21. Article. https://doi.org/10.1145/3774417

Smieja, J. (2023, March 17). The enormous opportunity of e-waste recycling. *Trellis*. https://trellis.net/article/enormous-opportunity-e-waste-recycling/

Stead, M., Coulton, P., Pilling, F., Gradinar, A., Pilling, M., & Forrester, I. (2022). More-than-Human-Data interaction: Bridging novel design research approaches to materialise and foreground data sustainability 25th international. In *Academic mindtrek conference*. https://doi.org/10.1145/3569219.3569344

Storey, F., & Storey, J. (2016). Spirituality and video games: Re-inventing initiation in the digital age. In J. Mata-McMahon, T. Kovač, & G. Grace (Eds.), *Spirituality: An interdisciplinary view* (pp. 151–161). Brill. https://doi.org/10.1163/9781848883710_014

Streitz, N. A. (2007). The disappearing computer. In *HCI remixed: Reflections on works that have influenced the HCI community*. The MIT Press. https://doi.org/10.7551/mitpress/7455.003.0014

Sturm, D. (2015). Playing with the autoethnographical:performing and re-presenting the fan's voice. *Cultural Studies ↔ Critical Methodologies*, *15*(3), 213–223. https://doi.org/10.1177/1532708614565454

Swalwell, M. (2017). Moving on from the original experience. Philosophies of preservation and Dis/play in game history. In M. Swalwell, A. Ndalianis, & H. Stuckey (Eds.), *Fans and videogames: Histories, fandom, archives*. Taylor & Francis Group.

Szolin, K., & Griffiths, M. D. (2022). Why imaginary worlds? The role of self-exploration within online gaming worlds. *Behavioral and Brain Sciences*, *45*, e302. https://doi.org/10.1017/S0140525X21002077

Taylor, T. L. (2006). *Play between worlds: Exploring online game culture*. The MIT Press. https://doi.org/10.7551/mitpress/5418.001.0001

ten Cate, D. H. (2025). *'Anecdotal evidence': A holistic approach to the ecological analysis of videogames*. DiGRA. https://doi.org/10.26503/dl.v2025i2.2427

The Sims 4. (2014). *PC [Game]*. Electronic Arts.

Thiel, S.-K., & Lyle, P. (2019). Malleable games - A literature review on communities of game modders. In *9th international conference on communities & technologies - Transforming communities*. https://doi.org/10.1145/3328320.3328393

Walker, I. (2023, December 6). Infamous Baldur's gate 3 anti-LGBTQ+ mod removed from Nexus Mods. The dweebs continue to be not welcome. *Polygon*. https://www.polygon.com/23991023/baldurs-gate-3-bg3-no-alphabets-mods-nexus-anti-lgbtq

Weiser, M. (1991). The computer for the 21st century. *Scientific American*, *265*(3), 94–105. http://www.jstor.org/stable/24938718

Wells, K. (2025, January 12). The rise of retro gaming. *PowerUp Gaming*. https://www.powerupgaming.ca/blogs/news/the-rise-of-retro-gaming?srsltid=AfmBOopPtJYrQmigURZF3ZYDk_rrHyjfyXBUyx09xZkzykuqizEId0_S

Worldcraft 2.0. (1998). *PC [Software Development Kit]*. Valve/Sierra Studios.

Yodovich, N. (2022). Like father, like daughter: The intergenerational passing of doctor who and star wars fandom in the familial context. In B. Kies & M. Connor (Eds.), *Fandom, the next generation*. University of Iowa Press.

Zervas, K., & Maronitis, K. (2025). Digital bonds: A gamers' perspective on the role of online gaming communities in fostering social interaction and identity. *International Review for the Sociology of Sport*. https://doi.org/10.1177/10126902251349297

Chapter 16

Sustainable Design: Creating Responsible Products and Services With Fans

Nicolle Lamerichs

HU University of Applied Sciences Utrecht, Netherlands

Abstract

Design is a vital element of fandom and participatory cultures. By producing fan art, Fanfiction and costumes, fans not only express their passion for their favourite narratives but also express themselves creatively. Fans increasingly work towards fairer, responsible and regenerative design practices, which can also be conceptualised as 'sustainable fandom'. This movement includes critical discourse around companies, knowledge sharing around production and consumption, and an interest in greening of one's own fan activities. This also includes a critical perspective on the use of digital technologies and a mindfulness of digital circularity. Moreover, fans launch their own new sustainable products, services and communities.

This chapter brings together different theories of design and sustainability, and analyses sustainable developments in fan culture. Furthermore, I provide a tool, a Sustainable Fandom Canvas, which readers can use to analyse and innovate fan practices. This ideation tool can be used by companies to co-create with fans as well. After introducing the tool, I discuss into its three focal points (social benefits, ecological benefits and innovation) through different cases to provide examples of how this Canvas can be used. By providing these tools and perspectives, fans and organisations can be empowered to create sustainable solutions in their communities.

Bridging Design and Fandom, 249–260

doi:10.1108/978-1-80592-659-720261016

Keywords: Sustainable fandom; sustainability; sustainable design; fandom; design canvas

Introduction

The culture of fans can be described as a participatory culture, one that relies not only on the consumption of source material but also on the production of new designs. Just like other consumer cultures, the question of what is produced and consumed, and how this can be done in responsible ways, enters the picture. This brings us to the question of sustainability and other design practices that help renew and restore the ways in which we produce our fan practices and commodities.

Sustainability has three key components, namely environmental, economic and social (Thompson & Norris, 2021). These are also referred to as people, planet and profit as well in the triple bottom line model, first conceptualised by Elkington (1994). Environmental (planet) relates to ecology, earth and its planetary boundaries. Businesses are being challenged by climate change, increasing pressure on resources, declining biodiversity and growing inequality. The social elements of sustainability (people) focus on inequality, poverty and social justice, among others, without which we cannot have fair work, production and materials. The economic side (profit), finally, captures how different companies deal with these tensions in their own practices, regulations and organisational cultures. In this volume, Changede and Jacobs explain these perspectives in detail, with an additional fourth dimension of 'personal meaning' stemming from the quadruple bottom line model by Stuart Walker (2011). Personal meaning is, of course, fundamental to fandom, where sustainability is often aligned with one's own identity and values.

However, many scholars and practitioners increasingly point out that sustainability, or the idea of 'sustaining' our world, is not enough. We need to rejuvenate our resources. The circular economy, for instance, refers to designs where waste is minimised, and we aim for maximum reusability of products (Weetman, 2020). This reuse is also central in the doughnut economy, which not only emphasises recycling but also points to the limits of our labour and natural resources (Raworth, 2017). Beyond these sustainable discourses and theories, regenerative models are proposed as well (Konietzko et al., 2023). The idea of these models is that resources are restored and even renewed. I will refer to these different models throughout the chapter, with sustainability as an umbrella term.

To realise a more sustainable design, interventions are often needed in multiple areas. This requires changes to multiple layers and even to the system itself. In her seminal work *Thinking in Systems*, Donna Meadows (2008) argues that systems need to be dynamic to become future-proof and sustainable. She stresses that dynamic systems have the following characteristics: 'Resilience, self-organization, and hierarchy are three of the reasons dynamic systems can work so well. Promoting or managing for these properties of a system can improve its ability to function well over the long term – to be sustainable' (p. 85).

To create long-term change, the systems underlying our designs need to be analysed and the relationships of different actors within these systems understood.

In this research, attention to system thinking is crucial. It helps to analyse different actors, such as high-level consumers and fans, and how they impact the sustainability of a system. The practices of fans, for instance, influence larger ecosystems such as brands, for example, through discussion, appropriation and adding to products and ideas. Since fans are often influencers, early adopters and critics, they are an exceptionally interesting group to study in a systemic way. This allows us to see how they behave around a design, such as a product or service. In other words, to see how sustainable design can be formed, fandom can be a unique pilot case.

Fandom, Design and Applied Research

Fandom produces an immense amount of content, design and art. Fans create many designs every day. Fan art, memes and fan movies are well-known examples that have been studied frequently (e.g. Booth, 2018; Stein, 2015). However, fans also have a unique material culture of crafts and self-made merchandise. From binding their own books ('fanbinding') to crafting costumes or fashion, fans create designs in many media and for many different reasons, such as self-expression and trade. Changede and Jacobs explore these fan activities in a sustainable context as a way of generating personal meaning (this volume).

As Bridget Cherry (2016) writes in the context of arts and crafts in fandom: 'Fan handcrafting is both mimetic and non-mimetic, it moves between affirmational and transformational works, and it is material and yet also textual. Further, in light of the material objects made and the way they are incorporated into the fans' everyday lives, they also function as a bridge from text to lived experience' (p. 24). Fan designs, then, are made not only as a form of creative expression but also as an appreciation of character love and stories. Design in fandom has many roles, including performative, social and affective.

Material culture, in other words, is deeply entangled with fan culture. Designs by fans come in many different forms and media, from costumes and performances to the creation of visual fan art. Fan designers are equally diverse and range from hobbyists to professionals, active on platforms such as Etsy. Within this space, sustainable designers are a sub-set who pair their specialisation with a passion for sustainability and ecology. An example of this is 'eco-cosplay' (Lamerichs, 2025) in which participants seek different ways of undertaking costume design. By upcycling elements of their outfit, thrifting or using sustainable materials, cosplayers take a more circular approach to their hobby. Bottles that would otherwise be waste can be turned into buttons, paper can become a prop and thrifted jackets can be retailored to fit a beloved character.

However, sustainability in fandom is not just limited to material production. It also relates to other behaviour, such as travel and fan tourism. Think of the conventions, concerts or theme parks that fans might visit and how they reach those destinations. Some events have actively started to address transport. Heroes Dutch Comic Con (2025), for instance, has a sustainability vision, which includes notes on recycling, bringing your own water bottle, and energy use. They also stress transport: 'Whenever possible, walk, cycle or use public transport to come to the event. If you need to use your car, take a colleague or friend with you!' Furthermore, the convention provides a list of preferred hotels in line with their sustainability standards. This is just one example. Within this volume, Bethan Jones provides a more detailed study of sustainability in fan tourism.

Digital sustainability is also an increased discourse that relates to fans. Fandom is a thriving part of today's large creator economy, consisting of thousands of streams, videos, photographs and texts that users upload online on a daily basis. Modern fandom is best described as a data-driven participatory culture, which relies on different platforms that harness not only a user's content, but also their data. For example, generative AI is increasingly used for the production of fan art, which raises critical questions around authorship, ownership and the digital carbon footprint of fans (Lamerichs, 2023; Mussies, 2025).

These digital platforms not only shape environmental sustainability negatively but also impact social sustainability. Participation has become more complex in the context of digital platforms, which profit immensely from the digital participation, content and data of their users (Schäfer, 2021). This development is primarily driven by platformisation, which captures how different platforms increasingly adopt different features to become large economic and governmental players (Nieborg et al., 2019). The business models that emerge around platforms have often been described as a platform economy (Steinberg, 2019) and even a form of 'platform capitalism' (Srnicek, 2016). The content that fans design, produce and upload is not separate from these developments. Fan data is harnessed on different social media platforms, where it is scraped, automated and remixed, often without a fan's knowledge or consent.

The digital space of fandom is one that we need to pay attention to, since it is far from sustainable at the moment. Fan designs are consistently profited from and misused by third parties, raising questions of ethics, labour and social justice.

Approach

This chapter adopts an applied design research approach (Joore et al., 2022). This method of action research combines design tools with an applied research stance. While building new knowledge is still central in this approach, applied research also focuses on co-creating solutions with different stakeholders. I add to applied design research with other ideas and approaches, essentially adopting a 'bricolage approach' (Jacobs, 2020). The notion of systems thinking, for instance, allows me to also analyse different actors in specific cases (e.g. fans and brands) and how to activate them.

This approach is paired with my own tool, a Sustainable Design Canvas, that provides further activation inspiration for readers. I encourage readers to make use of this tool for their own workshops, brainstorming and designs. Furthermore, I explore its three focal points (social benefits, ecological benefits and innovation) with different cases to provide further inspiration and reflection. I hope that by providing this design and knowledge, fans can become change-makers within their own unique spaces and work towards circular solutions.

Sustainable Fandom Canvas

The Sustainable Fandom Canvas captures insights on sustainability in fandom (see Fig. 16.1). By including different topics and prompts, fans can brainstorm about their own solutions, designs and services. In other words, it is an ideation tool that readers can use to explore sustainable ideas in relation to initiatives of their choice. The goal of this canvas is to optimise different areas of a service or initiative and consider sustainability from different angles, such as social, digital and environmental. The idea is to use fans and other consumers as co-creators in these models. Where can they be involved more? Who has been included or overlooked so far?

When creating this template, I was inspired by design and business tools such as the Business Model Canvas (Osterwalder & Pigneur, 2010) as well as Design Thinking models. The Canvas works towards a renewed, regenerative promise of a design. The top boxes of the Canvas act as headers that the ones below relate to, ending in a key promise or solution at the bottom. The social and environmental columns also build up towards innovation on the right as a space for critical thinking and reflection. The version of this Canvas that is published in this volume can be used or adapted (appropriately credited) by readers in classes

Social benefits What are the key social and inclusive benefits of your initiative? How does it speak to different consumer groups? Can you extend the segments further?	Ecological benefits What are the ecological benefits of your initiative? Who benefits? Can you estimate the carbon footprint with a calculator? Is it the same per consumer group?	Innovation Can you use the insights on the left to sharpen your initiative? How would you revise its value proposition?
Fandom Who are the key consumers? Are there high-affinity consumers (e.g. fans) or non-users? How are these relationships maintained? Can they be strengthened?	Material footprint What is needed for the production and supply chain? Which steps use a lot of resources? Can sustainable alternatives be found (e.g. renewable, local)?	Values How would you describe the key values and ideas of your initiative? (e.g. connection, creativity, fantasy, leadership)
Co-creation Where can you co-create more with fans? How can consumers add even more value to your initiative? In what phase (e.g. design, promotion, marketing) and in what experiences?	Digital footprint What is the digital footprint? How are posts/socials used and new technologies (e.g. generative AI)? What can be changed to minimize the footprint? Look up alternatives.	Ecosystem What are new ideas to connect with consumers and fans? Are there ways in which you can promote your initiative more to them and involve them?
Key Partners Visualize the key partners and their intended impact here	Experiences Are there other eco-factors to consider (e.g. services, travel, hospitality)?	Sustainable promise Summarize your ideas. How will you optimize your initiative?

Fig. 16.1. Sustainable Fandom Canvas.

or workshops. I would recommend using this tool with several workshop hosts to facilitate the process and think along with participants.

The aim of the Sustainable Fandom Canvas is to work towards optimisations in the designs of products and services, meaning that it is ideally suited for fans, businesses, educators or researchers. For example, the Canvas can be used by groups of fans to optimise their designs or services, such as the organisation of a fan convention. Furthermore, it can be a helpful tool for organisations that want to work on their sustainability practices and strategies and want to involve fans in the co-creation processes. Finally, educators and researchers could use it in classrooms to reflect on sustainability from different lenses through a case related to fandom that is close to a student's heart. From a research perspective, they can use it as an analytical tool to dive deeper into a fandom or initiative and examine its sustainable benefits.

The Canvas can be used in two ways in workshops, and I encourage readers to think of more ways to implement or adapt this material. Firstly, the Canvas can be used in its entirety as a sheet that participants can fill in. By having access to the full Canvas, they have a sense of overview, can follow the order of the rows or columns, and set priorities. If possible, print large versions of the Canvas or ask participants to use the categories on a flip-over sheet. This way, they can brainstorm, add sticky notes and put them on the wall for others to see. Participants can also draw connections between boxes and work towards the key promises at the bottom. A second way to use this tool is to cut the first three rows out as cards and use these as prompts for participants. These cards can also be given blindly to inspire and give more surprise and focus.

The Sustainable Fandom Canvas was tested at a workshop at the 2025 DiGRA (Digital Games Research Association) conference in a workshop on Responsible Game Fandom. Participants were researchers, educators, game designers and/or fans themselves. They could choose fan cultures, games and services of their choice to optimise. They chose widely between different game communities, local fan initiatives and their own products and designs.

For example, two colleagues applied the case to a Polish fan convention that they organise, to consider how the event could deal differently with waste, travel and other elements of the experience. They found their core strengths to be their passionate volunteers, their public location and focus on local fans. They wanted to make the event more accessible and sustainable, for instance, by rethinking transport and waste. Overall, participants found the canvas 'helpful', 'inspiring' and those who had never used canvases or similar tools could envision using it in class.

Social Benefits: Co-Creation and *Doctor Who* Fandom

Fandom has a rich history of participation and co-creation. From organising conventions to creating unique art, the contributions of fans have made an impact on official brands and their products. As an example of co-creation and its social benefits, I would like to zoom in on a short case around Doctor Who, a franchise that is innately tied up with its fandom.

When the BBC cancelled the series in 1989, it was fans who kept this property going and kept momentum for The Doctor and their companions (Perryman, 2008). Two initiatives were central during the hiatus and the revival of the television series. First, the spin-off novel ranges (published first by Virgin and then by the BBC). Many fan-authors who wrote for this range continued by writing the revived television series, including Mark Gatiss, Paul Cornell and Russell T Davies. Big Finish Productions is another good example, a fan initiative that later became a licensed part of the *Doctor Who* productions. Both the novels and audio dramas helped establish the revival of the series on television as the new *Doctor Who* (2005–2022) series.

'Big Finish' is a story of fan success. Prior to the establishment of the company, many of their employees worked for the unlicensed 'Audio Visuals' series that produced fannish audio plays. They befriended the previous cast and crew and managed to obtain the copyrights for the audio material of the series. They established 'Big Finish' to produce their own official audiobooks. The creative team invited fellow fans, previous actors and writers to join their endeavours. In this fan-driven context, many of the current *Doctor Who* writers and actors met.

Doctor Who is a large franchise, built around the energy and dedication of fans, which partly led to the revival of the series. It is an ecosystem consisting of large production companies such as BBC, fan-driven companies like Big Finish and fan practices. The participation of fans led to different products, some of which are officially licensed. As Matt Hills shows in this volume, there is also a wealth of unlicensed fan-created merchandise and designs (Hills, this volume).

Doctor Who is an example of how different stakeholders can benefit from a major intellectual property and many different creatives can become part of such a world. Rich social cultures can form around existing products, and companies can stimulate this fan behaviour. Participation is a hallmark of fan culture and something that can be treasured in many types of services, innovations and products. From beta-testing games to creating their own fan art, the participation of fans can take many forms. If we want to make the most of our ideas, we need to involve fans and allow them not only to form communities but also to become a part of the design process (see Fig. 16.2).

Ecological Benefits: Rethinking Fan Art

Fan art is an important domain of fan culture. On platforms such as Instagram, artists upload art and designs based on their favourite characters and often showcase their own merchandise as well. Fan art is a rich space of participation, rife with affect. Fans buy or commission these pieces because they relate to their favourite characters and stories, leading to a healthy life cycle of these beloved products. As a fan practice, these fan designs relate to the fan identity of the maker but also of the consumer as a collector and patron.

Example 1: Doctor Who

Social benefits

Longstanding franchise sparking fantasy, community and participation. Family-friendly, escapist and nostalgic to some viewers.

Fandom

Intergenerational fandom of diverse consumer groups. Highly active, create different products (e.g. fic, art, audio). Professionals overlap with fan community.

Co-creation

Fans are highly engaged and some of their works are also licensed (e.g. Big Finish, Virgin). Some become official creatives on the television series or other products. Co-creation is central in Doctor Who

Key Partners

- Companies: BBC, Virgin, Big Finish.
- Fan clubs, e.g. DWAS, DTTA
- Conventions, e.g. Flux, London MCM
- Online platforms/communities

Fig. 16.2. Social Benefits and *Doctor Who* Fandom.

Fan art has a varying footprint, depending on the materials used. Materials for buttons, stickers and other merchandise are sometimes ordered globally from web shops, adding to the footprint. However, new approaches to circularity and material also come from artists themselves by rethinking their own designs. For example, many cosplayers have started to question the sustainability of their costumes, their travel behaviour to conventions, and their performances (Lamerichs, 2025). In the case of visual fan art and fan merchandise, different materials can be used. Some fans look into sustainable 3D printing or eco-friendly materials, such as wood or paper. These eco-friendly production techniques are often incorporated as a unique selling point in the marketing of their products.

Fan art can be paired with sustainable messaging as well, emphasising how the art or merchandise was made, highlighting its locality or its materiality. A good example is the work of Sugar Bunny, an artist who specialises in cute manga-style apparel and merchandise. She uses wood for her standees and pins. About her cute wooden cow standees, she writes: 'These eco-friendly wood stands are professionally printed on walnut for a textured vintage appearance' (Sugar Bunny Shop, 2025b). Sugar Bunny offers wooden pins and many other items as well. She also specialises in simple cotton towels that dry quickly and are an ideal replacement for paper towels (Sugar Bunny Shop, 2025a). By promoting herself as a sustainable artist and by providing insights on sustainable design and use, Sugar Bunny can inspire other artists and consumers.

Digital circularity now has a prominent place in the discourse around fan art. It has become easy to generate one's own fan art through use of generative AI. Platforms such as Midjourney and Stable Diffusion can be prompted to generate art in the style of a Ghibli film, a Doctor Who novel cover or Sailor Moon fan art. The use of AI is a notable concern to many fans due to its undesired remixing of existing fan art and fan data. Furthermore, generative AI has a high carbon footprint, increasingly discussed by fans, and is sometimes sold at conventions and online, thus competing with art produced by human fan artists. Many conventions and artists by now take a stance against such tools. One of my previous studies analyses these emerging discourses in more detail (Lamerichs, 2023). AI is not the only tool that raises concerns in fan art. The tokenisation of fan art, by means of blockchain, also leads to controversies due to its excessive energy use.

Overall, fans are rethinking sustainable fan art from different perspectives – through their own design practices, digital circularity and sustainable messaging. Fan art also depends on artist allies and conventions, meaning that travel behaviour can also be examined. Fan organisations, fan artists and fan consumers can advance this space together. While some artists reflect on the production of their merchandise, this is not yet a common discourse. As stated in the Sustainable Design Canvas, fan designers can reflect on what production techniques and tools they use, what waste they create and how to reuse certain materials (see Fig. 16.3). Fandom luckily already has a healthy market of selling and reselling wares on eBay, Vinted and other platforms. By taking inspiration from different fan cultures and best practices, even more changes can be made in what we buy and discard.

Innovation: Sustainable Events and Music Fandom

The previous elements are brought together in new innovations in the area of sustainability, community and digitalisation. Coldplay's Music of the Spheres

Example 2: Fan art

Ecological benefits
Fan art can have a notable footprint, depending on the products used. It also is a space where local artists can be supported. However, fan art is often cherished by the fans buying and commissioning it, leading to a healthy life cycle of these beloved products. Fan art is paired with collecting and affect.
Material footprint
Fan art has a varying footprint, depending on the materials used. Materials for buttons, stickers and other merchandise are sometimes ordered globally, adding to the footprint. Local and renewable materials can be used for merchandise. Sustainable awareness is growing, with some artists reflecting on material use and carbon footprint and promoting their art as sustainable.
Digital footprint
The use of AI is a notable concern to many fans. Artist alleys, conventions and online communities sometimes take active stance against AI, sharing concerns about data and scraping, as well as environmental impact of such tools. Other technologies, such as blockchain and streaming, also have impact.
Experiences
Conventions, events and meetings are central for many artists. Encouraging sustainable travel and other alternatives help.

Fig. 16.3. Ecological Benefits and Fan Art.

World Tour (2022) is a great example of a sustainable design to which fans contribute. This world tour was set up from the get-go as an eco-friendly experience. The band committed to sustainable travel and encouraged fans to do the same. They planted a tree for every ticket sold, allowing their music and fandom to contribute to the environment (Grace, 2021).

Fan practices were also reconsidered from a sustainable perspective. For instance, at concerts, fans dance and generate a lot of movement, which can be harnessed. Coldplay collaborated with Energy Floor to turn the dancing of fans into renewable energy. As Energy Floors (2025) states on their site: 'The Energy Centres consist of 44 sustainable kinetic dancefloor tiles assembled in a circle for fans to dance to generate energy. The Centres also include 15 stationary bikes for fans to cycle on to create energy'.

Finally, merchandise was produced in a sustainable way for the tour. For example, PixMob invented an ultrabright LED wristband, made of compostable plant-based plastic. They state that their wristband has a 400% lower carbon footprint than regular plastic. Over four million fans used these beautifully lit wristbands during the tour, which sparkled through the crowd. They state that '86% of wristbands were recycled to be reused on average at every show', encouraging reuse rather than preserving the bracelets (Pixmob, 2025).

Coldplay is just one example of a band that embraces sustainability and innovation to thrive (see Fig. 16.4). Fan practices are used here in restorative ways, for instance to harness energy. The band seeks partners from the industry that fit this cause and help advance sustainability in different areas of their tour. Within music fandom, and fandom overall, many innovations can still be made towards regenerative fan practices. This is where we can consider different innovations as a collective.

Example 3: Coldplay

Innovation Coldplay's Music of the Spheres World Tour Sustainable concert tour facilitated with multiple partners, considering the full concert journey and experience
Values Circular Social Connection No waste
Ecosystem Renewable fan activities, such as dancing on the energy floor Compostable wristband, reused and recycled Sustainable transport facilitation and messaging for fans Coldplay band as sustainable role-models / influencers, providing additional inspiration for the community
Sustainable promise Coldplay provides a sustainable concert experience and reconsiders fan activities (e.g. dancing, merchandise) from an innovative perspective

Fig. 16.4. Innovation and Coldplay.

Conclusion

As awareness around sustainable design grows, creativity and design in fan cultures are also shifting. By bringing together the innovative energy of fans, designers and professionals, we can make sure that fandom contributes to a better world. As I have shown, fandom can create awareness, stage interventions and become part of a co-creation process. However, to truly achieve a more sustainable fandom, companies also need to take ownership. This is where systems thinking is crucial, to see where we can create changes and identify challenges in complex networks and communities. This is a joint effort between fans, brands and other stakeholders.

I hope that the Sustainable Fandom Canvas can act as an actionable tool for change. By focusing on three domains – social, environmental and innovation – users of the canvas can explore and activate different elements that relate to sustainability. This could also mean tensions arise. Certain innovations, for example, implementing generative AI, might have consequences for the environment. If these tensions emerge, sit with them: analyse their potentials and drawbacks. This canvas is just a starting point for a larger co-creation process.

Design research and fan studies, then, are complimentary approaches. Their combination can lead to powerful designs, interventions and movements, for instance, in the field of sustainability. By embracing co-creation, we can build new participatory cultures that focus on imagination, belonging and sustainable impact.

References

Booth, P. (2018). *A companion to media fandom and fan studies. A companion to media fandom and fan studies*. Wiley.

Cherry, B. (2016). *Cult media, fandom and textiles: Handicrafting as fan art*. Bloomsbury.

Energy Floors. (2025). *Coldplay*. https://energy-floors.com/coldplay/

Grace, A. (2021). Coldplay's eco-friendly tour will be partly powered by fans' dancing. *New York Post*. https://nypost.com/2021/10/14/coldplays-eco-friendly-tour-to-run-on-fans-dancing/

Heroes Dutch Comic Con. (2025). Sustainability. https://www.dutchcomiccon.com/info/sustainability/

Jacobs, N. (2020). Interdisciplinary methodologies for the fan studies Bricoleur. In J. E. Largent, M. Popova, & E. Vist (Eds.), *Fan studies methodologies* (Vol. 33). Transformative Works and Cultures. https://doi.org/10.3983/twc.2020.1665

Joore, P., Stompff, G., & ,van den Eijnde, J. (Eds.). (2022). *Applied design research: A mosaic of 22 examples, experiences and interpretations*. CRC Press.

Konietzko, J., Das, A., & Bocken, N. (2023). Towards regenerative business models: A necessary shift? *Sustainable Production and Consumption*, *38*, 372–388.

Lamerichs, N. (2023). Generative AI and the next stage of fan art. *Image*, 37. https://image-journal.de/generative-ai-and-the-next-stage-of-fan-art/

Lamerichs, N. (2025). Sustainable fandom: A virtual ethnography of sustainable cosplay and material culture on Instagram. In D. Ciesielska, N. Lamerichs, & A.

Zarzycka (Eds.), *Affect in fandom: Fan creators and productivity* (pp. 89–109). AUP.
Meadows, D. H. (2008). *Thinking in systems*. Earthscan.
Mussies, M. (2025). AI, Fanart and intellectual property – An analysis of ownership in the age of machine creativity. Crime, Law and AI. https://www.intjournalcrimelawai.com/ai-fanart-and-intellectual-property-an-analysis-of-ownership-in-the-age-of-machine-creativity
Nieborg, D., Poell, T., & Deuze, M. (2019). Platformization of making media: Production, practices, and professions. In M. Deuze & M. Prenger (Eds.), *Making media: Production, practices, and professions* (pp. 85–96). Amsterdam University Press.
Osterwalder, A., & Pigneur, Y. (2010). *Business model generation A handbook for visionaries, game changers, and challengers*. Wiley.
Perryman, N. (2008). Doctor who and the convergence of media. *Convergence: The International Journal of Research Into New Media Technologies*, *14*(1), 21–39.
Pixmob. (2025). *Coldplay*. https://pixmob.com/projects/coldplay
Raworth, K. (2017). *Doughnut economics: Seven ways to think like a 21st-century economist*. Random House.
Schäfer, M. (2021). *Bastard culture! How user participation transforms cultural production*. Amsterdam University Press.
Srnicek, N. (2016). *Platform capitalism*. Wiley Blackwell Publishing.
Stein, L. (2015). *Millennial fandom: Television audiences in the transmedia age*. University of Iowa Press.
Steinberg, M. (2019). *The platform economy: How Japan transformed the consumer internet*. University of Minnesota Press.
Sugar Bunny Shop. (2025a). Salty britches floor sack tea towel. *Sugar Bunny Shop*. https://www.sugarbunnyshop.com/products/salty-britches-flour-sack-tea-towel
Sugar Bunny Shop. (2025b). Tiny moos cow wood standees. *Sugar Bunny Shop*. https://www.sugarbunnyshop.com/products/tiny-moos-cow-wood-standees
Thompson, P. B., & Norris, P. E. (2021). *Sustainability: What everyone needs to know*. Oxford University Press.
Walker, S. (2011). *The spirit of design: Objects, environment and meaning*. Earthscan.
Weetman, C. (2020). *A circular economy handbook: How to build a more resilient, competitive and sustainable business* (2nd ed.). Kogan Page Ltd.

Afterword: Futures of Fan Studies and Design Research

Naomi Jacobs

The work collected in this book, I hope, demonstrates the breadth of possibilities that begin to emerge when design research and fan studies are brought together and productively combined. However, it is only a starting point for this area of research. In each of the topics highlighted in this book, there are clear opportunities for development at the intersections of design research and fan studies. Across and between the sections of this book, topics of platforms, technology, materiality and sustainability re-occur. Some key emerging topics are only briefly touched on but suggest opportunities for future work – for example, both design and fandom are now seeing significant impacts from the rapid update of artificial intelligence (AI) tools (Black & Jacobs, 2025; Yu et al., 2025). Work in this collection indicates the productivity of thinking about AI with an approach that considers both design and fan perspectives. The role that the design of platform affordances plays in supporting, shaping and restricting fan practice and behaviour is also ripe for further exploration, as was highlighted through the vigour and excitement surrounding related conversations and presentations at the 2025 Fan Studies Network North America Conference. Similarly, as tourism becomes a significant economic driver in many regions, and the economic power of fandom becomes both larger and more widely recognised, there are many reasons it is important to use design to consider how fan visitors shape our built environments, our natural environments and the intersections between the two.

What is also notable about the work covered in this collection is its breadth in terms of methodologies and methods. Research methods used in these chapters include quantitative (meta)data analysis, ethnography and autoethnography, document analysis, case studies and research through design. I have previously written about the value of being open to a wide variety of methodological approaches in fields such as fan studies and design research (Jacobs, 2020), and I hope that this will continue to draw attention from scholars.

There remain, however, opportunities for more of this methodological sharing and cross-fertilisation. One underexplored area to date is the use of speculative design approaches in relation to fandom. Speculative design is a design approach which arose from the critical turn in design research and was popularised by Anthony Dunne and Fiona Raby. Rather than directly creating change through design, it seeks to provoke and critique through design: used 'not to show how things will be but to open up a space for discussion' (Dunne & Raby, 2014). In these approaches, we are not predicting a singular future but considering multiple possible futures that exist in potentia and may be impacted by our choices now. Speculative design has a close association with speculative fiction and science fiction; genres that have been a heavy focus of fan studies work because of the visibility of their fan cultures. This is not necessarily a coincidence. Fans have an affinity with genres that show alternative ways of being: be that futures or alternative presents. And design is inextricably bound up with storytelling and collective imagining that is expressed through and by media. For example, we can look to Star Trek as an example of representing both social and technological change in its speculative imaginings, and inspiring or cautioning against such change. A direct example of this is the Tricorder X Prize which ran from 2012 to 2017 and offered $10M to developers of a medical diagnostic device based on the fictional version in the show (X-Prize Foundation, n.d.).

Design Fiction (Bleeker et al., 2022) is a method within speculative design that may be of particular relevance as an approach which could be productively used with fan studies, particularly for research through design in fandom. In this method, tangible objects are created as 'diegetic prototypes' (Kirby, 2010; Sterling, in Bosch, 2012) allowing people to immersively interact with and critique potential futures. These physical manifestations represent a fictional shift in the world, which may reflect alternate pasts or presents, or speculated futures (Jacobs, 2020). I suggest that tapping into the transformative creativity of fans would be an ideal site for collaborative design fiction research.

At the time of writing, a search of work relating to both speculative design and fandom yields very few results. While a small amount of research is starting to use speculative approaches in relation to fandom (e.g. Fiesler, 2018; Jacobs, 2024) or to consider how fan approaches can strengthen design fiction and speculative design (e.g. Tanenbaum et al., 2012; Vistisen & Jensen, 2018), this is an area that is ripe for further exploration and development.

Speculative approaches, and design fiction, help us to consider and explore multiple and potential futures. I hope that the work in this book opens up a space to help explore futures that might exist for fandom, design, fan studies and design research and productively imagine together to help us move towards preferable futures.

References

Black, S. R., & Jacobs, N. (2025). Fans and AI: Transformations in fandom and fan studies. *Transformative Works and Cultures, 46*.

Bleeker, J., Foster, N., Girardin, F., & Nova, N. (2022). *The manual of design fiction*. Near Future Laboratory.

Bosch, T. (2012, March 2). *Sci-Fi writer bruce sterling explains the intriguing new concept of design fiction*. Slate Retrieved https://slate.com/technology/2012/03/bruce-sterling-on-design-fictions.html. Accessed on December 18, 2025.

Dunne, A., & Raby, F. (2014). *Speculative everything*. The MIT Press.

Fiesler, C. (2018). Owning the servers: A design fiction exploring the transformation of fandom into 'our own. *Transformative Works and Cultures*, *28*.

Jacobs, N. (2020). Interdisciplinary methodologies for the fan studies bricoleur. *Transformative Works and Cultures*, *33*(1).

Jacobs, N. (2024). Archiving the ephemeral in digital public space: Using speculative design to consider collaborative fan play in the metaverse. *Proceedings from the Document Academy*, *11*(1), 3.

Kirby, D. (2010). The future is now: Diegetic prototypes and the role of popular films in generating real-world technological development. *Social Studies of Science*, *40* (1), 41–70.

Tanenbaum, T. J., Tanenbaum, K., & Wakkary, R. (2012). Steampunk as design fiction. In *CHI '12: Proceedings of the SIGCHI Conference on Human Factors in Computing Systems* (pp. 1583–1592). https://doi.org/10.1145/2207676.2208279

Vistisen, P., & Jensen, T. (2018). Designers as fans: Bottom-up online explorations of new technology concepts as a genre of design fan fictions. *First Monday*, *23*(12). https://doi.org/10.5210/fm.v23i12.9298

X-Prize Foundation. (n.d.). *Qualcomm tricorder XPRIZE*. https://www.xprize.org/competitions/tricorder. Accessed on December 18, 2025

Yu, C., Zheng, P., Peng, T., Xu, X., Vos, S., & Ren, X. (2025). Design meets AI: Challenges and opportunities. *Journal of Engineering Design*, 1–5.